FROM CLASSROOM TO APP STORE

TEACHING YOUR KIDS HOW TO BUILD AN APP FOR YOUR SCHOOL

By Doug Stitcher

CREATIVE EDUCATIONAL PRESS LTD

PUBLISHED BY: Creative Educational Press Ltd
2 The Walled Garden, Grange Park Drive, Biddulph, Staffs, ST8 7TA

Tel: 07789938923
Fax: 01782 379398

PRINTED BY: York Publishing Services Ltd.,
64, Hallfield Road, Layerthorpe, York, YO31 7ZQ

DESIGN: Amy Doorbar

PROOFREADING: Tom Storey and Julie Peat

Doug Stitcher www.facebook.com/angelapplications
dougstitcher@angelapplications.co.uk
@theRenegade78

Alan Peat www.alanpeat.com
info@alanpeat.com
www.facebook.com/alanpeatltdapps
@alanpeat

ISBN: 978-1-911169-06-2

Also available from Creative Educational Press Ltd (www.thecepress.com):

Writing Exciting Sentences: Age 7 Plus by Alan Peat
A Second Book of Exciting Sentences by Alan Peat & Mathew Sullivan
50 Ways to Retell a Story: Cinderella by Alan Peat, Julie Peat and Christopher Storey
Get Your Head Around Punctuation (...and how to teach it!) by Alan Peat
The Elves and The Shoemaker 1897 illustrated by John Harrold
Writing Exciting Ghost Stories: Age 9 Plus: Ghost Story Plot Skeletons by Alan Peat (co-author Julie Barnfather)
Teaching Outstanding Persuasive Writing by Alan Peat
Developing Writing Through Comics by Mathew Sullivan
The Magic Stone by Alan Peat (illustrated by John Harrold)
50+ iPad Lessons for Exciting Sentences by Alan Peat & Lee Parkinson
50+ iPad Lessons for Teaching Non-fiction by Alan Peat & Lee Parkinson
50+ iPad Lessons for Teaching Fiction by Alan Peat & Lee Parkinson
Melvin McGee: Zombie Hunter by Mathew Sullivan
A Photocopiable Book of Mathematical Word Games by Alan Peat
The Ultimate Guide To Non-Fiction Writing by Alan Peat & Mathew Sullivan
Word Games at Key Stage 2 by Alan Peat
Teaching Poetry with 4 – 8 year olds by Alan Peat
Teaching Poetry with 7 – 12 year olds by Alan Peat
Improving Story Writing at Key Stages 1 & 2 by Alan Peat
First Class Maths by Gareth Metcalfe

DOUG STITCHER

Doug Stitcher is currently the Acting Deputy Head Teacher of a Wirral primary school. He has been an ICT subject leader since 2001 and worked in a number of schools providing ICT and Computing support. Doug has also produced a variety of apps and software for his family-run business Angel Applications for the last six years as well as developing the huge range of apps for Alan Peat Ltd.

Doug has a passion for teaching children to code and hopes this, his first book, will inspire teachers across the country to teach their pupils to build their own app.

In his spare time, of which he has very little, Doug enjoys spending time with his family, playing guitar, listening to country music and watching his beloved Peterborough United play.

"Aut viam inveniam aut faciam"

CONTENTS

INTRODUCTION

So you want to teach your kids to code? You've dabbled in Scratch, you've experimented with Python – even though you don't really know what Python is. And you've found a few apps that let your children move stuff across the screen. But I bet part of you has thought about teaching the students to create an app.

Not a 'web app', not a 'Scratch app'. But a real-life, bonafide iPhone or iPad app. That's what you want, isn't it?

I know. You're not a coder, or a software engineer, if you're trying to sound posh. You're a teacher. As a teacher, you were once a trainee teacher and probably spent many hours teaching yourself about Henry VIII's wives the night before you were going to face an important lesson observation. You're used to learning stuff and then teaching it to the children like you studied it for a degree.

Coding is no different. Sure, elements of it are technical and geeky. But everyone knows that one day the geeks will take over the world.

The beauty of this book is that I'm a teacher too. You know what it's like when you meet a teacher on holiday; you talk shop and instantly become best friends. So this is similar – only I'm talking to you in a book.

As a teacher, I was given the role of ICT Co-ordinator in my NQT year. Now, you're not supposed to lead a subject in your NQT year and I didn't really know what I was doing. So I learnt. I researched. And I found that it was something I enjoyed. The only issue was that I wasn't an expert. This frustrated me as I felt like I should be. It made me try harder to be ahead of the game.

I started off my making animations in Flash. Then I taught the class to do it – it was the quickest way of cementing my own learning. I refined this to making games in Flash and again, I taught the children to make games. And then a guy called Steve Jobs changed everything.

I got my first iPhone. And I heard that it was possible to make applications for it but you had to use an Apple computer. So I bought a cheap Mac Mini and set it up in my computer suite at home and began playing around.

At school, we have a technician by the name of Chris James. He's an incredibly talented man with a background in computer engineering and knows more about computers than anybody I've ever met. So he seemed like the obvious choice to work with. I ran into school one morning knowing it was our turn for an afternoon of IT support. I told him I'd had a brilliant idea, we could start a company making apps. People could pay us to make apps for them!

His response, 'Nah, it'll never catch on.'

Fortunately, we are still friends. And my app company did catch on.

I suppose what I'm trying to tell you is that although right now, at the start of this book, the idea of being able to create your own iOS app and teach that to the children is unbelievable, you can do it. And I will help you.

And unlike a book from some computer guru, I'll be there well after you've read it. You can find me all over the internet and I'll happily help you out any step of the way **@therenegade78**.

HOW THIS BOOK WORKS

Most 'How to Code' books assume prior technical knowledge. I don't. Most 'App Development' books use lots of technical jargon. I don't. I only use as much as is required. Throughout the book, we will be referring to lots of technical things but teaching them to the children will quickly reduce their love of coding to nothing more than rubble.

In each lesson, you will get step-by-step instructions, terminology to share with the class, terminology for your own subject knowledge and a child-friendly approach to coding using analogies and phraseologies to which the students can relate.

We could talk about classes, arrays and IDEs until the cows come home, but that's not going to help you unless you can explain it to the children.

Think about algorithms. A simple web search will reveal that the term 'algorithm' is:

Derived from the name of the mathematician Muhammed ibn-Musa Al-Khowarizmi, an algorithm is a list of instructions, procedures, or formulas used to solve a problem. Today, algorithms are used millions of times every day for a variety of tasks. For example, an algorithm could look at an incoming email to determine if it is spam or a legitimate email and discard only spam messages. Ada Lovelace is credited as being the first person to develop an algorithm for a machine.

Great. But getting the class to come up with a set of instructions for the Hokey Cokey and then seeing what happens when another group follow those instructions is probably a more effective way of getting the concept across.

And that's the key here. Everything will be simplified to a level that is easy for you to understand, but more importantly, to a level that you can then pass on to the pupils with confidence.

Screenshots will support each step and will be available online by using the QR code at the end of each lesson. This will allow you to easily model to the class but I hope you won't need that resource. I hope that by following the steps yourself, you will be confident enough to model the skills involved just as you would model writing the opening paragraph of a newspaper report.

Over the course of the lessons in this book, you will create a real-life app. There's even a chapter at the end about putting your real-life app on the App Store – a feat that took me several weeks to accomplish with my first app.

Some of the lessons do not build into the app but will equip you, and your class, with essential skills.

We will also be using some third-party code. That's code that I didn't write and you didn't write but is available for others to use free of charge within their own apps. Why? Because that's what real coders do. If somebody has found a way to read an RSS Feed and put it into an app, and they're happy to share it, then use it.

And that's important bit. You are going to teach your students to build an app for your school. Now, when I told my wife about that, she looked at me like I'm slightly crazy. Why? Our app company builds apps for schools. So by telling you how to do this yourself, I'm effectively talking myself out of an order for a school app.

But just as children write better if there is a real life purpose, so they will code better.

I will give you everything you need. All the instructions as lessons.

Lots of books about coding give access to the code, in case the reader messes it up. Well, I know that you won't. And if you do, you keep trying until you get it right.

In Chapters 2 and 3, I will provide you with lessons that you can directly teach to the children in order for them to become familiar with the process of creating apps.

As we progress through the book, I will primarily being teaching you so that you can use the skills you acquire and the images to effectively model the process of creating a school app. How much you involve your students is completely up to you. But there is no reason why they cannot do everything I will show you to do.

I would recommend you follow all the steps in each chapter and become familiar with them before attempting to re-create them with your class or group of children. Remember, all the screenshots are available by scanning the QR code at the end of each chapter.

WHAT YOU'LL NEED

We're building an app to run on an iPhone, iPod touch or iPad. Therefore, there are some things that you need:

- An Apple computer: If your school doesn't have one, try to get a Mac Mini. They're the same price as a regular PC but you'll need to provide your own monitor, keyboard and mouse.

- A device to test the app on - An iPhone or iPad. You can avoid this step but it is bad practice to submit an app to the App Store without testing it on a device. This is because the simulator – we'll talk about that later – doesn't have the same capabilities as an iPhone or iPad.

- *Xcode*: This is Apple's software used by developers to create apps. It's actually an IDE (Integrated Developer Environment), but you don't need to know that. Oh, and it's FREE.

- An Apple Developer Account: You only need this if you want to submit your app to the App Store. It costs £79 per year.

SWIFT OR OBJECTIVE-C

You can code apps in *Xcode* in two languages: Objective-C, which has been around since the conception of the App Store; or Swift, which is a new language devised by Apple. I couldn't possibly teach you to code in two languages so I had to pick one.

You might think it makes sense to go with the newer language, Swift. And to a certain extent you'd be right. Swift is easier in terms of its syntax – much like human languages follow rules of syntax – and is newer so is likely to be supported by Apple for longer.

However, Objective-C has been around for a long time. There is a wealth of articles online in support forums and on 'learn to code' sites. If you get stuck in Objective-C, I can guarantee somebody else has had exactly the same problem. And somebody else has fixed it.

So we're going to use Objective-C throughout this book. You will learn to love it. Possibly.

And that's about it, so hold on to your hats, I'm about to take you on a journey that will begin with the simplest of apps and end with the pupils in your class helping you to create your own (App Store appropriate) app.

CHAPTER ONE
GETTING STARTED

In this chapter, we'll set up the environment you need to create apps. Again, I'm going to assume you know very little but I will presume you are reasonably computer literate.

So you've set up your shiny new Apple Mac. Any Mac will do: Mac Minis are your cheapest option, (I personally use a 15 inch MacBook Pro). This is often the biggest hurdle in deciding to develop iOS apps. To build using *Xcode*, and there are other ways of building apps, you must use an Apple computer. But don't worry – you will learn to love it.

Step 1: Set up your Apple ID

The first thing we need to do is set up an Apple ID at **https://appleid.apple.com/account**. Now before you rush into doing this, do you have an iPhone? do you have an iPad? do you have an iPod? If you do, then you probably already have an Apple ID so you can quite happily skip this step.

Step 2: Install Xcode

The title of this step is misleading in its simplicity. Installing *Xcode* is easy but takes forever. It's a large file (more than 4GB) and if you've not got good broadband, expect it to take an hour or two.

1.01

It's easy to find. Open the App Store on your Mac. Be careful, if you're used to using iTunes to find apps for your mobile devices, you might try and open iTunes.

You're looking for the big blue icon with an 'A' made out of a crayon, paint brush and ruler.

Search for Xcode in the box on the top right:

1.02

The first app that shows up in the search should be this one:

1.03

I've already got *Xcode* installed, so mine says **OPEN** but yours will say **GET**. Go ahead and press it.

You will prompted for your Apple ID. Enter the password and the app will download.

One thing about *Xcode* I need to mention is that, while it takes up a lot of space when you download it, it continues to eat up your hard drive space as you use it. It creates lots of files that it needs as it goes along and in doing so, can easily take up to 30GB of your hard drive space.

It falls outside the remit of this book to explain how to manage that, but a quick Google search for 'Free up space used by Xcode' will provide you with all the information you need if it becomes a problem.

Before you teach a thing to your class of over-excited ten-year-olds who think that the first lesson will see them making the next Angry Birds, you need to get acquainted with *Xcode* and its different screens and options.

In this chapter, I will give you an overview of each *pane*. We will then look in more detail at certain areas and options within each pane.

So let's dive in. Open *Xcode*. You'll see its icon in your *Applications* folder, for which there is normally a shortcut right next to the trash icon on the *Dock*.

You'll see the welcome screen:

1.04

Mine has a list of apps already created on the right-hand side. I've cut that bit off. You'll see three options on the left and you want the middle one, *Create a new Xcode project*.

You'll be faced with another set of options:

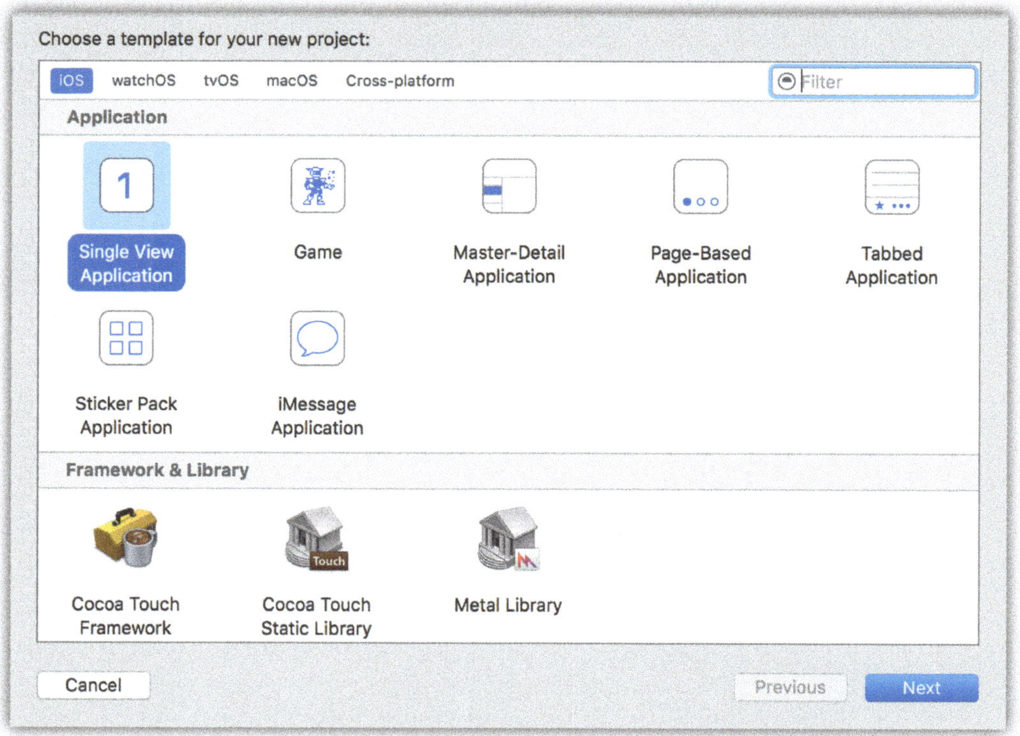

1.05

You will see five different types of apps you can build; iOS (iPhone and iPad), watchOS (Apple Watch), tvOS (Apple TV), macOS (Apple Macs) and Cross-Platform (games for all these devices at once). We are going to be building an iOS app so we can leave iOS selected at the top.

In the centre, you'll see there are a number of templates. I'm not going to go into what they all do. All you need to know is that we are going to be using a *Single View Application* template. That's the one I use the most.

Go ahead and press *Next*. You'll now see this set of options:

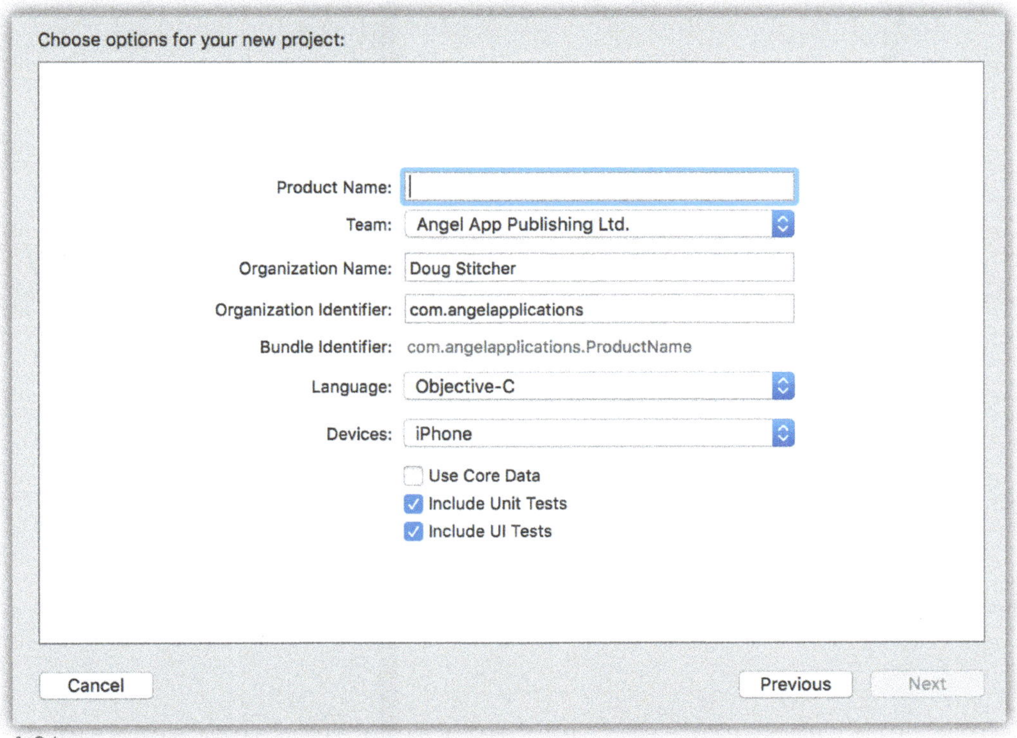

1.06

Looks a bit complicated, I know. Your screen will be pre-populated with your name in *Organization Name* but you'll probably need to add the other bits. For our first app, enter the following information:

Product Name: Hello World
Team: None
Organization Name: Your Name (It may be obvious, but if you are Jane Smith, for example, enter 'Jane Smith') *
Organization Identifier: com.yourname
Language: Objective-C
Devices: iPhone

** Take it as read that, for the rest of the book, when I ask you to enter 'Your Name' this means YOUR name!*

Leave the two bottom boxes checked and press *Next*. *Xcode* will then ask you where you want the project to be saved. Choose a folder on your computer. I place all my apps in the *Documents* folder. Whichever folder you choose will become the default location for saving your apps.

And finally, you're ready to meet *Xcode*...

Getting to know Xcode

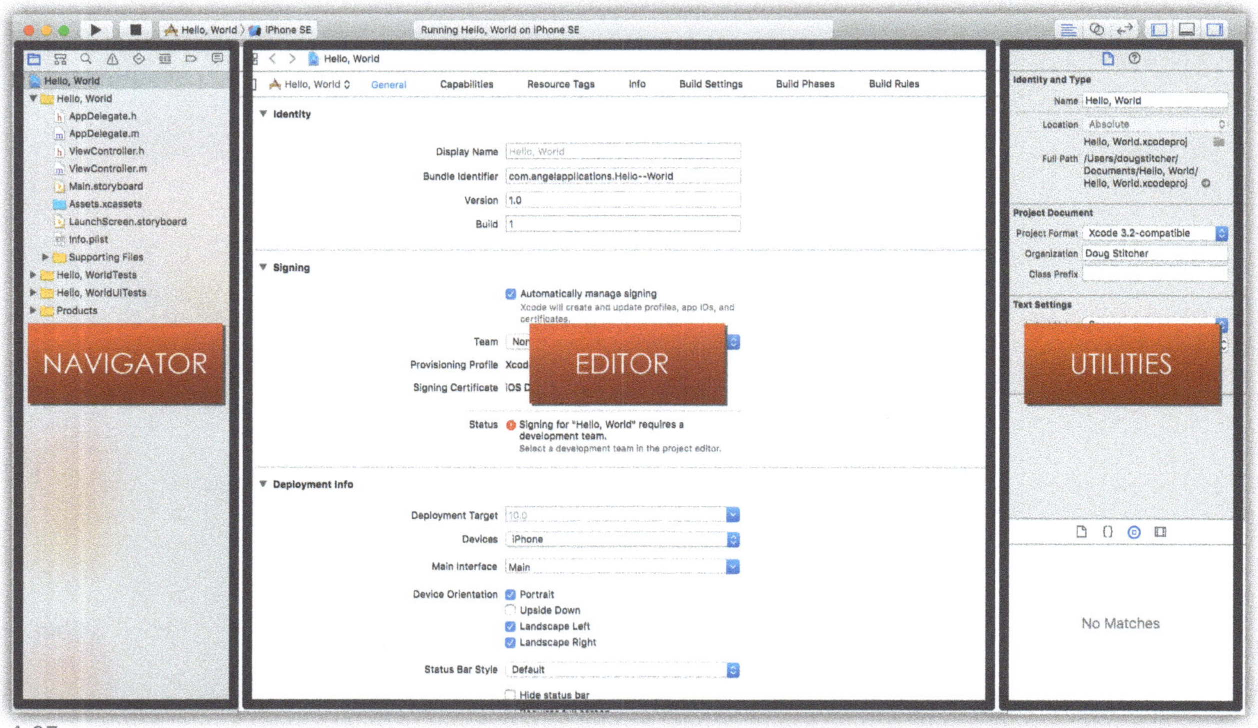

1.07

Xcode, in all its beautiful Appleness, is split into three main areas: I call them sections for the children, but they are technically known as *panes*.

When explaining these panes to the class, stick to child-friendly language as far as you can. This is what I tell them:

***Navigator*:** This is where you will find all your files. That's your files containing your code, any images, sound effects or videos that you add and any 'helping code'. That is what I call third party libraries for the benefit of the students.

***Editor*:** This is where you edit your code or make changes to the design of your app.

***Utilities*:** This is where you can tweak options, like the font size, or add new objects to your design, such as a new button.

Don't worry if it all looks a bit overwhelming at the moment. Remember the first time you used a new version of Office? You got the hang of it. The same applies here.

It's also important to remember that there are a lot of advanced options throughout *Xcode* and the app building process that we don't need to worry about.

Have a look at the top right corner. You should see a set of icons like this:

1.08

These icons let you toggle certain parts of *Xcode* to be hidden or visible.

The first three icons are related just to the *Editor* pane. The default, as displayed in the first screenshot of the *panes*, is the icon with blue lines highlighted. This is how you will probably use *Xcode* most of the time.

The two circles interlinked divide the *Editor* pane into two parts where one displays one file of code and the other displays another file of code that is linked somehow to the first. I use this occasionally, but it's unlikely you will need to press this.

The two arrows compare two versions of the same file. It's used to identify changes over time between files. Again, you won't need this.

The second set of icons will be more useful to you. They will hide, or show, different *panes*. The icon with the vertical line on the left will hide the *Navigator* pane. The icon in the centre with a horizontal line will hide the *Debug* pane. This only shows once you've tested your app for the first time. I'll explain more about it later. The icon on the right with the vertical line on the right hides the *Utilities* pane.

Why do that? Sometimes as you develop your app, you will need more screen space, particularly if you are building an iPad app that runs in landscape. So *Xcode* creates the facility to hide *panes* to give you more room.

It's a handy feature but when I first started using *Xcode*, I occasionally lost *panes* and couldn't get them back so I thought it might help to share this with you from the outset.

There is no point me showing you any more bits of *Xcode* right now. So we'll come back to it when we build our first app in the next chapter.

Right now, it's time for a bit of background subject knowledge. It's not the most exciting or practical part of the book but it's important for you to know if you are going to come across like you're an app coding genius in front of your class.

The anatomy of an app

I'm going to explain how an app is created for iPhone. I'm going to assume you have little prior knowledge. If you happen to be a computing expert and you're reading this, you may notice that I have brushed over elements or missed things out. But then, if you're a computing expert, probably you wouldn't need to read this book.

When programming in *Objective-C*, we use the *MVC* design pattern. It's way too technical to go into here or with the children but if you're so inclined, you can read more at **https://developer.apple.com/library/ios/documentation/General/Conceptual/CocoaEncyclopedia/Model-View-Controller/Model-View-Controller.html.**

As far as the pupils need to know, we create a *user interface*; the part of the app that you see and interact with. We then create code to control the *user interface*.

Take an app the students are familiar with, say, *Angry Birds*. It has a *user interface*; the screens with birds and pigs on. Behind that are files containing code that tell the birds how to move, the objects how to fall and the pigs how to die.

When we're creating iOS apps in *Objective-C*, we create our code to control each screen using two files: a *header* file and an *implementation* file. What we actually create is known as a *class* but at this point in your journey, I would avoid delving too deeply into classes. That said, should you like to find out more, have a look at **http://blog.teamtreehouse.com/beginners-guide-objective-c-classes-objects**.

To explain this more clearly, go back to *Xcode* and select the file in the *Navigator* pane called *ViewController.h*:

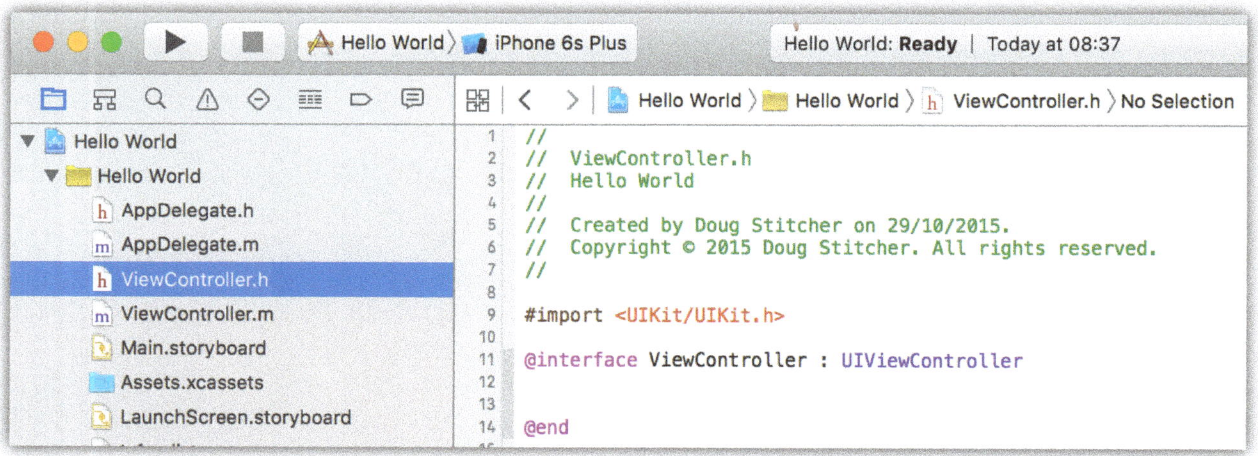

1.09

This is your *header file (ViewController.**h**)*. Its job is to define variables and objects that you will use in your *implementation file (ViewController.**m**)*.

In the *Editor* pane, you will see there isn't a great deal in there yet. That's because at the moment, the pre-generated code from *Xcode* does no more than create the *class ViewController*. In a little bit, we're going to make that *class* do some stuff.

Click below in the *Navigator* pane and choose *ViewController.m*:

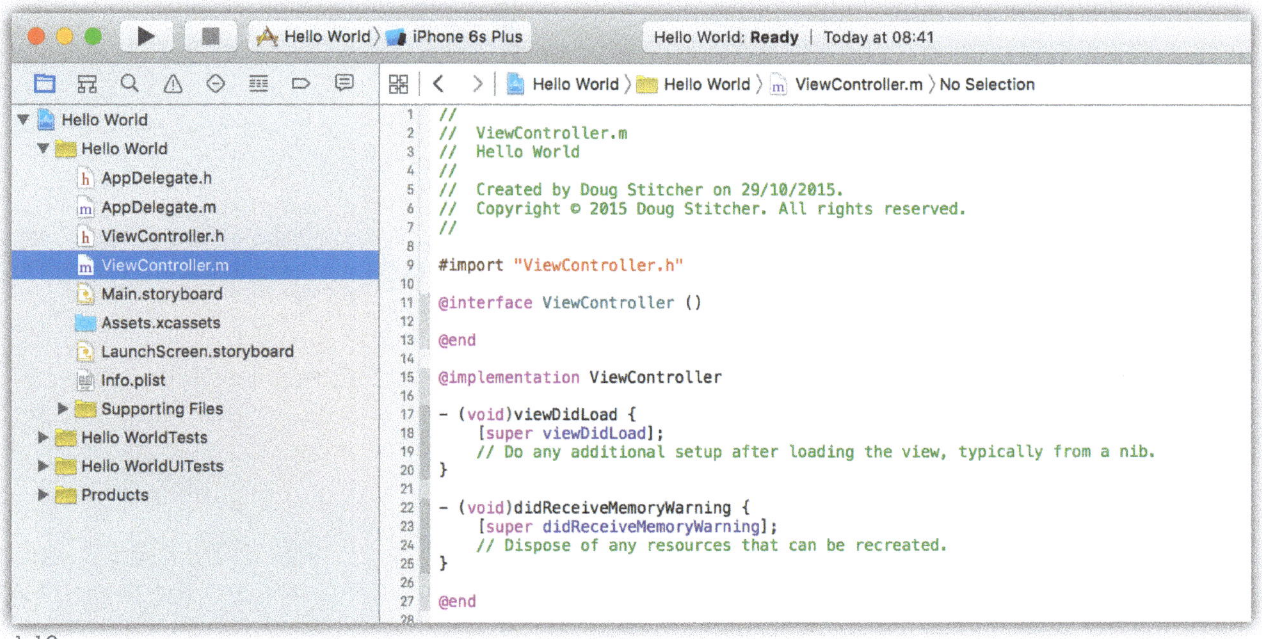
1.10

This is your *implementation file (.m)*. This is where the magic happens. There's a bit more pre-populated here. Two *methods* called *viewDidLoad* and *didReceiveMemoryWarning*. We'll talk a lot about methods later.

Together, the *.h* and *.m* files control our *user interface*. They don't have to have a physical *user interface* to control but for the sake of this book, we will always link our code to a *user interface*.

So where is the *user interface*? Just below *ViewController.m*, you'll see a file called *Main.storyboard*, select it:

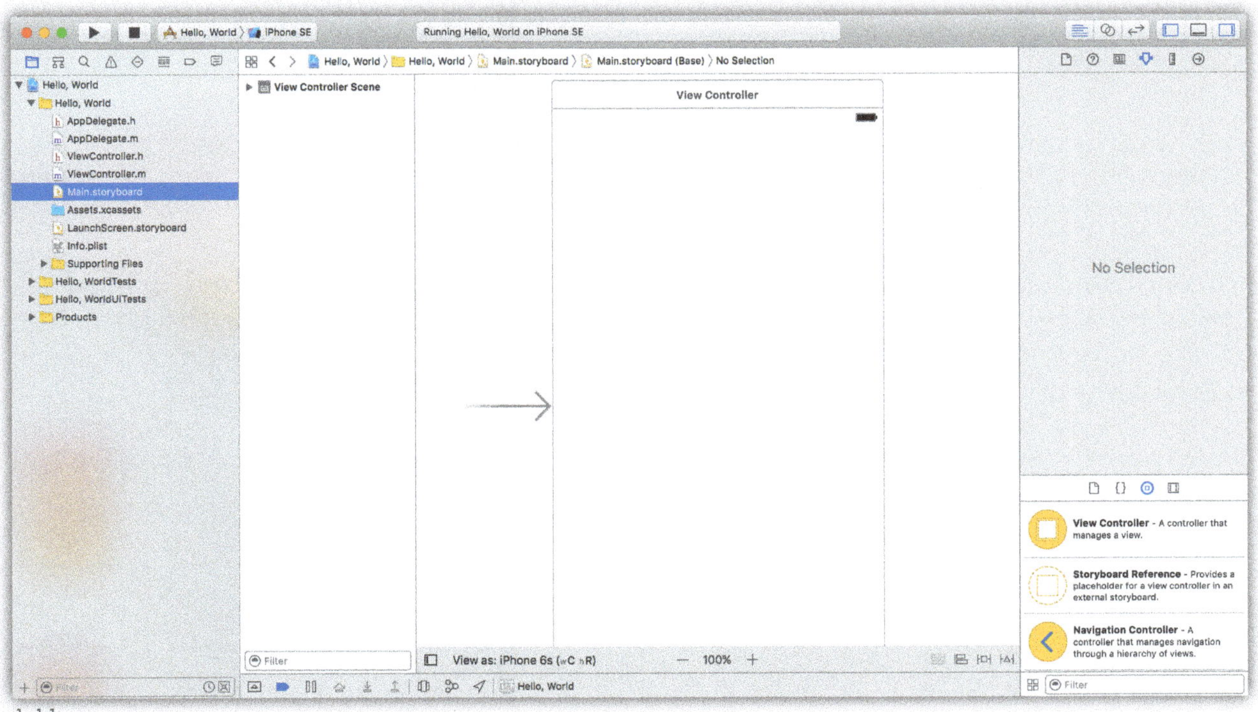
1.11

What you are looking at is what Apple call *Interface Builder*. This is where we design the graphical elements of our app.

If you look in the *Editor* pane, you'll see a large white box, this represents a screen layout. It's rectangular because Apple have recently introduced a feature for making one layout for each type of device: iPhone, iPad etc. But when we build our app, we're going to turn this feature off. It will be much easier for the class.

The large white box, which is actually called a *View Controller*, is controlled by the code in *ViewController.h* and *ViewController.m*. When I first started learning, I found this a bit confusing.

This is because of how Apple have named things when an app is created. *Xcode* always gives you a *header* and *implementation* file called *ViewController*. And they always give you a blank screen in the *.storyboard* file that is a *View Controller* and controlled by the files called *ViewController*!

So it's important to understand that in our sample app, *ViewController.h* and *ViewController.m* could be called anything; 'MyApp.h' and 'MyApp.m' for example. But they will control a *View Controller* in *Interface Builder*.

When we build our first app, I will show you how to attach any *View Controller* to the correct *header* and *implementation* files.

I'd read this bit again if I were you. It's important to what we're going to do and it's a little complicated because of the way Apple have named their files.

I also mentioned something called a *.storyboard* file. But I didn't explain it. Let's have a closer look at what this means.

Storyboards and Nibs

We have looked at how the code we will write is held in two files (the *header* file and the *implementation* file), but the design of our app is usually completed in one of two ways: a storyboard or a *.xib* file (pronounced 'nib').

You'll have noticed that our sample app has a file called *Main.storyboard* and Apple would prefer us to use storyboards. So what is a storyboard? As its name suggests, it's a bit like an animator's storyboard where each screen layout for each section of your app is linked together.

Here's a zoomed-out version of the iPad storyboard I created for Stuart Spendlow's *Penguinpig* app:

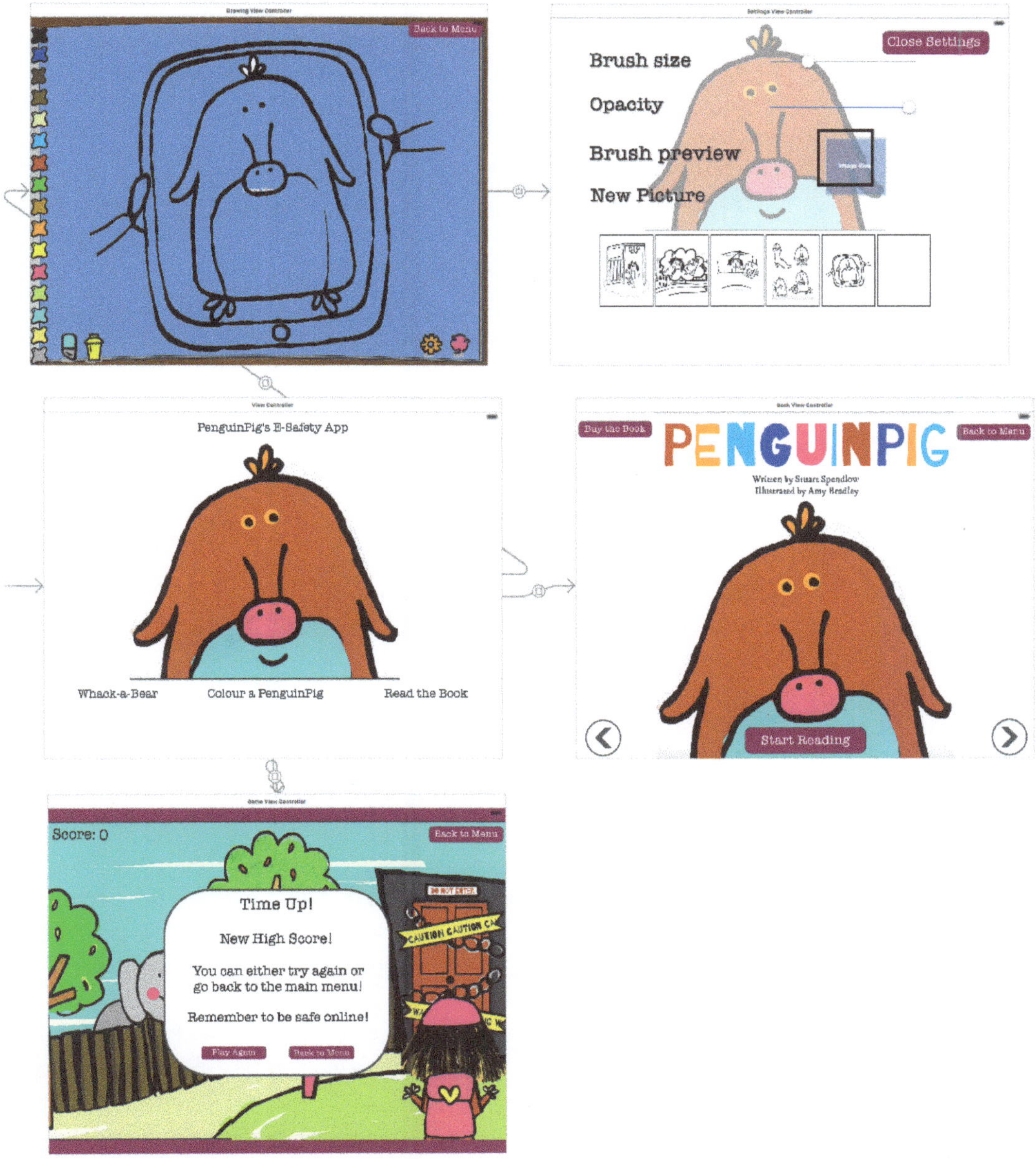

1.12

You can see five *View Controllers*. Each one represents a different screen in the app, and each one is linked to a pair of *.h* and *.m* files controlling what happens on the screen.

Storyboards were introduced a few years ago. Before that you would create a *.xib* file alongside your *.h* and *.m* file. So each *class* would have three files associated with it. You can still do this now if you choose to. A *.xib* is a bit like a one screen storyboard; you can only add the design for one screen of your app. You'd then need a new *.xib* file to add another screen. Aside from that, the process of designing your *user interface* is pretty much identical in both *.xibs* and Storyboards.

However, for the sake of this book, we will focus on creating Storyboards. It's much more efficient and easier to work with and, perhaps most importantly, requires less coding than separate *.xib* files.

You will make your first storyboard in the next chapter.

Different screen sizes

Once upon a time, there was one iPhone; the one with a clown fish as the home screen. It had one screen size.

Then Apple brought out the iPhone 5, which had a bigger screen. And then they brought out the iPad, which had a bigger screen again.

Then, just as all the app developers were okay with three screen sizes, those good folks in California brought out the iPhone 6 and iPhone 6 Plus.

And then they brought out the iPad Pro, and so on...

This has massive implications for app developers. You have to support certain screen sizes to be approved by Apple.

When we're talking about screen sizes, we use the term pixels. Those of you who know about these things will know that pixels aren't a measurement of size, but to make life easier for you and your class, we will act like they are.

By far the best guide to iPhone screen sizes I have found online, and use regularly for reference, is at **http://www.paintcodeapp.com/news/ultimate-guide-to-iphone-resolutions**.

As developers, we have to be aware of the capabilities of every device we are targeting. So throughout this book, we are going to focus on just two devices: the iPhone 4 and the iPhone 5. Creating an app for these two devices will allow our app to be installed on all iPhones without having to spend too much time creating extra user interfaces.

Let's look at the screen sizes we will be working with. Both the iPhone 4 and iPhone 5 are *retina* devices. This means that they display double the number of pixels than the actual screen size. All you need to know from this is that we must create all artwork at double the size we want it to appear on the screen, or else it will look blurry and pixelated. And that's never good.

So let's start with the iPhone 4. This was the first big update to contain retina screens. The screen size of the iPhone 4 is 320 x 480 pixels. If we wanted to create a background image to fill the screen, we'd create it at twice that size; 640 x 960 pixels.

Likewise, if we wanted to create a 100 x 100 pixel image for a button, we'd create a 200 x 200 pixel image.

The iPhone 5 – this was where Apple made the screen longer but the same width – has a size of 320 x 568 pixels. So a background image to fill the screen would need be double that at 640 x 1136 pixels.

Apple recently introduced the iPhone SE - this is the same size as the iPhone 5, iPhone 5C and iPhone 5S so throughout the book, when I refer to iPhone 5, I am also referring to the iPhone SE in terms of screen size.

GEEK ALERT

You do not need to read this paragraph:

For reference, the iPhone 6 and 6 Plus have the same aspect ratio as the iPhone 5 so most developers start by making iPhone 6 Plus art and scale it down for the iPhone 6 and iPhone 5. Unfortunately, the iPhone 4 has a different aspect ratio so artwork will always need to be produced separately.

By now, you're probably banging your head against the nearest hard object and thinking that maybe this whole app thing wasn't such a good idea. Don't worry. While the different screen sizes cause a fair few issues for developers, there are plenty of ways of overcoming them. And, in fact, when we build our school app, we're only going to make a storyboard for the iPhone 5. We're then going to copy it and resize for the iPhone 4.

At this point, I should tell you about something called *Auto Layout*. I haven't mentioned it so far because I hate it. Why do I hate it? Because it's confusing.

The premise makes sense. You make one storyboard for all devices. Sounds easier, but whenever you place an object, like a *button* or a *label*, on the screen, you have to set its relative position. For example, the button should always be 100 pixels from the left-hand side. And then on all devices, the button is 100 pixels from the left-hand side. But as you start adding more and more objects, it becomes difficult to manipulate the objects as you'd wish.

I find it hard to use, although I do use it sometimes. You might find it even harder to use. And the pupils in your class? I'd stay clear. Unless you want 30 hands up and 30 little voices yelling, 'Why won't my button go there?'

Unfortunately, it's a feature that *Xcode* enables by default so we will have to manually turn it off.

I should point out that using *Auto Layout* is best practice. But I should also emphasise that this book isn't about best practice. It's about finding a way to teach young children how to code an iOS app and giving you the introduction you need to develop your skills further.

So there will be a few times in this book where we do something in a way that a software engineer would question. But whether you drive to your destination in a Ford Escort or a Jaguar XF, does it matter as long as you get there?

And that's it. That's everything you need to know to get started. Don't get me wrong, there's a lot more stuff to learn but the best way to learn it is through examples and practical activities so that's what we'll do.

REMEMBER

Xcode has three main panes: Navigator (for loading files), Editor (for editing code or user interfaces) and Utilities (for changing aspects of code or design).

Each screen of your app is controlled by a class made up of two files: the header file and the implementation file.

The header file has the .h extension (like .doc on a Word file) and the implementation file has the .m extension.

You can design your app's user interface using storyboards or nibs (.xibs).

An iPhone 4 has a screen size of 320 x 480 pixels but needs art at double that.
An iPhone 5 has a screen size of 320 x 568 pixels but needs art at double that.

We don't like Auto Layout because it's hard.

http://www.alanpeat.com/build-an-app/Chapter1

CHAPTER TWO
YOUR FIRST APP

In this chapter, we're going to make our first app. It's going to be incredibly simple with just two screens. And in the tradition of software development, we're going to make a 'Hello, World' app.

For years, when developers have learned a new programming language they have begun by creating an app that displays 'Hello, World', or a variation of this phrase, on the screen.

As you're going to be making this app with the children, you might want to let them replace 'World' with their name (or, if you're a particularly egotistical teacher, your name. Either is fine with me).

The aims of this lesson will be:

- To familiarise the class with *Xcode*.
- To add a *UILabel*.
- To run the iOS Simulator.

For the students, I wouldn't recommend using the term *class*, refer to it as a new screen. So let's dive in.

I would recommend spending some time going over the three *panes* of *Xcode* prior to building this app.

The first thing we are going to do is make our opening screen. This is the screen that the user will see straight away and it is their first chance to interact with our app.

In the *Navigator* pane, find the file called *Main.storyboard* and click on it once. Be careful not to double click or a new window will open.

Your screen should look like this:

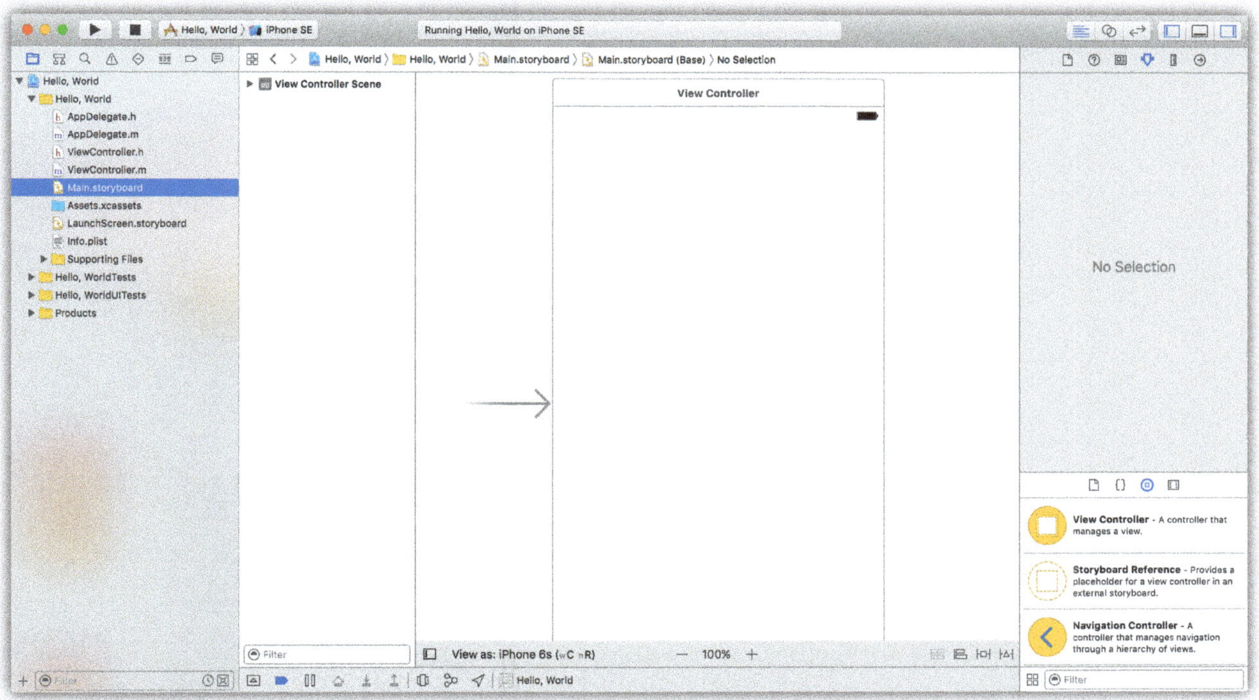

2.01

You'll notice the white box is the size on an iPhone 6 - in fact, if you look at the very bottom of the Editor Pane, you'll see some text saying 'View as: iPhone 6s' - if you click on this text, you will see a variety of other sizes you can choose from:

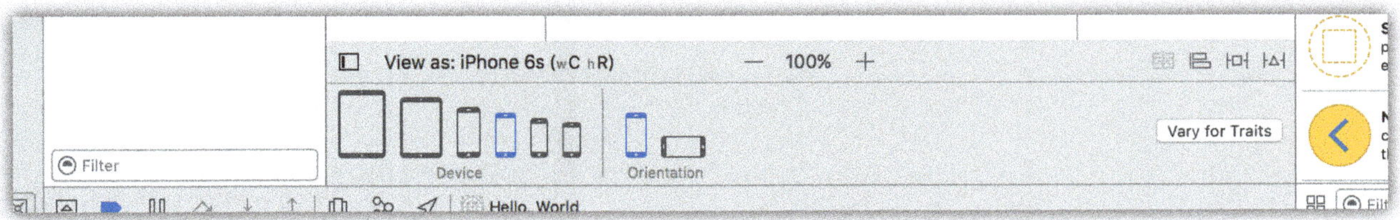

2.02

We're going to make our first app for an iPhone 5 (or iPhone SE) so select the second smallest iPhone image:

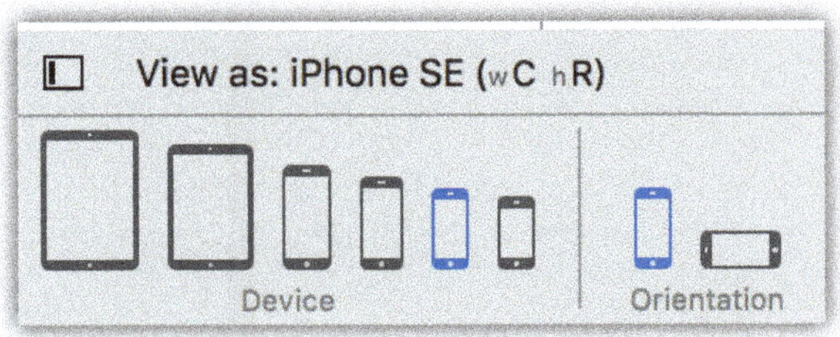

2.03

The white box in the middle of the Editor Pane will change to look like an iPhone 5 screen (it will get slightly smaller).

We need to change the shape of our screen. So look closely at the *Utilities* pane and find an icon that is shaped like a piece of paper:

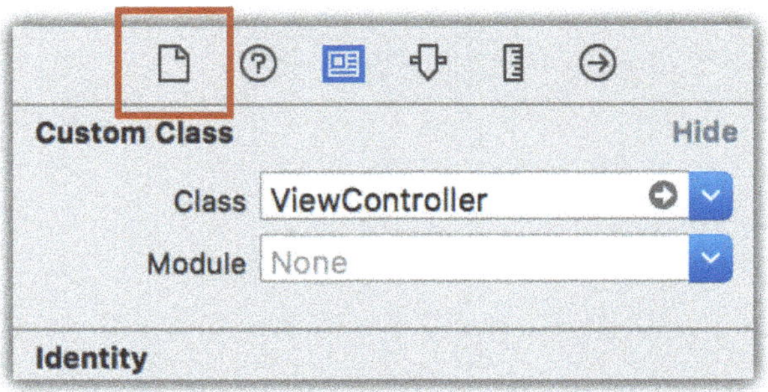

2.04

This is called the *File Inspector* tab and it changes the *Utility* pane to the *File Inspector*.

Now we're going to turn Auto Layout off so that you end up with this:

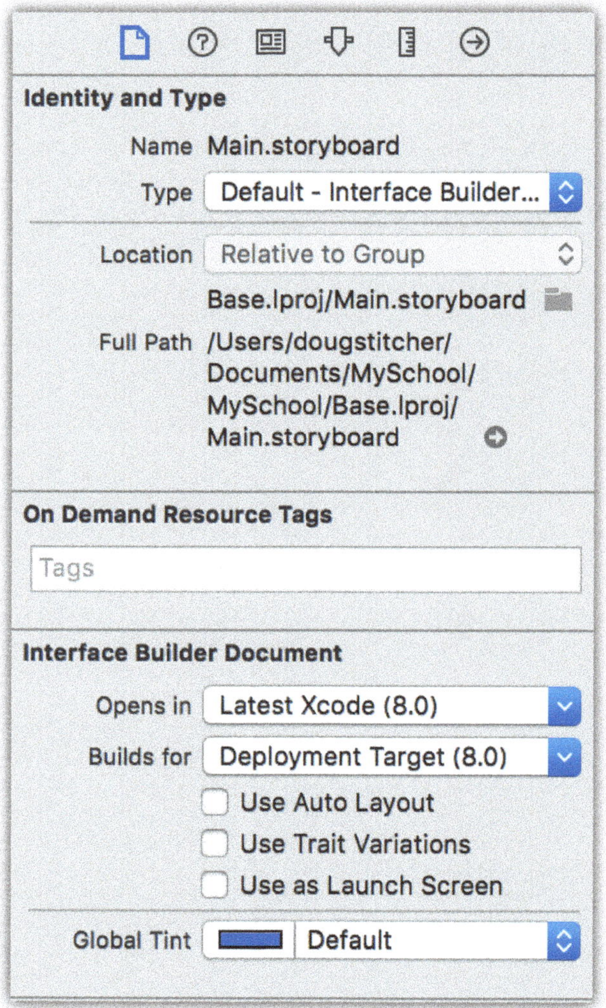

2.05

To do this, underneath *Interface Builder Document*, you'll see two checked boxes:

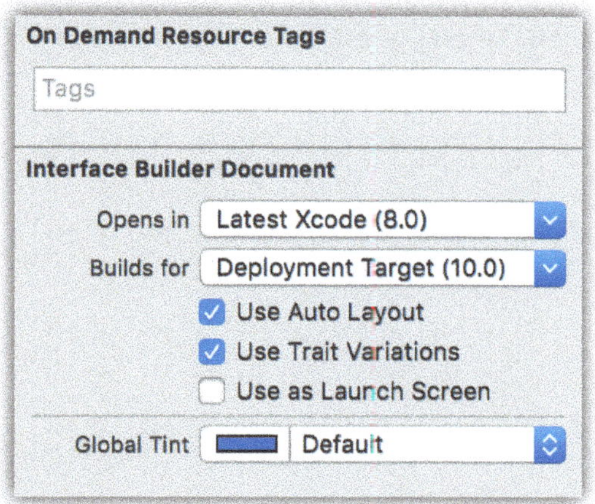

2.06

Uncheck the Use *Auto Layout* box and an alert dialogue box will pop up:

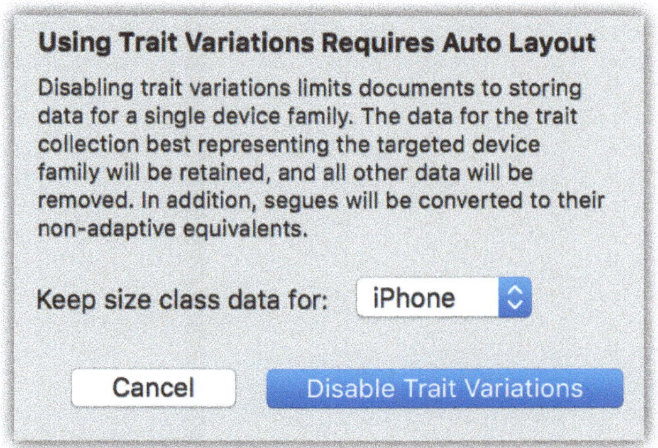

2.07

Press the blue *Disable Trait Variations* button and you're done. *Auto Layout* is now disabled and we can start to build our app.

Did you notice how when you pressed the *File Inspector* tab, the bottom of the *Utility* pane didn't change? Try it now. You'll see that the bottom third of the *Utility* pane always stays the same.

This is the *Library* section of *Xcode*. Fortunately, we don't need to worry about any of the tabs except the one that is already selected, the square inside a blue circle. This is our *Object Library* and it's here that we'll find loads of cool stuff to put into our app.

Scroll down until find an object called *Label*.

Click and drag from *Label* to the middle of your iPhone screen in the *Editor* pane.

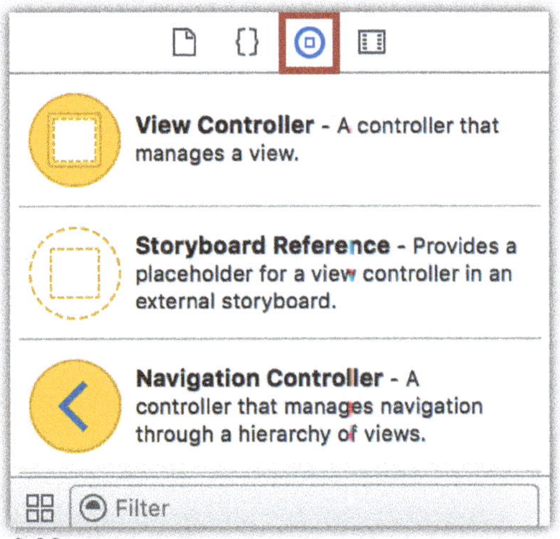

2.08

The end result should look something like this:

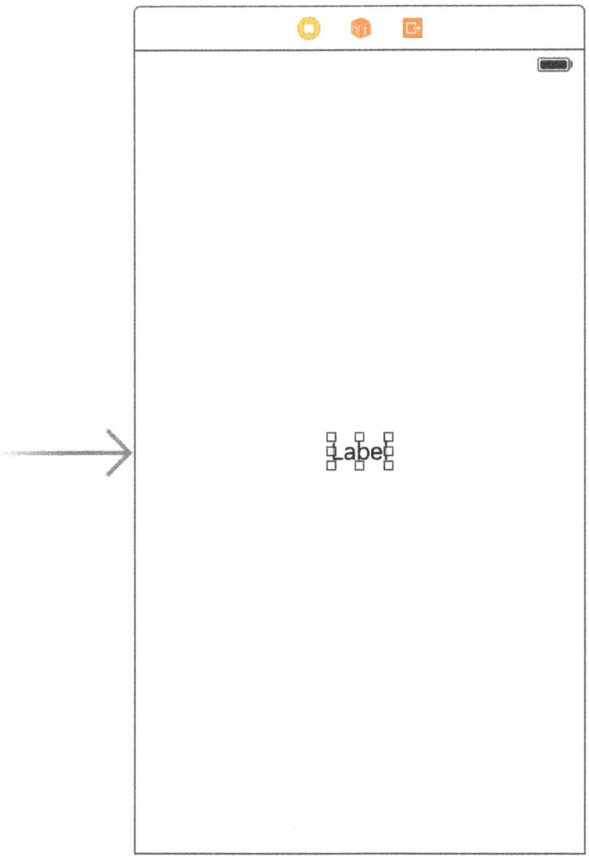

2.09

Did you see those blue dashed lines that appeared as you were dragging the label? They're a neat feature of *Xcode* and they allow the careful positioning of objects. I used them in the example above to place the *Label* directly in the centre of the screen.

We want to change the text of the *Label* from 'Label' to 'Hello, Your Name'. We can do this in two ways: we could double click on the label itself or we could select the label then press the *Attributes* tab in the *Utilities* pane.

Doing so will reveal this:

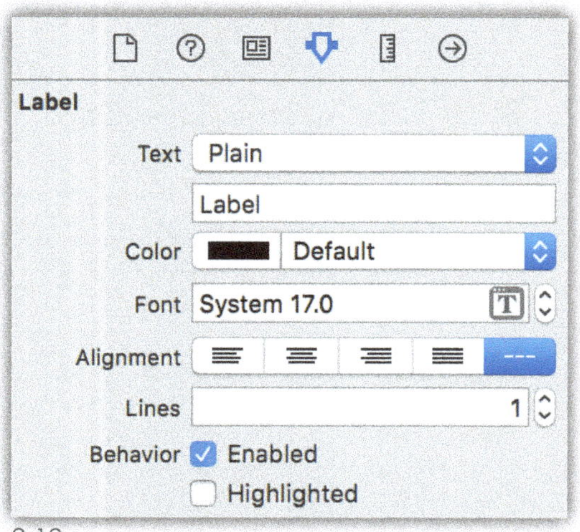

2.10

You can change the text, by editing the word 'Label'. You can change the colour and you can change the font, size and alignment.

In *Labels* – the posh name is *UILabel* where UI stands for *User Interface* – they are always set to display one line of text only. If you want more lines, increase the number in the *Lines* box. Alternatively, make it zero to have an unlimited number of lines.

For what we're trying to do here, you won't need to change it to zero.

Once you've changed the text from 'Label' to 'Hello, Your Name', you'll notice that the label no longer fits all your text in:

This is easily fixed. Click on the label and use the handles to resize it so that your text fits in.

You will probably find that you then need to reposition the *Label*. Try using the blue lines to centre the label horizontally and vertically.

If you've done everything correctly, your screen should look a little like this:

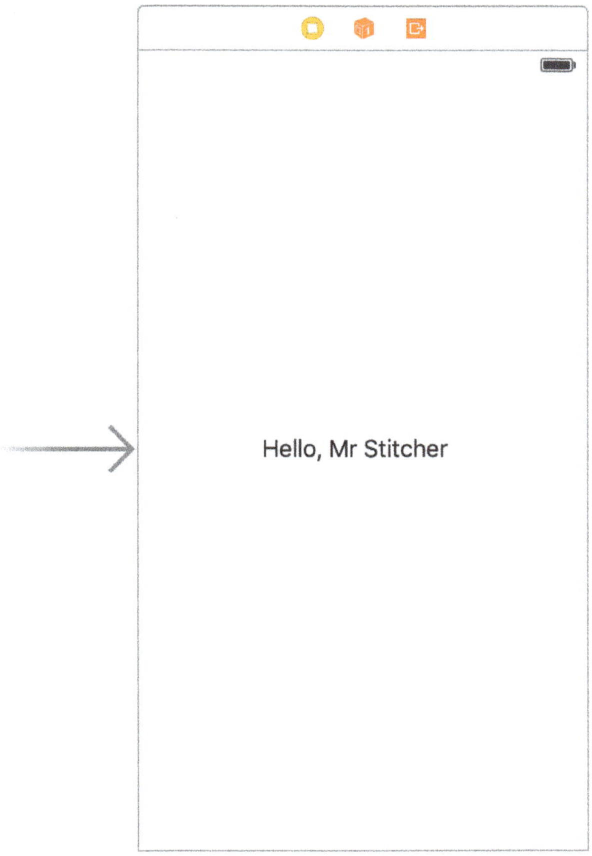

2.11

Probably by now, your class will have started playing around with the font and colour of the label. Let them, it's fun. But use it as a teaching point. Apple produce a set of design guidelines **https://developer.apple.com/library/ios/documentation/UserExperience/Conceptual/MobileHIG/** and their focus is on user experience. Point out that while curly, colourful fonts look pretty, they are not always easy for the user to read and understand.

We're ready to build our app. To do this, we are going to run our app on an *iOS simulator*.

Have a look at the top of *Xcode* just crossing between the *Navigator* and *Editor* panes:

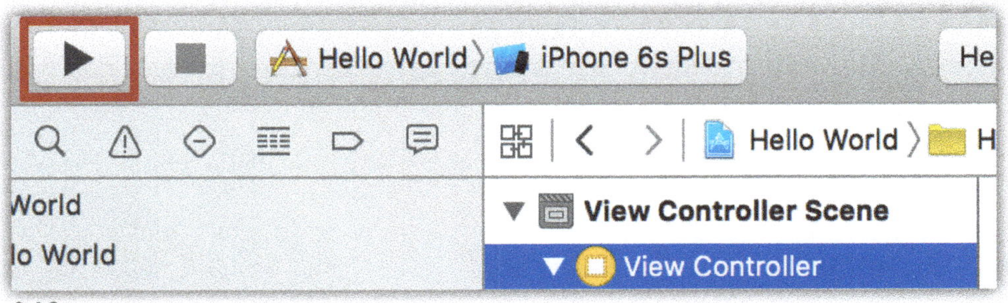

2.12

You should be able to see a *Play* button, this runs our app. But don't press it yet.

Next to the name of our app ('Hello World'), you can see that it says *iPhone 6s Plus*. That's telling us that pressing *Play* will run our app on the iPhone 6s Plus simulator. But we have designed our app to run on iPhone 5. So we need to choose the correct simulator.

To do this, click on *iPhone 6s Plus*.

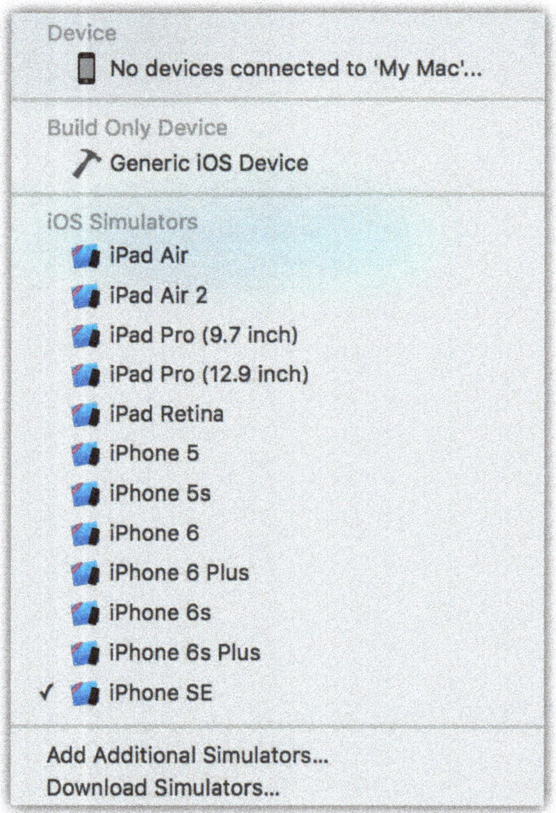

2.13

You'll see a list of available *simulators*. If your iPhone or iPad is connected to your computer with a USB lead, it will appear in the list at the top under *Device*.

As you can see, every device is available as a simulator from iPhone 5 onwards. This is because we are currently building an app for iOS 10 which was released in September 2016. Devices prior to the iPhone 5 are not capable of running iOS 10 and so do not appear in this list. However, when we build our school app, we will build it for iOS 8 so we will be able to use the iPhone 4s simulator.

That's fine. We're going to build apps that will work on the most recent devices.

So go ahead and select *iPhone 5* or *iPhone 5s*, it makes no difference which one you choose.

And now for the moment of truth... hit that big *Play* button that is just screaming to be pressed.

After a few seconds, the simulator will boot up and your app in all its simple glory will run. A new window will appear and a new icon will appear in the dock:

This is the iOS simulator icon. The simulator runs as a separate program on your Mac so you will need to access this icon if you want to close or find the window again.

2.14

Assuming everything went as planned, your first app should be happily displaying in the iPhone 5/5s simulator and should look like this:

2.15

Move the mouse around. Press away. Nothing happens. Why not? We've created an app with no code at all. An app that simply displays a label on the screen.

It's not much, I know, but every long journey begins with one step!

It's taken us several pages to get to this point, but the process of creating this app should take no more than about five minutes once you've got the hang of where everything is.

SAVING YOUR WORK

Xcode saves as it goes along. But you can't always trust it so it's a good idea to save manually. You can save individual files by going to File > Save – while the file you want to save is open in the Editor pane.

Xcode keeps track of which files haven't been saved by making the small icon to the left of the file name grey.

A quick way to save everything is to press the *Play* button. It will autosave all files before building the app onto the simulator.

Next steps

In this next exercise, you're going to learn how to use storyboards to link different screens, how to create a new *class* and how to add some more objects.

It's always a good idea to plan out apps in the same way you'd plan a piece of writing. So before we go ahead and add our next part, let's briefly discuss what we are going to try to achieve.

We're going to change our app to make it more interactive and in doing so, you're going to pick up quite a lot of new skills. Here's a brief overview of what our new app will do:

- The 'Hello, World' text will be changed to ask you what your name is.
- We'll add a text field so the user can answer the question.
- We'll add a *Submit* button so the app can do something with the information.
- We'll go to a new screen.
- We'll display the text 'Hello,' with the user's name after the comma.

I know that doesn't sound exciting but you will be amazed how delighted the children will be to see that the app knows their name. I taught my ten-year-old how to do this a couple of weeks back and she acted like she'd just invented *Siri*.

So expect lots of 'oohs' and 'ahhs' as you teach this. Oh and quite a lot of hands up as simple typing errors cause apps to crash.

Depending on how well your class got on with the first task, this lesson could either carry straight on from the first one or be split over two sessions. There's quite a bit to cover.

The aims of this lesson will be:

- To add a *UITextField*.
- To add a *UIButton*.
- To create a new *class*.
- To write code in *Objective-C*.

That's right. We're on to writing code.

The first thing I need you to do is go to your 'Hello, World' app and find your *Storyboard* file:

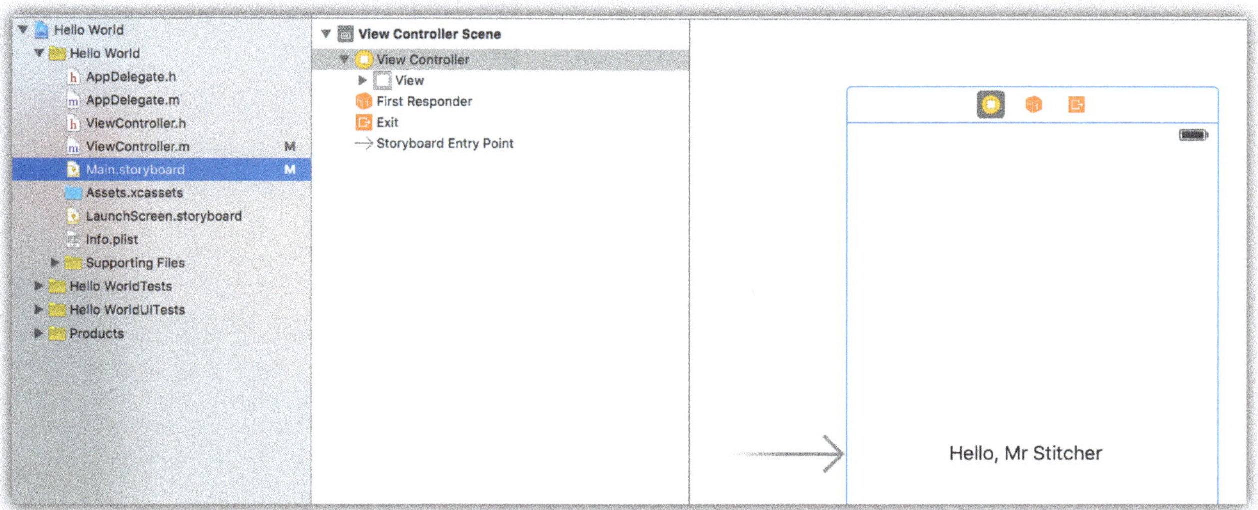

2.16

Now, select the label in the *Editor* pane, my one says 'Hello, Mr Stitcher'. Then, in the *Utilities* pane, select the *Attributes* tab:

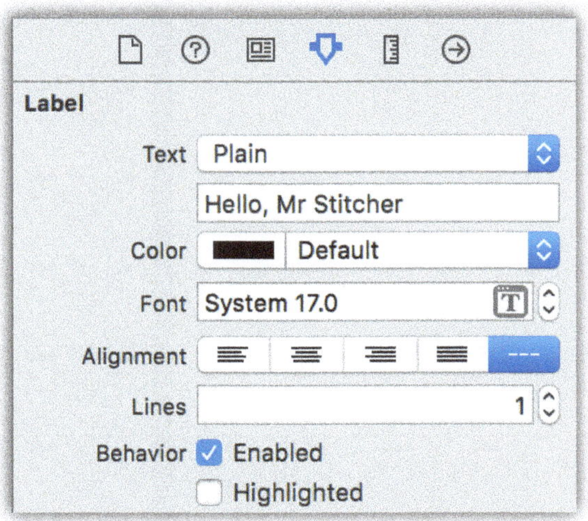

2.17

Select the text that says 'Hello, Mr Stitcher' and change it to 'What is your name?' or words to that effect.

Your *Label* will probably need resizing now:

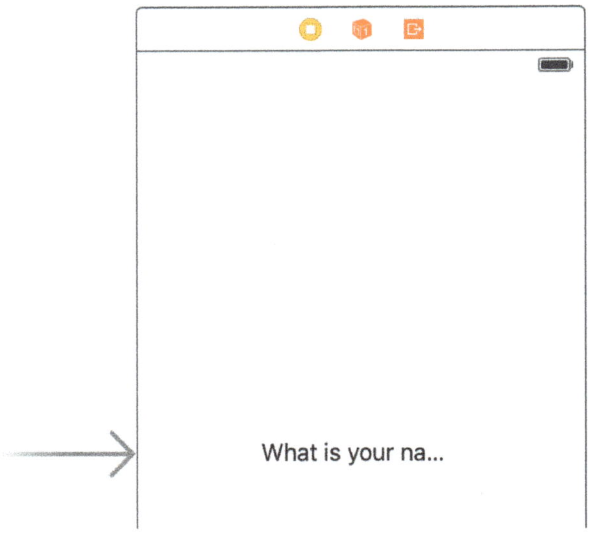

2.18

We did this in the last lesson, but if you've forgotten and can't be bothered looking back, just select the label and use the handles to make it longer.

Once you've resized it, drag it and use the blue guidelines to position it centrally on the screen. We're going to need a bit of space below this label, so I need you to lift the label up nearer to the top of the screen, something like this:

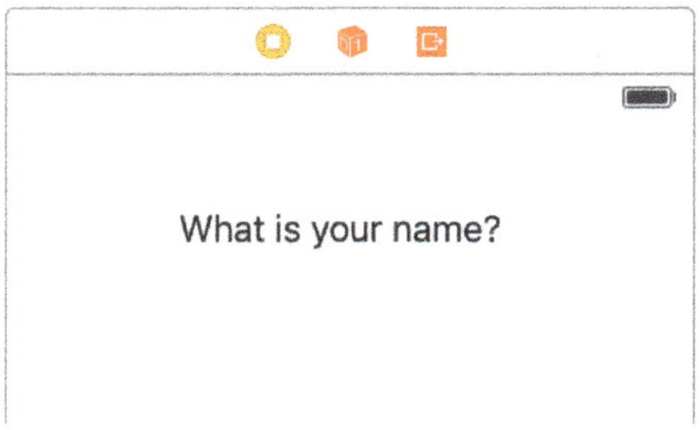

2.19

There we go. That was easy.

It's a good time to mention that our *UILabel*, the posh word for our label, is displaying *static* text. This means the text will never change during the life of our app. Later in this lesson, we will be adding some *dynamic* text. The text will change depending upon the way the user interacts with the app.

We've got our question. We need to add a way for the user to respond. The most common way of doing this is by adding a *UITextField*, UI just means *User Interface* and any objects in our app that do the job of changing how the user interacts with our app begin with the letters 'UI'.

Go back to the *Utilities* pane and locate the *Object Library* in the bottom third of the pane:

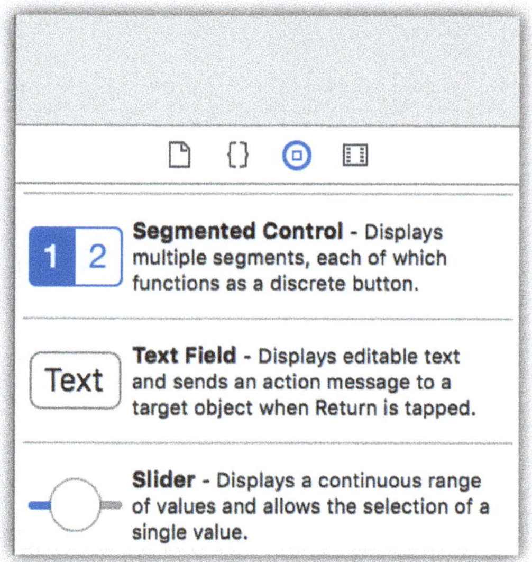

2.20

If you scroll down, you should see *Text Field*. That's the one we want. Drag it from the *Object Library* to your screen, which should still be open in the *Editor* pane.

Position your *text field* somewhere below your label displaying your question.

Your screen should look a bit like this. I've left in the top of the *Attributes* section in the *Utilities* pane so you can see some of the options:

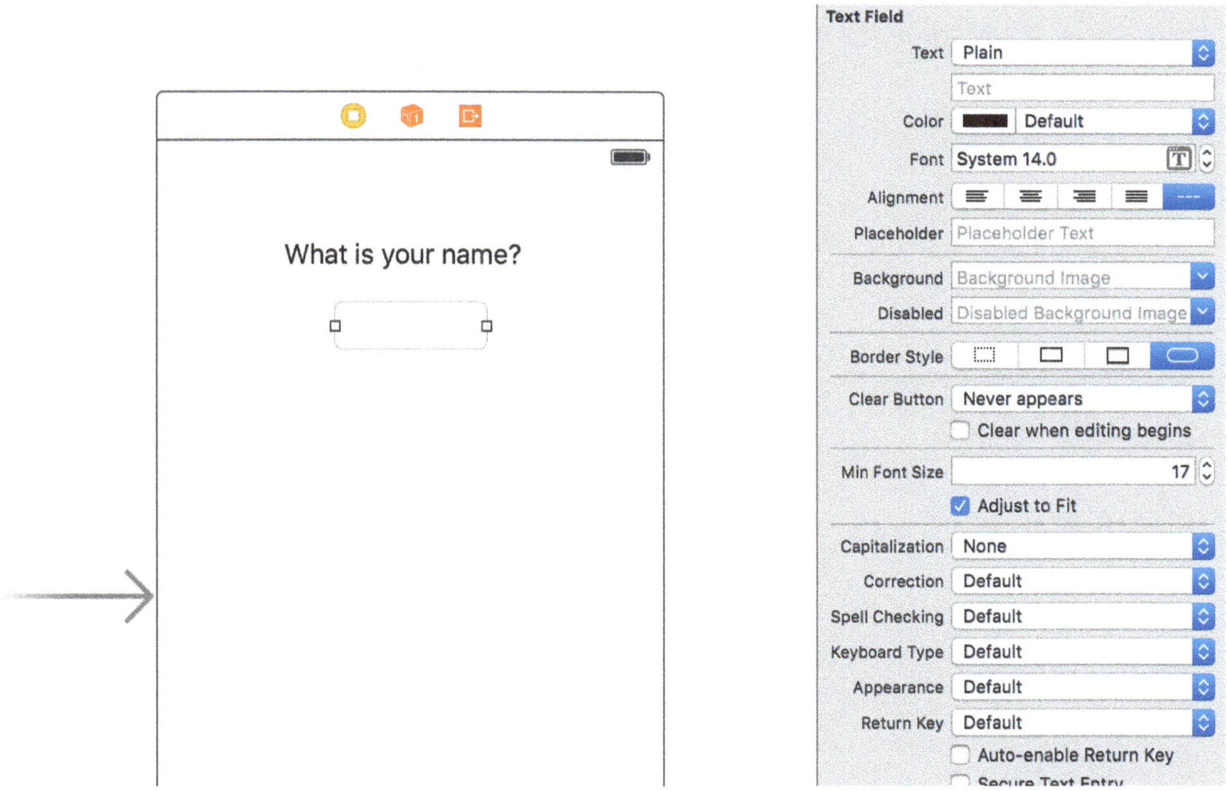

2.21

There's a bit more to change on a *Text Field* so let's go through some of the key *properties* that you can change depending on the purpose of your text field. Remember, our text field is designed to collect the name of somebody.

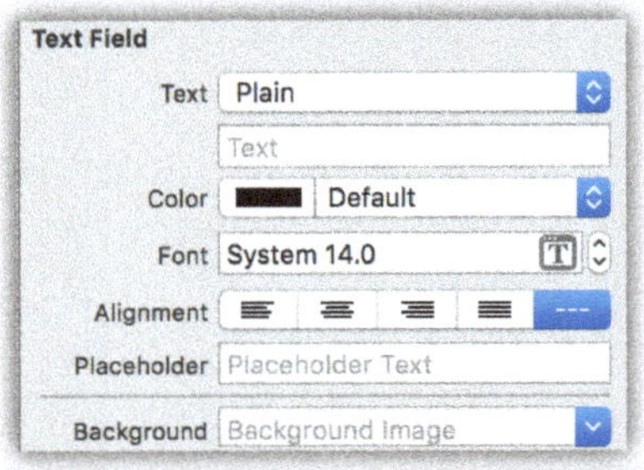

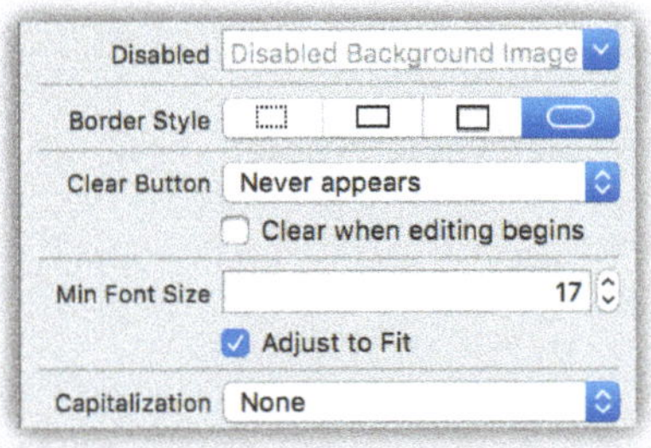

Text - Plain	Here you can choose between plain text or 'attributed text' where you can change some of the more advanced options. We don't need to change this from plain.
Colour	You know the children will want to change this – get ready for garish pinks and impossible-to-see yellows.
Font	The default font is an Apple font called San Francisco that can only be used in apps at present. By all means, change it.
Alignment	Much like in *Word*, you can centre the text or align it left or right or justify it. For this text field, I'd recommend left align or centred.
Placeholder Text	This lets you leave some text in the box so the user knows what to do with it. For example, you could put 'Enter your name' – as soon as the user begins typing, the placeholder text will vanish.
Background Image	You can add a background image to the text field – for example, you may want to make the box coloured depending on what the box is for.
Disabled Image	This is how the text field appears when the user isn't allowed to type into it. We don't need this for this app as they are always allowed to use it.
Border Style	This changes the appearance of the textfield. The default is the rounded rectangle that you've already used.
Clear Button	This refers to the little cross that appears when you're typing that will clear the text. You can have it appear all the time, never or just when you're typing.
Min Font Size	This is the smallest size you will allow the font to shrink to if the words being typed into the text field don't fit. After that size is reached, the text gets cut off with dots e.g. Your Na... Leaving the 'Adjust to Fit' button checked will resize the text to your minimum font size.
Capitalisation	This feature lets you specify whether words, sentences or nothing is automatically capitalised. For names, go with 'words'.

Clearly, there are a lot of properties. This is true for many of the objects we can add to our apps but fortunately, we do not need to use them all. As we move through the different activities, I'll draw your attention to those that do need changing.

The one thing you will need to do is make your text field a little wider. While the text will auto shrink to fit the box, if you are entering a particularly long name, it will cut the name off with dots. And we don't wan't that.

Your screen should look like this:

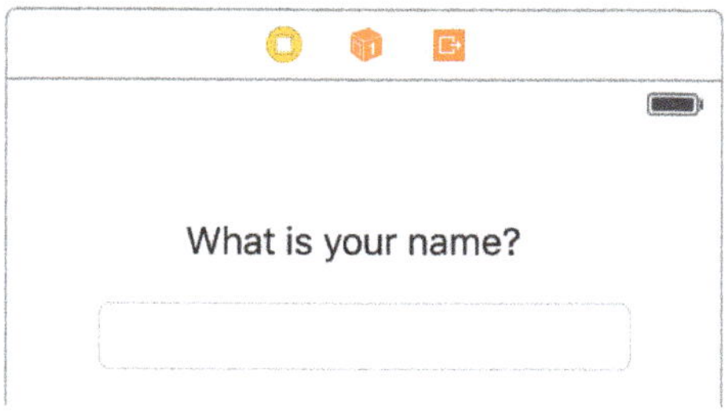

2.22

You might be wondering how the keyboard will appear when the user clicks on the *text field*. This is down to a little bit of Apple magic. Press the *Play* button above the *Navigator* pane. This will run the app in the *iOS simulator*.

With the app running, press your mouse in the *text field* and notice how the keyboard appears. You can also type in the box. Again, all this without a single line of code.

It's worth noting here that when you want a text field to bring the keyboard, it **becomes the first responder**. This doesn't have anything to do with emergency services, but it's some terminology to get used to. Likewise, when we want to get rid of the keyboard, we **resign the first responder**. I know it's a bit technical but as long as you are aware of it at this stage, you do not need to fully understand it.

Now we're ready to add some real life bonafide code to our app. I would suggest supporting students by having snippets of code for them to copy and paste. Almost all code will go wrong with as little as one typo.

Before we code, a couple of things to note. Firstly, you, and your class, may not understand everything we do. I will explain what the code does but don't panic if it looks like gibberish for a while.

Secondly, everything we code is case-sensitive. Capital letters and lower-case letters are read as such and it's not uncommon for an app to crash because of a misplaced letter.

Cast your mind back to page 14, when we were looking at the *implementation* file (.m) and the *header* file (.h). We're first going to add some code to the header file. There are two things we need to tell it:

- We've got a *UITextField* on our storyboard
- We're going to be using some of the features of a *UITextField*

Once the *header* file knows this, it passes that information on to the *implementation* file and we can do our cool stuff in there.

Therefore, I'd like you to select *ViewController.h* from the *Navigator* pane:

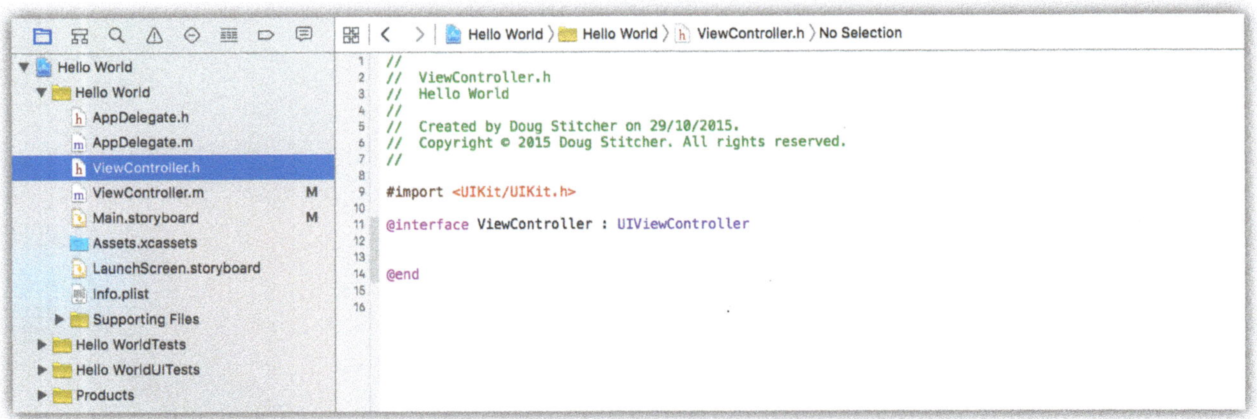

2.23

The first thing we're going to do is tell the file that we are using *UITextFields*. This opens up lots more features that we could use later on if we so wanted. In our app, this isn't essential but it's good practice.

If we didn't tell the file this, we wouldn't be able to make the keyboard disappear when we finish typing for example.

Look at line 11 (the line numbers are in the grey column to the left of the *Editor* pane):

You should see this code:

@interface ViewController : UIViewController

I'd like you to change the code to this:

@interface ViewController : UIViewController <UITextFieldDelegate>

All I've done is add <UITextFieldDelegate>

Don't worry about what this means beyond the fact that it's telling the .m file we're playing with *Text Fields*.

Next I need you to add a swirly bracket '{' after the > on the same line:

@interface ViewController : UIViewController <UITextFieldDelegate> {

Press the *return* key and you will notice another swirly bracket appears a couple of lines down automatically, closing the brackets for us.

The complete code should look like this:

```
#import <UIKit/UIKit.h>

@interface ViewController : UIViewController <UITextFieldDelegate> {

}


@end
```

2.24

Check yours carefully. A good way of testing is to run the app. It won't run on the iOS simulator if there's a mistake.

So we've used the .h file to tell the .m file that we're going to be playing around with *Text Fields*.

The next thing we need to do is tell the .h file that we've already created a *UITextField* and placed it on our screen in our *StoryBoard* file. For this bit to make sense, you need to know that when you are editing your screen layout, like when you dragged your *Label* around, you are working in a part of the app called *Interface Builder*. When *Xcode* was first released, you'd edit your screens in a separate app called *Interface Builder* but a few years back, Apple put the ability to do this directly in *Xcode*.

As a result, whenever we refer to *Interface Builder*, we're talking about the screen you see in the *Editor* pane when you are editing a *StoryBoard* file (or a .xib file).

I've made that as clear as mud, so let's go back to the *ViewController.h* file and add the following code between the two swirly brackets:

IBOutlet UITextField *myTextField;

```
@interface ViewController : UIViewController <UITextFieldDelegate> {
    IBOutlet UITextField *myTextField;
}
```

2.25

Let's talk this code through.

The *IBOutlet* bit simply tells the app that we have an object (in this case, our *text field*) in *Interface Builder*, that's what the IB stands for. It's called an *Outlet* but it's just a posh way of saying 'Something cool in Interface Builder'.

The next bit (in dark purple) *UITextField* is telling the app what type of object we have. In this case it's a *text field*. You might be wondering why we haven't put our *Label* here. The reason is because the label contains static text so we don't need to change it with any code. Therefore, our .h and .m files don't need to know whether it even exists.

We use an asterisk to tell the app that we're going to give our text field a name, in this case 'myTextField'. You could call it anything you want; even something like 'Bob'. Notice how I've used a lower case letter to start the name and then any new word begins with a capital.

The most common mistake children make with this code is they call the text field something like 'my text field' with spaces. This will throw up errors so make sure they keep it as one word.

Finally, we finish every line of code with a semi-colon. This is pretty standard in most programming languages. Again, not doing this will throw up errors.

And that's it in this file.

The next thing we need to do is make sure that the text field on our *StoryBoard* file is *connected* to our code. This is easy to do so click on *Main.storyboard* in the *Navigator* pane.

Press the little right-facing arrow next to *View Controller Scene*:

2.26

It will expand to show this:

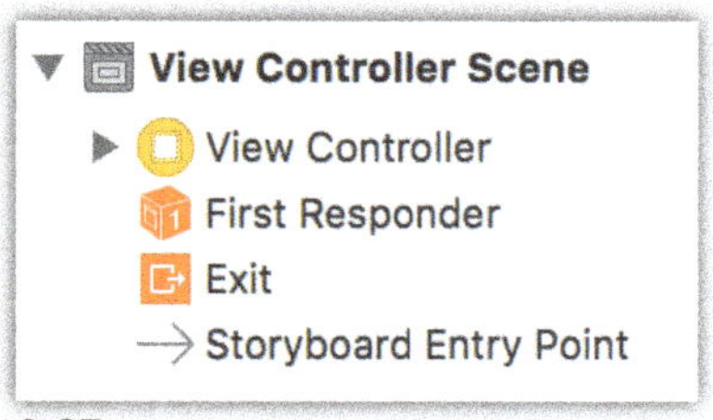

2.27

You can continue to expand by pressing the arrow next to the yellow circle and *View Controller*. This will show you all the objects on your screen (currently a *UILabel* and *UITextField*). However, for this bit, you don't need to do that.

Select your *Text Field* on the main iPhone screen in the middle of the *Editor* page. You'll notice that the list of objects automatically expands and that the text field is selected.

If you're using a *MacBook* or magic *Trackpad*, then with two fingers, drag from the yellow circle that says *View Controller* to your text field. If you're using a regular mouse then press *ctrl* and drag with your mouse at the same time:

A blue line should appear from the yellow circle to your text field and then a little black box will pop up:

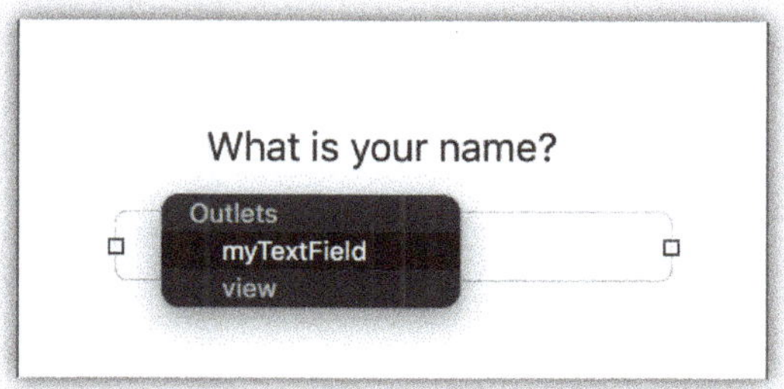

2.28

This is giving you a list of the *outlets* you've declared in your .h file. Go ahead and select *myTextField*.

You won't get any instant feedback that you've done this correctly. So let's use the *Connections inspector* in the *Attributes* pane to check.

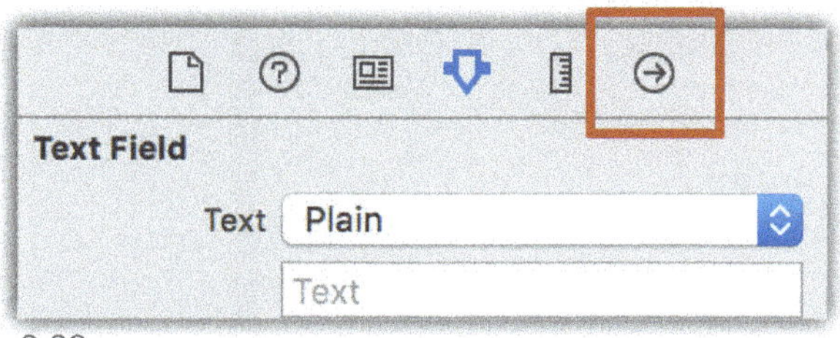

2.29

Press the button on the far right, the arrow inside a circle. This will change the *Utilities* pane to display the *Connections inspector*. About midway down the *pane*, you will find where you've successfully connected your text field:

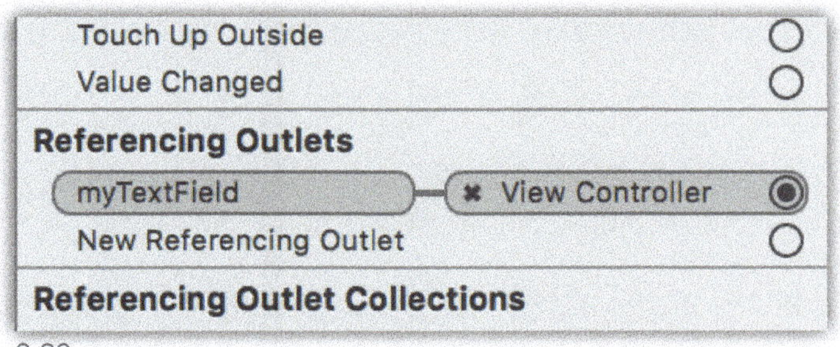

2.30

Notice it's called a *referencing outlet* – that's because we have referenced it in our .h file.

Once you've done that, reselect the *Attributes inspector* by pressing the fourth button from the left (highlighted below), that's the one we've been using most of the time so it's handy to have that one open.

Thus far, we've added a *UITextField*, told our .h file we're playing with text fields, told our .h file we have a *text field* and what we'd like to call it and also connected our text field to our .h file by dragging in *Interface Builder*.

Next we need to add a button to press to submit our user-entered data (in this case, that's the pupil's name).

To get the button, go to the *Utilities* pane and then look in the *Object Library* in the bottom third of the screen.

Scroll down until you see the object called *Button*:

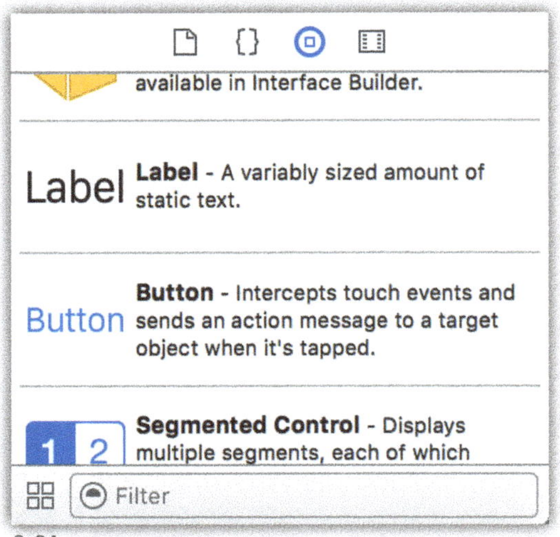

2.31

Remember, all our *user interface* elements have the prefix 'UI' to remind us that they are used to allow the user to interact with our app, so while we call this a *Button*, it's actually a *UIButton*.

Go ahead and drag the button to the iPhone 5 screen you can see in the middle of the *Editor* pane:

Have a look at where I've put mine. Can you foresee any issues with this?

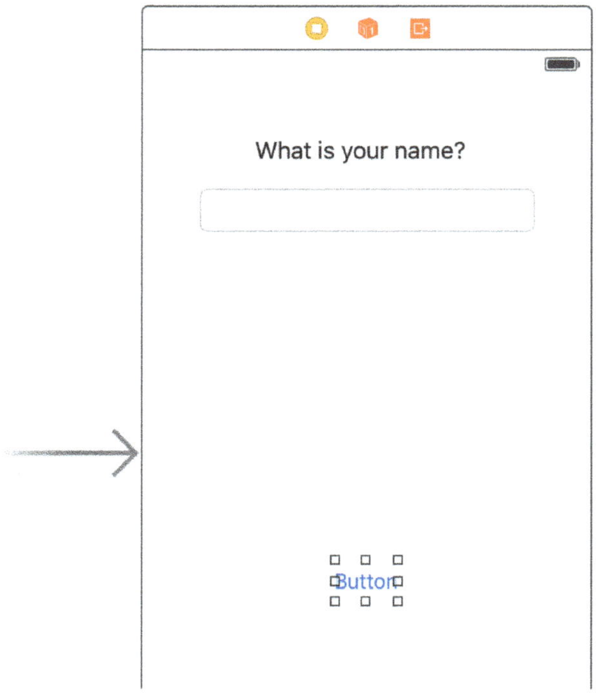

2.32

When the user presses in the textfield, a keyboard will pop up.

Drag yours to roughly the same position as mine and press the *Play* button to run the app on the simulator.

Now press the *text field*.

What do you notice?

Yep, the keyboard covers the button we've just added. There are ways to make the screen lift up when the keyboard is open, but we're not going down that road with this so, instead, just move your button so it lies centrally horizontally and just beneath the textfield.

With your button in position, give it a new title. You may need to resize your button after this to make it fit. As with our label, there are two ways of altering the text:

1. Click on the button itself and type the new title, for example 'Submit';

2. In the *Utilities* pane, select the *Attribute inspector*, which you've probably already got open, and change the text of the title:

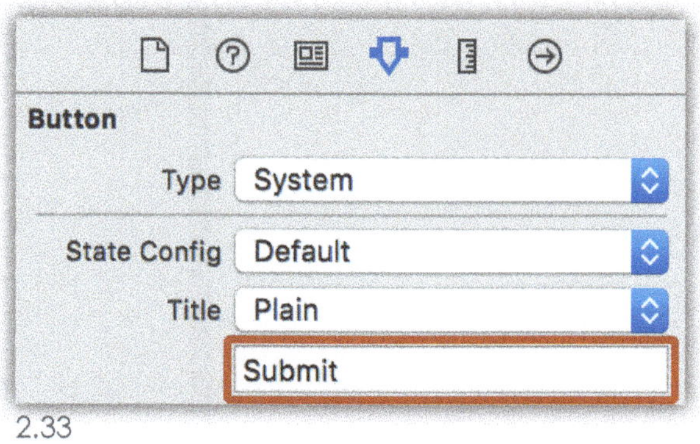

2.33

If you've changed the title to 'Submit', you will need to resize your button, so do that and it should look something like mine:

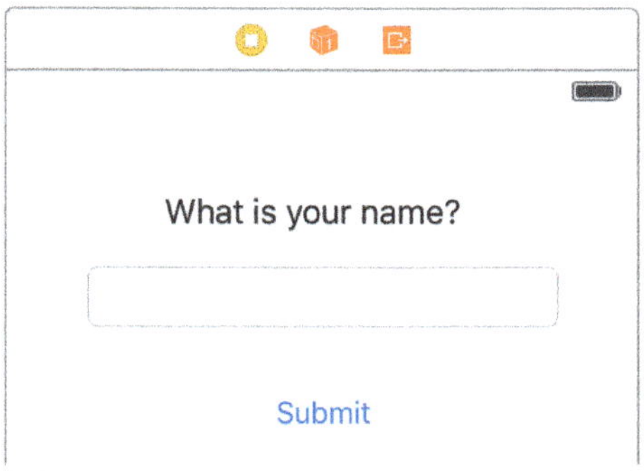

2.34

You've now added a *UILabel, UITextField* and *UIButton* to your app. You've linked your UITextField to your code and you're ready for the fun bit.

We're going to write a *method*. A method is a block of code that runs either on the press of a button or when told to run by another method.

There are two types of *methods* in *Objective-C*: *instance methods* and *class methods*. I'm not going to go into the difference between the two in this book but if you're interested in the difference between instance and class methods, have a look at **http:/tinyurl.com/objcmethods**.

We will be using two types of *instance methods* throughout our app development and on the next page, we'll have a look at two different ways of writing instance methods. You can safely skip it if it gets too heavy, but it's worth a quick skim.

Before we write our method to collect the user's name, let's have a look at the structure of two typical methods:

METHOD 1

An IBAction (Interface Builder Action)

An IBAction is a *method* that we write and then link it to an object on our screen, much like how we linked the UITextField earlier.

```
- (IBAction)myMethod:(id)sender{

        //My code here

}
```

We put a minus sign at the start and then 'IBAction' in brackets before we give our method a name. In this case, it's imaginatively called 'myMethod'. We then use a colon before putting (id)sender and a swirly bracket.

The ':(id)sender' means that we can get some information from the button that calls this method – this can be useful if we want several buttons to call the same method. We can track which button called the method.

In between the swirly brackets, we add the code that we want to do stuff when the method is called.

METHOD 2

A 'void' Method

When we don't necessarily want our method to be triggered by pressing a button (although we can still do this as I will explain later), we use a 'void' *method*. You don't need to know too much about what 'void' means, other than simply that the method doesn't return a value. Instead, it just tells objects to do things.

Our apps will predominantly use IBAction and Void methods.

```
- (void)myMethod{

        //My code here;
}
```

You'll notice, our void method also begins with a minus sign and then the word 'void' in brackets. We give our method a name, add a swirly bracket, add some code in and close it with a swirly bracket.

Now you know a little bit more about *methods*, it's time to write one. It's always a good idea to get it straight in your head what you want to achieve before writing the method so let's run through that now:

- The user enters his/her name and presses *Submit*.
- We collect the name from the *text field*.
- We store the name so we can get it on our next screen, which we haven't made yet.

Doesn't sound too complicated.

We will be writing an *IBAction* method which we will put in *ViewController.m*. Why? Because this is the *implementation* file that controls what we've put on the screen. Open the file:

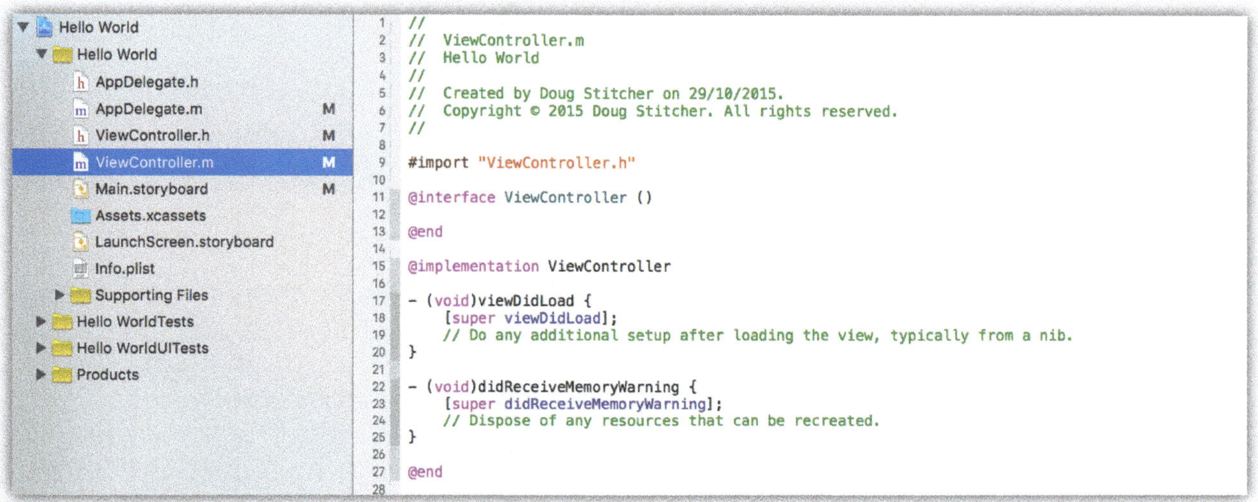

2.35

You'll notice there are already two void *methods* in there: *viewDidLoad* and *didReceiveMemoryWarning*.

ViewDidLoad is for anything you want to happen after the screen loads for the first time. We will be using that later on. The method didReceiveMemoryWarning is so we can do something if the app starts using too much memory on the user's device and is looking like it might crash. We won't need to use that one. I'd like to say that this is because our code will be so efficient, we won't run out of memory, but really it's just because our apps won't do anything very memory intensive.

We're going to stick our method in between the two methods that are already there. I tend to keep viewDidLoad at the top – it makes sense as it's the method that we call first.

I'd like you to copy my method. Be careful with the spacing and cases. I'll explain it after you've typed it:

```
- (IBAction)submit:(id)sender{
    [[NSUserDefaults standardUserDefaults] setObject:myTextField.text forKey:@"username"];
    [myTextField resignFirstResponder];
}
```

2.36

This isn't the complete code but it's a big part of it. We'll add some more in a minute. So, what does this mean?

We declare our method as an *IBAction* and keep track of the *Button* that called it:

```
- (IBAction)submit:(id)sender{
```

2.37

The *method* is going to be called 'submit'. Notice the swirly bracket. The next bit of code is a bit more complicated:

```
[[NSUserDefaults standardUserDefaults] setObject:myTextField.text forKey:@"username"];
```

2.38

Here, we are doing something fancy. We are saving the contents of our *text field* into a special place where we can store information for use on another screen, or *class*.

In this code we tell the app that we want to use something called *NSUserDefaults*. That's a space reserved for storing settings in games. For example, whether the user wants sound on or off. But you can use it for storing lots of different things. I should point out that there are other, more efficient ways of passing information between different screens. But remember, we're trying to keep this simple and achievable for you and your class.

Once we've said we're using *NSUserDefaults*, we set the object that we want to save. In this case it is the text in our *text field*. To access this, we use the code *myTextField.text*. We then have to say which NSUserDefault we want to save it to. As we haven't got any set up yet, we can call it what we want. So I've decided to call mine *username*. You can call it anything you want.

And finally, our last bit of code:

```
    [myTextField resignFirstResponder];
}
```

2.39

This is straightforward. All we are doing is telling our app that once we've pressed the *Submit* button, the keyboard should go away. If we don't do this, when we open the next screen, the keyboard will still be there.

Finally, a closing swirly bracket. }

As our app currently only has one function, getting the user to type their name, let's make the keyboard appear when our screen first loads.

Go to the *viewDidLoad* method and change it so it looks like this:

```
- (void)viewDidLoad {
    [super viewDidLoad];
    [myTextField becomeFirstResponder];
    // Do any additional setup after loading the view, typically from a nib.
}
```
2.40

By adding *[myTextField becomeFirstResponder];* all we are doing is telling our app to bring up the keyboard when it starts.

Try it. Go ahead and press the *Play* button to run the app on the simulator.

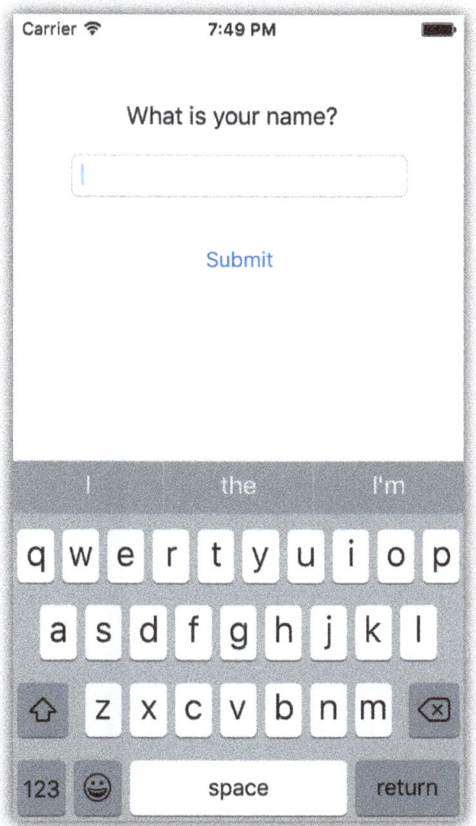

2.41

How cool is that? You've just made the keyboard appear all by itself. I was so excited when I learnt how to do that, but then I don't get out much.

Type something into the box and press the blue *Submit* button. Anything happen? Nope.

That's because we haven't linked our *IBAction* to the button. So let's do that now. Open your storyboard file. Select the *Submit* button then using a two-finger drag (or pressing *ctrl* and dragging), go from the button to the white square in a yellow circle. There are actually two places you can do this:

2.42

Either one of them is fine as they both represent the same thing.

Once you've done this, a little black box will pop up:

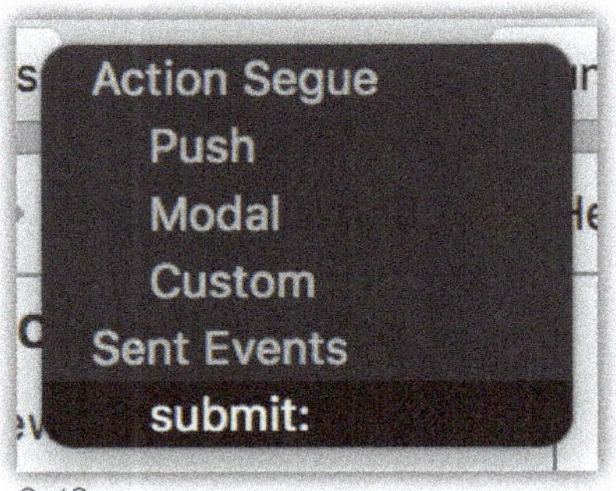

2.43

Select *submit:* which is under the *Sent Event* heading. The box will disappear. If you want to check that it has worked, repeat the dragging process and you should see a small white dot next to submit. Your *IBAction* is now linked to your button.

One other interesting thing to look at is back in *ViewController.m* so open up that file:

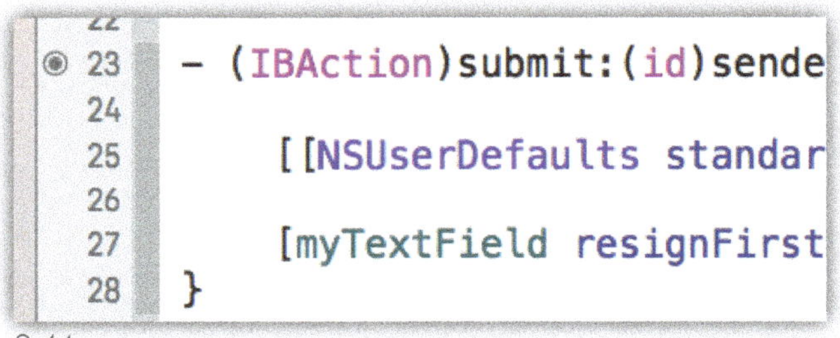

2.44

See that circle on line 23? That was empty before you linked the *method* to the button. It now has a grey dot inside it telling you that this method is linked to something in *Interface Builder*. This is a handy feature if you need to remind yourself of which methods you've linked and which you haven't.

You could run the app again. The button will save the name to *NSUserDefaults* but you won't know about it as we haven't added any code to do anything with the saved name.

So let's do it.

This is what we are going to do:

- Add a new *class*. This new class will control a new screen for us.
- Add a *Label* to our new screen.
- Tell that label to display our user's name in a *UILabel*.
- Add some code to open the new screen.

The first thing to do is create our new *class*. These are the .h and .m files that will control our next screen. It's easy to do:

2.45

Go to the *File* menu at the top of the screen and select *New > File*. Or, as you can see, use the keyboard shortcut by pressing the *CMD* button and 'N' at the same time.

You'll then be given a wealth of choices for the new file you can add:

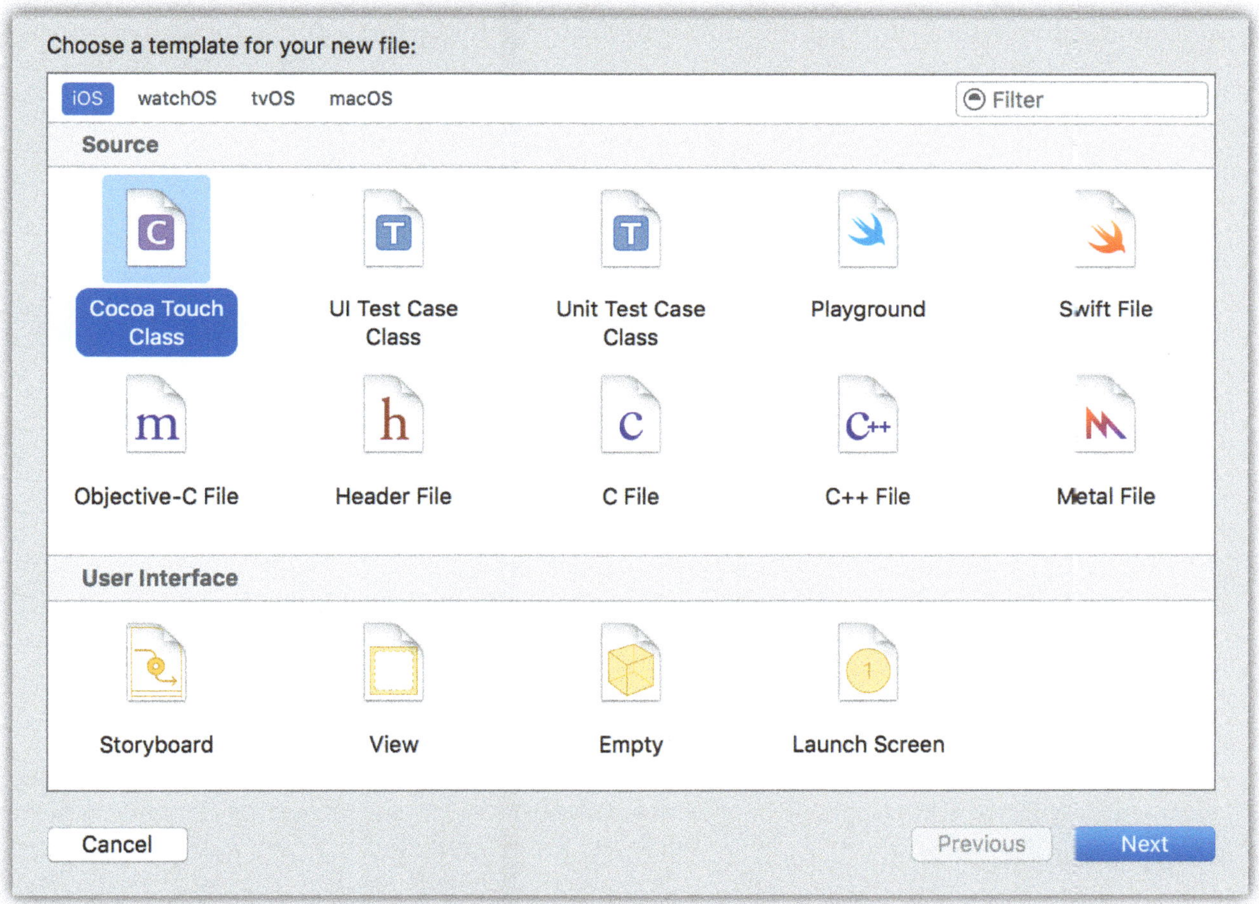

2.46

Fortunately, we want to add a new *Cocoa Touch Class* so leave that selected and press *Next*.

On the next screen, you'll be asked to name your class. We're going to call it *NameDisplayViewController*. Notice how our class names begin with capital letters. They don't have to, but it's the convention so let's not go against the grain. Do NOT select 'Also create XIB file for user interface' as we're using storyboards in this app.

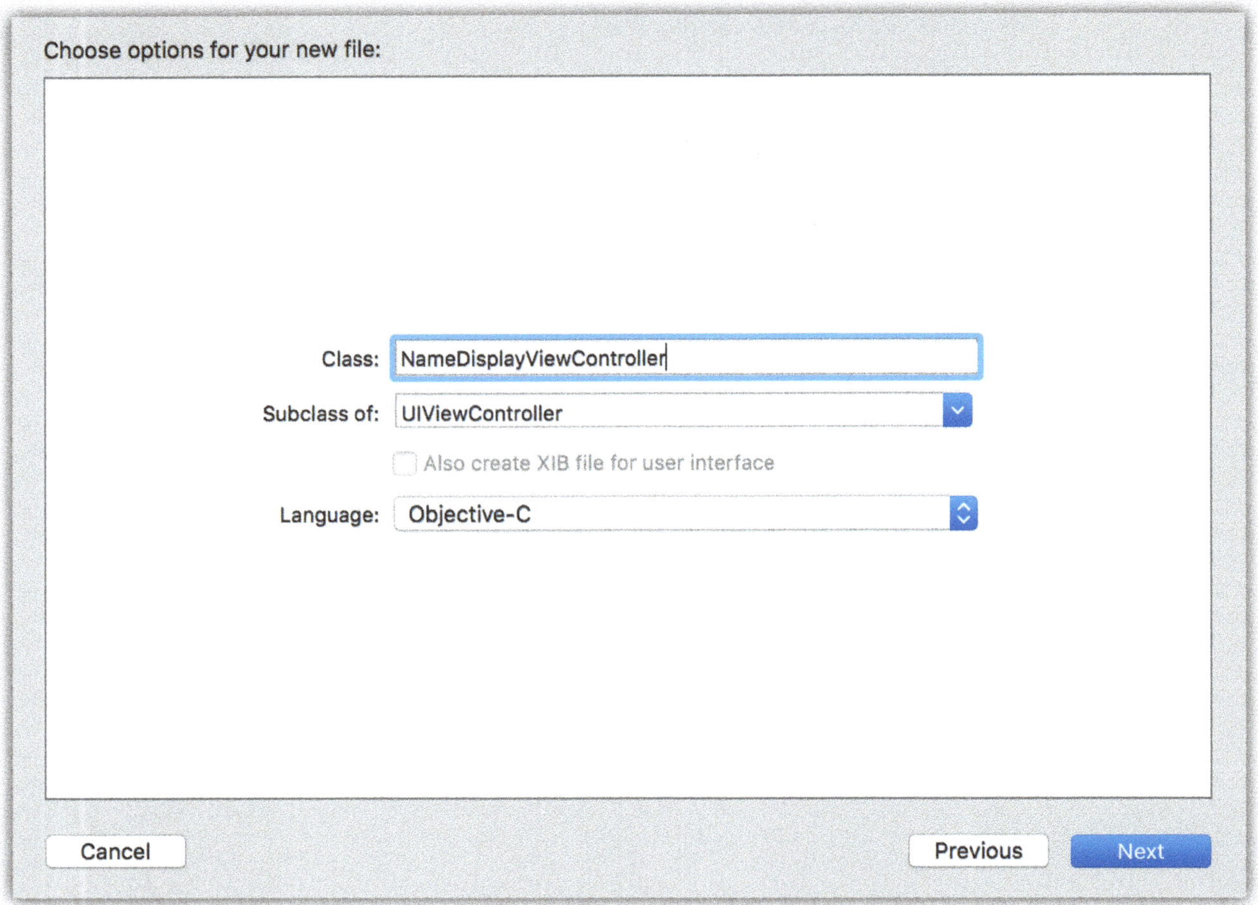

2.47

Press *Next*.

The next screen just asks you where to save the file. It always selects the folder where your project can be found so you don't need to change anything here. Just press *Create*.

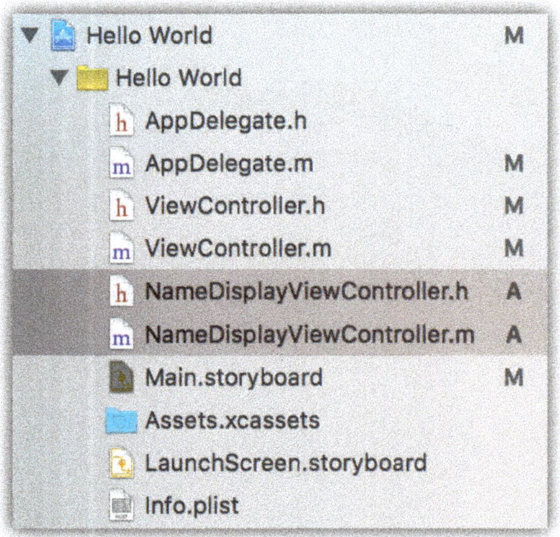

2.48

Your new *header* and *implementation* files will appear in the *Navigator* pane. Where they appear depends on the last file you had selected. They will always appear below the last file you were using. If you've followed everything I've told you so far then you were using *ViewController.m* last so they should appear below that file.

Your files in the *Navigator* pane should look like the image on the left.

You have just created a new class.

We now need to add this class to a screen layout on our storyboard. This is straightforward once you get the hang of it so I'll explain it step by step.

First things first, open up the *storyboard* and find the object *View Controller* in the *Object Library*:

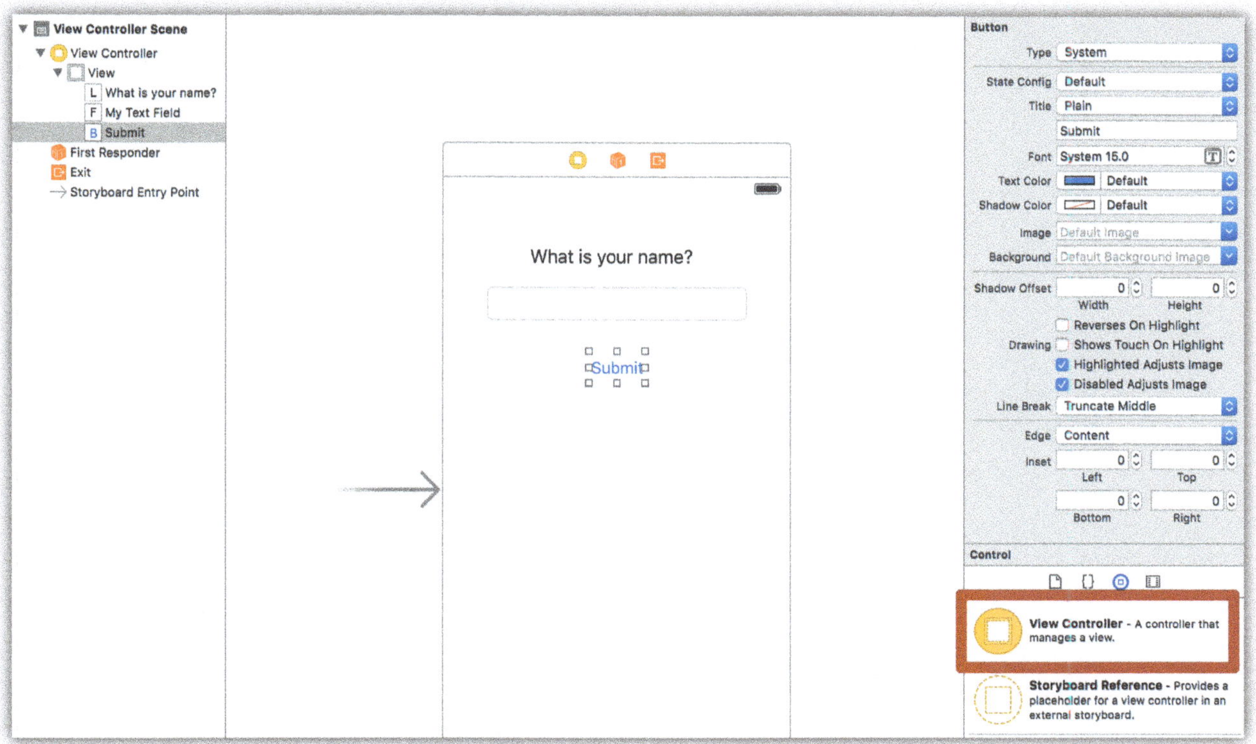

2.49

Drag it into the *Editor* pane just to the right of your first screen:

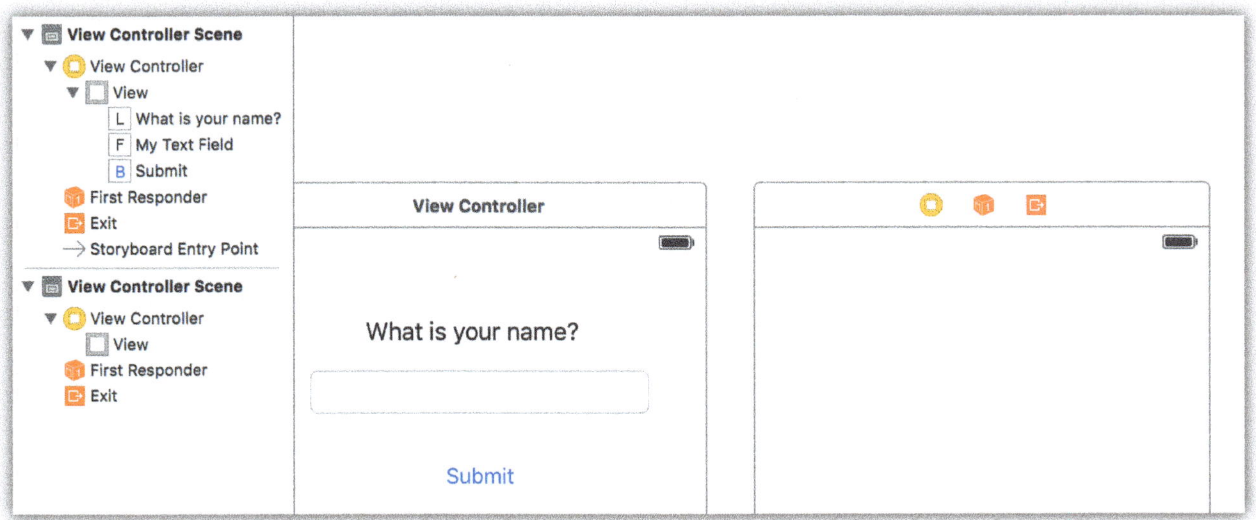

2.50

Your new *View Controller* will settle nicely next to your old one. But, rather confusingly, if you look to the left where the list of files is, you'll see there are two *scenes* called *View Controller Scene*. That's because the default name for a *View Controller*, like the one you've just dragged in, is View Controller. And our first class was called 'ViewController' so that's okay. It makes sense that the scene in the *storyboard* has the same name as the class that controls it.

So we need to tell *Xcode* which class is controlling our new *View Controller*.

To do this, click in the top of the new *View Controller* avoiding the three buttons. Pressing the first button, the white square in a yellow circle, will have the same desired effect. It should get a nice blue outline:

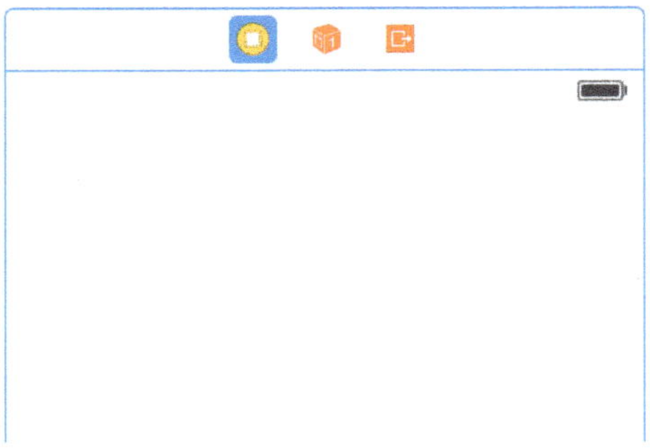

2.51

Go to the *Utilities* pane and select the *Identity inspector* tab:

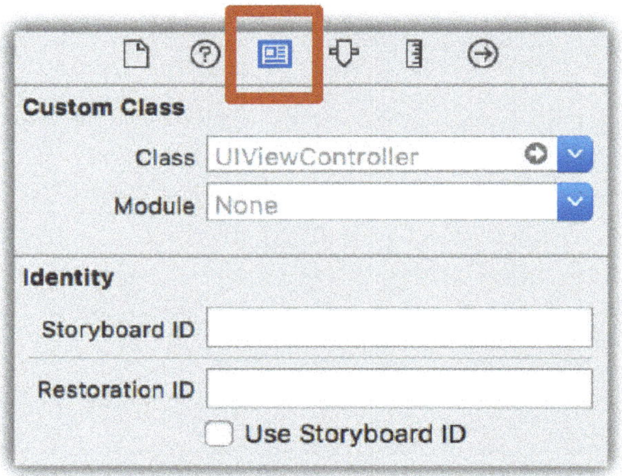

2.52

Next to where it says *Class*, enter *NameDisplayViewController*. It should auto complete this for you.

Next to where it says *Storyboard ID*, enter *NameDisplay*. We will need this later on.

It should now look like this:

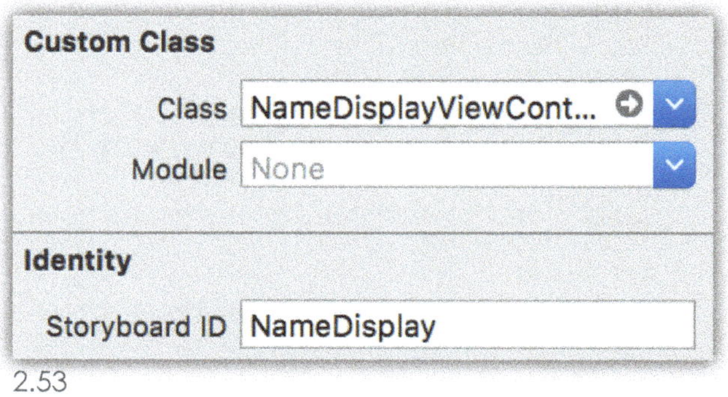

2.53

We now have two *View Controllers* in the *Editor* pane on our *storyboard*:

1. *View Controller*: This is our first screen and is controlled by the code in *ViewController.h* and *ViewController.m*.
2. *Name Display View Controller*: This is our second screen and is controlled by the code in *NameDisplayViewController.h* and *NameDisplayViewController.m*.

Interestingly, *Xcode* automatically names these by adding spaces to the names of your classes. Just glance next to the *Editor* pane:

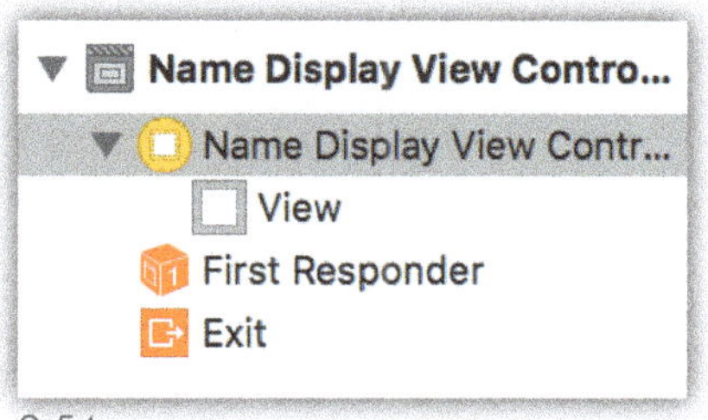

2.54

We didn't type that in without spaces. It is done for us. A little present from Apple.

Remember what we created this second screen for? We want to display some text that says 'Hello,' and then the user's name taken from the previous screen.

To do this, we need to add a *Label*. This time, our label is going to display *dynamic text*. That is text that will change depending upon what the user types on the previous screen. This means we'll need to alter some properties.

First, drag a *UILabel* from the *Object Library* to your *NameDisplayViewController*:

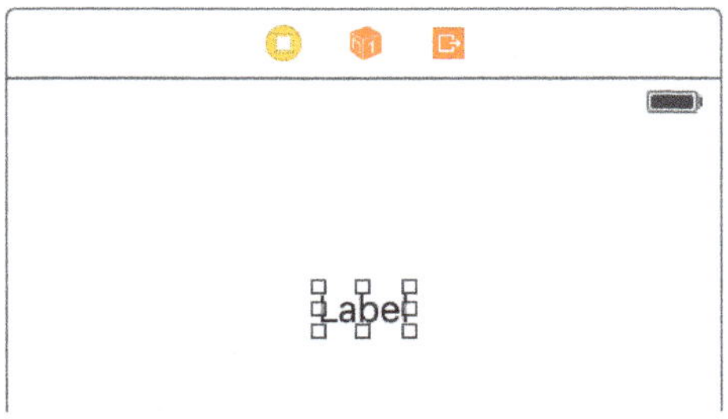

2.55

It doesn't really matter where you place it as we're not adding a keyboard to this screen but it will need resizing. Remember, it's going to say, 'Hello, [name]' and 'name' could be really long. So drag it by the handles to stretch it close to the edge of the screen on either side:

2.56

With the Label in position, we need to change some of its properties. I'm going to tell you how to do this, but before I do, have a look and see if you can do it without my help.

These are the two properties we need our label to have:

- It should centre the text.
- It should resize the font if the text is too long (so we avoid the ellipsis that appear when there's not enough space).

In the *Utilities* pane, click on the *Attributes tab* to open up the *Attributes inspector*. That's the one that looks like a shield.

Have a look for the two properties we want to change:

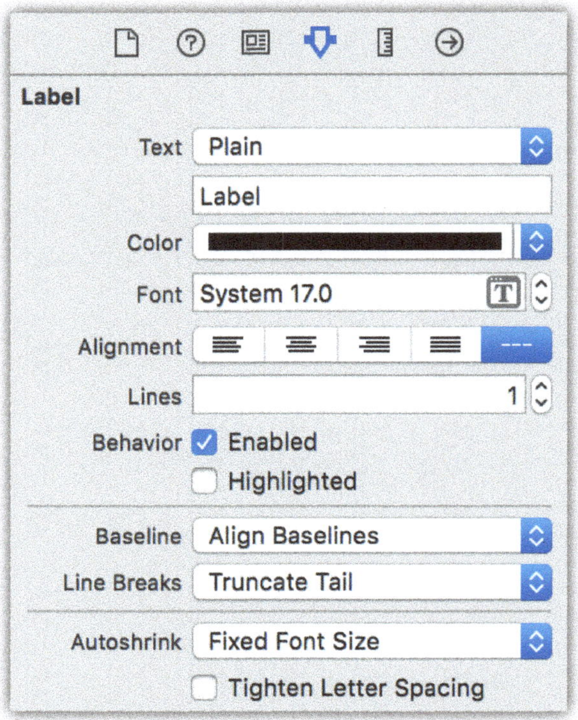

2.57

They should be reasonably self-explanatory. To change the text so that it is centred, press the *Centre* button in the *Alignment* section, much as you would in *Microsoft Word*.

And to make the text resize, go to the drop-down menu next to the *Autoshrink* property. Choose *Minimum Font Scale* and leave the value at 0.5. Your *Attributes inspector* should look like mine:

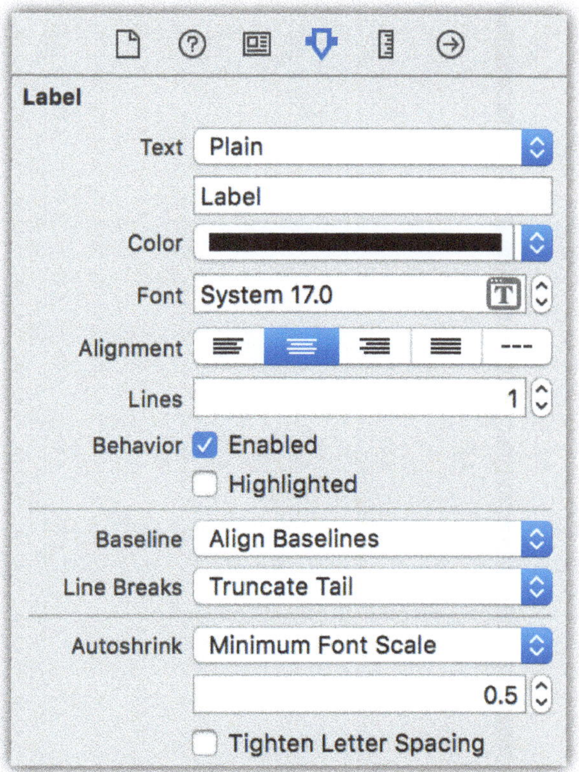

2.58

To explain the *Minimum Font Scale*, if the text is too big for the *Label*, the app will resize the font up to our minimum scale. In this case, the minimum scale is 0.5 which means the app will shrink the font up to half of its original size. As our font size is 17.0, the smallest our font will be resized to is 8.5. If you want a smaller font size than that, decrease the decimal value, for example 0.25 will allow the font to be reduced to a quarter of its original size. Conversely, increase the decimal number if you want to prevent the font getting too small.

And there you have it. Our label is set up and we're nearly ready to go.

We still have a couple of tasks to do:

- We need to tell our *ViewController.m* to load *NameDisplayViewController* after pressing the *Submit* button.
- We need to tell *NameDisplayViewController* to put the correct text into the label we've just added.
- We need to connect our new label to *NameDisplayViewController.h*.

Let's add a bit more code to *ViewController.m*. In the *Navigator* pane, select *ViewController.m*:

2.59

We're going to add a bit more code to our *IBAction* called *submit*. Put your cursor at the end of *[myTextField resignFirstResponder];* and press *return* to start a new line.

Now copy the code below:

```
UIStoryboard *myStoryboard = [UIStoryboard storyboardWithName:@"Main" bundle:nil];
UIViewController *myViewController = [myStoryboard instantiateViewControllerWithIdentifier:@"NameDisplay"];
[self presentViewController:myViewController animated:YES completion:nil];
```

2.60

This looks a bit complex but it isn't. In the first line, we create a new variable to remember the name of our storyboard. In this case, our storyboard is called *Main*.

Then we tell the app that we have a *View Controller* we want to talk about, the View Controller that we have given an identifier of *NameDisplay*. Remember when we did this as we set up our second View Controller?

And our final line of code simply 'presents' our second view controller on top of the previous one. With the pupils, you can tell them we've 'loaded' the next screen. It's not quite what happens, but at this point, I wouldn't worry about it.

The complete *IBAction* code should now look like this:

```
- (IBAction)submit:(id)sender{

    [[NSUserDefaults standardUserDefaults] setObject:myTextField.text forKey:@"username"];

    [myTextField resignFirstResponder];

    UIStoryboard *myStoryboard = [UIStoryboard storyboardWithName:@"Main" bundle:nil];
    UIViewController *myViewController = [myStoryboard instantiateViewControllerWithIdentifier:@"NameDisplay"];
    [self presentViewController:myViewController animated:YES completion:nil];

}
```

2.61

Check it carefully for any mistakes. And then press that big ol' *Play* button to run the app on the simulator.

So with the app running, press the *Submit* button. Up pops your second screen. You've created a transition between two screens.

There are a few ways of doing this, and we have used just one of those ways. But this code will come in handy as you move on to more complicated apps.

One thing is wrong though. The *UILabel* on *NameDisplayViewController* still says 'Label'. Why? Because we haven't told it to do anything else. Let's do that now.

The first thing to do is open up *NameDisplayViewController.h*.

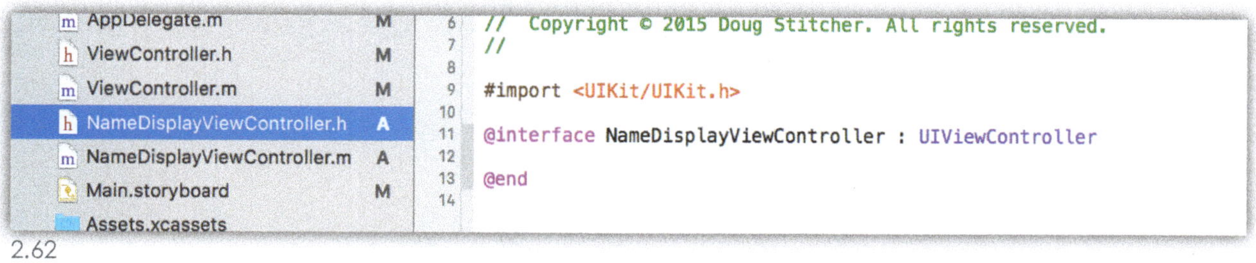

2.62

Remember when we edited *ViewController.h*? We're going to do something similar here. Add a swirly bracket after the purple *UIViewController* and press *return*. Pressing *return* will cause another swirly bracket to appear.

In between those brackets, we need to tell our app that we have a *UILabel*, the label we added to display 'Hello, name'.

Enter this code between the swirly brackets:

```
IBOutlet UILabel *nameLabel;
```
2.63

The code should look like this:

```
#import <UIKit/UIKit.h>

@interface NameDisplayViewController : UIViewController{
    IBOutlet UILabel *nameLabel;
}

@end
```
2.64

We need to go back to our storyboard and link our label. By the way, I've called it 'nameLabel' but you could call it anything you want.

So in the *Navigator* pane, click on *Main.storyboard*.

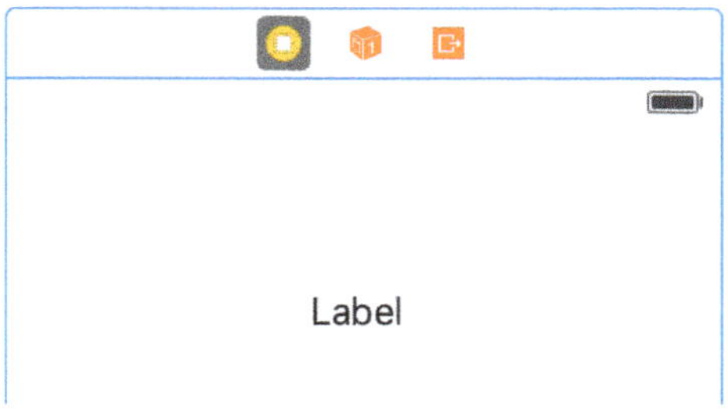

2.65

Make sure you've selected *Name Display View Controller* by ensuring that there is a blue line around the outside of it.

Then, with a two-finger drag (or *ctrl* and drag if you're using a regular mouse), go from the square in a yellow circle to the label:

This box should appear:

2.66

Select *nameLabel* and the box will disappear.

We have one last thing to do. We need to tell *NameDisplayViewController* to change the text in *nameLabel* to say 'Hello' and then whatever name the user entered on *View Controller*.

Go to the *Navigator* pane and click on *NameDisplayViewController.m*. You should see this:

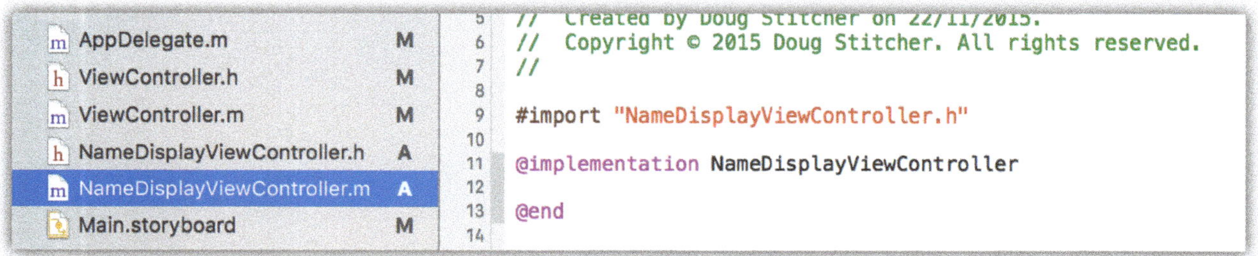

2.67

As you can see, there are no *methods* in this file. Sometimes, *Xcode* will automatically add *viewDidLoad* methods depending on how you added the file.

Actually, it is only the *viewDidLoad method* we need as we want the app to change the text of our label when the view first appears.

Therefore, add the following code in-between the *@implementation* line and the *@end* line:

```
- (void)viewDidLoad {
    [super viewDidLoad];

    NSString *userName;

    if (![[NSUserDefaults standardUserDefaults] objectForKey:@"username"]){
        userName = @"stranger";} else {
        userName = [[NSUserDefaults standardUserDefaults] objectForKey:@"username"];}

    nameLabel.text = [NSString stringWithFormat:@"Hello, %@", userName];
}
```

2.68

It looks a bit complicated, so let's talk it through.

After the standard *[super viewDidLoad];* we declare a new variable called *userName*. It is a *string*. In other words, it will hold some words as text and store them until we need them.

We then do something a bit complicated. We check to see if the user has entered their name or not. In our app, even if the user enters nothing as their name, the app will save their name. So if they leave it blank, their name will be saved as blank.

So this code isn't really necessary, however, it is good practice to make sure we cover every eventuality.

The '!' before *[[NSUser Defaults...]]]* refers to if there isn't anything saved in the NSUserDefault we've called *username*. Then we tell the app that if there isn't anything saved, our string '*userName*' should be set as *stranger*. Then the app would say 'Hello, stranger'.

We use the word 'else' to say what to do if we DO have something saved. And then we set userName as the contents of our username *NSUserDefault*.

USING 'if' STATEMENTS

Using 'if' statements is a way of telling our app to do something depending on certain conditions.
They have a very clear format:

if (the condition that applies) {
code to something here;
} else {
code to do something if the condition in the normal brackets isn't met;}

So the condition always goes in normal brackets, for example, in a maths app, it might be if (theAnswer == 10). And the methods go in swirly brackets.

With that done, we can set the contents of our label and that's just what the last line of our code does.

Let's look at it in isolation:

```
nameLabel.text = [NSString stringWithFormat:@"Hello, %@", userName];
```
2.69

We access the text property of our label by writing *nameLabel.text*, this means that we are setting the text of the label.

We set the label with an *NSString* (this is just how we say a *string* – which means 'letters or words'). Our NSString has to begin with @". We then typed 'Hello, ' – the next bit '%@' means we're going to add another string to our string but we don't say what that string is yet.

We close the string with inverted commas. We add a comma and then we type the name of the variable that we want to go where we put the '%@'.

If that doesn't make sense, don't worry. When learning to code, it often just takes time for concepts to click.

Go back to the last page and check that you've entered the code properly. Any major errors will be shown by *Xcode* automatically as either a yellow highlight (this is a warning and can sometimes be ignored) or a red highlight (this is an error and means your app will not build).

When you're happy with everything, go ahead and press the *Play* button.

You've built an app with two screens that pass information. Here's my screen:

2.70

You should be pleased with yourself. None of that was easy and you've managed to build an app that takes information from the user and does something with it. You should have learnt an awful lot doing this and it should make the building of our school app a little bit easier.

Don't get me wrong, there's a lot more to cover but if you can do this, what's stopping you making more complicated apps? That's right, nothing.

http://www.alanpeat.com/build-an-app/Chapter2

CHAPTER THREE
PLANNING YOUR SCHOOL APP

Now we're going to get to the good bit: your school app. Designing any app isn't an easy job. There are many things you need to take into account. This in itself constitutes a valid learning objective for the pupils and I would spend a lesson looking at a variety of (throughly vetted) apps.

Get the students to identify what makes them easy or hard to use. Can they spot common design elements, for example, is the *Back* button always on the left?

A good task would be for you to do some crawling through the App Store and find some rubbish apps. There are loads out there. Quite a few of the million or so apps are built by independent developers, some of whom have no technical knowledge at all. As a result, their apps are often poorly designed and crash.

Apple have a strict approval process when it comes to letting apps into the App Store. They even produce a set of guidelines: **https://developer.apple.com/app-store/review/guidelines/** Have a look and give the class a carefully edited version of the list.

It's important to bear in mind that the review process is not automated. It is done by human beings and, as such, it can be inconsistent. For example, I once had an app rejected for reason 2.12: *Apps that are not very useful, unique, are simply web sites bundled as Apps, or do not provide any lasting entertainment value may be rejected.*

To be fair to Apple, they were right. The app did nothing more than display some websites. It was free and useful-ish so I didn't feel bad. But I thought I'd use it to test the system. So I resubmitted the app having made no changes whatsoever.

The app was approved the following week.

When I started making school apps, it became apparent that they were prone to rejection as they didn't provide anything useful beyond news from the school. This meant that I needed to find a way around the approval system and that's why our school app is going to have a feature that isn't related to your school in any way; a simple note-taking and drawing screen. Don't worry. You won't need to code it, I'm going to give you the code for free.

So, you've looked at some apps – feel free to look at some of my school apps by searching for Angel App Publishing in the app store – and you've looked at the Apple Review Guidelines. You're ready to start planning your app.

In this chapter, we will cover the following skills:

- Using a web tool to create an app *wireframe*.
- Considering the user experience when designing an app.

I would suggest that you use the content of this chapter to scaffold a series of lessons enabling the children to fully understand the process of app design. Interestingly, in this chapter we won't be doing any coding but that doesn't mean that we won't be learning important skills that we can apply as we build our app.

So, let's map out our app. What kinds of things do we want in it? Normally at this point expect the class to suggest things like an *Angry Birds*-type game or *Candy Crush* made out of the school logo.

Clearly, that's not going to make a useful school app and is beyond what is possible for us to code in a short time. I would direct them to something like this:

TITLE OF SCREEN	FUNCTIONALITY
Latest News	Provide some headlines of news from school that when you press opens up a full page view of the news.
Contact Us	Send an email with a pre-populated subject and recipient address i.e. the school's email address; Call the school directly from within the app.
Find Us	A map showing the school's location.
Website	Display the school's website in the app.
School Jotter	This is our note-taking facility – designed primarily to get through the app approval process.

The skills you will learn as we build all these sections can be transferred to add more screens should you so choose. For example, once you've learned how to add a website to your app, you could add multiple websites such as links to Ofsted.

For the sake of this next section, we're going to assume that we're making a five button app that will load each of the screens listed above.

We're going to create a *wireframe* for our app. A wireframe is a basic version of our app with no code and limited amounts of artwork. It will help us plan our app in terms of where our buttons will go and what they will lead to.

The beauty of this is that the pupils can learn to do it quickly and without any prior coding knowledge.

Let's get started. On a computer, it doesn't matter if it's a PC or Mac, open your internet browser and head to **https://ninjamock.com/home/index?v=2**. There are lots of free, and paid-for, wireframe building sites out there. I've chosen this one as it's simple to use.

You should see this (The look of the website is subject to change as the developers evolve it. These screenshots are correct as of August 2016):

3.01

It's worth mentioning here that you can design a wireframe without setting up an account. However, if you want to save your work and come back to it, you will need to set one up. That said, if you use the same computer with the same login and you have cookies enabled, the website should remember your design without saving it.

I'd suggest setting up one account that all the class can access but bear in mind that their free account only lets you create three projects, so you may need to set up multiple free accounts.

If for whatever reason you don't want to do this, everything we're about to do can be done in *Word*, *Publisher* or even just on paper.

We're going to sketch out our app. This is essential if we are going to build an app that makes sense to the user. It's a bit like writing a story. We need to plan out the essential elements before we dive into the narrative.

I'm going to assume that you're using *NinjaMock* to create your wireframe, but if you're not, just flick through the next few pages and take a look at the images of my mock-up.

To get started, press the *Start Designing Now* button and choose *iPhone* from the following screen:

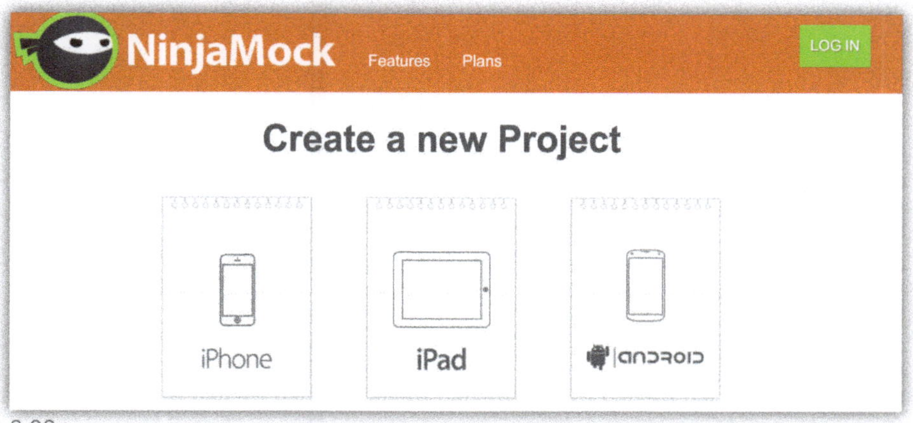

3.02

You could choose *iPad* but to keep things simple, let's just sketch out our app on an iPhone.

Once you've selected your device type, you will see the main *NinjaMock* interface. The site allows you to drag and drop elements to your screen and re-arrange them, as well as linking them to other screens.

There's no need to add any code.

Let's have a look around:

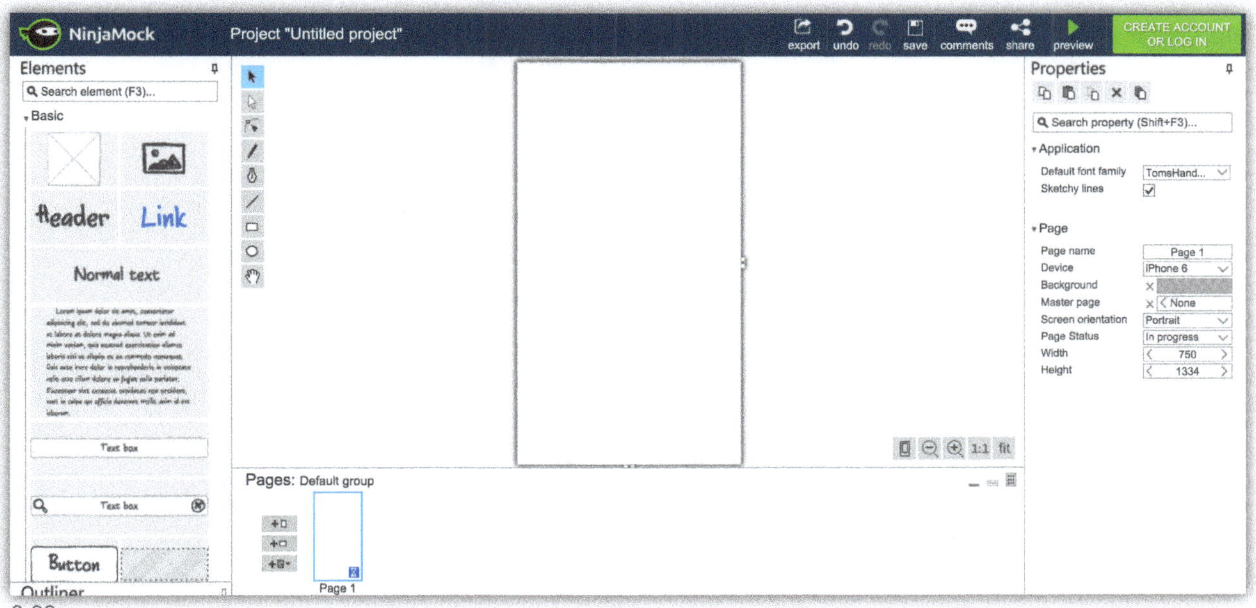

3.03

The page is split into three panes, much like *Xcode*. On the left, we have our *Elements* pane. This is where we can drag items onto our screen.

In the centre, we have our *Editor* pane. This is where our screen is and where we arrange our added elements.

And on the right, we have our *Properties* pane. This is where we can set different properties of the elements we use.

Let's get started. Drag the *Header* element onto your screen in the *Editor* pane:

3.04

It will appear in a blue box, a lot smaller than in the screenshot above. Use the blue handle to resize it.

Double click on the word *Header* and it will become highlighted. Enter the name of your school. You may then need to resize the box again to make it fit on the screen:

3.05

Now scroll down the *Elements* pane and find the buttons icon:

3.06

Drag five of these to your screen:

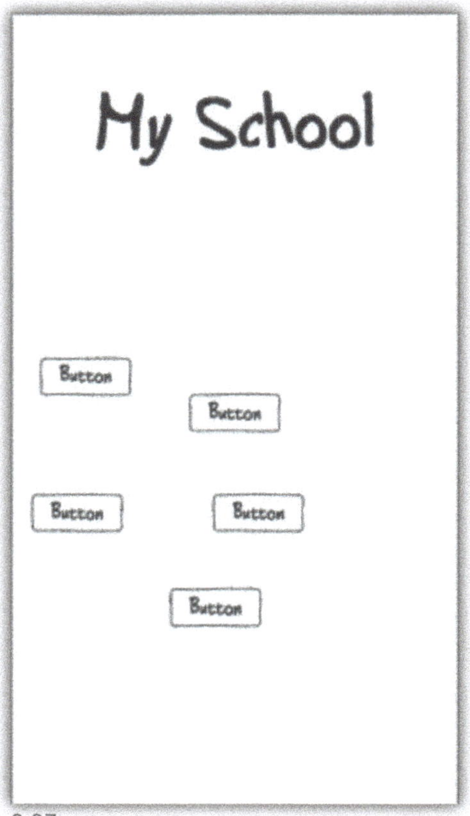

3.07

You can resize them, move them about and generally play with them.

Use the *Properties* pane to change the text in the buttons by selecting a button and changing the 'text' property. Or you can double click on the actual buttons:

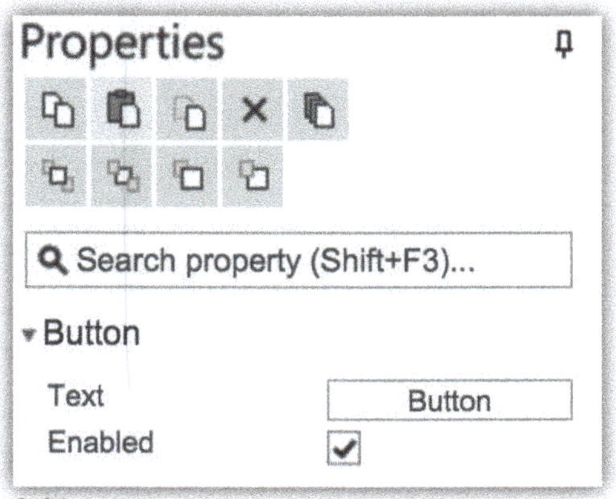

3.08

Go back to our list of screens at the start of this chapter and give your buttons appropriate names. Then move the buttons around until you're happy with the design.

After a bit of tweaking, it should look something like this:

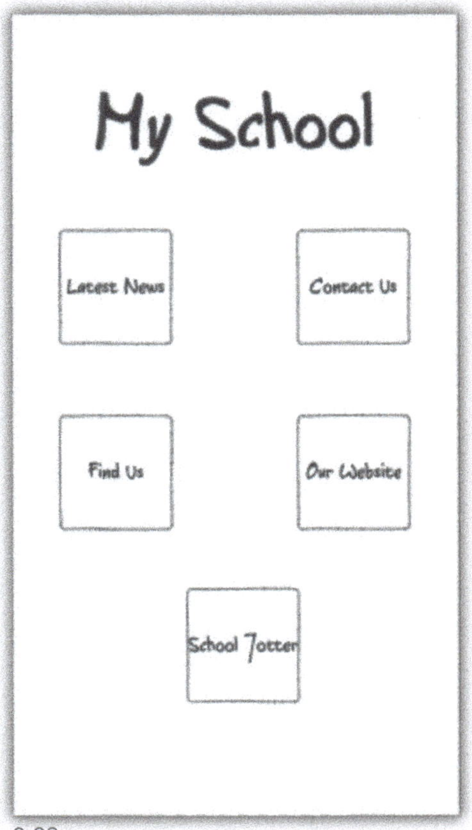

3.09

I've made the buttons square but you don't have to. And I've arranged them in a 2-2-1 formation; feel free to move them around.

The next step in designing our *wireframe* is to add some more pages. Have a glance below the *Editor* pane:

3.10

Here you can see an overview of your screens: known as pages in *NinjaMock*. Go ahead and press the *Add New Page* button, highlighted above.

A new page will appear to the right:

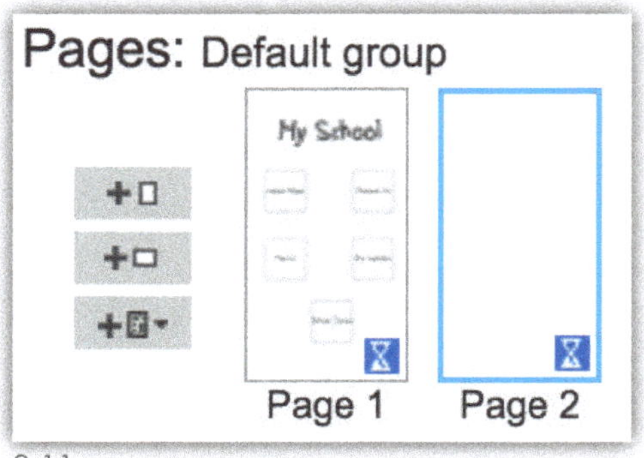

3.11

If you take a look in the *Properties* pane with that page selected, you'll see this section:

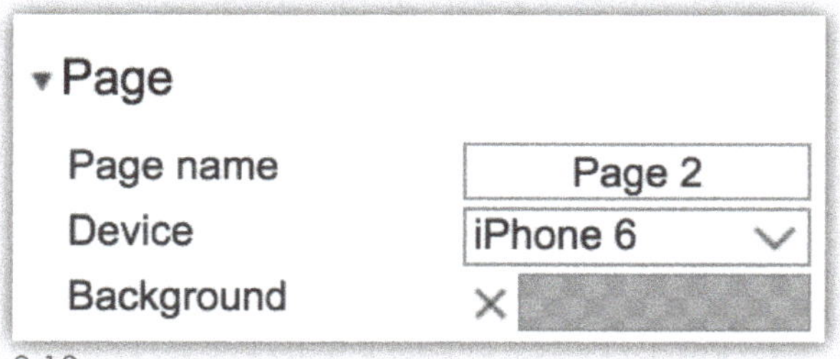

3.12

Feel free to give this page a more descriptive name. I'm going to call mine 'Latest News Page':

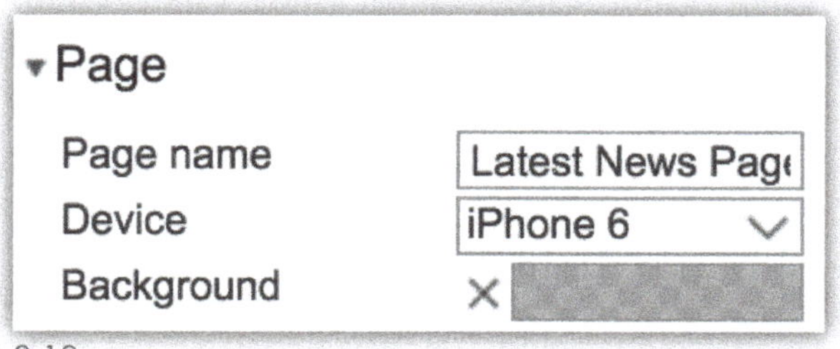

3.13

Glance back to the Pages section and you'll see that 'Page 2' has changed to 'Latest' as the whole title cannot fit.

Next we can make our buttons do something. Click back on *Page 1* and then select your *Latest News* button. The *Properties* pane will change:

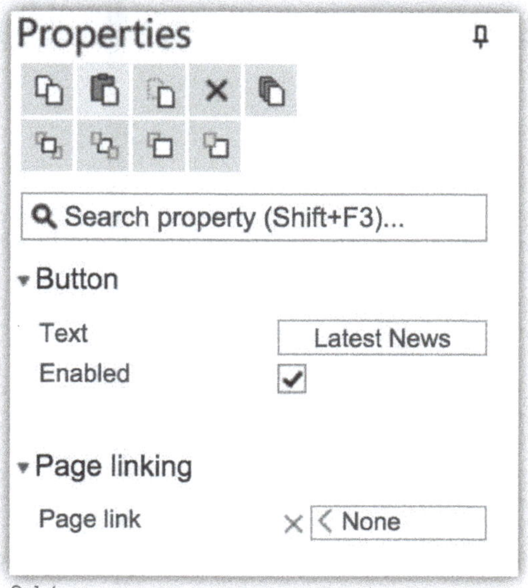

3.14

Underneath where it says *Page Linking*, click on the word *None*. This box should pop up:

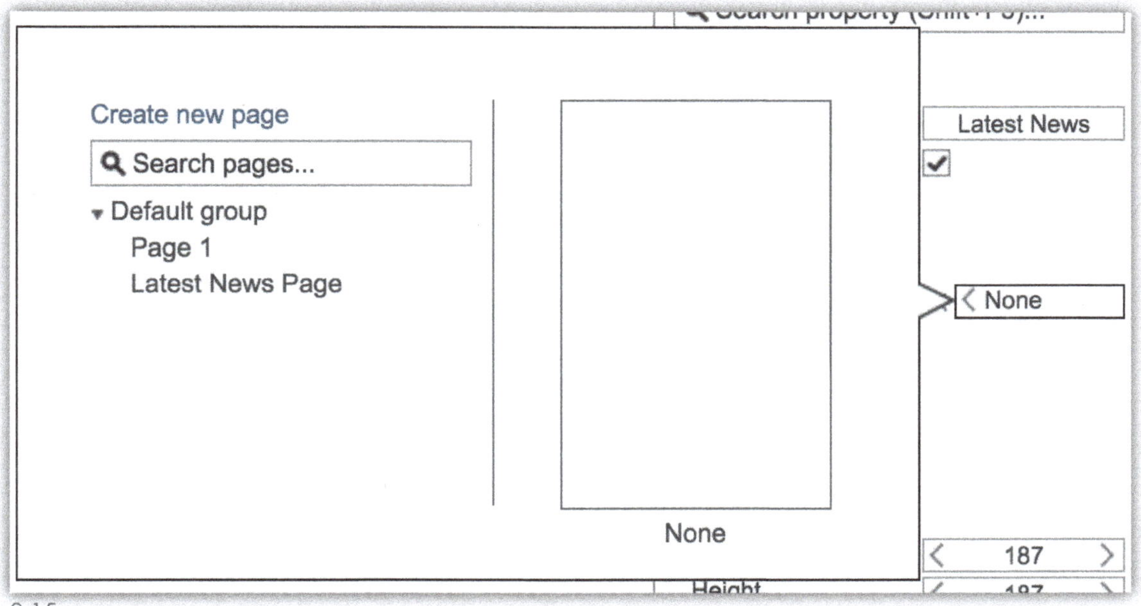

3.15

Select *Latest News Page*.

Now, in the top right of the screen, select the *Preview* button, that's the big green triangle:

3.16

You'll see a preview screen that looks like this:

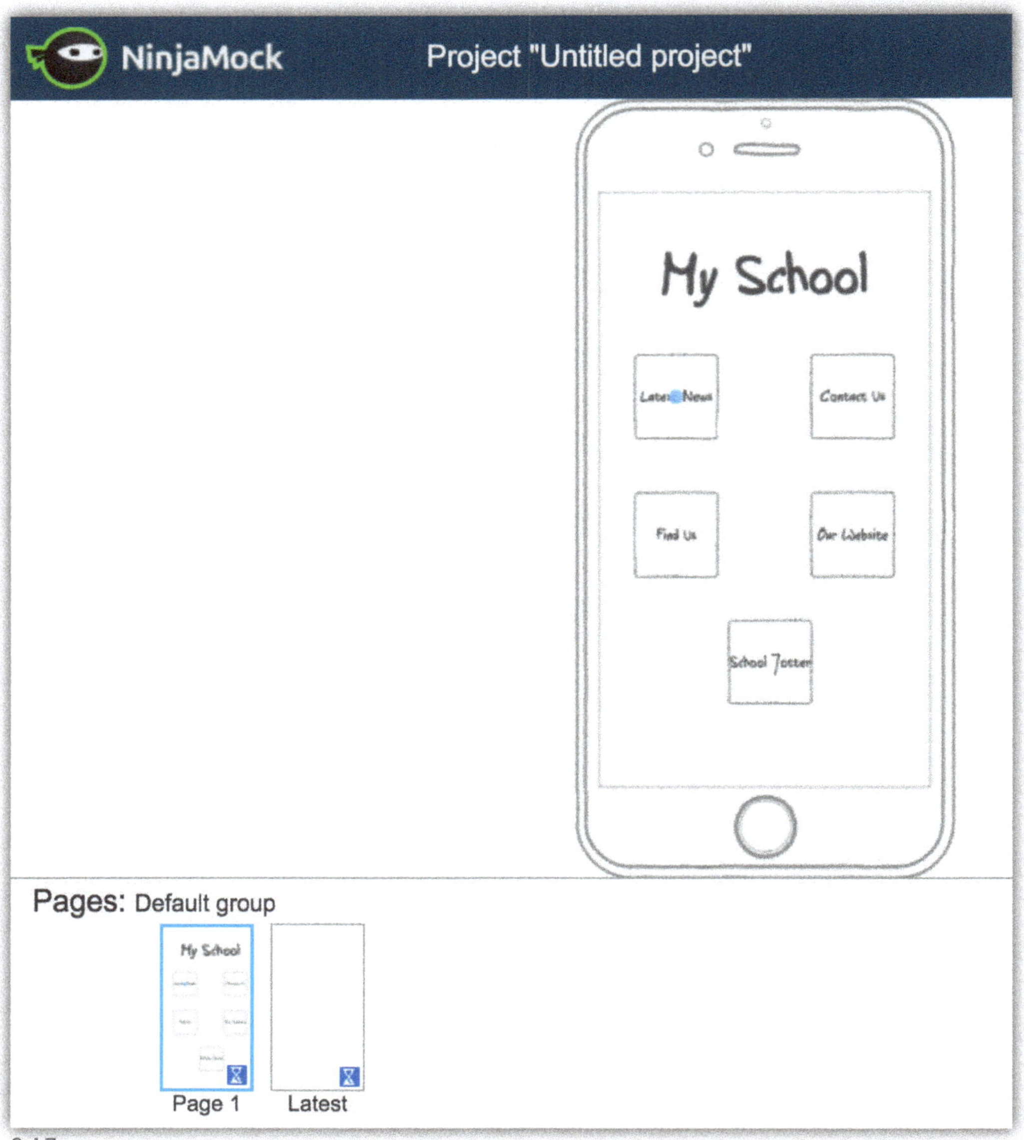

3.17

You'll notice a small blue dot on the *Latest News* button. This shows you that the button links to a page. Press it and the *Latest News Page* will appear on the cartoon iPhone. As we've not added anything to that screen yet, it will appear blank.

And that's about all you can see here. So press the red *Stop* button on the top right:

3.18

This will take you back to the project editor screen.

You can now plan out the rest of your screens. To help you out, I've done a few of my own. You could display these and see if the students can emulate them or improve them, but it should give you an idea about where we are headed with our app.

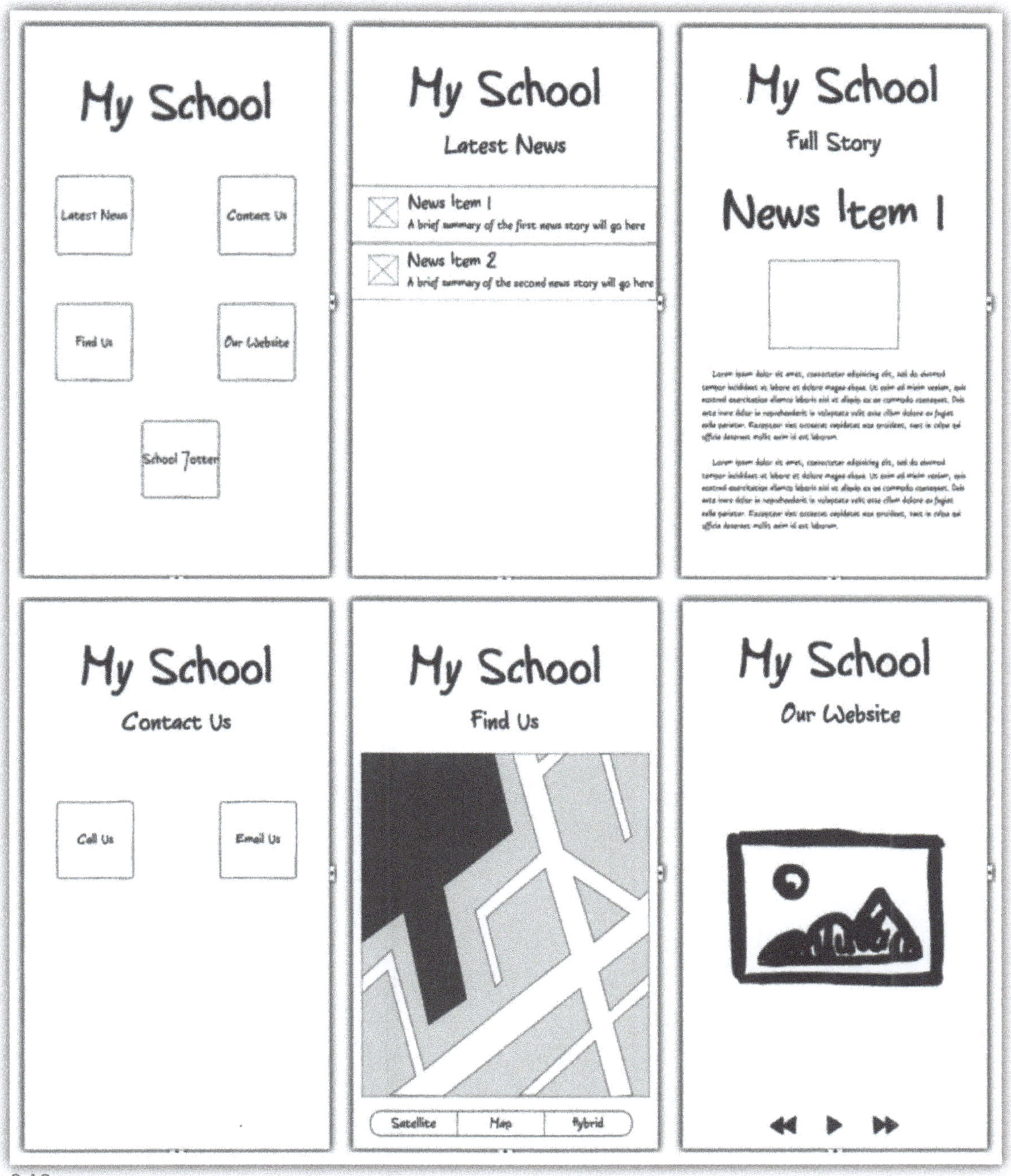

3.19

All of the screens above were made using elements from the *Elements* pane. I had never really used *NinjaMock* before creating these and they only took me a few minutes to create.

You can also add your own images if you want to.

The class will enjoy trying out new combinations and experimenting with the design. The whole time, they will be learning about app design and thinking about user experience.

If you link all the buttons up to the pages you create, you will be able to preview your app as a functional version that lets you navigate between screens.

Running the preview on my app highlights one major flaw though. I've not added a *Back* button to any of the screens.

Hopefully, your pupils will forget to do this too. It emphasises the importance of planning for every possible interaction your user could or would want to make.

Adding a *Back* button is as simple as adding another button and linking it to the home screen, or in the case of the full story for the news item, link it back to the list of available stories.

And that's it. You've created a *wireframe*, or mock-up, of your school app. We now have a roadmap to help us build our fully functional school app. Over the course of the next few chapters, we're going to build each one of these screens.

This isn't going to be easy. We're going to use a combination of disciplines to create the functionality we need.

Let's have a look at each page and plan out what is involved. This will hopefully put the whole project into context for you and the children.

Home screen

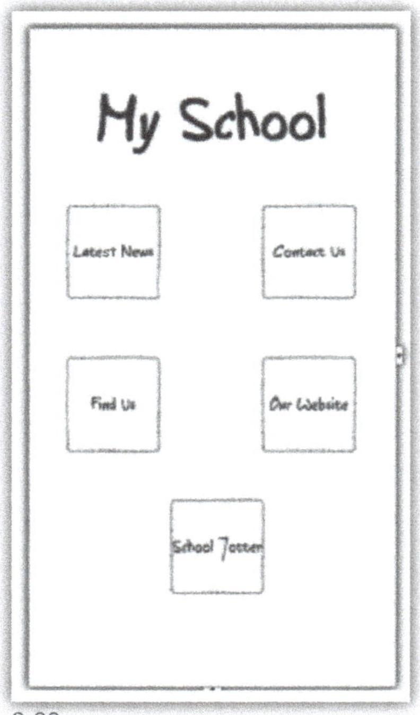

3.20

This is the easiest of our screens. To make this screen, we will need to:

- Create some images for our *Buttons*.
- Create a *header* image that we will use on all of the other screens within the app.
- Link our buttons to the other pages in the app.

Of all the pages, this one has the least coding and it's the most fun in terms of adding your own design touch to it.

Latest news

This is probably our most complicated section. It is made up of two separate screens.

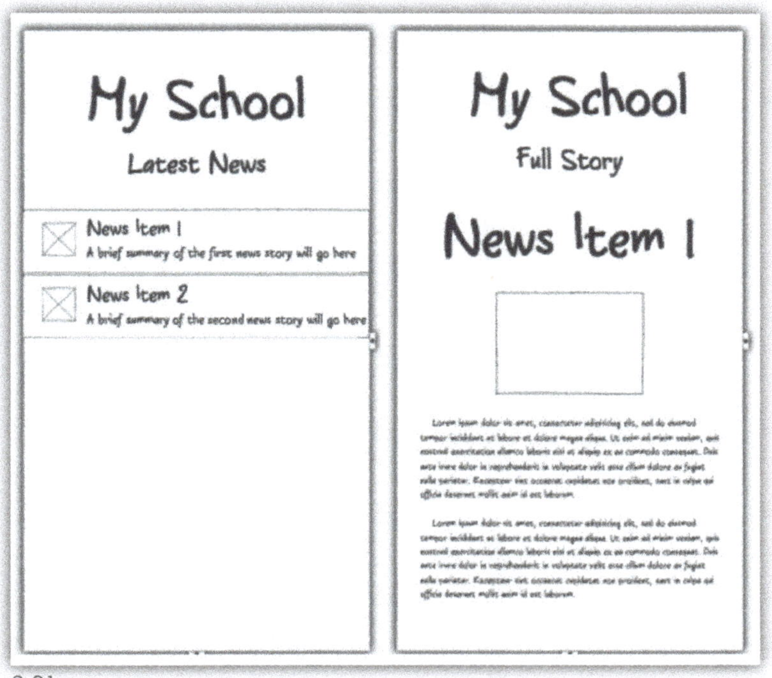

3.21

We will need to:

- Create a special web-based feed called an *RSS Feed* that will send news items to our app.
- Use a third-party library to read the news from our RSS Feed.
- Create a *UITableView* and fill it with a summary version of our news information.
- Create a screen to display the full detail of any story in our list of news items.

Contact us

3.22

This is an easy one. On this screen, we will have two *Buttons*: one will open the iPhone's phone app and dial your school's phone number and the other will open up the iPhone's email app and send an email to your school with a pre-populated subject.

Some things you will need to do:

- Add a *framework*: This is some extra code provided by Apple that isn't included in our apps by default. This is to save space. But we will need to add the *UIMessage* framework to cope with sending emails;
- Link our buttons to a couple of *IBActions* to send the email or call the school.

Find us

3.23

This isn't too tricky a screen. It simply displays a map.

However, to make it work, we will need to:

- Add the *MapKit* framework. Remember, Apple don't include all the frameworks when you start a new app.
- Add the code to display the map and get the user's current position.
- Add a *UISegmentedControl*. That's the button at the bottom which is split into three parts.
- Tell the app what to do when each of the segments is pressed.

Our website

3.24

A straightforward screen, this one. We're going to use something called *WebKit* to stick a web-browser into our app which we will then code to automatically load your school's website when the screen opens.

We'll also need to add some navigation buttons at the bottom. To go back or forward and to refresh the page.

One thing is worth thinking about now; does your school site link to other pages on the web that may not be suitable for young children? If so, you may need to change the age-rating of your app as Apple insist on apps that provide unrestricted web access being rated as suitable for 17 years and over only.

Usually, school sites are safe but you may want to check the external links.

There you have it. We have planned our app, we have looked at some of the skills you will need to produce it – trust me, it will make a lot more sense once we get started – and you are now familiar with using wireframes.

There's only one thing left to do… build our app.

http://www.alanpeat.com/build-an-app/Chapter3

CHAPTER FOUR
SETTING UP THE APP

We're now ready to set up a new *Xcode* project for our school app. The procedure is much like the one we followed when we built our first app. But I'm still going to talk you through all the steps. There is no right or wrong way to set a project up – how you do it when you build your own apps is up to you.

When getting your pupils to set up the project, you may wish to follow the instructions below and save then copy the project file from your document folder to a shared drive to which your pupils have access. Alternatively, you could easily walk through these steps with them. The advantage of the children following your lead is that they get used to the process and will then be able to replicate it as you move on to create other apps in the future.

I mentioned that we will be adding *frameworks* – special tools that let us do things like send an email or look at a map. I would normally add all my frameworks as I set my project up. However, so you can see why we are adding them, we'll add them as and when we need them.

Let's get started. If you've already got *Xcode* open, go to the *File* menu and select *New > Project*:

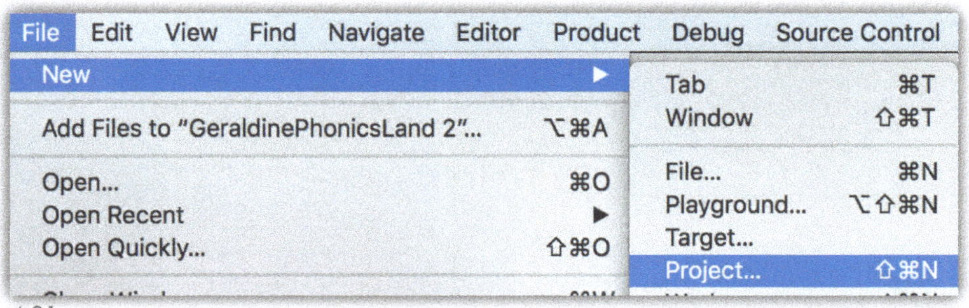

4.01

If not, select *Create a new Xcode project* from the *Xcode* welcome screen:

4.02

As with our first app, we want to create a *Single view application*:

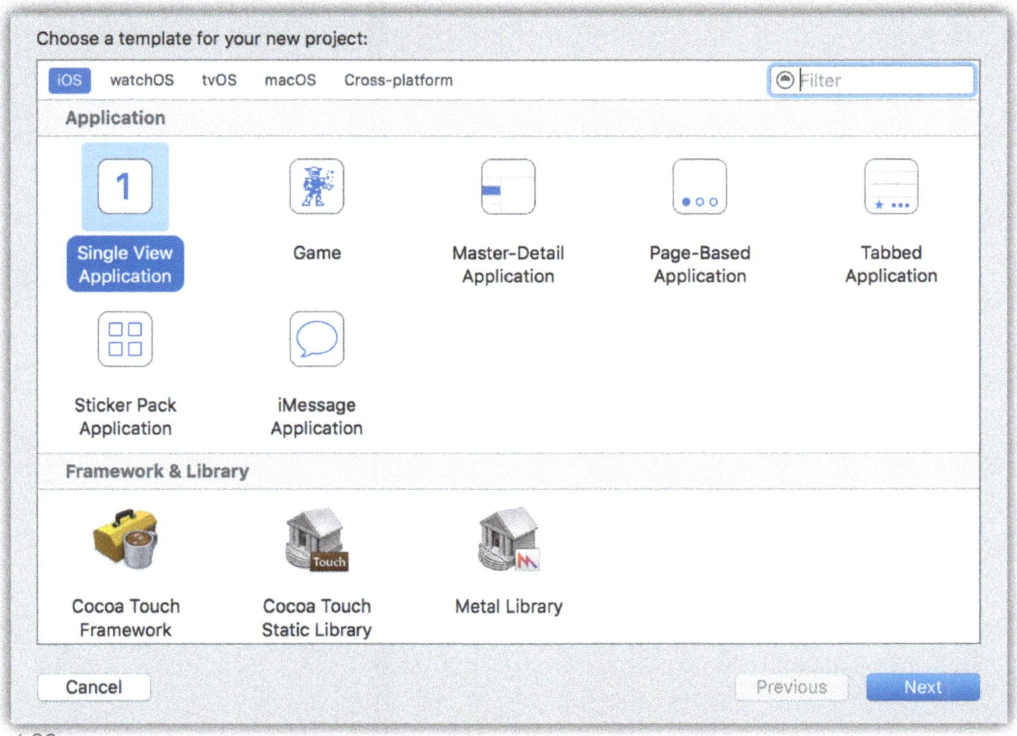

4.03

Press *Next*.

Give your project a name, I suggest your school name. Next to *Devices* – change *Universal* to *iPhone* as we are only going to build our app for iPhone for now. Then press *Next* again.

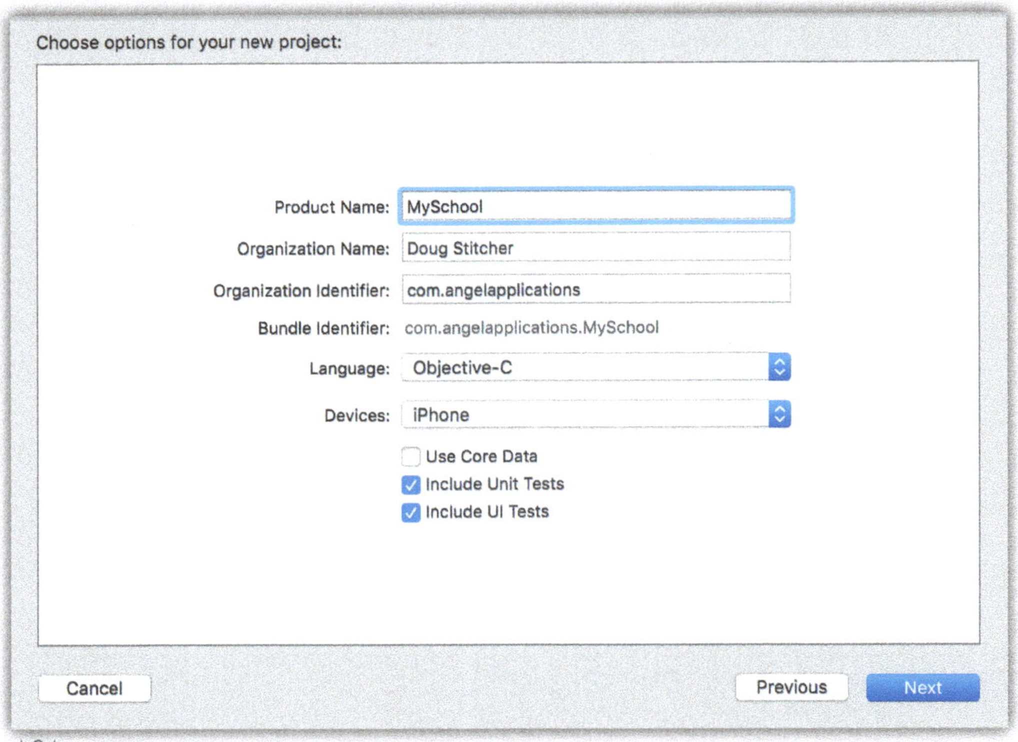

4.04

On the next pop-up, press *Create*. We're ready to go:

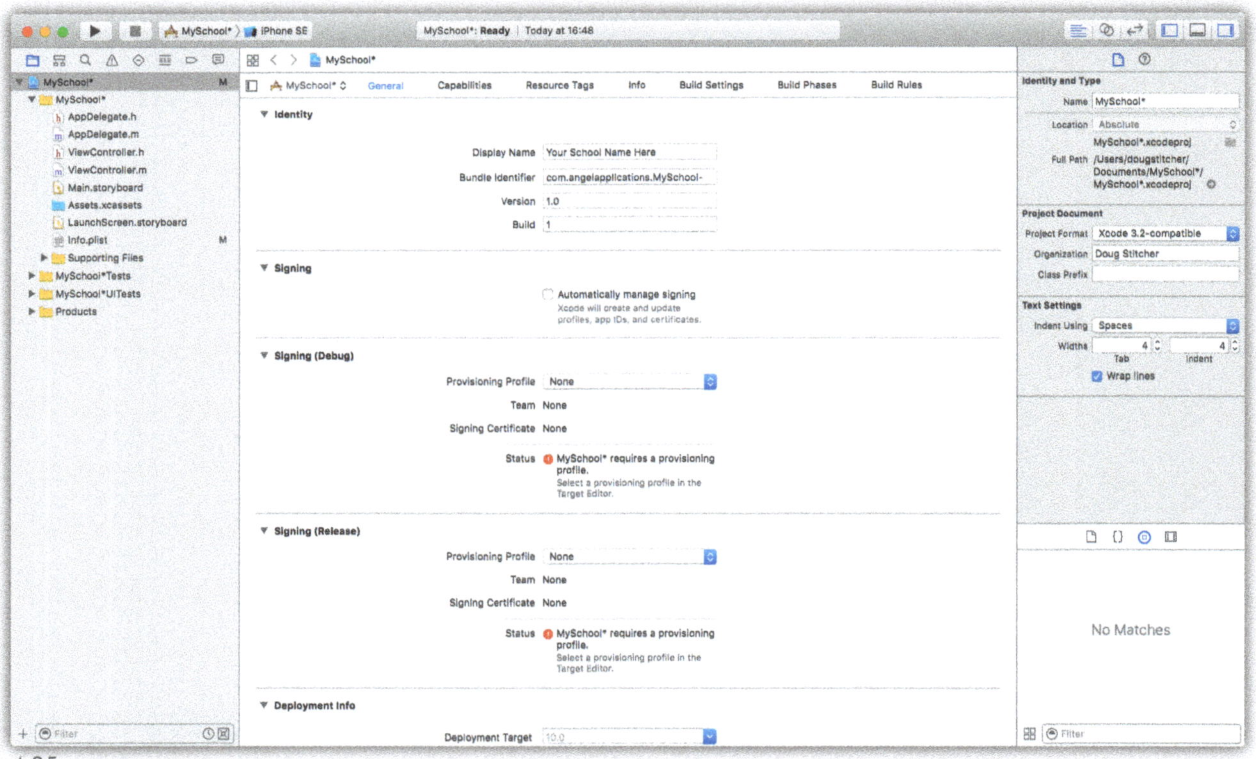

4.05

Before we get started on designing our app, a word or two about screen sizes again. We're going to target 3.5 inch devices and 4 inch devices. In other words, iPhone 4 and iPhone 5 (and all variants thereof). I would take this opportunity to ask the children about screen sizes. You could display a variety of different iPhones and iPods - just use Google Images to find an array of images comparing different models.

One of the really interesting things about iPhone development is that Apple consciously decided to make the iPhone 5 (that's the four inch screen) their biggest screen, saying that if you couldn't use your thumb to reach everywhere, it was too big.

They changed their tune when it became apparent that there was a demand for larger sizes, as Android 'phablets' began to take off. The design of Apple products and the marketing behind them is often just as valid a teaching point as the coding itself and links nicely with the new computing curriculum.

Our app will still run on iPhone 6 and 6+ and their 'S' iterations. But it means we only have to make two storyboards, one for iPhone 4 (3.5 inch screen) and on for iPhone 5 (4 inch screen).

We'll come back to this. But for now, have a quick look at some of the settings displayed in the *Editor* pane:

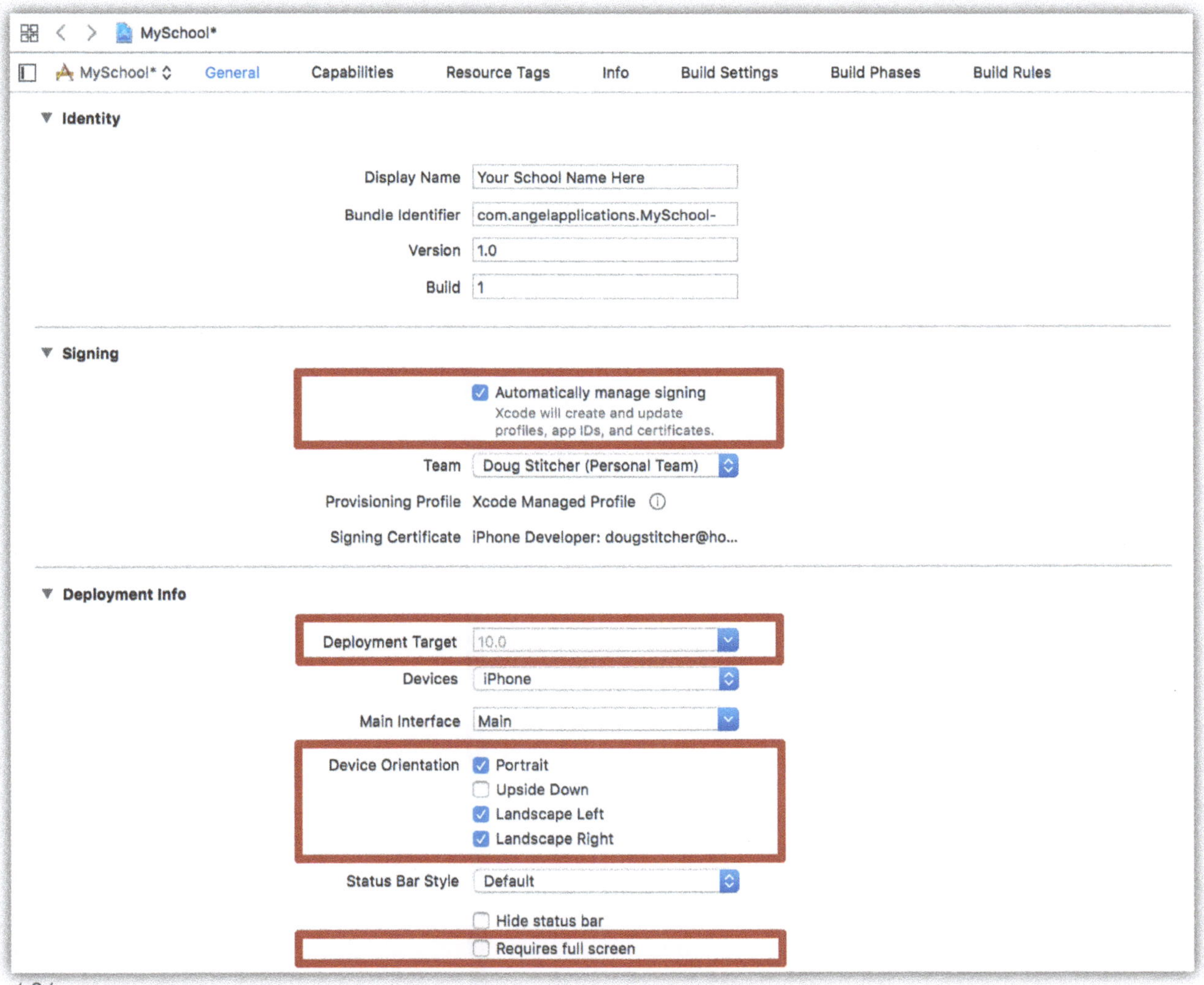

4.06

We only need to edit a few of these. I've highlighted the ones we're going to change in the screenshot above. That's not to say we won't need to come back and change more later, but right now, could you change the following:

(1) Change *Deployment Target* to 8.0. This will allow the app to run on more than 90 per cent of iPhones out there. By default, *Xcode* sets the target operating system as the most recent one which most people won't have updated to yet.

(2) Set *Device Orientation* to *Portrait* and *Upside Down* and uncheck *Landscape Left* and *Landscape Right*. This will ensure the app displays properly. We won't be adding support for a landscape display so we need to uncheck those two boxes.

(3) Select '*Requires Full Screen*'. This feature is actually for iPad apps. Without this button selected, the app would support split view features on iOS 9 iPads. Ours won't so we need to tick the box to say that our app can only run in full screen mode.

(4) Untick 'Automatically manage signing'. Whilst this is a useful new feature of Xcode, it will be better for us to go through the process properly.

We're ready to build our home screen..

http://www.alanpeat.com/build-an-app/Chapter4

CHAPTER FIVE
BUILDING OUR HOME SCREEN

Remember our plan for the home screen? This is what we are going to create next. The first step is to create our header image. At this point, it might be a good idea to have your class sketch out their design ideas. Ask them to think about button styles, experiment with fonts and map out some button layouts. Do they want square buttons or round buttons? I would also look at some similar apps (or screenshots thereof) and discuss the design of the buttons here.

With the introduction of iOS 7 - remember, when your iPhone completely changed how it looked - Apple introduced a much flatter style of design. Buttons stopped being rounded and having a 3D effect and became flatter and generally of one main colour. They also became brighter!

Your pupils will really enjoy experimenting with design and it's an excellent opportunity to link to art and to delve more deeply into the work of Sir Jonny Ive (Apple's British-born head of design).

There are plenty of image editors out there. I use *Adobe Fireworks* but this costs a fair amount of money so, for the sake of this book, we will use free resources.

One particularly easy-to-use editor is found at **https://ipiccy.com/feature/free-online-image-editor**. You might want to have a look and play around. Now, *iPiccy* is web-based so you don't need to use Apple computers to access it. If you only have limited access to Apples, you could still have children creating the artwork on Windows PCs.

Let's have a go at using *iPiccy* to create our *header* image. The first thing you need to know is the dimensions in pixels we need. If you cast your mind back to when we talked pixels, you may remember that the iPhone screen is 320 pixels wide but we want double that to create retina artwork. Height-wise, I'd go for about 80 pixels, remembering to double it, so the image for our header needs to be about 640 x 160 pixels. Feel free to alter the height, but keep the width.

Here, I would model this to the children and then let them run with it. Give them some time to experiment and to work together to compare their ideas. You may even want to open this up to the rest of the school, allowing them to vote for their favourite designs.

On iPiccy, select *Make a design*:

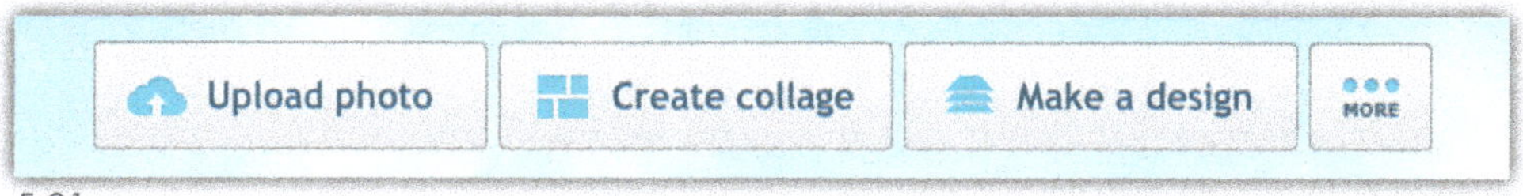

5.01

You'll then be prompted to set the dimensions of your image:

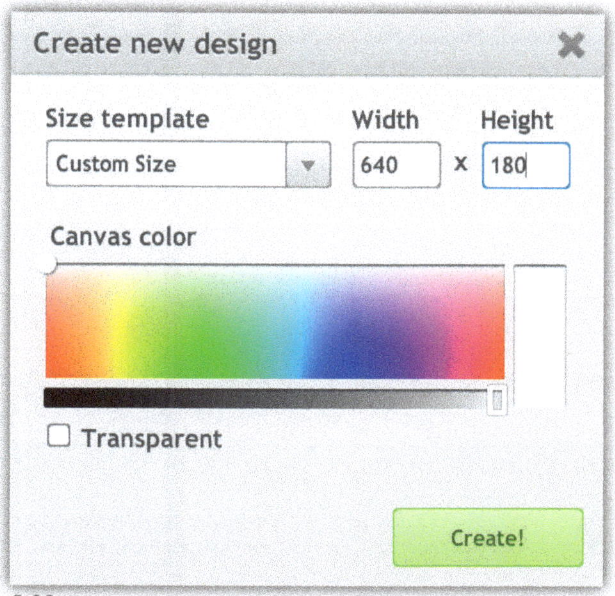

5.02

You can also select the colour of the canvas, which is the background of your image. If you're planning on covering the whole canvas then you don't need to worry about this, but otherwise choose a colour linked to your school.

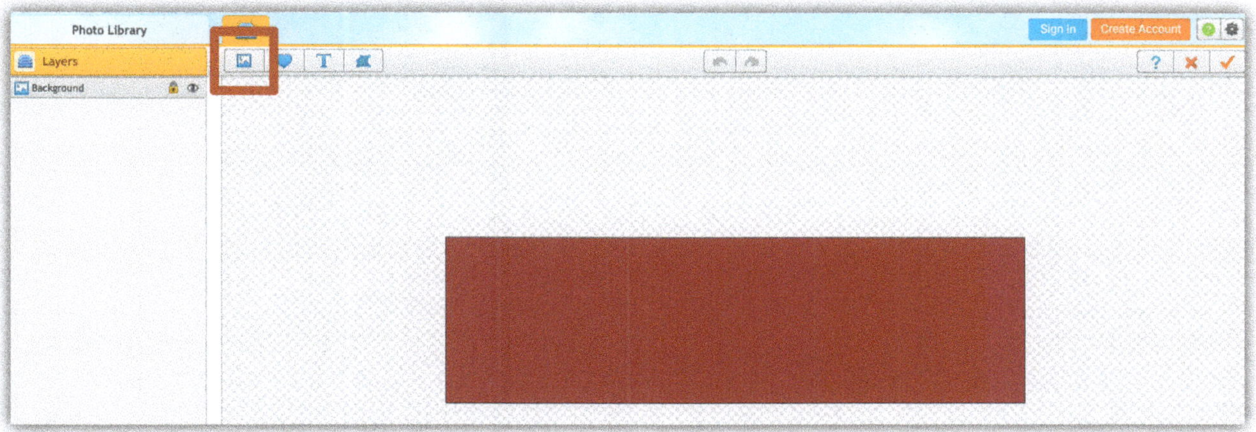

5.03

I've made my *header* maroon.

You'll probably want to add your school logo. To do this, press the image button I've highlighted. You'll then need to follow the instructions from *iPiccy*, which can be a little fiddly, especially if you're working on a Mac.

But once you've done everything it asks you to do, you're ready to upload your school logo. If you don't have it saved on your computer, get a copy from somewhere. I used Google to find my school's logo.

You'll know you've done everything right when you see this on the left-hand side:

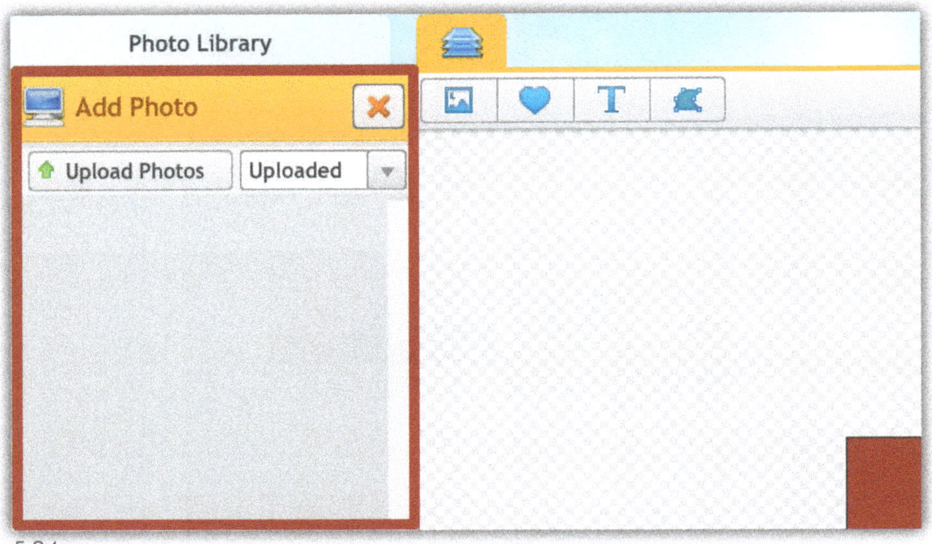

5.04

Select *Upload Photos* and locate your school's logo in the *Finder* window that pops up. Select it and it will upload. The screen will change to this:

5.05

You can see my school's logo. It's worth mentioning here that my logo is gold on a white background – NOT a transparent background. This means that when I add it to my header, it will be a gold logo on top of a white box on top of the maroon header. To avoid this, get hold of a logo with a transparent background.

It's then just a case of dragging your image on top of your header and positioning it and sizing it as appropriate.

A word of warning. You will need to incorporate a *Back* button and a *Refresh* button on either side of your header, so leave some space.

Mine looks like this:

5.06

I'm going to add some text beneath the logo. It doesn't need to be fancy.

Click on the 'T' button.

5.07

There are loads of options here. Some of the fonts are great and the kids will love messing with them.

Here's my finished header image:

5.08

Of course, you can spend hours on this and run it past the School Leadership Team or whoever decides things at your school. But for the sake of our app, this will suffice.

Last thing to do now, save it.

5.09

Press the tick on the right of the screen. This will take you back to the main screen. At the top, you will see a picture of a floppy-disk.

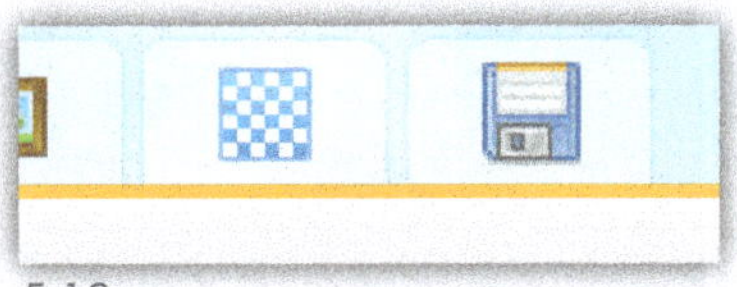

5.10

Press it.

This box will appear:

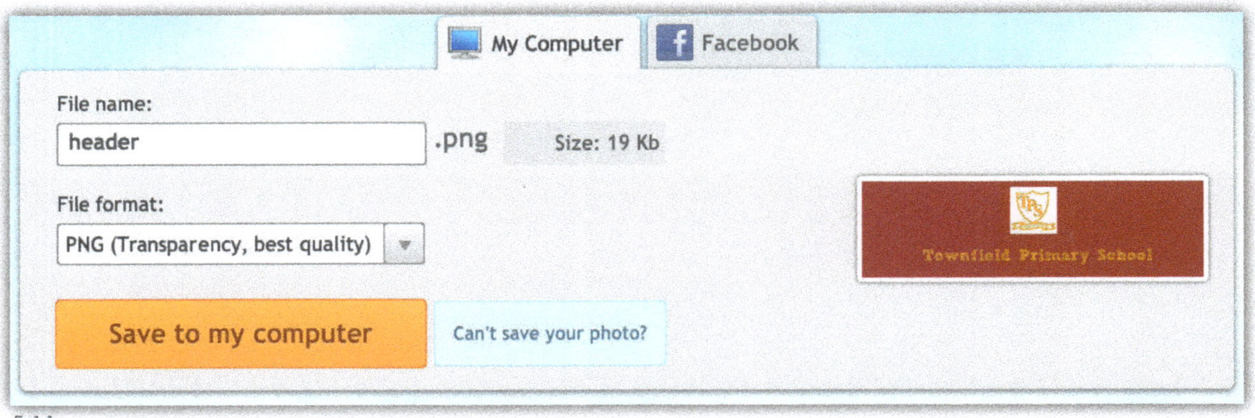

5.11

Call the file 'header' and select *PNG* for the file format. iOS handles PNG files better than *JPGs* but it doesn't really matter unless you want transparency.

Click *Save to my computer* and save it to somewhere you'll remember. You'll need the image soon. It's a good idea to create a folder on your desktop to save all the images we're going to make. Something like this:

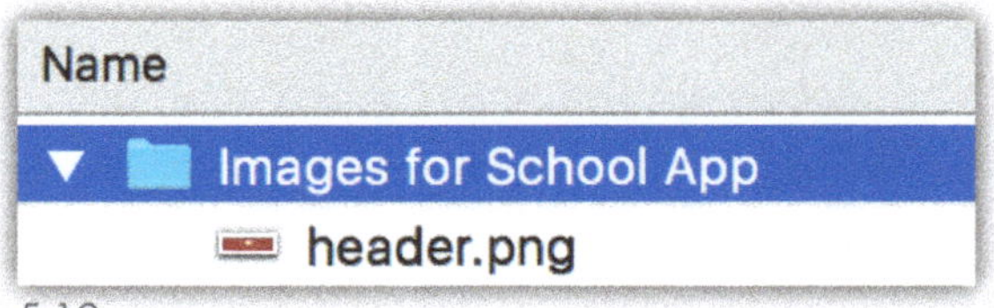

5.12

While we're using *iPiccy*, let's go ahead and make our *Buttons*. Remember, for our home screen, we need five buttons:

- Latest News
- Contact Us
- Find Us
- Our Website
- School Jotter

I'll show you how to make the first one – you can then repeat the process for the others. And that really is how I would do this with my class. I would create one button and then ask the children to copy the process to create their own.

When I've taught this, it's taken around three lessons to get all of this artwork made so you may wish to block it in or have a word with ICT Co-ordinator to see if you can get a morning in the ICT suite!

Remember that, as *iPiccy* is web-based, you don't need to use Apple computers to access it so if you only have limited access to Apples, you could still have children creating the artwork on Windows PCs.

Go back to *iPiccy*, and start a new project by selecting *Make a design*.

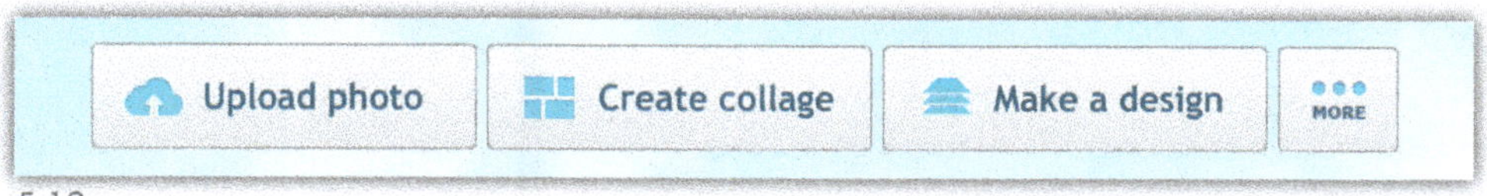

5.13

This time, we're making *Buttons*. We've planned square buttons but they can be any shape you like. For the sake of this tutorial, I'm going to stick with square ones. Use the following options:

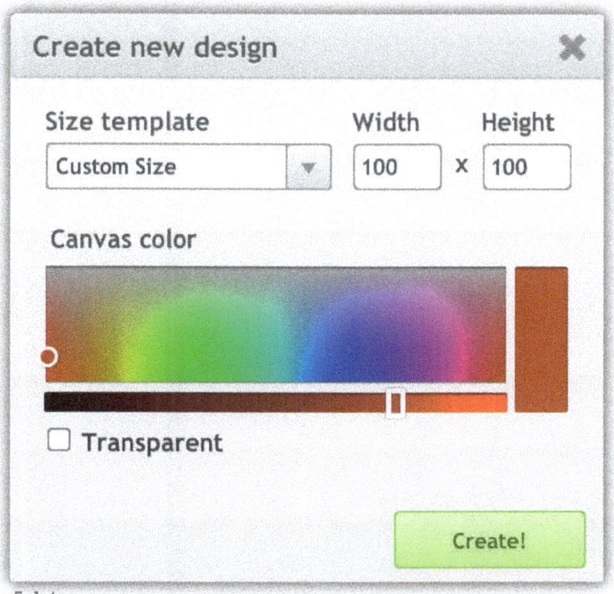

5.14

I've set the width and height at 100 pixels each and the background to be the maroon of my school. If you want a square button, you can either set its colour by setting the canvas colour as I've done, or draw a square and set its fill colour as the colour you want. If you want a button of a different shape, make sure you select a transparent canvas by checking the box.

You should see a screen like this:

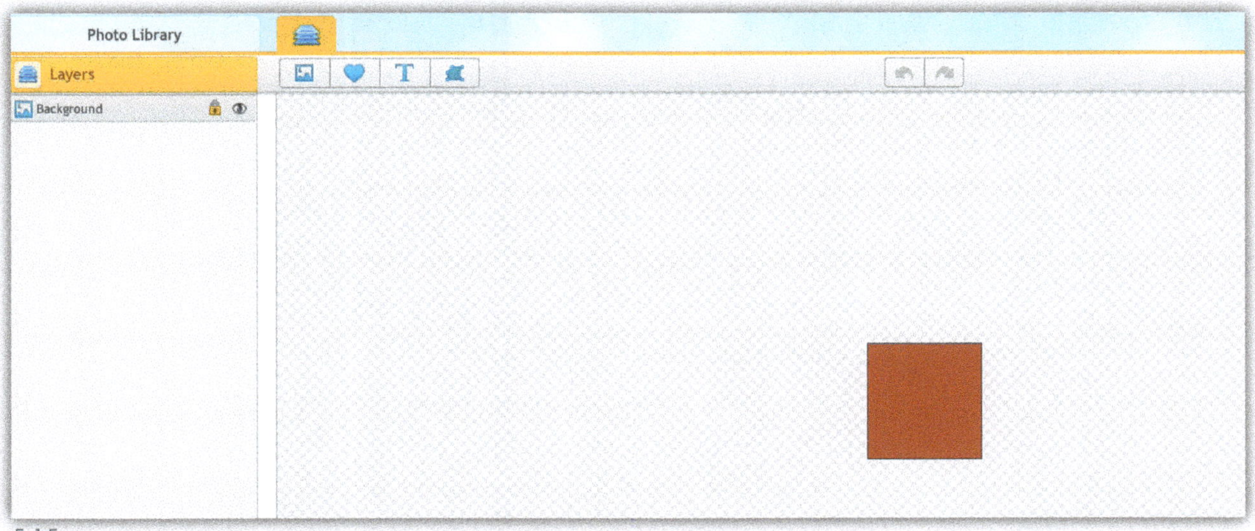

5.15

As it stands, all I need to do is add the text to my button. But if you wanted a different shape, press the picture of a heart and choose the shape you want from the left-hand side.

I'll add my text by pressing the 'T' button next to the heart:

5.16

You can play around with the fonts and colours as you see fit.

When you're happy, press the tick in the top right:

5.17

And then press the save button:

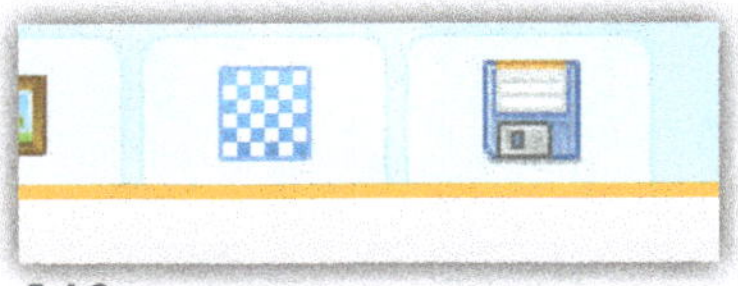
5.18

5.19

Have a look at how I save my button:

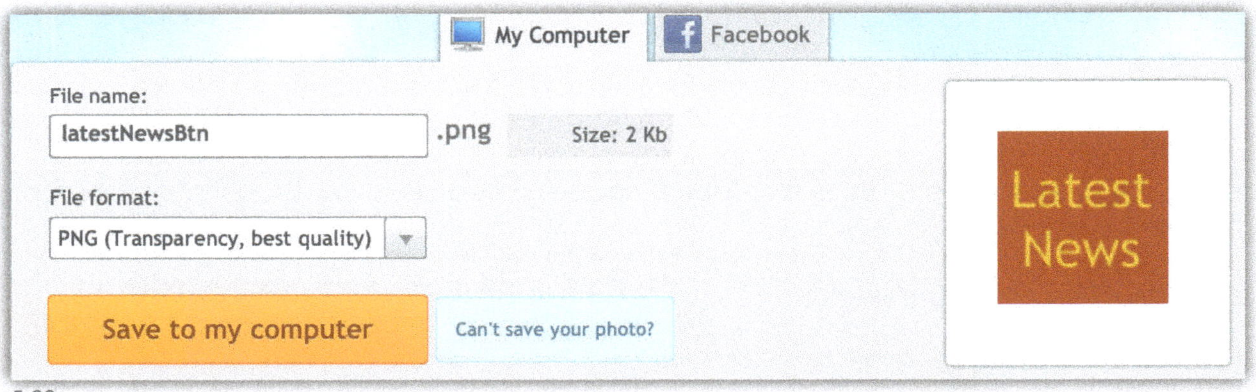

5.20

I've used the naming convention of starting with a lowercase letter and then using a capital for each subsequent word.

I've also selected to save as a PNG. This is especially important if your button isn't square. Press Save to my computer and save it to the same folder as your header:

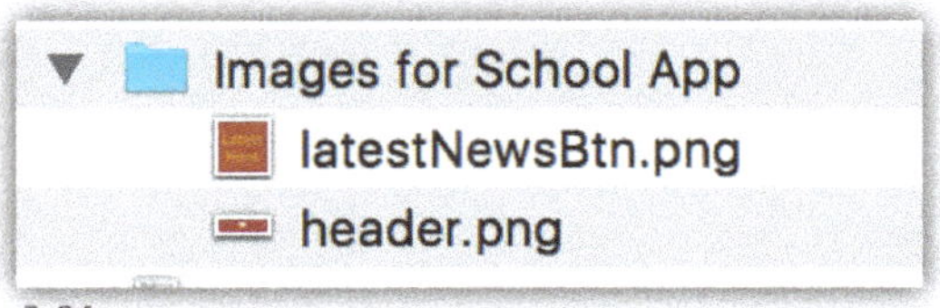

5.21

Go back to your internet browser, and you should see this screen:

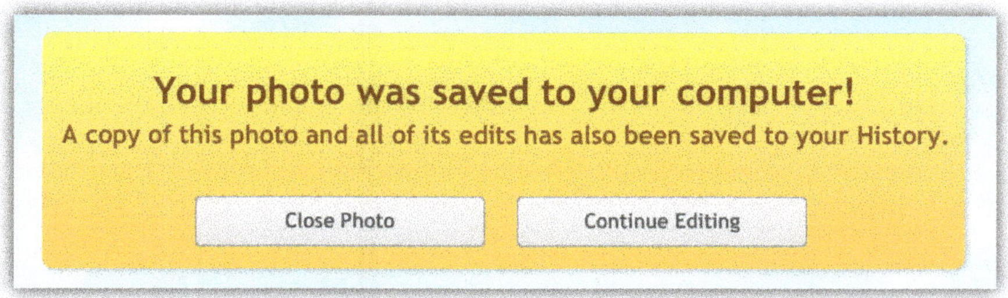

5.22

Select *Close* Photo.

Repeat this process to produce the other four buttons you need. Once we have all five buttons and our header, we are ready to build our home screen.

If you are building this app as a collective with your class, you will need to decide which images you will use within the app before following the instructions below. Alternatively, you may want to allow each group of children to create their own complete app before deciding which one to add to the App Store.

The process for adding images is relatively easy; you should only need to model this once to your class before they get the idea!

The first thing we need to do is add our images to the app. Go back to your *Xcode* project.

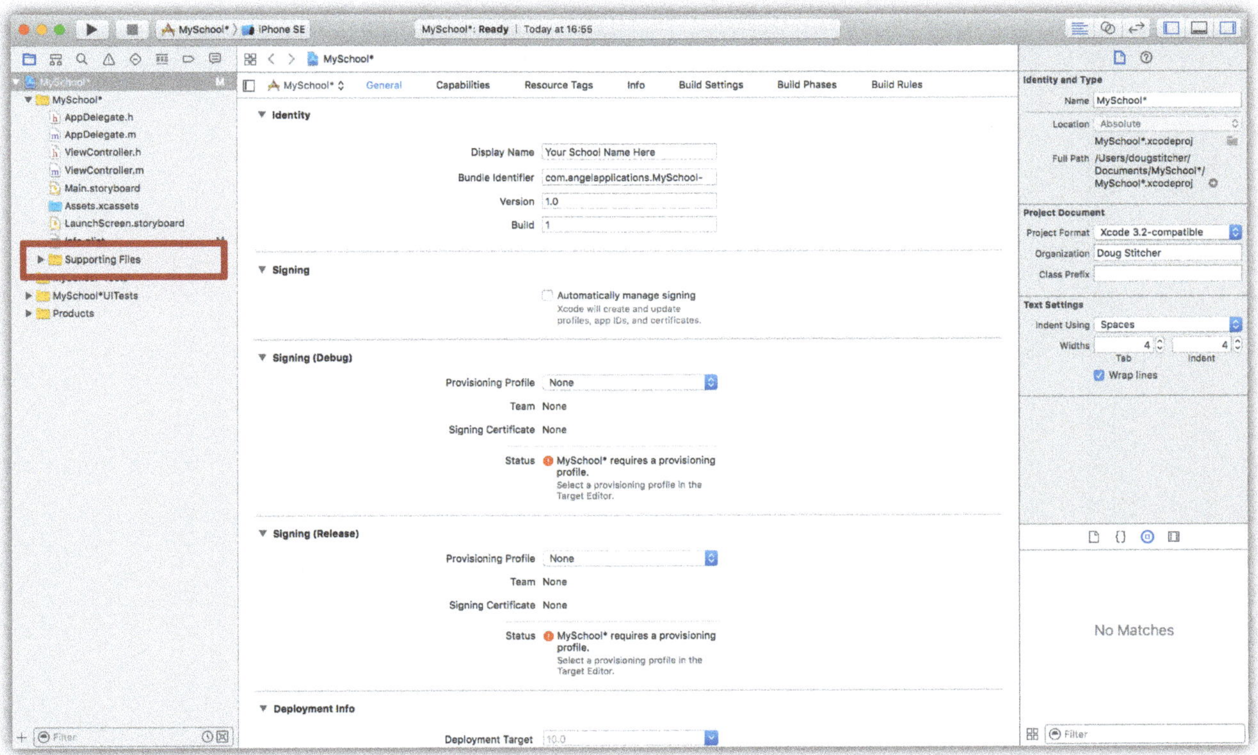

5.23

See that folder called *Supporting Files*. It's the one I've drawn a box around. We're going to drag our images there. Open your folder of images in *Finder*. Your view may look different depending on how you have Finder set up. Mine shows my items in a list but you may have an icon layout instead.

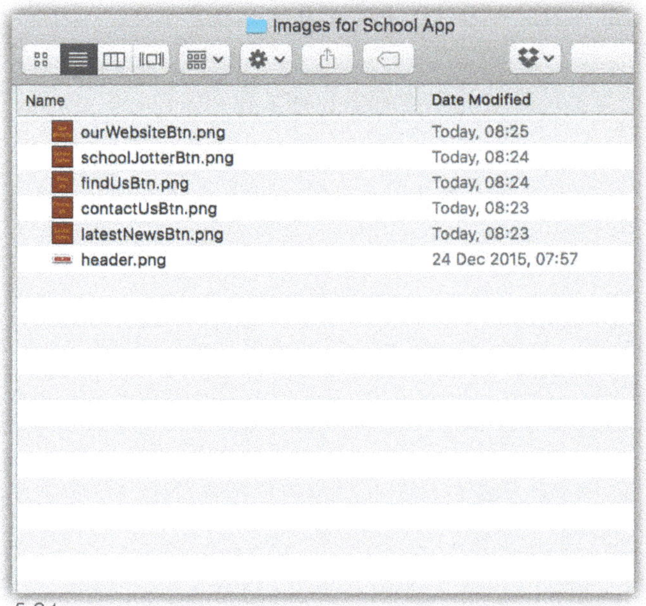

5.24

Select all the images, either by dragging a box around them all, or by pressing *Cmd* and 'A' at the same time.

Now drag the files from *Finder* to the *Supporting Files* folder in *Xcode*. A small line will appear under *Supporting Files*. Release the mouse and the files will be added, then the following pop-up screen will be displayed:

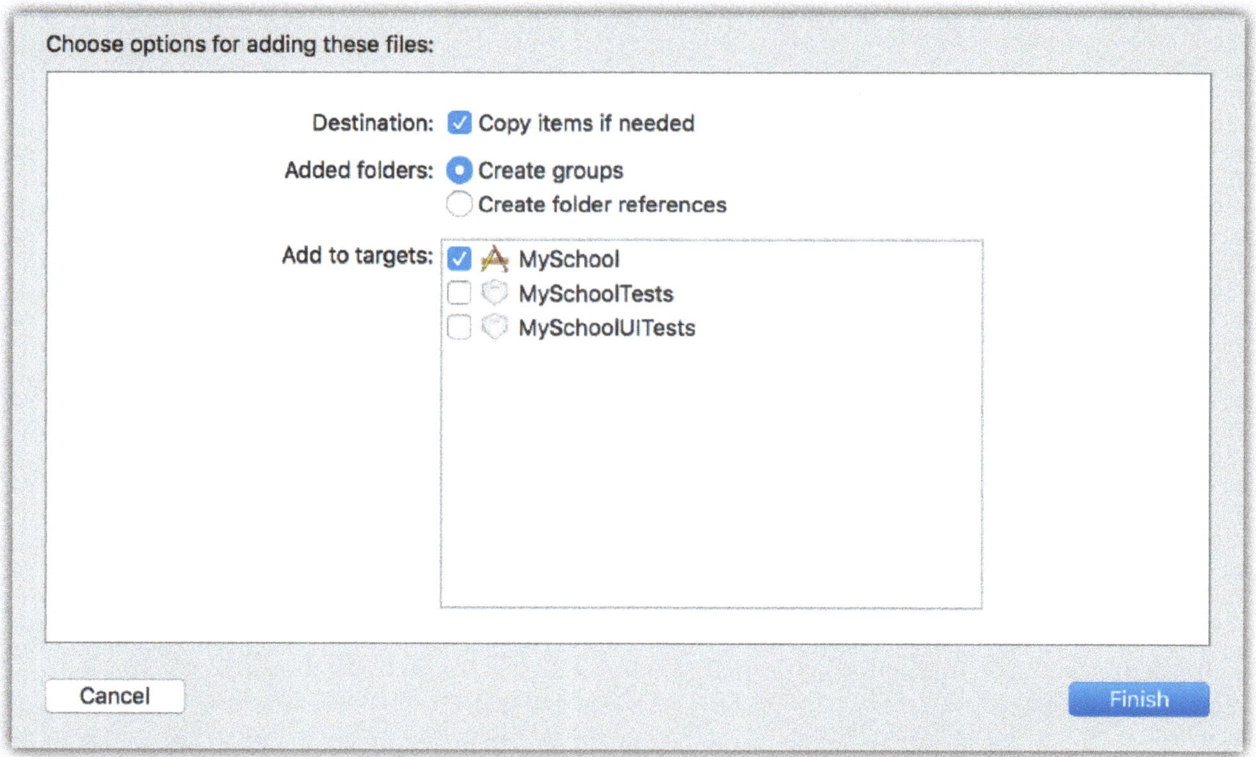

5.25

This screen is displayed whenever you add files to your app. You always want these three boxes ticked: *Copy items if needed*, *Create groups* and *MySchool*. Remember that the next time you add items to your app.

If everything has gone to plan, your files in the Navigator pane should look something like this:

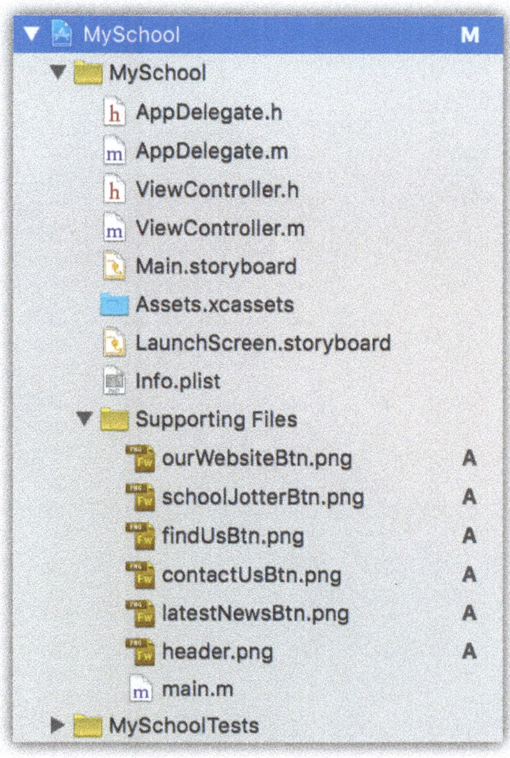

5.26

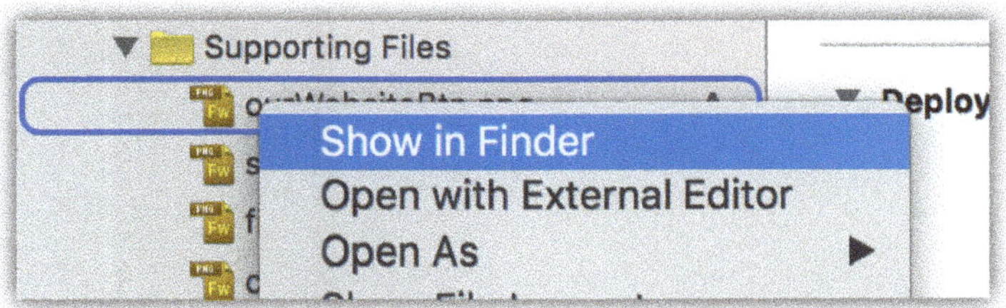

5.27

It's also handy to know how to find the original file. Say you wanted to edit an image you'd added, the quickest way is to show the image in *Finder*, open it, edit it and save it. This will save you having to go through the whole importing images process every time.

Now we need to use the images in our app. This is where the fun begins. You'll feel like you're building your app at this point.

First step, let's add the header image to the top of our app. Find the *Main.storyboard* file in the *Navigator* pane:

5.28

If you look in the *Editor* pane, you will see the storyboard. To start with, we're going to build our app for iPhone 5 only (this is the 4 inch screen). The first thing we need to do is change the shape of our screen. We have done this before, but I'll go through it again just to remind you.

In the six tabs at the top, press the one that looks like a piece of paper. It's the first one. This will change the *Utility* pane to display the *File Inspector*.

Underneath *Interface Builder Document*, you'll see two checked boxes:

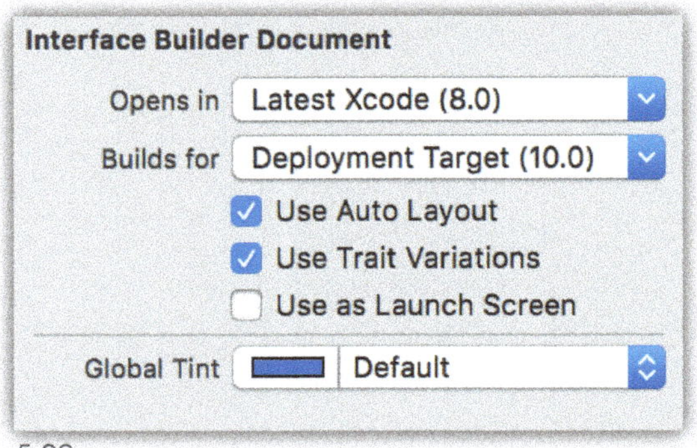

5.29

Uncheck the Use *Auto Layout* box and an alert dialogue box will pop up:

Press the blue *Disable Trait Variations* button and you're done. *Auto Layout* is now disabled and we can carry on.

I know it's a pain. But we won't have to do all of this again.

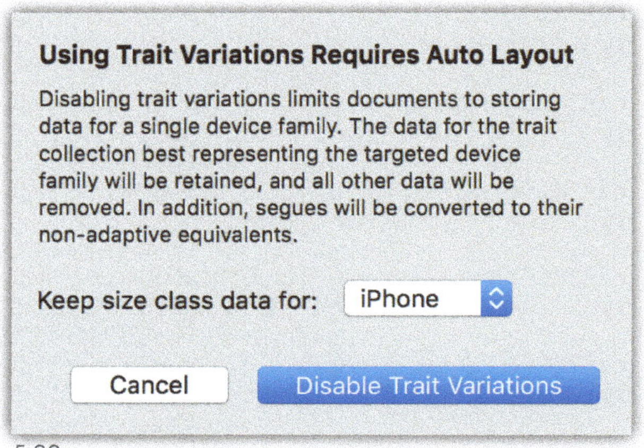

5.30

As we're going to build our first screen for iPhone 5, we need to change our view to look like an iPhone 5 (Apple now refer to this as the iPhone SE). To do this, click on the small grey bar at the bottom of the Editor Pane:

5.31

You'll then see a selection of screen sizes:

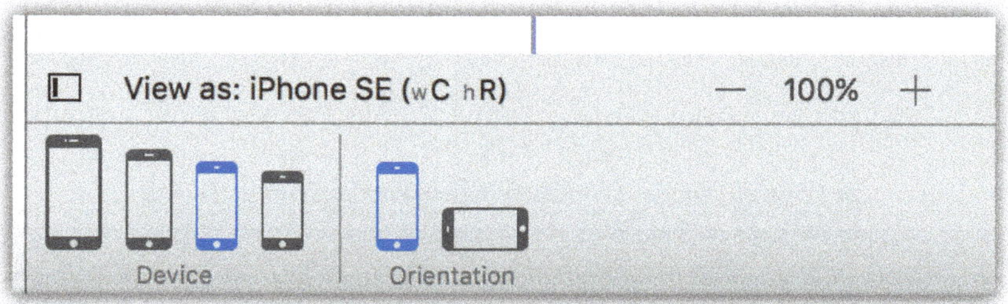

5.32

Select the second smallest device - this represents the iPhone 5/5s/SE. Your view should change to be the size of an iPhone 5/5s/SE like this:

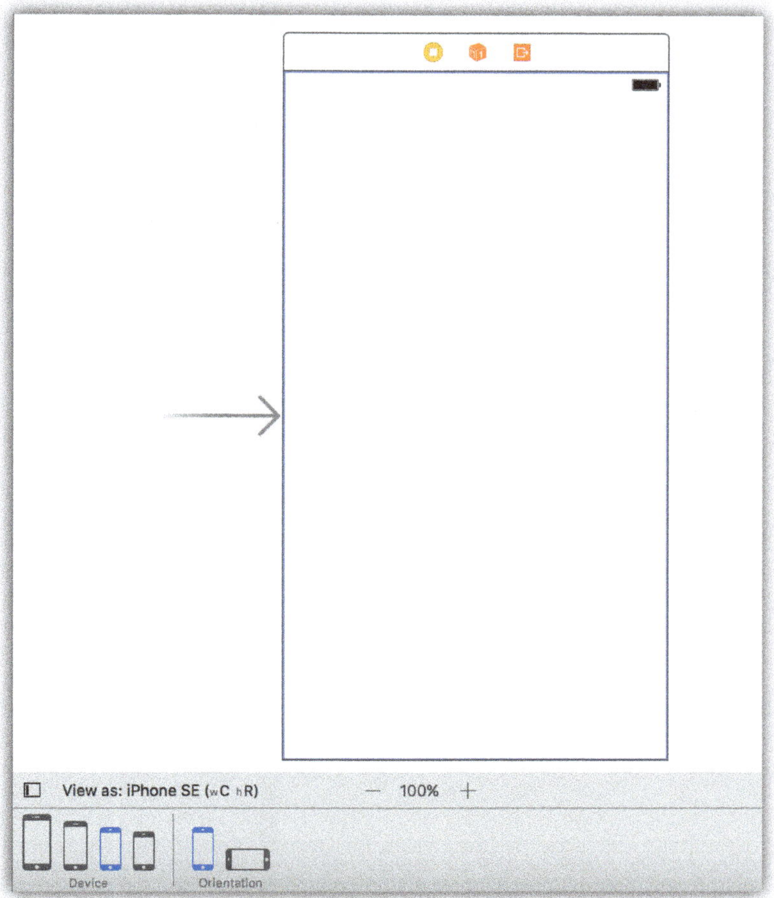

5.33

Let's add the header image. Go to the *Object Library* in the bottom third of the *Utility* pane:

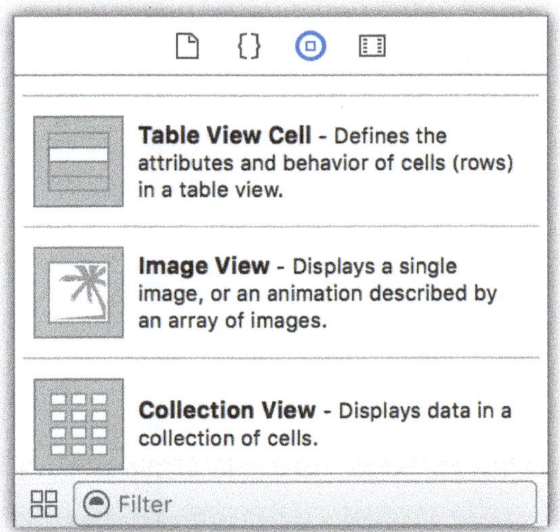

5.34

Scroll down until you find the object called *Image View*. This is technically a *UIImageView* and we will use one any time we want to display an image. Like our *UILabels*, the content of the *Image View* can be either *static* or *dynamic*. Our *header* image isn't going to change, so it will be static. But when we create our *RSS Feed* reader for *Latest News*, the images displayed will vary depending upon the images in the news feed.

Drag an *Image View* onto the iPhone screen in the centre of the *Editor* pane:

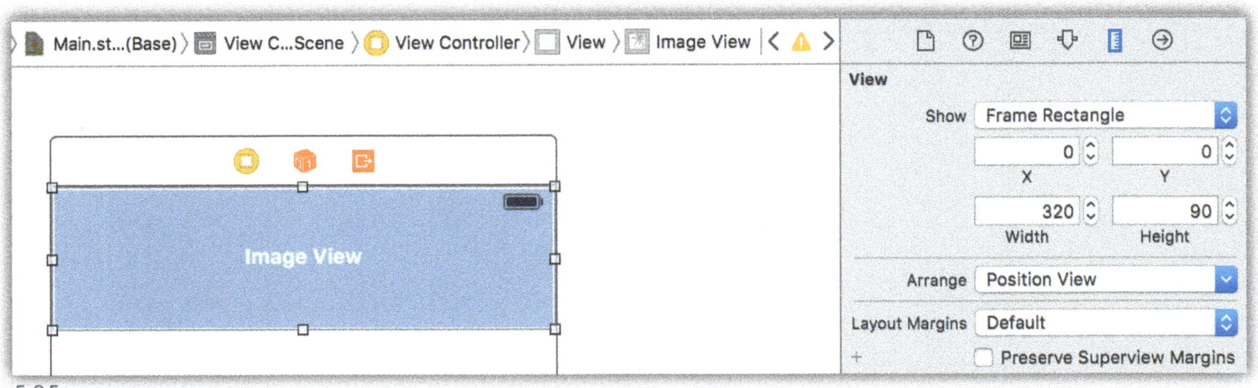

5.35

We made our header image 640 x 180 pixels. To display it we need to make it half that size, or 320 x 90 pixels. You can size by dragging the handles. But if you want to be more accurate, press the button that looks like a ruler in the *Utility* pane. You'll then see the x and y positions of the selected view, in this case, our *Image View*. These are the horizontal and vertical positions. They should both be set at zero. That will put the *Image View* at the top left of the screen. If you move the *Image View* around a bit you will see these values change.

Beneath the x and y positions, you'll see a *width* and *height box*. Set these values at 320 for the width and 90 for the height. Press *return* and the *Image View* will resize appropriately.

The last step is to put our image in the *Image View*. You can do this two ways. One is with code and is a bit tricky. The other is in *Interface Builder* and is dead easy. We'll be using the latter.

Go to the *Utility* pane again and press the *Attributes* tab:

5.36

Make sure the *Image View* on the iPhone screen in the *Editor* pane is selected. You should then see this:

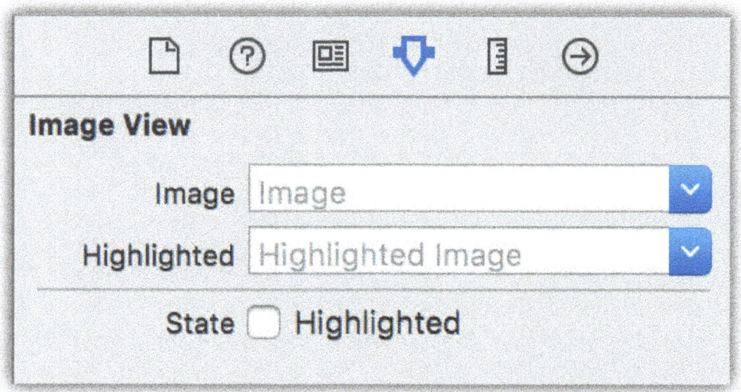

5.37

In the text box that is called *Image*, type the name of your *header* image. It should autocomplete for you. Mine is called 'header.png'.

Make sure you write the file name exactly as it appears on the file. It is case-sensitive so you will need to be careful. Press *return* and your image will appear:

5.38

Next, it's time to add your buttons. The process is similar. I'll show you how to do one and then you can do the rest yourself.

The first step is to go back to the *Object Library* in the bottom third of the *Utility* pane and find the *UIButton* option:

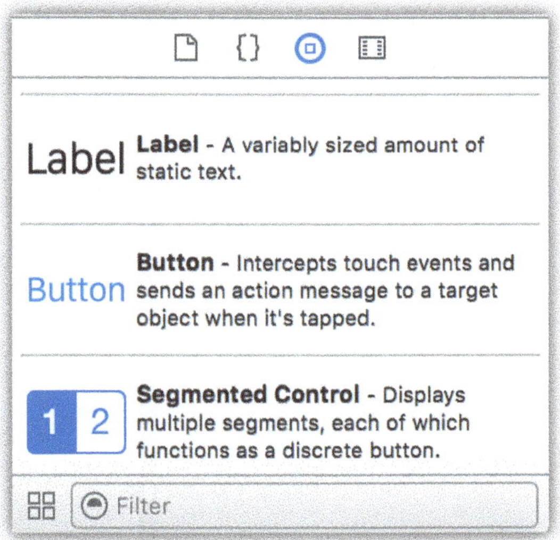

5.39

Drag a Button onto the iPhone screen somewhere beneath the header image:

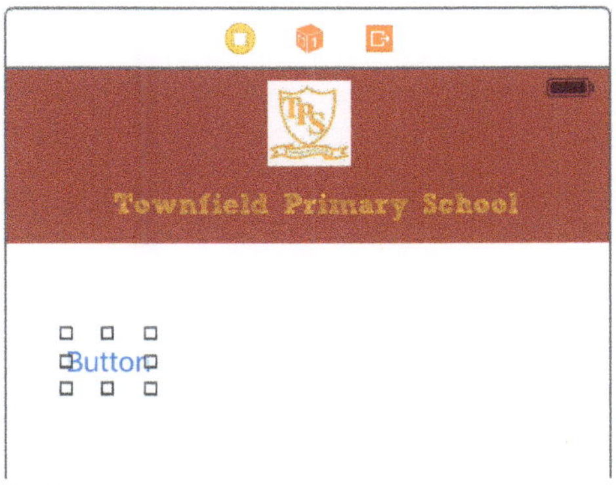

5.40

You'll notice that the button is quite small and contains the text 'Button' instead of our button image. That's what we need to fix. So with the *Button* selected, press the *Attributes* tab. You may already have the attributes selected from when you added the header image.

Only a couple of things to do here. First, delete the word 'Button' under the *Title* option. Press *return* and the button should lose its text.

Then, go to Image and enter the name of your Latest News button image. Mine is called 'latestNewsBtn.png'.

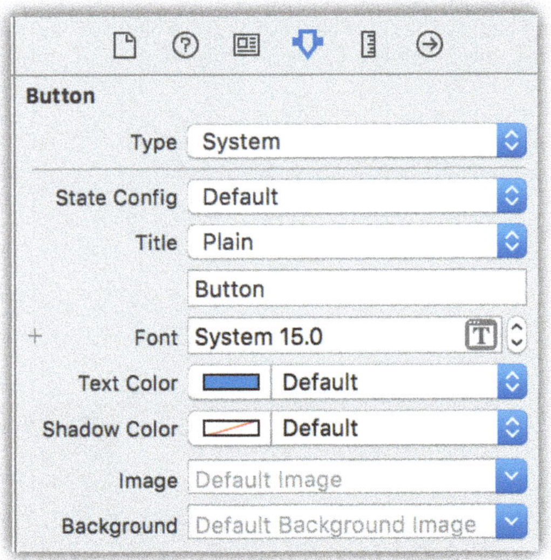

5.41

It should look something like this:

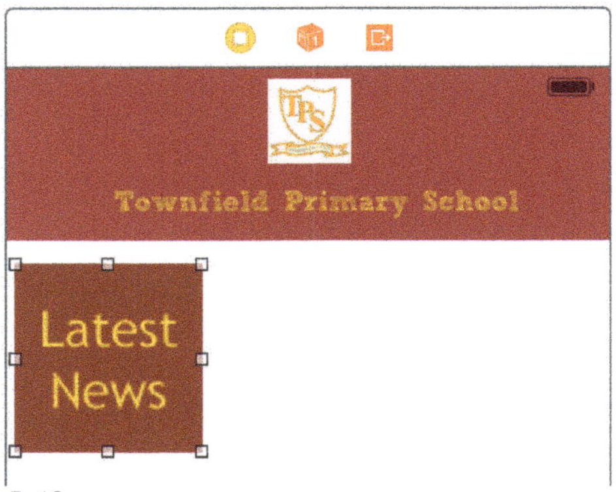

5.42

All that's left to do is move your button around to where you want it.

We need to add the other four buttons. You've got two options here. You can repeat the above process four times and you'll be done.

Or, and this is my preferred method, we can copy our *Latest News* button four times and change the image.

To copy the button, you have to use keyboard shortcuts. A right-click will bring up the connections menu we use to link buttons to actions. Select the button, you'll know it's selected when the handles appear around it, as in my screenshot above. Press *Cmd* and 'C' at the same time.

This copies it to the clipboard. To paste it, press *Cmd* and 'V' at the same time. Your new button will appear 10 pixels down and 10 pixels across from the original button:

5.43

Don't worry, we'll move it in a second. Press Cmd and 'V' three more times. This will paste a further three buttons:

5.44

You can select each button and move it around the screen. Do this to all five buttons until you are happy with the layout. You can always change this later.

Your screen should look something like this:

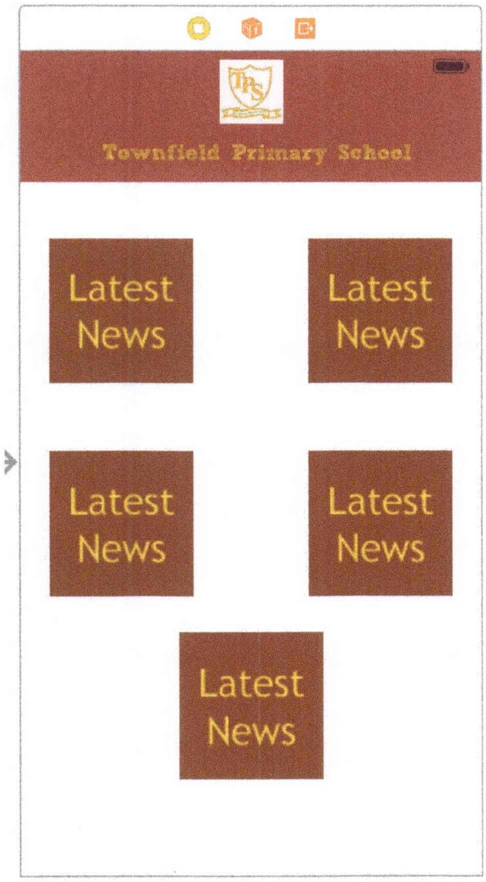

5.45

The only issue is that all the buttons say 'Latest News'. Click on the second button and go to the *Utilities* pane, making sure you've pressed the *Attributes* tab.

Change the image to your *Contact Us* button image:

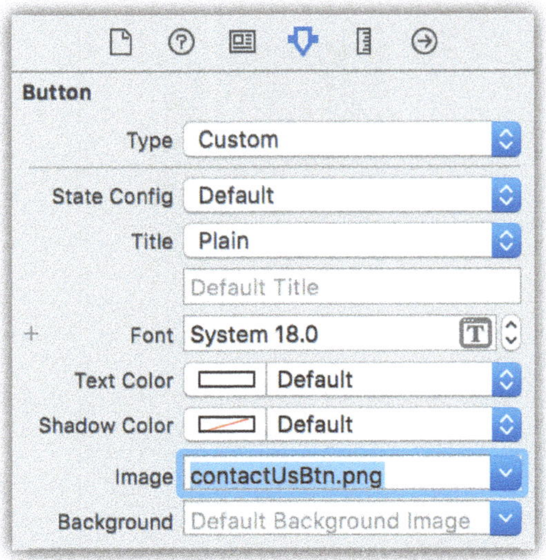

5.46

That is the only thing you need to change. Repeat this with the other buttons until all five buttons are correct.

And you're done.

Your final screen should look like this:

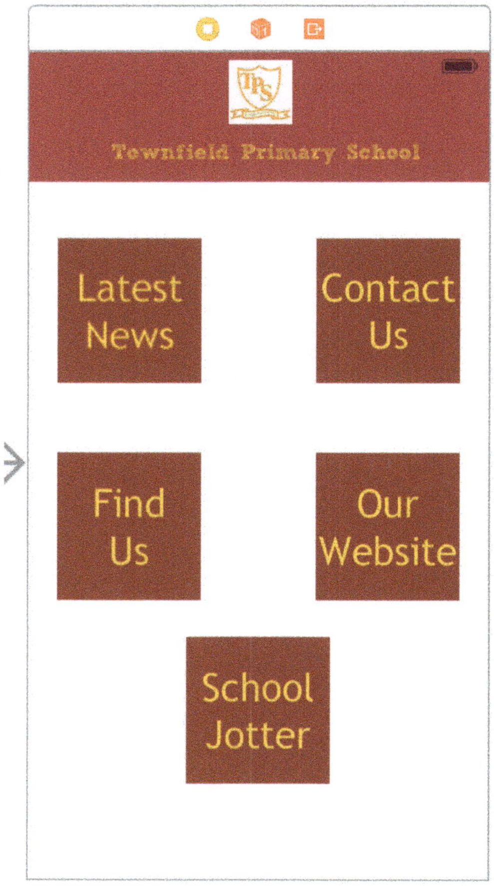

5.47

Believe it or not, that is the home screen finished. The only thing left to do is to link each button to the correct screen. We'll do that later.

I haven't spent much time on my design, but you can tweak the look and feel of your buttons and header images. This is the perfect time for your students to start to try some ideas out. They could try arranging the buttons in different formations, explore different sizes and change the images for the buttons to some other ones they have designed. This is all part of the whole process.

One final thing to show you is how to change the background colour. It's currently white. If your school uses white in its colours, you might want to leave it.

As I mentioned, my school's colours are maroon and gold. My headteacher would be very cross if I left the background white. So to keep her happy, let's change it.

The background colour is a property of an object that is added automatically for us called a *UIView*. It's the view into which we put our *header* image and five buttons.

To access it, click anywhere on the iPhone screen that isn't a *Button* or an *image*. Keep an eye on the *Utility* pane:

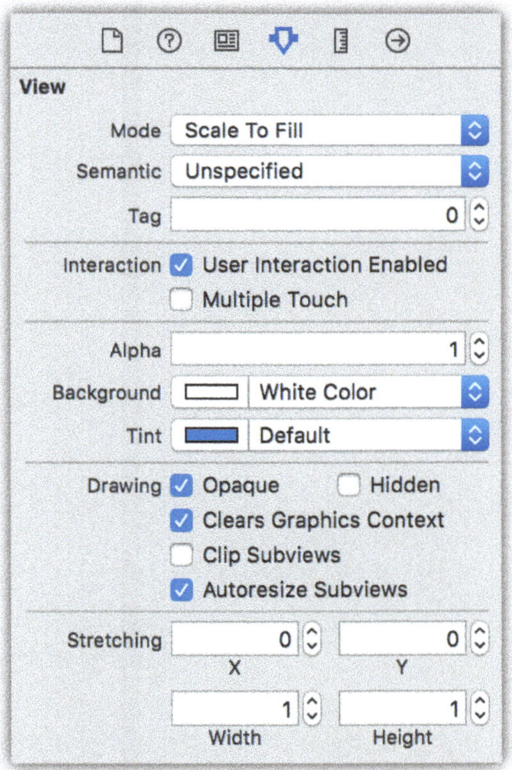

5.48

The option we want to change here is the one called *Background*. It's set as *White Color* by default. Press over the words *White Color* and a colour picker will appear:

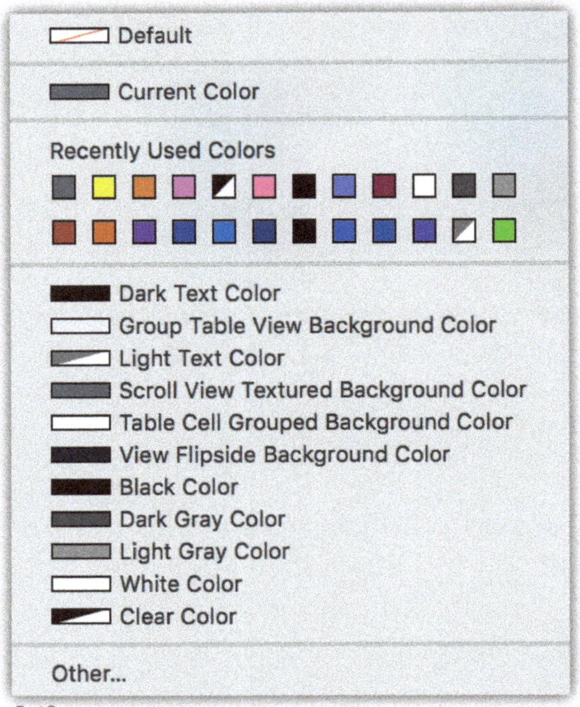

5.49

If the colour you want isn't here, select *Other...* at the bottom and you'll get some pallets to choose from.

Here's an example of what you'll see:

5.50

I like using the crayon option. The pupils like it too. Choose a colour and your background will change. You'll then need to close the pallets by clicking the small circular button in the top left of the window.

My final screen looks like this:

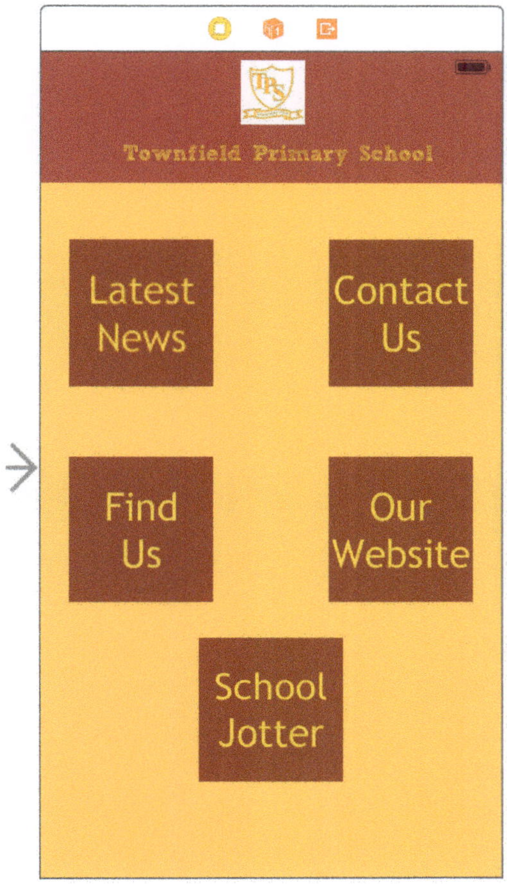

5.51

Yes, I know. It's hideous! But it doesn't matter. The screen is built and we haven't written a line of code yet.

Your pupils will really feel like they've accomplished something at this point (despite the lack of the code).

If you're feeling more adventurous, why not create a background image and add another *Image View* beneath your buttons to hold it?

If you're not feeling more adventurous, stop now and make a cup of tea.

Next up, creating our *Latest News* screen.

http://www.alanpeat.com/build-an-app/Chapter5

CHAPTER SIX
BUILDING THE LATEST NEWS SCREENS

We're about to embark on the hardest part of the app.

Let's remind ourselves of what this part of the app does:

(1) It reads an RSS Feed of news that you have added. The app will be optimised to read a WordPress blog. We'll look at how to create a WordPress blog for free but you may already have your own school blog to use.

(2) It displays an image from the news item alongside a heading and a summary of the news.

(3) Pressing the news item loads another screen that displays the whole content of the news story and a larger copy of the image.

It sounds easy. It isn't. But I intend to make it look like it is.

Setting up the WordPress Blog

This part of the process is essential if your school doesn't already have a blog. However, the setting up of it isn't really something you'd need to teach your children to do. Instead, once it is up and running, you could involve them in the creation of the posts that the app will read. So the following set of instructions are really only intended for you, the teacher.

Let's set up a free *WordPress* blog using WordPress's website.

Go to **https://wordpress.com/** to get started:

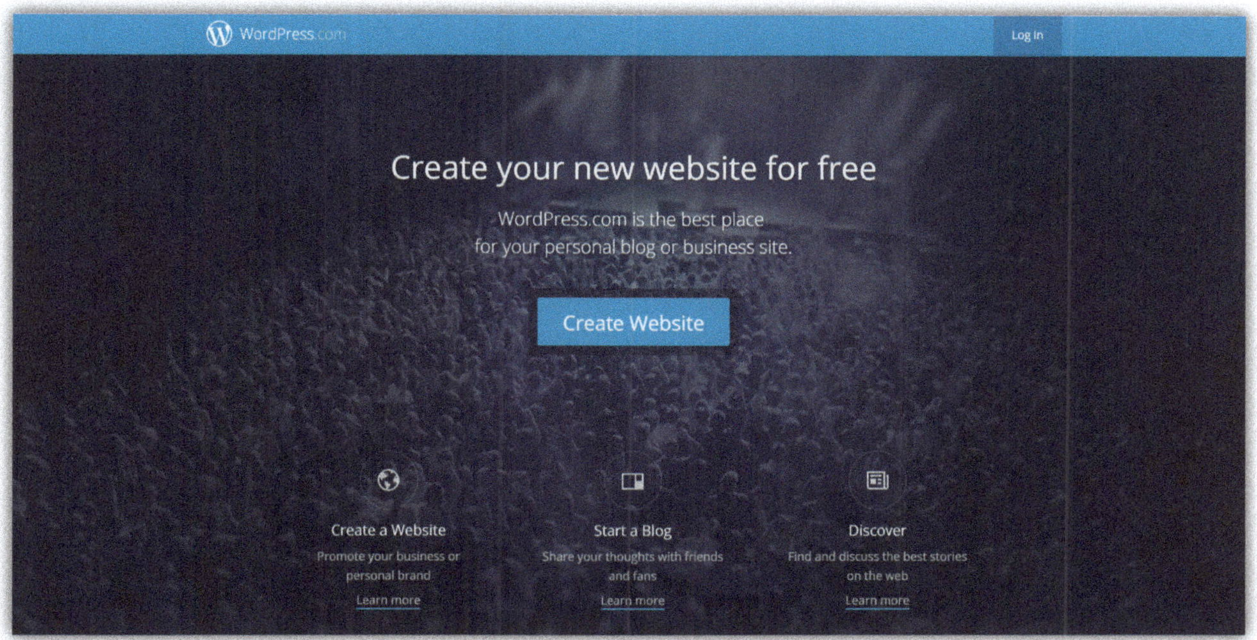

6.001

You know what I want you to do. Press the big blue *Create Website* button.

You'll be taken to a select a theme page:

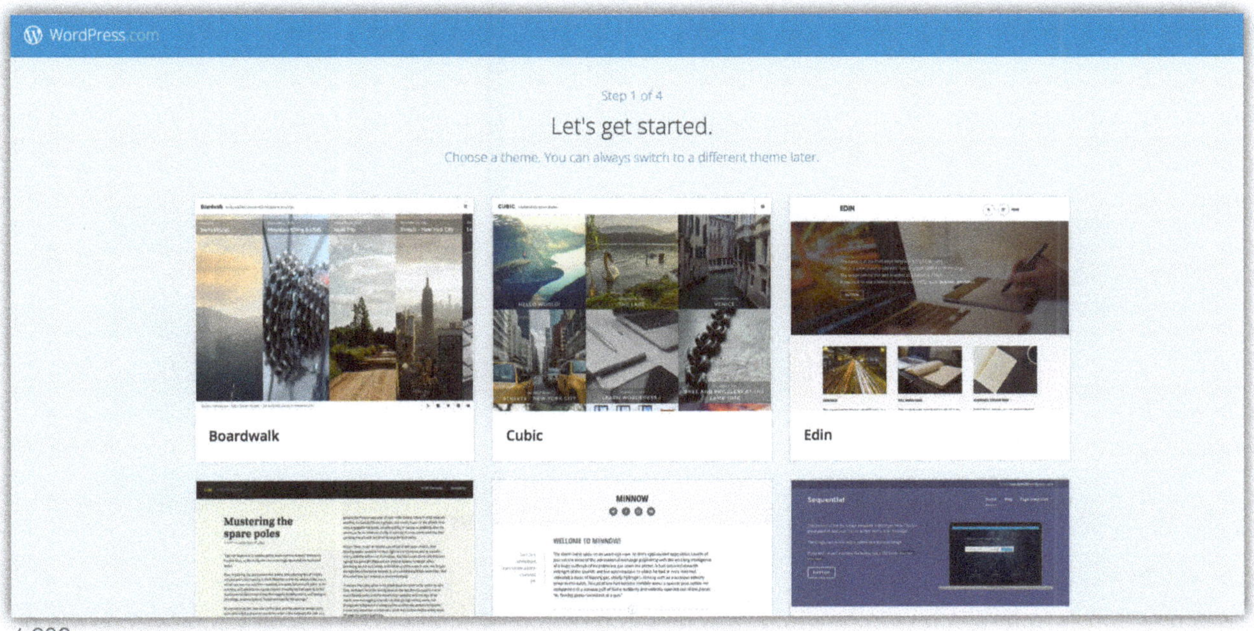

6.002

This bit really doesn't matter. Your *WordPress* blog isn't going to be overtly visible in the app. It's going to hold the latest news content but the app is going to strip that information down so the theme you choose here is irrelevant.

You can scroll down to the bottom of the page and choose *Skip*.

Step 2 will load:

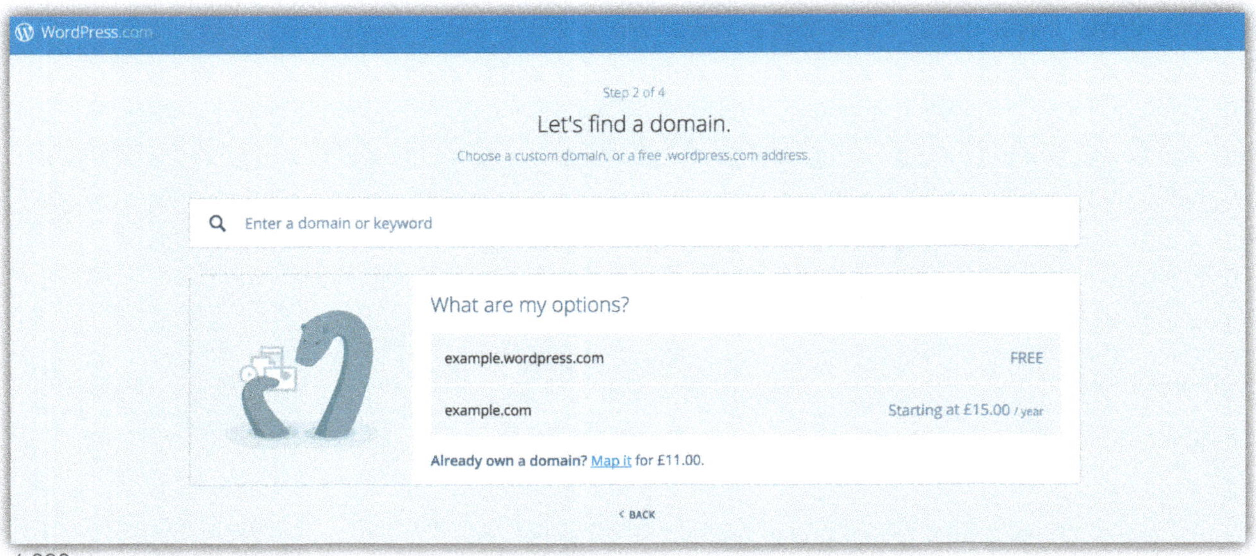

6.003

Here you get to set the domain name for your blog. For the sake of the app, choose the free option. Nobody will ever need to know the link to your blog except you as you build the app so you might as well choose the **example.wordpress.com** one. Enter your school name in the top search box.

You'll be presented with some options:

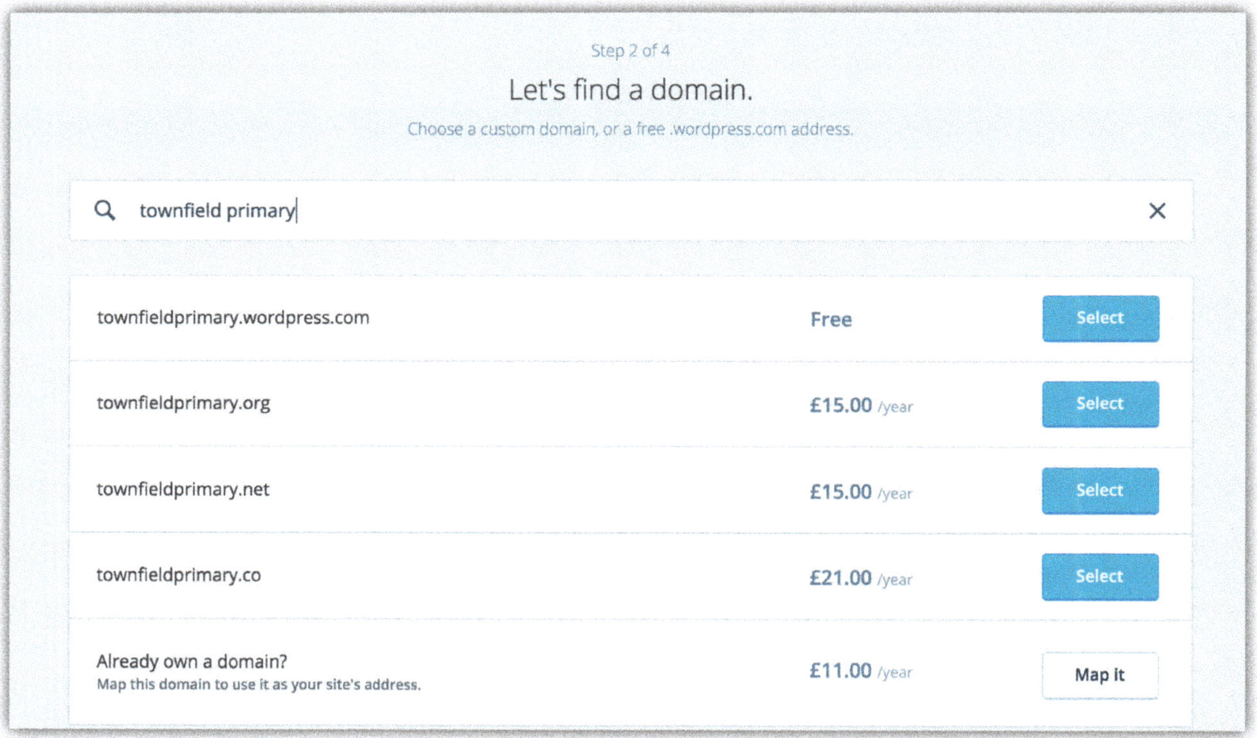

6.004

I'm going to choose the free option (in my case, **townfieldprimary.wordpress.com**). If somebody else has a similar domain, you'll be presented with other options you can choose.

Press the blue *Select* button.

Step 3 will ask you to choose a payment plan:

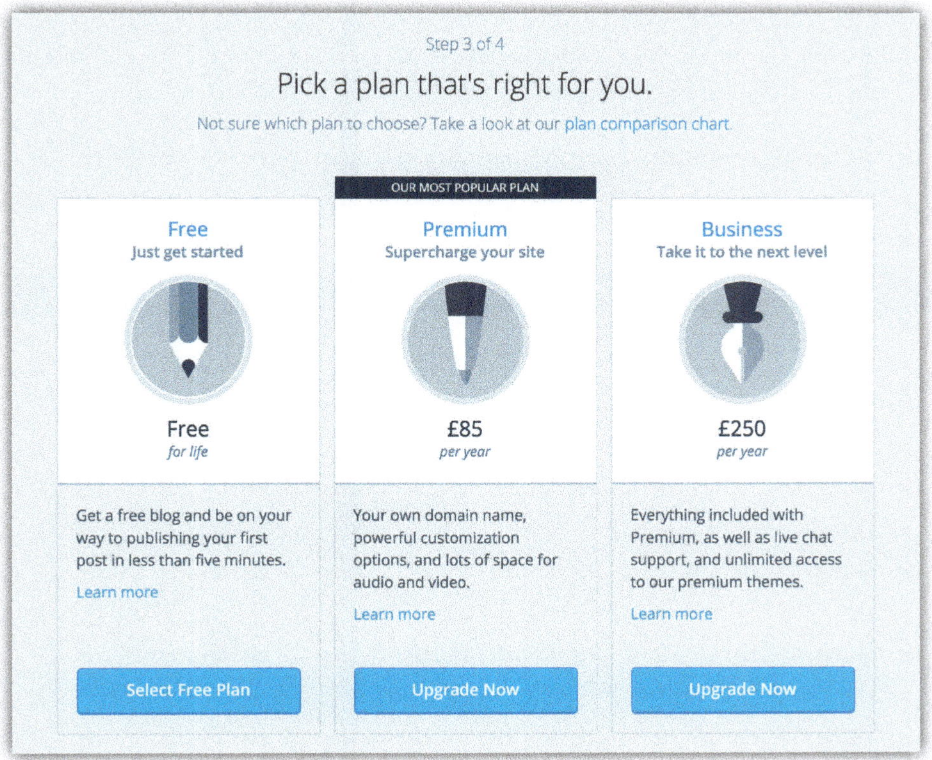

6.005

The free plan is supported by adverts. But again, that doesn't matter. Our blog isn't visible in the app, just its content. So go ahead and hit *Select Free Plan*. Unless you're feeling flush of course.

Finally, you need to set up your account credentials:

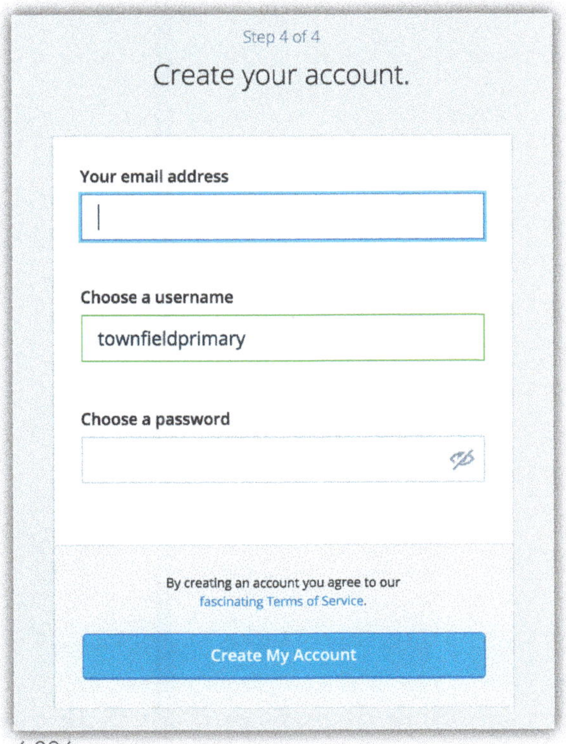

6.006

Go ahead and create your account.

In all likelihood, the students aren't going to access the blog to create the latest news information so set it up with secure details. The only information the children will need is the *URL* (the link) of your *RSS Feed,* which we haven't created yet.

Once you've entered your details, *WordPress* will send you a verification email which you need to click on before it will allow you to post. Do this and you'll see this page:

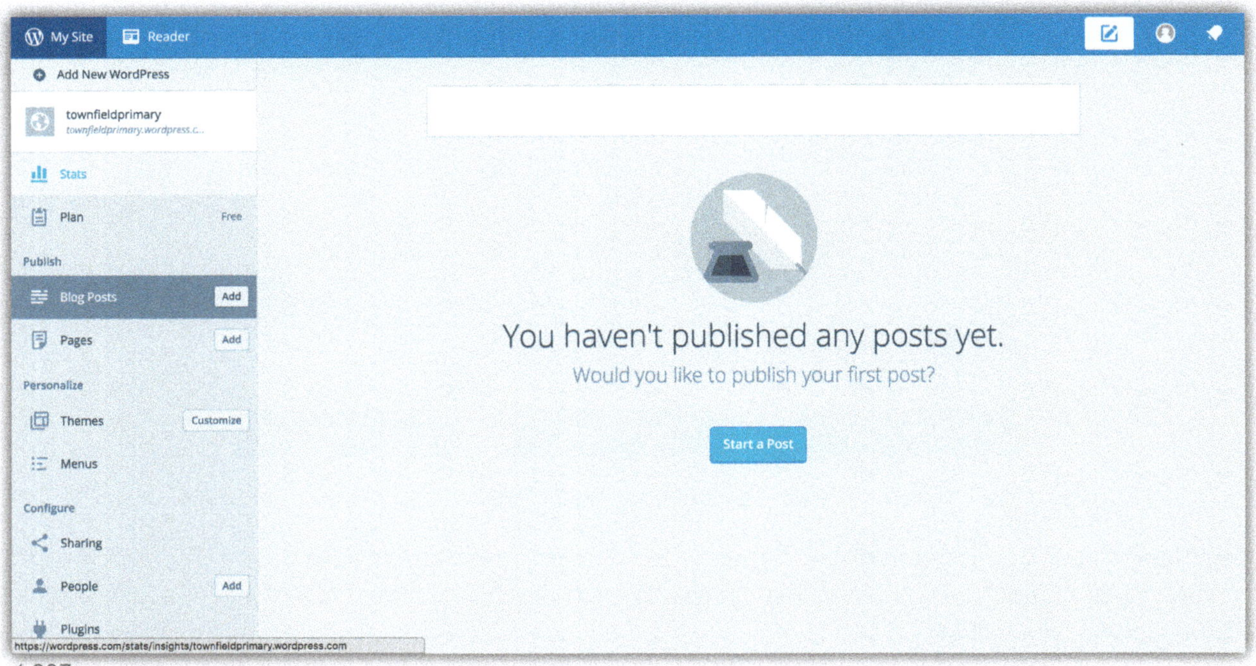

6.007

Our WordPress blog will work by displaying *posts*. Each post will be an item in our *Latest News* section. So let's get started and create a new post. Press the *Start a Post* button. You'll see an editor to create your first post. Here's mine:

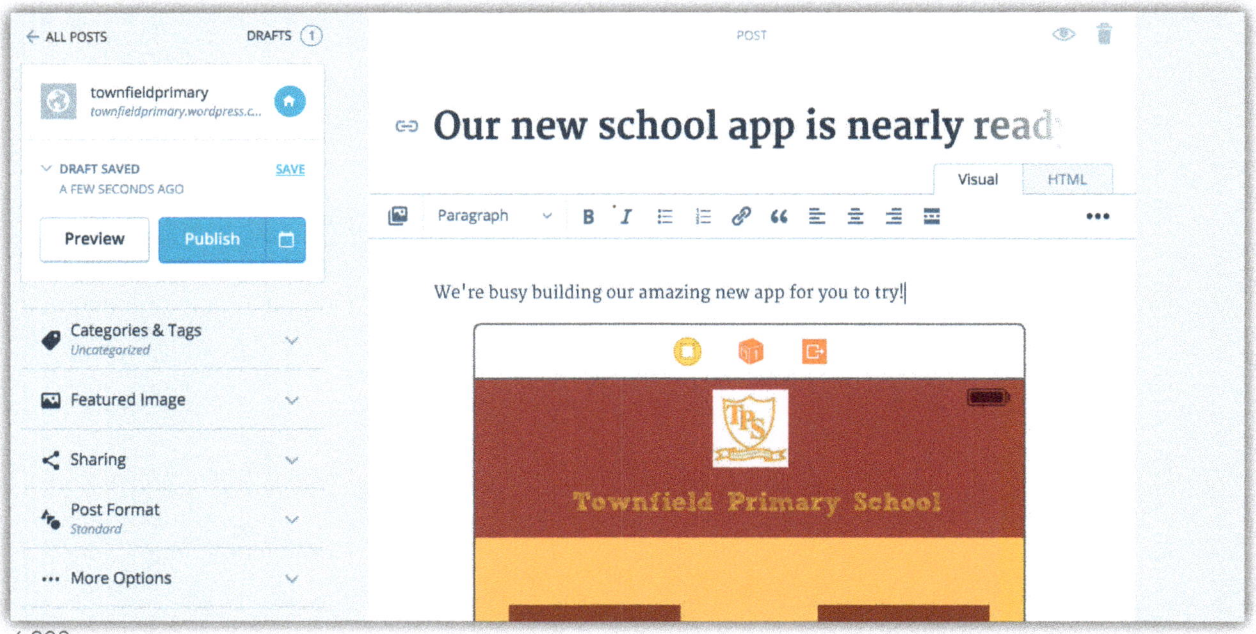

6.008

I simply typed a title in the top box, added some text and then pressed the image button. That's to the left of the word 'Paragraph'. Then I followed the on-screen instructions to add an image.

Once I'm happy with my first post, I'm going to press the *Publish* button on the left. You can view your new post online by pressing the *View Post* button:

6.009

You'll then see the web version of your news post:

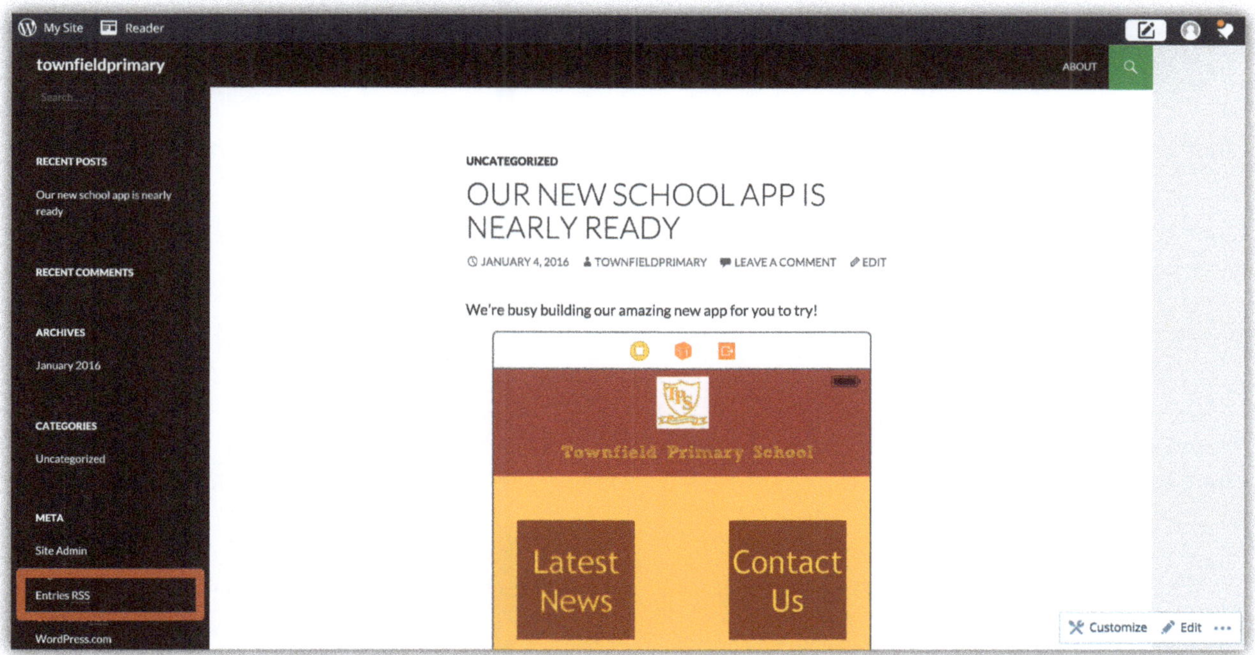

6.010

But the most important part of this page is the bit I've highlighted; a link called *Entries RSS*. Click on the link.

You'll see a page of gibberish:

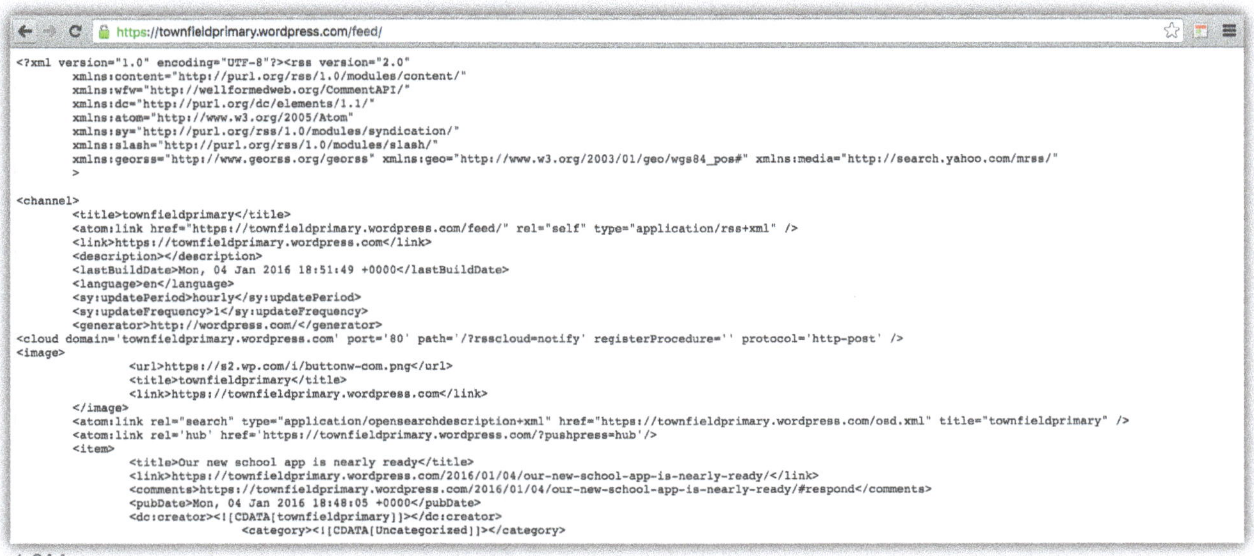


```
<?xml version="1.0" encoding="UTF-8"?><rss version="2.0"
	xmlns:content="http://purl.org/rss/1.0/modules/content/"
	xmlns:wfw="http://wellformedweb.org/CommentAPI/"
	xmlns:dc="http://purl.org/dc/elements/1.1/"
	xmlns:atom="http://www.w3.org/2005/Atom"
	xmlns:sy="http://purl.org/rss/1.0/modules/syndication/"
	xmlns:slash="http://purl.org/rss/1.0/modules/slash/"
	xmlns:georss="http://www.georss.org/georss" xmlns:geo="http://www.w3.org/2003/01/geo/wgs84_pos#" xmlns:media="http://search.yahoo.com/mrss/"
	>

<channel>
	<title>townfieldprimary</title>
	<atom:link href="https://townfieldprimary.wordpress.com/feed/" rel="self" type="application/rss+xml" />
	<link>https://townfieldprimary.wordpress.com</link>
	<description></description>
	<lastBuildDate>Mon, 04 Jan 2016 18:51:49 +0000</lastBuildDate>
	<language>en</language>
	<sy:updatePeriod>hourly</sy:updatePeriod>
	<sy:updateFrequency>1</sy:updateFrequency>
	<generator>http://wordpress.com/</generator>
<cloud domain='townfieldprimary.wordpress.com' port='80' path='/?rsscloud=notify' registerProcedure='' protocol='http-post' />
<image>
		<url>https://s2.wp.com/i/buttonw-com.png</url>
		<title>townfieldprimary</title>
		<link>https://townfieldprimary.wordpress.com</link>
	</image>
	<atom:link rel="search" type="application/opensearchdescription+xml" href="https://townfieldprimary.wordpress.com/osd.xml" title="townfieldprimary" />
	<atom:link rel='hub' href='https://townfieldprimary.wordpress.com/?pushpress=hub'/>
	<item>
		<title>Our new school app is nearly ready</title>
		<link>https://townfieldprimary.wordpress.com/2016/01/04/our-new-school-app-is-nearly-ready/</link>
		<comments>https://townfieldprimary.wordpress.com/2016/01/04/our-new-school-app-is-nearly-ready/#respond</comments>
		<pubDate>Mon, 04 Jan 2016 18:48:05 +0000</pubDate>
		<dc:creator><![CDATA[townfieldprimary]]></dc:creator>
				<category><![CDATA[Uncategorized]]></category>
```

6.011

This is your *RSS Feed*. It's in a language called *XML* and the app will read it and understand it. Look in the address bar of your browser and copy the link then save it somewhere. You will need it to make your news reader work later on.

Here's mine: **https://townfieldprimary.wordpress.com/feed/** – yours will follow the same pattern. You just need to add the word '/feed' after the .com.

For now, we're done.

You've created a *WordPress* blog to which you can add news and information. Now we need to make our app understand it.

This is where it gets tricky.

Adding the Third-Party Code to Our App

Remember at the start I told you we were going to add some code written by someone else to our app? This is the first time that we're going to do it.

A clever guy called Michael Waterfall has written some code that will grab the information from our feed and turn it into a format we can use within our app.

The original code that he wrote is freely available to download at **https://github.com/mwaterfall/MWFeedParser** but we're NOT going to use this code. Instead, you're going to use my modified version of the code.

That said, it's important with this code that you adhere to the copyright notice found at the above link and included here:

"Copyright (c) 2010 Michael Waterfall

Permission is hereby granted, free of charge, to any person obtaining a copy of this software and associated documentation files (the "Software"), to deal in the Software without restriction, including without limitation the rights to use, copy, modify, merge, publish, distribute, sublicense, and/or sell copies of the Software, and to permit persons to whom the Software is furnished to do so, subject to the following conditions:

The above copyright notice and this permission notice shall be included in all copies or substantial portions of the Software.

This Software cannot be used to archive or collect data such as (but not limited to) that of events, news, experiences and activities, for the purpose of any concept relating to diary/journal keeping.

THE SOFTWARE IS PROVIDED "AS IS", WITHOUT WARRANTY OF ANY KIND, EXPRESS OR IMPLIED, INCLUDING BUT NOT LIMITED TO THE WARRANTIES OF MERCHANTABILITY, FITNESS FOR A PARTICULAR PURPOSE AND NON-INFRINGEMENT. IN NO EVENT SHALL THE AUTHORS OR COPYRIGHT HOLDERS BE LIABLE FOR ANY CLAIM, DAMAGES OR OTHER LIABILITY, WHETHER IN AN ACTION OF CONTRACT, TORT OR OTHERWISE, ARISING FROM, OUT OF OR

IN CONNECTION WITH THE SOFTWARE OR THE USE OR OTHER DEALINGS IN THE SOFTWARE."

The copyright notice gives permission for the code to be used freely and sold or modified in any way as long as you don't use it for an app related to diary or journal keeping. This is because Michael has a successful app based on this concept using his code.

The first thing you need to do is download my files. When doing this with your pupils, I would suggest that you download the files in advance and place them somewhere the children can access easily to save them having to go online, downloading them and unzipping them.

To do that, go to **http://tinyurl.com/zzsvq2a** and you will see my files in a shared Dropbox:

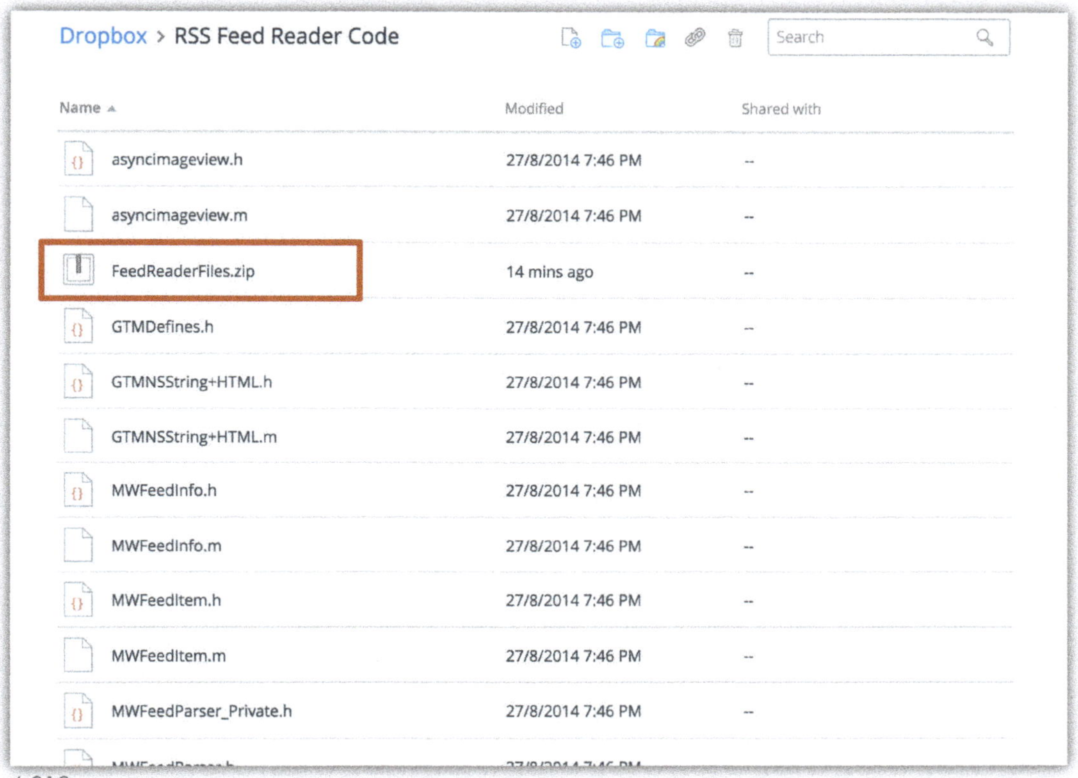

6.012

The files can be downloaded individually by right-clicking, or two-finger clicking, on the file name and selecting Download from the pop-up menu:

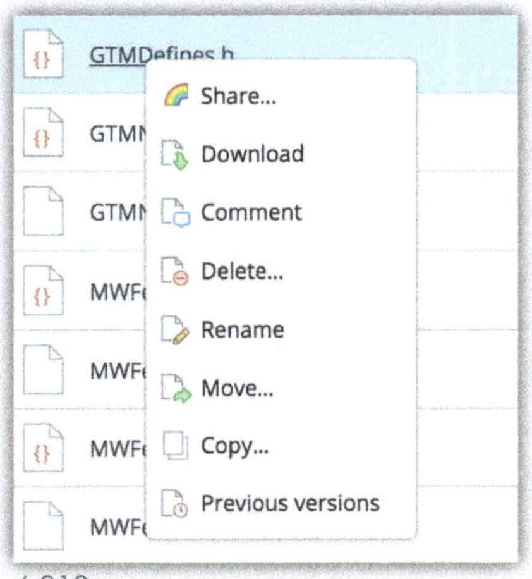

6.013

Alternatively, if you don't fancy downloading every file individually – there are 26 of them – then you can download the highlighted zip file called FeedReaderFiles.zip.

Once downloaded, you will need to unzip the files by double-clicking on the downloaded file.

Download all the files to a folder. It's a good idea to call it something you'll remember.

I'd also suggest putting these files somewhere easy for the class to access. You don't want them to have to download the files too.

You should now have a folder on your computer with all the necessary files:

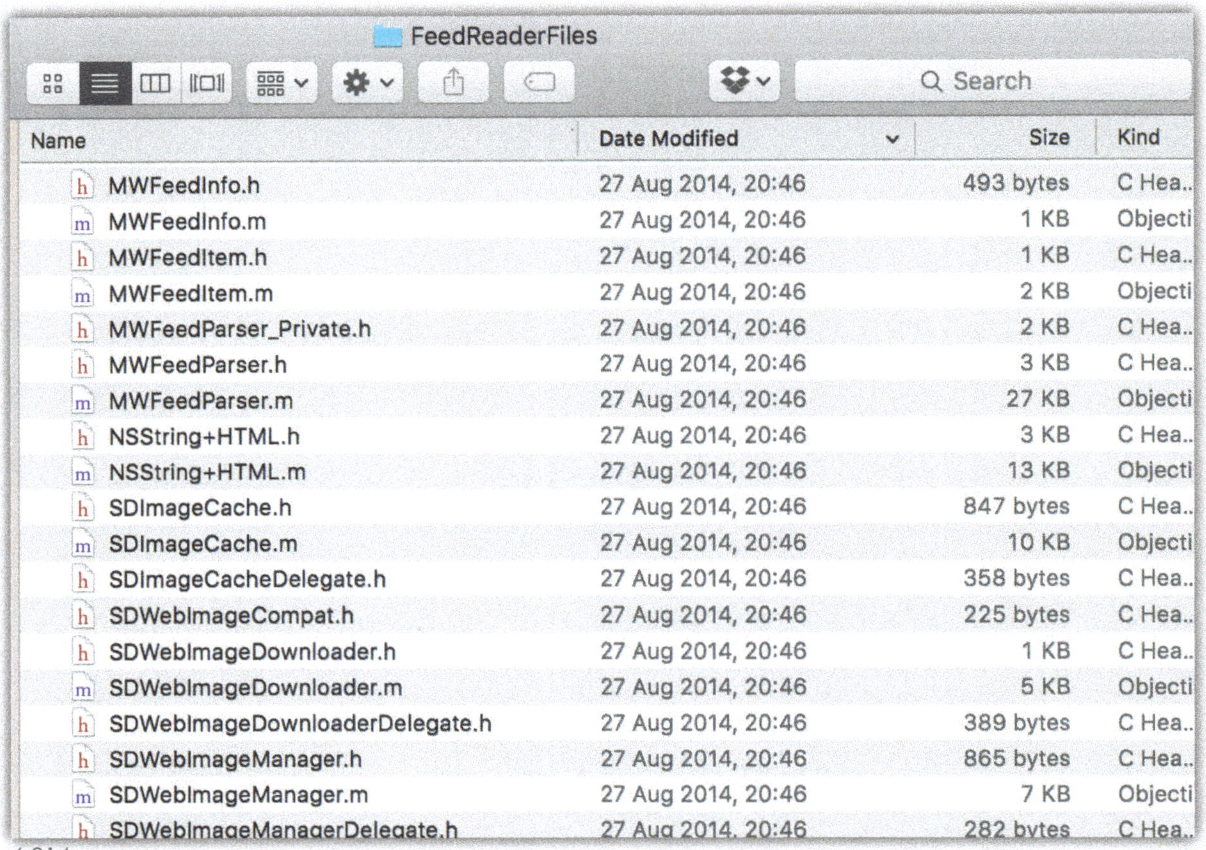

6.014

The next step is to add these files to your project; much like when we added the images earlier. Select all the files, either by drawing a box around them or pressing *Cmd* and 'A' at the same time. Then drag the files to *Xcode*, just between the *MySchool* folder icon and the *AppDelegate.h* file.

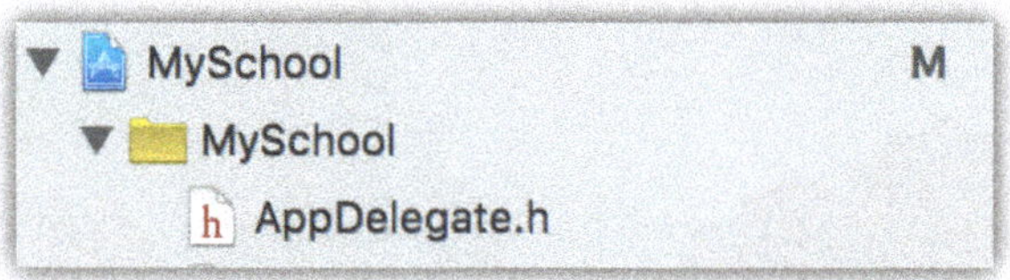

6.015

You'll then have a scary amount of files in your *Navigator* pane:

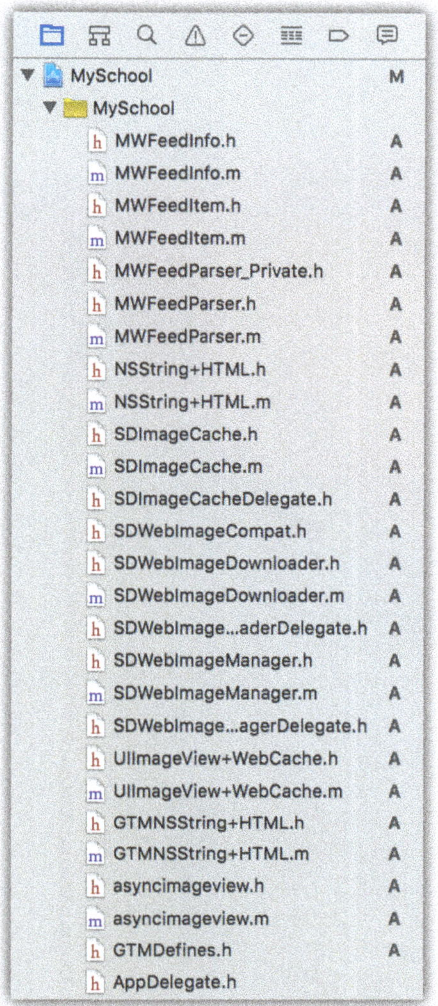

6.016

Don't worry. We'll organise them now. Click on the first of the files, *MWFeedInfo.h*, hold the shift button and select *GTMDefines.h*, that's the last file above *AppDelegate.h*.

All of the files in-between will be selected. Right-click, or two-finger click, over the selected files. A pop-up will appear; select *New Group from Selection*:

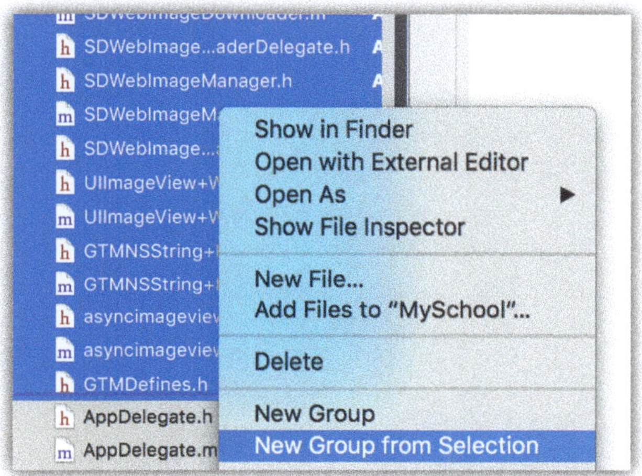

6.017

All your files will jump into a new group, imaginatively entitled 'New Group':

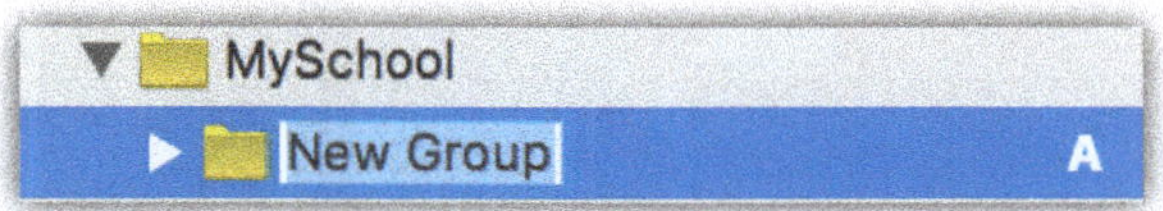

6.018

Rename the folder to something more meaningful like 'RSS Feed Reader'.

You have just added third-party code to your app; code that will enable us to build the *Latest News* section.

Now we've got to code it.

As with all the other screens, I'll walk you through it step-by-step but you should have already picked up quite a lot so rather than repeat myself, I'll refer you back to other chapters or things that we have done to help you as necessary.

The hardest part of what we are trying to do is coping with the sheer amount of code we will add. When devising this book, I toyed around with the idea of having the code somewhere for you to copy and paste but the problem with that is that you never really get a feel for the code. If you have to manually type it, you'll start to see how the text changes colour depending upon what type of code you're adding and how the language goes together.

I'll still explain things as we get to them so don't worry. I would walk through each step with your students. Depending on their age and ability, you may wish to provide them with code to copy and paste or let them type it in by copying your code.

The first thing we need to do is add a new *View Controller* to represent our screen that will display all the summaries of the news items. To do this, select *ViewController.m* in the *Navigator* pane and then right-click.

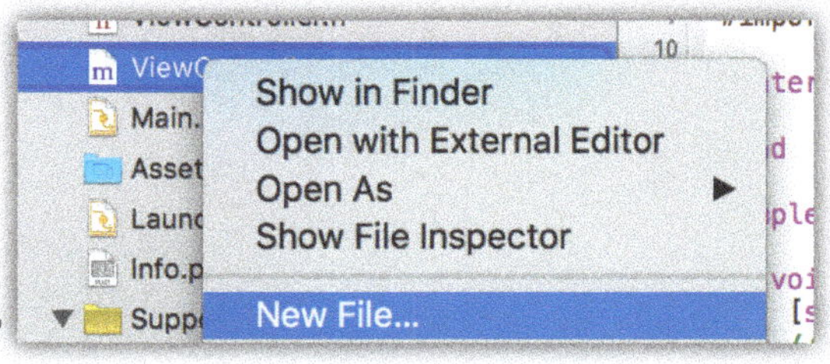

6.019

Select *New File* and in the pop-up that appears, make sure that *Cocoa Touch Class* is selected before pressing *Next*:

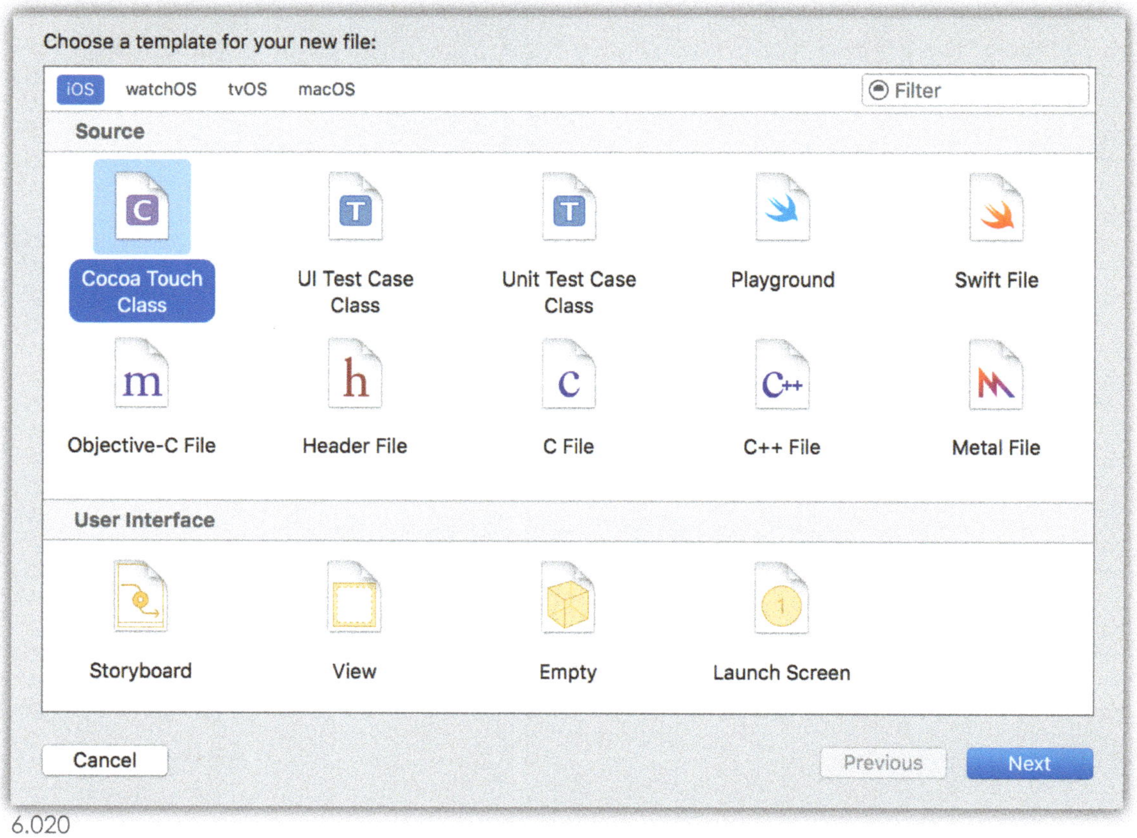

6.020

It's worth mentioning here that this is the procedure for adding any new *classes* (screens) so rather than repeat this again later on, I'll briefly remind you what to do. In our app, we're only going to add new files as *Cocoa Touch Classes* so you can safely press *Next* here.

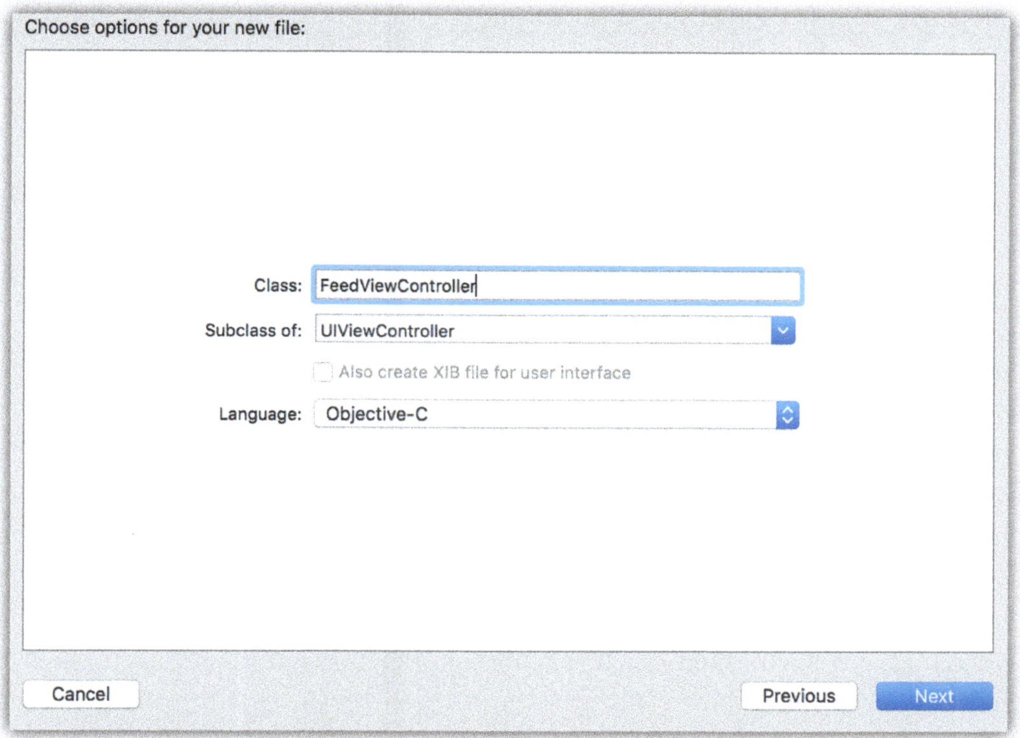

6.021

Name your class 'FeedViewController' and make sure the *Also create XIB* is NOT checked before pressing *Next*.

On the next screen, press *Create* and your two new files (your *implementation* file -.m and your *header* file -.h) will appear beneath the *ViewController.m* file in the *Navigator* pane.

Let's add some code. Open *FeedViewController.h*. It should look like this:

6.022

The first bit of code I want you to enter goes right underneath the *#import <UIKit.UIKit.h>* line on line 10:

```
#import <UIKit/UIKit.h>
#import "MWFeedParser.h"
```

6.023

All this does is make sure that the special code we imported earlier is included in this class. It means we can access all the features that Michael Waterfall wrote to help us read an *RSS Feed*.

You need to change the *@interface* line to this:

```
@interface FeedViewController : UIViewController <MWFeedParserDelegate> {

}
```

6.024

What we've done is we've added *MWFeedParserDelegate* in-between the < > which again lets us use code from Michael Waterfall's files. I've also added swirly brackets.

Let's look at it so far all in one go:

```
//
//  FeedViewController.h
//  MySchool
//
//  Created by Doug Stitcher on 05/01/2016.
//  Copyright © 2016 Doug Stitcher. All rights reserved.
//

#import <UIKit/UIKit.h>
#import "MWFeedParser.h"

@interface FeedViewController : UIViewController <MWFeedParserDelegate> {

}

@end

```

6.025

Check yours carefully to make sure it looks like mine.

We're ready to add some of the code to link to our *user interface* elements. Notice this time we are adding the code first. We will also add some *variables* that we will store data in later.

All the following code goes in-between the swirly brackets:

```
MWFeedParser *feedParser;
NSMutableArray *items;
IBOutlet UITableView *myTableView;
NSDateFormatter *formatter;
UIActivityIndicatorView *activityIndicator;
BOOL isRefreshing;
BOOL didFinish;
```

6.026

We've got a few things here. Let's go through them:

feedParser: This is the mechanism that will fetch our news items. Don't worry about exactly what it is.

items: This is an *array*. An array stores lots of things. In this case, it will store all of our news items and we will get them back from our array later on.

myTableView: A *UITableView* is the table you are used to on an iPhone, like in the Mail app. This will hold our news items.

formatter: We need this to display the date underneath each news story.

activityIndicator: This is the spinning symbol you see when you're waiting for your iPhone to do something.

isRefreshing: This is a variable known as a *Boolean*, it stores a YES or NO value. We will use this to tell if the news items are being refreshed or not.

didFinish: This Boolean will tell us when the app has finished loading the news. This will be quite useful later on.

```
MWFeedParser *feedParser;
NSMutableArray *items;
IBOutlet UITableView *myTableView;
NSDateFormatter *formatter;
UIActivityIndicatorView *activityIndicator;
BOOL isRefreshing;
BOOL didFinish;
```

6.026

For the moment, we are done with the header file. Let's add the screen to our *storyboard* so that we can start designing it.

Click on *Main.storyboard* in the *Navigator* pane:

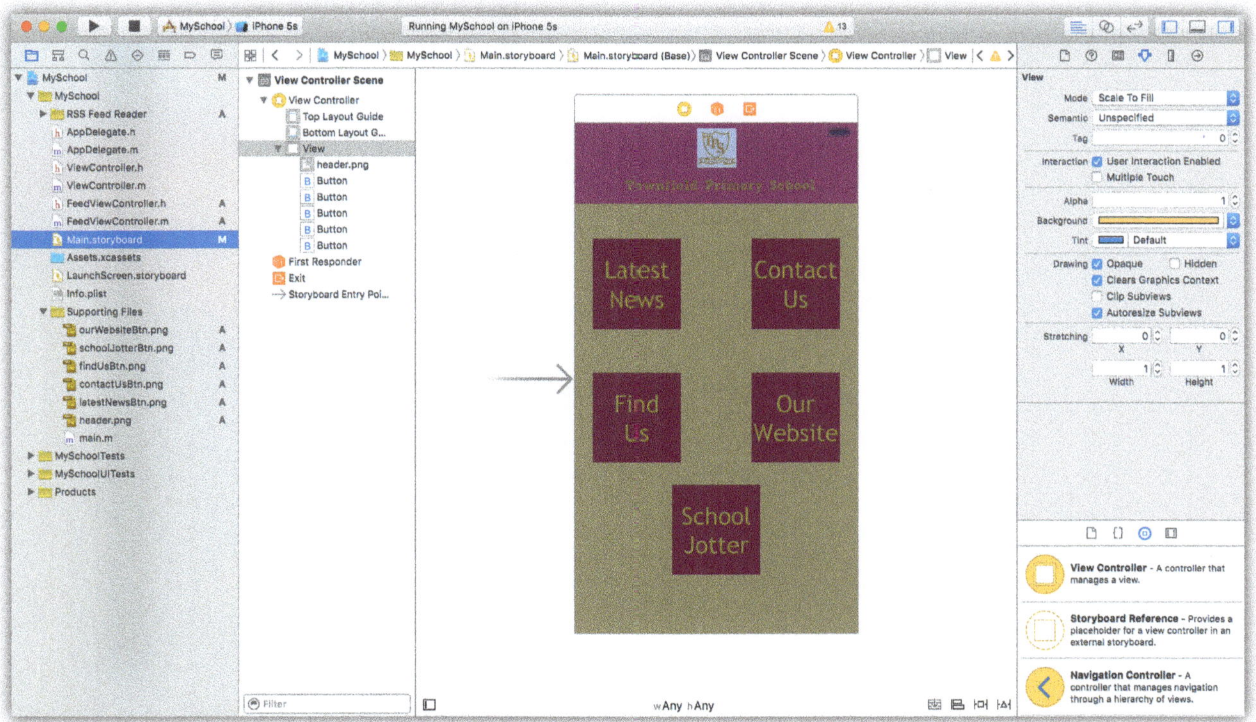

6.027

Go to the *Object Library* and scroll to the top. You'll find the *View Controller* item. Drag that slightly to the right of your home screen:

It will look a bit like this:

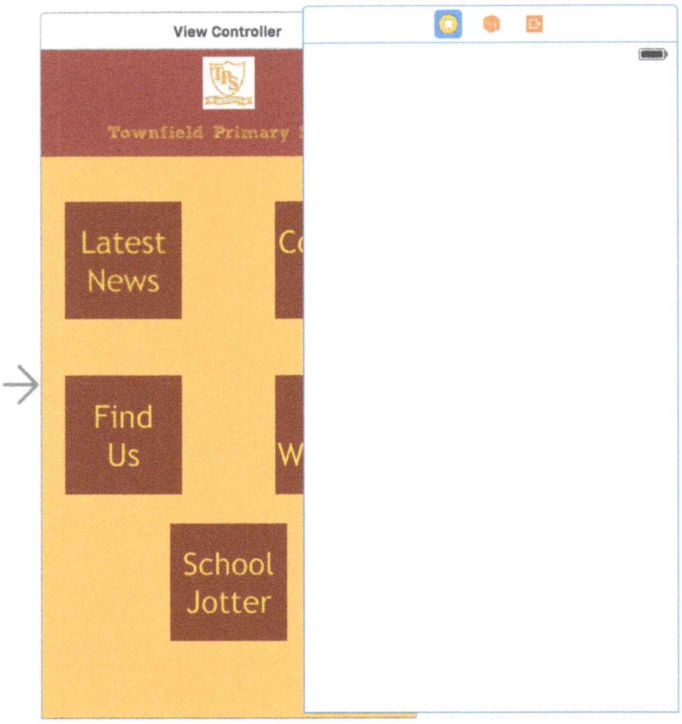

6.028

Select it and drag it to the side so it's nicely lined up with your home screen. You may need to scroll across to see your new screen properly:

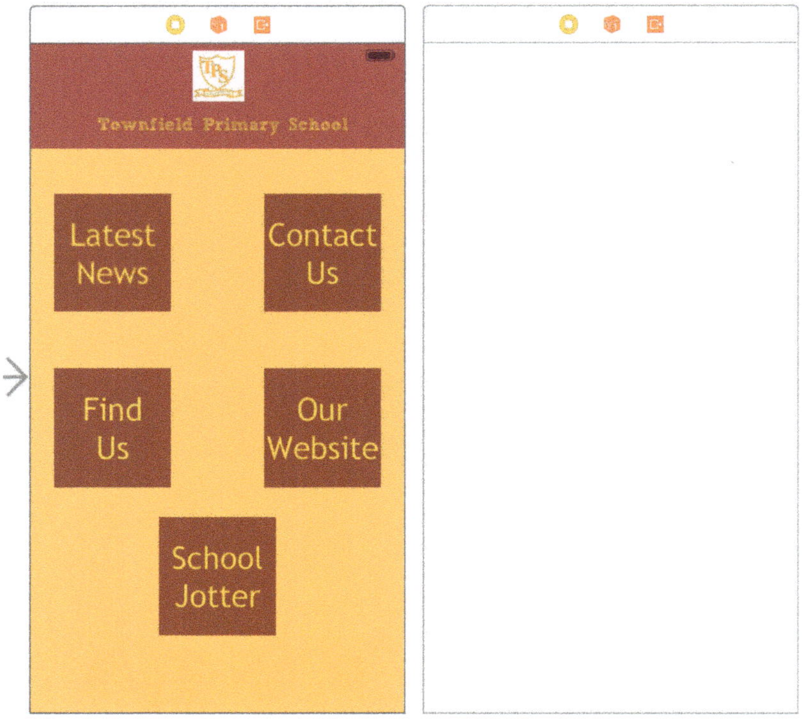

6.029

Next, we need to associate this screen with our *FeedViewController* class. It's easy to do.

Select the yellow circle containing the white square at the top of your new screen:

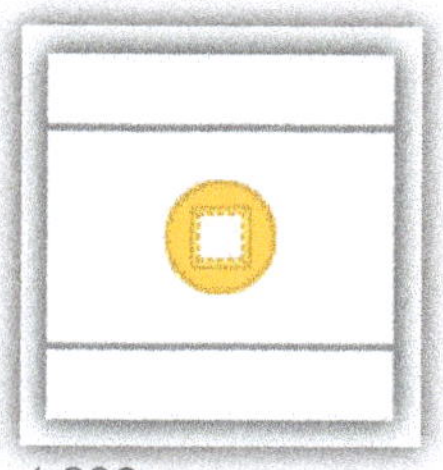

6.030

Go to the *Utilities* pane and select the third button from the left:

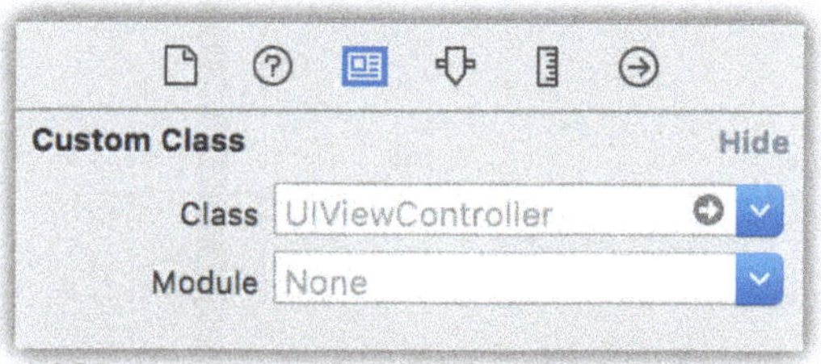

6.031

In the *Class* box, type in *FeedViewController*. It should autocomplete for you then press *return* to confirm your changes.

Your *View Controller* is now linked to the code in *FeedViewController* so let's start adding some things to our screen.

Firstly, we'd still like our header to appear on the new screen, so we can copy the *UIImageView* from our home screen to our new screen. To do this, select the header image on the home screen:

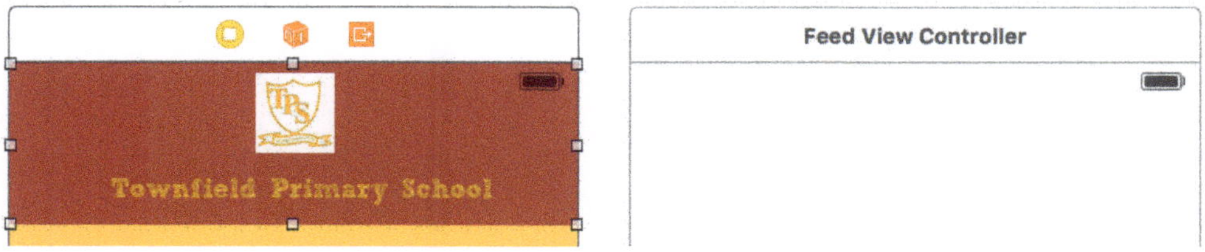

6.032

Now press *Cmd* and 'C' at the same time.

Go over to *Feed View Controller* and select anywhere on the large white screen. Now press *Cmd* and 'V' to paste the header image onto the new screen.

It will appear somewhere on the screen so you will need to move it to the same place as on the home screen:

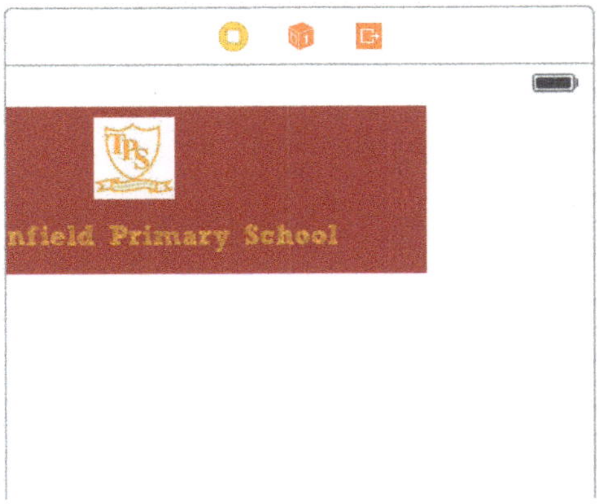

6.033

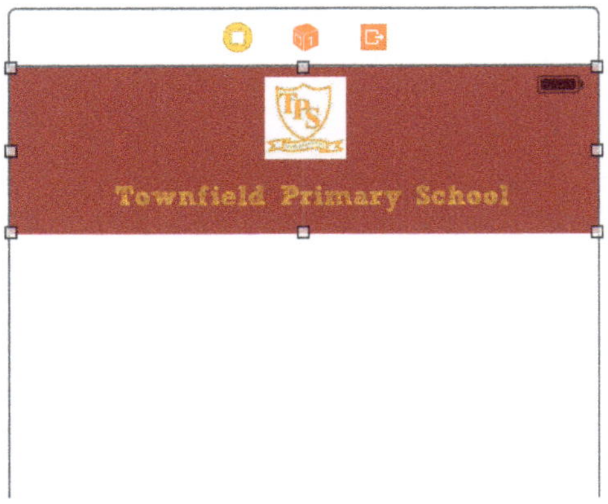

6.034

Remember, to align the header image, you can press the *ruler* tab on the *Utilities* pane and set the x and y position to zero as well.

Next job is to add our *UITableView*. Scroll down in the *Object Library* until you find this:

Useful tip: *You can search for specific objects by typing in the filter bar at the bottom of the library.*

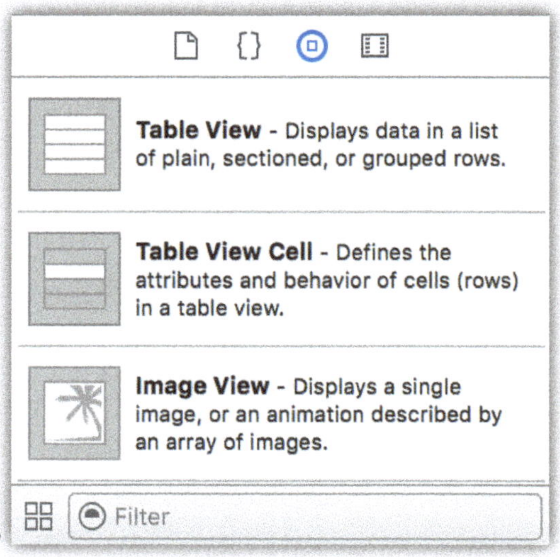

6.035

Select Table View and drag it on to the Feed View Controller.

It will appear in a small box, as in the left screenshot.

Resize it so that it fills the white space and goes to the edges.

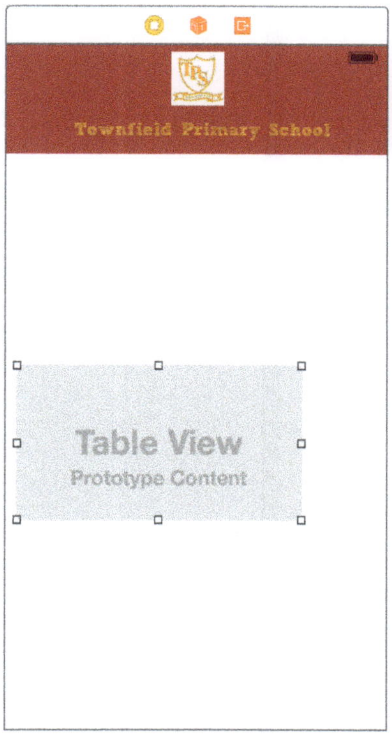

6.036

6.037

Be careful that it doesn't go over your header image or off the screen as this will ruin how it displays on the screen when it's filled with news items.

The last thing we need to do before we do some complicated coding is link the *Table View* we've just added to our *FeedViewController* files.

With a *Table View*, we have to do two things. Firstly, we have to right-click and drag from the yellow circle to the *Table View*. The following box will appear:

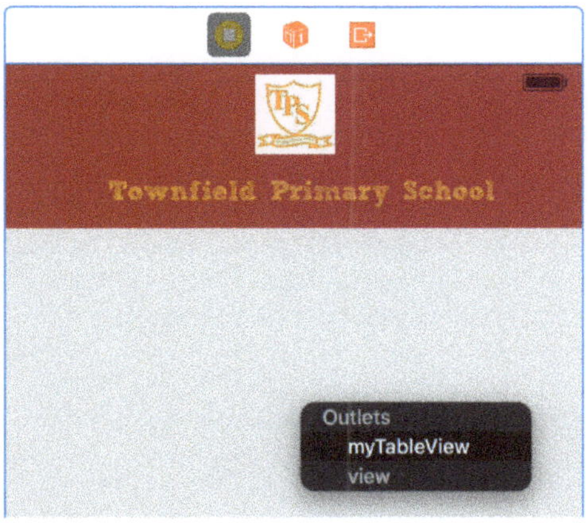

6.038

Select *myTableView*, the name we gave it in our .h file, and it will disappear.

Now go the other way; from the Table View TO the yellow circle with a right-click and drag. You'll see this black pop-up box:

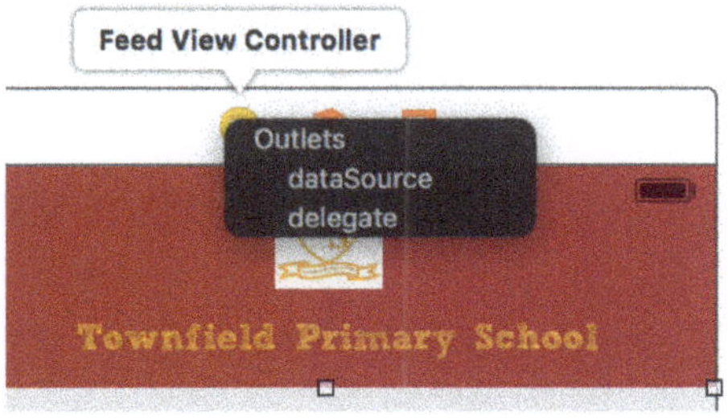

6.039

Select *dataSource* and the box will vanish. Repeat the process and this time, select *delegate* and the box will vanish again.

And there you go. We still need to add a *Refresh* button and a *Back* button, but for now we are done. Next we're going to add lots of code to our *FeedViewController.m* file.

Select *FeedViewController.m* from the *Navigator* pane. Your screen should look a bit like this:

6.040

You'll notice that there are no *methods* in here at all, so we need to add some.

We will start with the *viewDidLoad* method. Remember, this is a *VOID* method – it doesn't give us a result and it isn't linked to any button on the screen. This is the code that will run when the screen loads for the first time. Insert this code after the *@implementation FeedViewController* line and before the *@end* line:

```
- (void)viewDidLoad{

    [super viewDidLoad];

    NSString *rssfeed = @"https://townfieldprimary.wordpress.com/feed/";
    formatter = [[NSDateFormatter alloc] init];
    [formatter setDateStyle:NSDateFormatterMediumStyle];
    items = [[NSMutableArray alloc] init];
    myTableView.userInteractionEnabled = NO;
    feedParser = [[MWFeedParser alloc] initWithFeedURL:rssfeed];
    feedParser.delegate = self;
    feedParser.feedParseType = ParseTypeFull;
    feedParser.connectionType = ConnectionTypeAsynchronously;
    [feedParser parse];

}
```
6.041

What does this code do? Firstly, it stores a string, that's words and letters, in a variable called *rssfeed*. This string needs to be the link to your *RSS Feed* that you have created.

We then use *formatter* to gather the date information we will need. You don't need to worry about this too much.

Here we use *[[NSMutableArray alloc] init]* to activate the array *items* that we created before. We're telling our app that we'd like to use it.

We then use *userInteractionEnabled = NO* to prevent the user moving the table before we've loaded our news items.

The last five lines of coding use Michael Waterfall's code to fetch our *RSS feed* from the internet. At the moment, it does nothing with that information except store it in our *items* array. And that's our *viewDidLoad* code.

I don't want you to panic about the fact a lot of this code doesn't make a great deal of sense. When I first starting coding, I found snippets of code on the Internet that did what I wanted and over time, I got used to how they were structured and what they meant. When working with your students, I would simply explain what the code does without going into too much detail about how it does it.

As we go along, you will see things over and over again and that will give you a better understanding of what code does what.

We have a few more *VOID methods* to add. These methods handle the receiving of the information from the *RSS Feed*. Some of them don't actually do anything. But I've put them in as, at some point, you may wish to add extra code to these methods.

Let's do the first one. These methods should go under *viewDidLoad* in the order I show them to you:

```
- (void)feedParserDidStart:(MWFeedParser *)parser {
    //while it's parsing the feed this will display the info it gets
    //you can add any code here that want to run whilst the parser is running
    NSLog(@"Started Parsing: %@", parser.url);

}
```

6.042

This *method* is called *feedParserDidStart*. The bits in green are called *comments*. They begin with two forward slashes. They're not code; they are used by developers to remind them to do things or to point out what code does. You DO NOT need to copy the comments, they're just there to help you.

This method runs when the app starts looking for the *RSS Feed*. The code *NSLog* is a way of checking what's going on. In this case, when the app starts looking for the *RSS Feed*, you'll get a message in *Xcode* saying *Started Parsing*: and then the link to your *RSS Feed*. 'Parsing' is the posh word for analysing information. It just means that it has started to get our information.

Next, add this method:

```
- (void)feedParser:(MWFeedParser *)parser didParseFeedInfo:(MWFeedInfo *)info {
    NSLog(@"Parsed Feed Info: “%@”", info.title);

}
```

6.043

This sends *Xcode* information about the different news stories the app has found. Again, it doesn't display anything in the app.

Add this method now:

```
- (void)feedParser:(MWFeedParser *)parser didParseFeedItem:(MWFeedItem *)item {
    //this checks that there is something in the feed. If there isn't the array
    // items remains empty - this will stop it crashing if there are no feed items
    NSLog(@"Parsed Feed Item: "%@"", item.title);
    if (item) [items addObject:item];
}
```

6.044

This *method*, as the comments explain, checks whether there is anything in our RSS feed. If there is, it adds it to our *items* array. If there isn't, it does nothing.

Just two more of these to go. Add this method:

```
- (void)feedParserDidFinish:(MWFeedParser *)parser {
    //this is called when the parsing is all done
    NSLog(@"Finished Parsing");
    didFinish = YES;
    //allow the user to use the table again:
    myTableView.userInteractionEnabled = YES;
    [myTableView reloadData];
}
```

6.045

It's reasonably self-explanatory. This code is called when the app finishes *parsing*, looking for information.

We send a nice message to *Xcode* to say we've finished. Then we set our *Boolean didFinish* to *Yes* so our app knows we've finished.

We then allow the user to interact with the *Table View* again so they can scroll it up and down. Finally, we reload our *Table View* with the data we've just received. At the moment, we haven't set our *Table View* up properly, but we will be doing this shortly.

Time to add our last method for the reading of the information. It's a bit longer:

```
- (void)feedParser:(MWFeedParser *)parser didFailWithError:(NSError *)error {

    //Here is our error part - really important or Apple will reject the app.

    NSLog(@"Finished Parsing With Error: %@", error);

    UIAlertController *alert = [UIAlertController
                                   alertControllerWithTitle:@"Error"
                                   message:@"Cannot load the News Items. Please check you are connected to the internet."
                                   preferredStyle:UIAlertControllerStyleAlert];

    UIAlertAction *ok = [UIAlertAction
                         actionWithTitle:@"OK"
                         style:UIAlertActionStyleDefault
                         handler:^(UIAlertAction * action)
                         {
                             [alert dismissViewControllerAnimated:YES completion:nil];

                         }];

    [alert addAction:ok];
    [self presentViewController:alert animated:YES completion:nil];

    [items removeAllObjects];
    myTableView.userInteractionEnabled = YES;
    [myTableView reloadData];
}
```

6.046

But it's important. This code is called if something goes wrong. It could be a problem with the user's internet connection or maybe your *RSS Feed* isn't working properly. Regardless, if something goes wrong, your app has to handle it. Apple, when they test apps before approving or rejecting them, will check how your app performs when the internet is disabled.

As you can see from the code, if there is an error, we display a pop-up telling the user that something has gone wrong. You can change the text in red (red text represents a string) next to 'message' to any wording you like. I've left mine in there so you get the gist.

You've now added six *methods* to your *FeedViewController* class. All of them get the app looking for your information.

The next step is to add the code that controls how the *Table View* displays the information it receives.

I'm going to get you started with a nice easy *method*. Table Views are split into sections and rows. If you look at the *Mail* app on your iPhone, in the *Mailboxes* part you'll see two sections; one that contains all your *Inboxes* and one below that is titled *Accounts* and displays all the email accounts you have.

Our first method sets how many sections our *Table View* will display. And it's only one. Put this method below the last one we added:

```
- (NSInteger)numberOfSectionsInTableView:(UITableView *)tableView {
    return 1;
}
```

6.047

That was an easy one. So let's have another. This method sets how high each cell in our *Table View* is. On an iPhone, 90 pixels is about right, so add the following method beneath the last:

```
- (CGFloat)tableView:(UITableView *)tableView heightForRowAtIndexPath:(NSIndexPath *)indexPath
{

        return 90;

}
```

6.048

Next add the number of rows. This is a bit trickier because the app needs to display as many rows as there are news items. We have to check how many news items there are and then tell the app to display that many rows:

```
- (NSInteger)tableView:(UITableView *)tableView numberOfRowsInSection:(NSInteger)section {

    //Here, I check if there are more than 20 news items. If there are, I limit the display to 20
    // this is for performance but you can change this to suit.
    if (items.count > 20) {
        return 20;
    } else {
    //if there's less than 20 items, just display them all
    return items.count;}
}
```

6.049

The comments here explain the code pretty well. We display no more than the 20 most recent news items. You can display more, but the more you display the slower the app responds, particularly on older iPhones.

The next part is a little more complicated. Before we add the code to change the appearance of the *Table View*, we need to import a few extra files into our .m file. Scroll back to the top of the file.

Find the line #import *FeedViewController.h* and beneath it, add the following code:

```
#import "FeedViewController.h" //don't type this one - you've already done this one!
#import "NSString+HTML.h"
#import "asyncimageview.h"
#import "UIImageView+WebCache.h"
```

6.050

These three files handle how we will display the text and how we will load the images. You don't need to worry at all about exactly what they do.

It's time to add the code for the *Table View*. This is quite a long *method* so we will break it down into chunks.

Scroll down back to the method where you specified the number of rows we are going to display. Our new method will go after this.

Let's write the method name and the swirly brackets first:

```
- (UITableViewCell *)tableView:(UITableView *)tableView cellForRowAtIndexPath:(NSIndexPath *)indexPath {

}
```

6.051

Everything we add to this method will go between the swirly brackets. Now I'd like you to add this code. You don't need to copy the comments; they're just there to help you.

```
static NSString *CellIdentifier = @"Cell";

UITableViewCell *cell = [tableView dequeueReusableCellWithIdentifier:CellIdentifier];

//within the table we have four user interface items:
UIImageView *mainImage; //this is the thumbnail image from the feed
UILabel *mytitleLabel; // this is the headline of our news item
UILabel *mysummaryLabel; // this is a summary of the content of the news item
UILabel *mydateLabel; // this is the label that will display the date of the news item

if (cell == nil) {
    cell = [[UITableViewCell alloc] initWithStyle:UITableViewCellStyleDefault reuseIdentifier:CellIdentifier];
}

cell.accessoryType = UITableViewCellAccessoryDisclosureIndicator;
```

6.052

In the code above, we do a few things that you have to do with *Table Views*. Table Views are one of the most used ways of displaying information in apps. They work behind the scenes. Imagine a long list of emails. As you scroll down, it looks like there is row after row of emails that have been sitting in their respective rows. What actually happens is the app 'reuses' each cell as soon as it scrolls off the screen.

You don't need to understand this but it does have consequences. If we aren't careful about how we set up our Table View, information in one row will suddenly disappear and then re-appear in another cell, often over some other content.

What the code above does is make sure that we reuse cells in our Table View in the proper way.

I also set up the four *user interface* items that we will need. This is the first time we are going to use code to add *Labels* and *Image Views*. You don't have to do it in *Interface Builder*. Most people start off this way as it's easier but you can use code to describe what you want to add, for example a label and where on the screen you want it to appear. You can also set properties like the font, colour and text alignment etc. All in code.

Move the cursor under the last line of code you typed.

Copy this code, again, whether or not you copy the comments is up to you:

```
//set up the title of the news item label
mytitleLabel = (UILabel*)[cell viewWithTag:300]; //tag stops the label being overwritten with other text

if(!mytitleLabel){

    // set the size and position of the label
    mytitleLabel = [[UILabel alloc] initWithFrame:CGRectMake(80, -10, 210, 60)];
    // set its font
    mytitleLabel.font = [UIFont systemFontOfSize:14];
    // keep background colour clear so you can see the background image
    mytitleLabel.backgroundColor = [UIColor clearColor];
    //set the colour of the text
    mytitleLabel.textColor = [UIColor blackColor];;
    //set the number of lines - this will effect how big you need your cells. setting at 0 will give you unlimited
        lines!!
    mytitleLabel.numberOfLines = 1;
    mytitleLabel.tag = 300;

    //add the title label to the cell
    [cell.contentView addSubview:mytitleLabel];
}
```
6.053

This code is quite simple. We check if our *Table View* cell has a headline label, that's our *mytitleLabel*, and if it doesn't, we add one.

Then we set all the properties. Feel free to change any of these, although if you're not sure about them, leave them as they are.

You'll notice that I've mentioned keeping the background colour of the label clear. This is because later on, if we want to add a background colour to the row, we will need to make sure the label background doesn't obscure it.

Try playing around with the *mytitleLabel.textColor* = line. Delete *blackColor* and start typing 'blue'. The text will autocomplete to *blueColor*. There are quite a few of these you can use so you may wish to experiment to match the colour of your school. It may be worth noting with the children how 'colour' is spelt 'color' when we code as the software we code in is American.

I'm leaving mine as black.

We now need to do this for the *UILabel* that will display the summary:

```
mysummaryLabel = (UILabel*)[cell viewWithTag:400];

if(!mysummaryLabel){
    mysummaryLabel = [[UILabel alloc] initWithFrame:CGRectMake(80, 0, 210, 95)];
    mysummaryLabel.backgroundColor = [UIColor clearColor];
    mysummaryLabel.font = [UIFont systemFontOfSize:10];
    mysummaryLabel.textColor = [UIColor blackColor];
    mysummaryLabel.numberOfLines = 2;
    mysummaryLabel.tag = 400;
    [cell.contentView addSubview:mysummaryLabel];

}
```

6.054

The code is pretty much the same but we're using the *mysummaryLabel* and we've changed the tag to '400'. The *tag* is a way of giving different objects a reference so we can refer to them later on.

You've probably worked this out, but the next bit of code does the same for the label that will hold the date for when the news story was published.

```
mydateLabel = (UILabel*)[cell viewWithTag:500];

if(!mydateLabel){
    mydateLabel = [[UILabel alloc] initWithFrame:CGRectMake(80, 0, 320, 155)];

    mydateLabel.backgroundColor = [UIColor clearColor];
    mydateLabel.font = [UIFont systemFontOfSize:10];
    mydateLabel.textColor = [UIColor lightGrayColor];
    mydateLabel.font = [UIFont boldSystemFontOfSize:9];
    mydateLabel.tag = 500;

    [cell.contentView addSubview:mydateLabel];

}
```

6.055

Here, we've set the tag to 500 and changed the colour to light grey as we don't want it to be too prominent.

We need to add the code that puts our thumbnail *Image View* to the left of our news item:

```
mainImage = (UIImageView *)[cell viewWithTag:200];

if(!mainImage){
    mainImage = [[UIImageView alloc] initWithFrame:CGRectMake(8,5,62,62)];
    mainImage.contentMode = UIViewContentModeScaleAspectFit;
    mainImage.tag = 200;

    [cell.contentView addSubview:mainImage]; }
```

6.056

And that's it for setting up what the Table View will look like apart from one important line. This line goes directly beneath the above code:

```
cell.backgroundColor = [UIColor whiteColor];
```

6.057

This line sets the background colour of the whole row that will display our news item. I've set it as white so everything looks nice and crisp. But you can change this to any colour you want. For a full list of different colours plus some advice on other ways of coding colours, have a look at **http://foobarpig.com/iphone/uicolor-cheatsheet-color-list-conversion-from-and-to-rgb-values.html** – it's quite a useful page and shows you what the actual colours look like.

This will be an important part of branding your app.

We're making good progress. We've added lots of code to our *user interface*. We need to carry on adding code to this very long *method*.

The next lot of code handles interpreting the information the app finds when it reads our feed.

Directly underneath the last line of code we wrote, we are going to add this:

```
MWFeedItem *item = [items objectAtIndex:indexPath.row];
//first we check that there is info to fill the cells with! This stops it crashing if there's nothing to display!
if (item) {

    //Strip the html from the rss feed of its html tags - we don't need those
    NSString *itemTitle = item.title ? [[[item.title stringByStrippingTags] stringByRemovingNewLinesAndWhitespace]
        stringByDecodingHTMLEntities] : @"[No Title]";
    NSString *itemSummary = item.summary ? [[[item.summary stringByStrippingTags] stringByRemovingNewLinesAndWhitespace]
        stringByDecodingHTMLEntities] : @"[No Summary]";
    NSString *dateText = [formatter stringFromDate:item.date];

    //put the text into the cells
    mytitleLabel.text = itemTitle;
    mysummaryLabel.text = itemSummary;
    mydateLabel.text = dateText;
```

6.058

What does this do? It creates a new variable called *item*. This is not to be confused with *items*, thats our *array*. This new variable relates to every item in our feed.

We need to check that we have at least one item. If we don't, the app will freak out and crash. Assuming we have at least one item, we then find three parts of each news item: the *title*, the *summary* and the *date*.

We strip out all the *html code* from the text so that when we display it it doesn't look like all that gibberish we saw when we first looked at an *RSS feed*.

Finally, we put the three items into the three labels we set up before.

Simple? I know it isn't. When I created my first school app, I wasn't entirely sure what I was doing. I'm deliberately not bombarding you with too much technical stuff. At the moment, you just need to know what the code will do.

Next up, we need to add an *ActivityIndicator* to spin around while the images load. To do this, we add a little bit of code that makes it spin. When an image loads, it will sit on top of the ActivityIndicator and hide it.

Add this code directly beneath the last bit:

```
//add a spinner beneath the images so if they're taking a while to load, it is clear something is happening
UIActivityIndicatorView *spinner = [[UIActivityIndicatorView alloc] initWithFrame:CGRectMake(30,30,20,20)];
spinner.activityIndicatorViewStyle = UIActivityIndicatorViewStyleWhite;
[cell.backgroundView addSubview:spinner];
[spinner startAnimating];
```

6.059

In this code we put a *UIActivityIndicatorView* at a position of 30 on the x-axis and 30 on the y-axis and we set its width and height to 20 pixels. We set it to be white but you can change this to grey if your cell background is white (otherwise you won't see it!) and then we add it to the cell and start it spinning. Easy.

At last, we're onto the last bit of this *method*. This genuinely is the hardest part of our app which is why I put this chapter here. Once, we've finished the *Latest News* section, you'll find the rest of the app ridiculously easy.

The last piece of code for this method has the job of searching through the *RSS Feed* and finding an image. Once it's found, the app puts it in our *Image View* and if it can't find one, it uses an image of your choice as a place-holder. I tend to use my school's logo as the place-holder.

Here's the code:

```
    NSString *imageLink = item.content;
    NSRange textRange;
    textRange =[imageLink rangeOfString:@"src"];

    if(textRange.location != NSNotFound)
    {

        NSString *imageName = [[imageLink componentsSeparatedByString:@"src=\""] objectAtIndex:1];
        imageName = [[imageName componentsSeparatedByString:@"\""] objectAtIndex:0];
        [mainImage setImageWithURL:[NSURL URLWithString:imageName]];

    } else {
        mainImage.image = [UIImage imageNamed:@"schoolicon.png"];
    }

}

return cell;
```

6.060

You should notice that the image we use to fill the space if no image is found is called *schoolicon.png*. When you add your school logo to your project, either rename the file 'schoolicon.png' OR change the code to represent the filename of your school logo. Either option will work fine.

I will add my school logo as I'm tidying up at the end of this chapter.

The last line, *return cell*, tells the app to create a cell in our *Table View* that does everything we've spent the last hour or so writing.

That *method* should now be complete.

Here is the full code:

```
#import "FeedViewController.h"
#import "NSString+HTML.h"
#import "asyncimageview.h"
#import "UIImageView+WebCache.h"

@implementation FeedViewController

- (void)viewDidLoad{

    [super viewDidLoad];

    NSString *rssfeed = @"https://townfieldprimary.wordpress.com/feed/";
    formatter = [[NSDateFormatter alloc] init];
    [formatter setDateStyle:NSDateFormatterMediumStyle];
    items = [[NSMutableArray alloc] init];
    myTableView.userInteractionEnabled = NO;
    feedParser = [[MWFeedParser alloc] initWithFeedURL:rssfeed];
    feedParser.delegate = self;
    feedParser.feedParseType = ParseTypeFull;
    feedParser.connectionType = ConnectionTypeAsynchronously;
    [feedParser parse];

}

- (void)feedParserDidStart:(MWFeedParser *)parser {
    //while it's parsing the feed this will display the info it gets
    //you can add any code here that want to run whilst the parser is running
    NSLog(@"Started Parsing: %@", parser.url);


}

- (void)feedParser:(MWFeedParser *)parser didParseFeedInfo:(MWFeedInfo *)info {
    NSLog(@"Parsed Feed Info: "%@"", info.title);

}

- (void)feedParser:(MWFeedParser *)parser didParseFeedItem:(MWFeedItem *)item {
    //this checks that there is something in the feed. If there isn't the array
    // items remains empty - this will stop it crashing if there are no feed items
    NSLog(@"Parsed Feed Item: "%@"", item.title);
    if (item) [items addObject:item];
}

- (void)feedParserDidFinish:(MWFeedParser *)parser {
    //this is called when the parsing is all done
    NSLog(@"Finished Parsing");
    didFinish = YES;
    //allow the user to use the table again:
    myTableView.userInteractionEnabled = YES;
    [myTableView reloadData];
}

- (void)feedParser:(MWFeedParser *)parser didFailWithError:(NSError *)error {

    //Here is our error part - really important or Apple will reject the app.

    NSLog(@"Finished Parsing With Error: %@", error);

    UIAlertController *alert = [UIAlertController
                                alertControllerWithTitle:@"Error"
                                message:@"Cannot load the News Items. Please check you are connected to the internet."
                                preferredStyle:UIAlertControllerStyleAlert];

    UIAlertAction *ok = [UIAlertAction
                         actionWithTitle:@"OK"
                         style:UIAlertActionStyleDefault
                         handler:^(UIAlertAction * action)
                         {
                             [alert dismissViewControllerAnimated:YES completion:nil];

                         }];

    [alert addAction:ok];
    [self presentViewController:alert animated:YES completion:nil];

    [items removeAllObjects];
    myTableView.userInteractionEnabled = YES;
    [myTableView reloadData];
}



- (NSInteger)numberOfSectionsInTableView:(UITableView *)tableView {
    return 1;
}


- (NSInteger)tableView:(UITableView *)tableView numberOfRowsInSection:(NSInteger)section {

    //Here, I check if there are more than 20 news items. If there are, I limit the display to 20
    // this is for performance but you can change this to suit.
    if (items.count > 20) {
        return 20;
    } else {
    //if there's less than 20 items, just display them all
    return items.count;}
}

- (CGFloat)tableView:(UITableView *)tableView heightForRowAtIndexPath:(NSIndexPath *)indexPath
{

        return 90;

}


- (UITableViewCell *)tableView:(UITableView *)tableView cellForRowAtIndexPath:(NSIndexPath *)indexPath {


    static NSString *CellIdentifier = @"Cell";

    UITableViewCell *cell = [tableView dequeueReusableCellWithIdentifier:CellIdentifier];

    //within the table we have four user interface items:
    UIImageView *mainImage; //this is the thumbnail image from the feed
    UILabel *mytitleLabel; // this is the headline of our news item
    UILabel *mysummaryLabel; // this is a summary of the content of the news item
    UILabel *mydateLabel; // this is the label that will display the date of the news item
```

image is continued on the next page

```
    if (cell == nil) {
        cell = [[UITableViewCell alloc] initWithStyle:UITableViewCellStyleDefault reuseIdentifier:CellIdentifier];
    }

    cell.accessoryType = UITableViewCellAccessoryDisclosureIndicator;


        //set up the title of the news item label
        mytitleLabel = (UILabel*)[cell viewWithTag:300]; //tag stops the label being overwritten with other text

        if(!mytitleLabel){

            // set the size and position of the label
            mytitleLabel = [[UILabel alloc] initWithFrame:CGRectMake(80, -10, 210, 60)];
            // set its font
            mytitleLabel.font = [UIFont systemFontOfSize:14];
            // keep background colour clear so you can see the background image
            mytitleLabel.backgroundColor = [UIColor clearColor];
            //set the colour of the text
            mytitleLabel.textColor = [UIColor blackColor];;
            //set the number of lines - this will effect how big you need your cells. setting at 0 will give you
                unlimited lines!!
            mytitleLabel.numberOfLines = 1;
            mytitleLabel.tag = 300;

            //add the title label to the cell
            [cell.contentView addSubview:mytitleLabel];
        }


        mysummaryLabel = (UILabel*)[cell viewWithTag:400];

        if(!mysummaryLabel){
            mysummaryLabel = [[UILabel alloc] initWithFrame:CGRectMake(80, 0, 210, 95)];
            mysummaryLabel.backgroundColor = [UIColor clearColor];
            mysummaryLabel.font = [UIFont systemFontOfSize:10];
            mysummaryLabel.textColor = [UIColor blackColor];
            mysummaryLabel.numberOfLines = 2;
            mysummaryLabel.tag = 400;
            [cell.contentView addSubview:mysummaryLabel];

        }


        mydateLabel = (UILabel*)[cell viewWithTag:500];

        if(!mydateLabel){
            mydateLabel = [[UILabel alloc] initWithFrame:CGRectMake(80, 0, 320, 155)];

            mydateLabel.backgroundColor = [UIColor clearColor];
            mydateLabel.font = [UIFont systemFontOfSize:10];
            mydateLabel.textColor = [UIColor lightGrayColor];
            mydateLabel.font = [UIFont boldSystemFontOfSize:9];
            mydateLabel.tag = 500;

            [cell.contentView addSubview:mydateLabel];

        }


        mainImage = (UIImageView *)[cell viewWithTag:200];

        if(!mainImage){
            mainImage = [[UIImageView alloc] initWithFrame:CGRectMake(8,5,62,62)];
            mainImage.contentMode = UIViewContentModeScaleAspectFit;
            mainImage.tag = 200;

            [cell.contentView addSubview:mainImage]; }

        cell.backgroundColor = [UIColor whiteColor];


    MWFeedItem *item = [items objectAtIndex:indexPath.row];
    //first we check that there is info to fill the cells with! This stops it crashing if there's nothing to display!
    if (item) {

        //Strip the html from the rss feed of its html tags - we don't need those
        NSString *itemTitle = item.title ? [[[item.title stringByStrippingTags]                'stringByStrippingTags' is deprecated
            stringByRemovingNewLinesAndWhitespace] stringByDecodingHTMLEntities] : @"[No Title]";
        NSString *itemSummary = item.summary ? [[[item.summary stringByStrippingTags]          'stringByStrippingTags' is deprecated
            stringByRemovingNewLinesAndWhitespace] stringByDecodingHTMLEntities] : @"[No Summary]";
        NSString *dateText = [formatter stringFromDate:item.date];

        //put the text into the cells
        mytitleLabel.text = itemTitle;
        mysummaryLabel.text = itemSummary;
        mydateLabel.text = dateText;

        //add a spinner beneath the images so if they're taking a while to load, it is clear something is happening
        UIActivityIndicatorView *spinner = [[UIActivityIndicatorView alloc] initWithFrame:CGRectMake(30,30,20,20)];
        spinner.activityIndicatorViewStyle = UIActivityIndicatorViewStyleWhite;
        [cell.backgroundView addSubview:spinner];
        [spinner startAnimating];

        NSString *imageLink = item.content;
        NSRange textRange;
        textRange =[imageLink rangeOfString:@"src"];

        if(textRange.location != NSNotFound)
        {

            NSString *imageName = [[imageLink componentsSeparatedByString:@"src=\""] objectAtIndex:1];
            imageName = [[imageName componentsSeparatedByString:@"\""] objectAtIndex:0];
            [mainImage setImageWithURL:[NSURL URLWithString:imageName]];

        } else {
            mainImage.image = [UIImage imageNamed:@"schoolicon.png"];
        }

    }

    return cell;
}


@end
```

6.code1

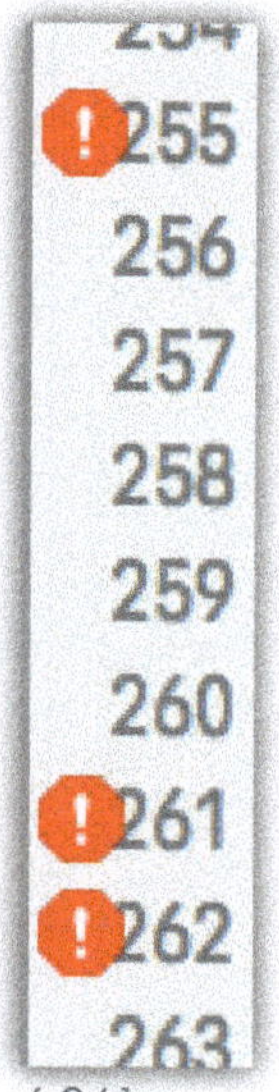

6.061

Go back and look at each part. If you see any of these red exclamation marks at the side on the left side of the *Editor* pane, it means you have an error.

Go back through the previous few pages and compare your code with mine. One small typing error could cause *Xcode* to go crazy and stick a red hexagon of doom next to your line of code.

Don't worry about yellow warning triangles. Ideally, you shouldn't have any of them either but some of our code may throw up a few warnings. Don't worry, it will still work.

And here's the good news; we only have one more method to write on this screen but to do it, we need jump ahead and create a new class first as we will be referring to this new screen in the last method.

We are about to write the final method on *FeedViewController.m* but we have a small problem.

The final method is called when the user presses a news item. It then loads the screen that displays the full news item. But before we can write this code, we need to create that screen, which we call, and refer to as, *NewsDetailViewController*.

That's what we're going to do next. As we'll be moving between different files, I'll make sure I make it clear which file we are working in before you add any more code. You will need to make this explicit to the pupils too or they will very quickly find themselves editing the wrong file!

Let's get started by creating *NewsDetailViewController*. Go to the *Navigator* pane and select *FeedViewController.m*. It's probably already selected.

Right-click on it and select *New File* from the pop-up menu:

6.062

Go through all the steps we have previously gone through and name your class, 'NewsDetailViewController':

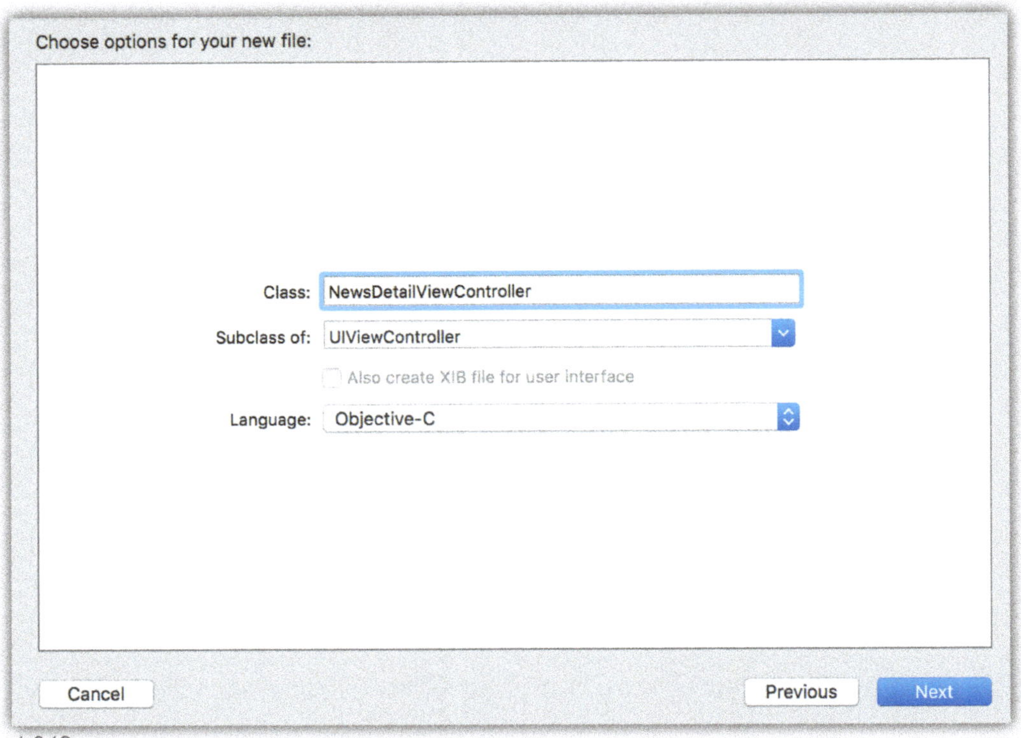

6.063

Press *Next* and then *Create* on the next screen. Your two new files should appear below *FeedViewController.m*:

6.064

We do have a fair bit of code to add to these two files but, for now, so we can complete *FeedViewController*, we're just going to add the bits we need.

Click on *NewsDetailViewController.h* and add this code to the top of the file:

```
#import <UIKit/UIKit.h>
#import "MWFeedItem.h"
#import "GTMNSString+HTML.h"
```

6.065

Then, change the rest of the code to this:

```
@interface NewsDetailViewController : UIViewController {

}

@property (nonatomic, strong) MWFeedItem *item;

@end
```

6.066

Now go to *NewsDetailViewController.m* and add this code at the top:

```
#import "NewsDetailViewController.h"
#import "NSString+HTML.h"
#import "asyncimageview.h"
#import "UIImageView+WebCache.h"
#import "GTMNSString+HTML.h"
```

6.067

And that's it in this file for now although we will come back to this in a bit.

Go back to *FeedViewController.m* and go to the top of the file.

Above all the *#import* lines of code, add this:

```
#import "NewsDetailViewController.h" // <----- THIS ONE :)
#import "FeedViewController.h"
#import "NSString+HTML.h"
```

6.068

All the code you've added on this page makes sure that every screen can access the code they need that is held in other files. I know it's looking a bit complicated but what you will find as we move through the app is that some of the code makes sense and some doesn't. The more time you spend teaching yourself the code, the more of it you will understand.

We now have our final *method* to add to *FeedViewController.m* so scroll down to the last method before the *@end* line. We will add the final method here.

And here it is:

```
- (void)tableView:(UITableView *)tableView didSelectRowAtIndexPath:(NSIndexPath *)indexPath {

    //first make sure you can only select a cell if there is any news there. If there isn't, don't let the user select a cell
    while (items.count <1){
        tableView.allowsSelection = false;
    }


    //Store the information from the news item we selected in a variable called 'item'
    MWFeedItem *item = [items objectAtIndex:indexPath.row];

    //Store the date of the news item so we can display it on the next screen
    [[NSUserDefaults standardUserDefaults] setObject:[formatter stringFromDate:item.date] forKey:@"dateString"];

    //Get the name of the storyboard so it doesn't matter if we're using an iPhone 4 or an iPhone 5
    UIStoryboard *storyBoard = self.storyboard;

    //Load the News Detail screen from our storyboard (we haven't created it yet!)
    NewsDetailViewController *vc = (NewsDetailViewController *)[storyBoard
        instantiateViewControllerWithIdentifier:@"NewsDetail"];
    vc.item = (MWFeedItem *)[items objectAtIndex:indexPath.row];
    [self presentViewController:vc animated:YES completion:nil];

    // Deselect the table so when we go back none of the stories will be selected
    [myTableView deselectRowAtIndexPath:indexPath animated:YES];

}
```

6.069

This is the code for when the user selects one of our news stories. I've put comments in explaining the code and there are probably parts of this that you get, and parts that you don't.

Once you've completed the code for this screen – and it's our most complicated one – we need to add a method for the *Back* button.

I guess that you're dying to test this app out but we're not quite ready yet.

Remember when you made your home screen with the five square buttons? So far those buttons don't do anything. Before we can test the app we need to link the *Latest News* button to our *FeedViewController* in our storyboard.

So head back to *Main.storyboard* in the *Navigator* pane.

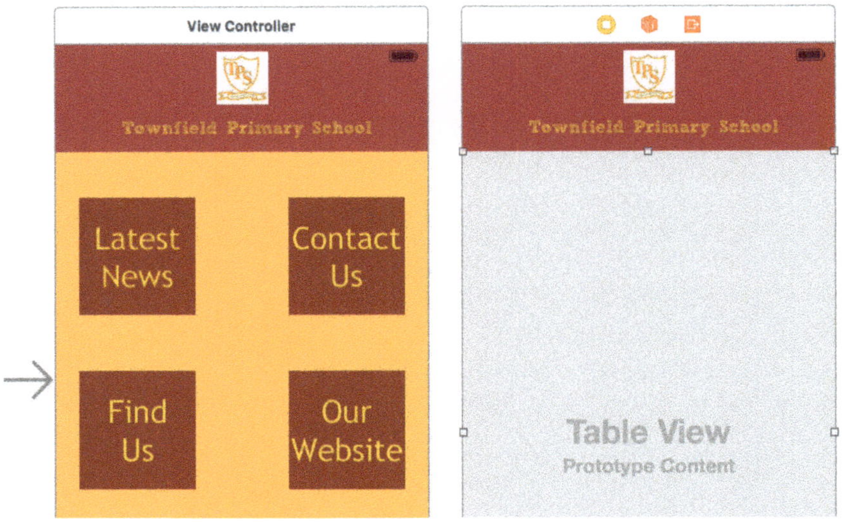

6.070

I'd like you to two-finger drag from the *Latest News* button to the screen for your *RSS Feed*.

When you do this, you will see this pop-up box:

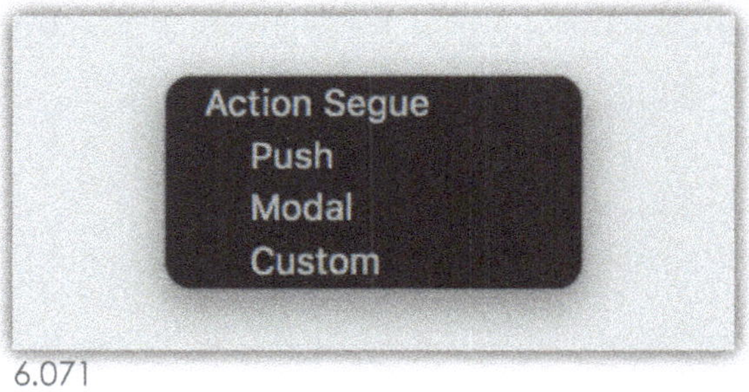

6.071

Select *Modal* and the box will vanish.

All you've done is told *Xcode* that when you press the *Latest News* button, you want the *RSS Feed* screen to appear *modally*. This means on top of the home screen. By default, the app will animate this. So the RSS Feed will pop up in front of the home screen. You can turn this animation off but we'll leave it on because it looks good.

And now, you are ready to test the app.

Press the play button above the *Navigator* pane. The app will load in the simulator. Remember, ONLY the *Latest News* button works at present so go ahead and press it.

Here is mine, using exactly the same code that you've just added:

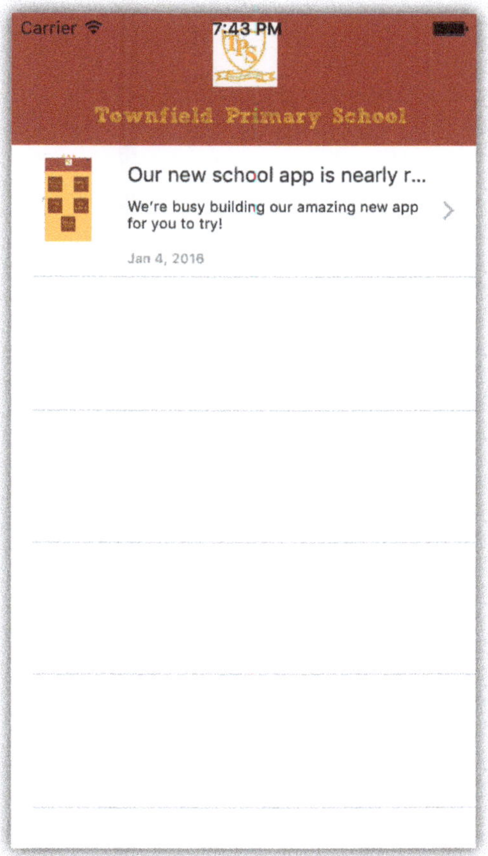

6.072

All that hard work seems worth it! You've built an *RSS Feed* in *WordPress* and then imported a third-party set of code, before using it to get the app to read the RSS Feed and display it in a *Table View*. You pupils will gasp in awe when they get to this point! But more likely, the app will crash. If this happens, just go back and check the lines of code. Look for a typing error or a missed line of code. Debugging is one of the most important skills children need to acquire when learning to code.

You'll notice that we don't yet have a *Back* button or a *Refresh* button. The *Refresh* button is optional – you are unlikely to be updating the app so often that your users will need to refresh the feed, unlike in a news app like the BBC where the stories are constantly changing.

The *Back* button is essential. Without it there is no way of sending the user back to the home screen from here.

A useful note here. Go back to *Xcode* and you will see a new window has appeared underneath the *Editor* pane:

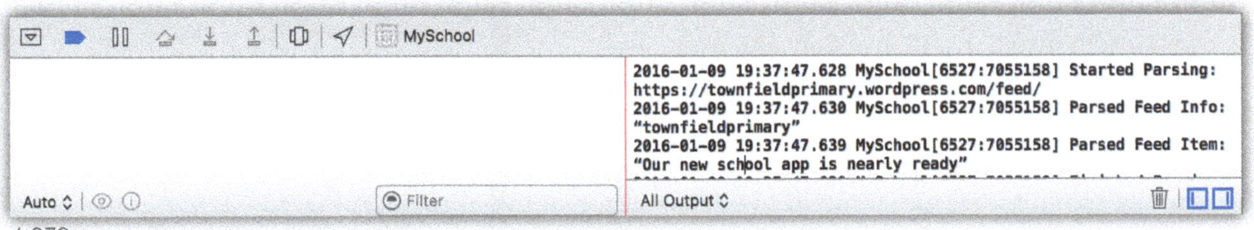

6.073

This is the *debugger*. It provides useful information as to why your app is crashing, if it is. It also displays anything you tell it to. Remember when we used *NSLog* earlier in this chapter? You can see the result of that on the right-hand window of the debugger.

Also, as we haven't yet added the screen for the page that displays the full story in detail, pressing the news item will cause your app to crash. Press on the news item to see what happens. Keep an eye on the debugger. You'll see information, that you may well not understand, appear in the right-hand window when the app crashes.

Once you've made the app crash, go to the debugger and scroll up.

You should be able to find this message:

```
2016-01-09 19:51:56.543 MySchool[6527:7055158] *** Terminating
app due to uncaught exception 'NSInvalidArgumentException',
reason: 'Storyboard (<UIStoryboard: 0x7fe8e8c0a030>) doesn't
contain a view controller with identifier 'NewsDetail''
```

6.074

This is *Xcode* politely telling you that the app has crashed because you haven't made the *NewsDetail* screen yet. We will make it, but we have our *Back* and *Refresh* buttons to make first.

You might have noticed that after crashing your app, the *Navigator* pane changed to this:

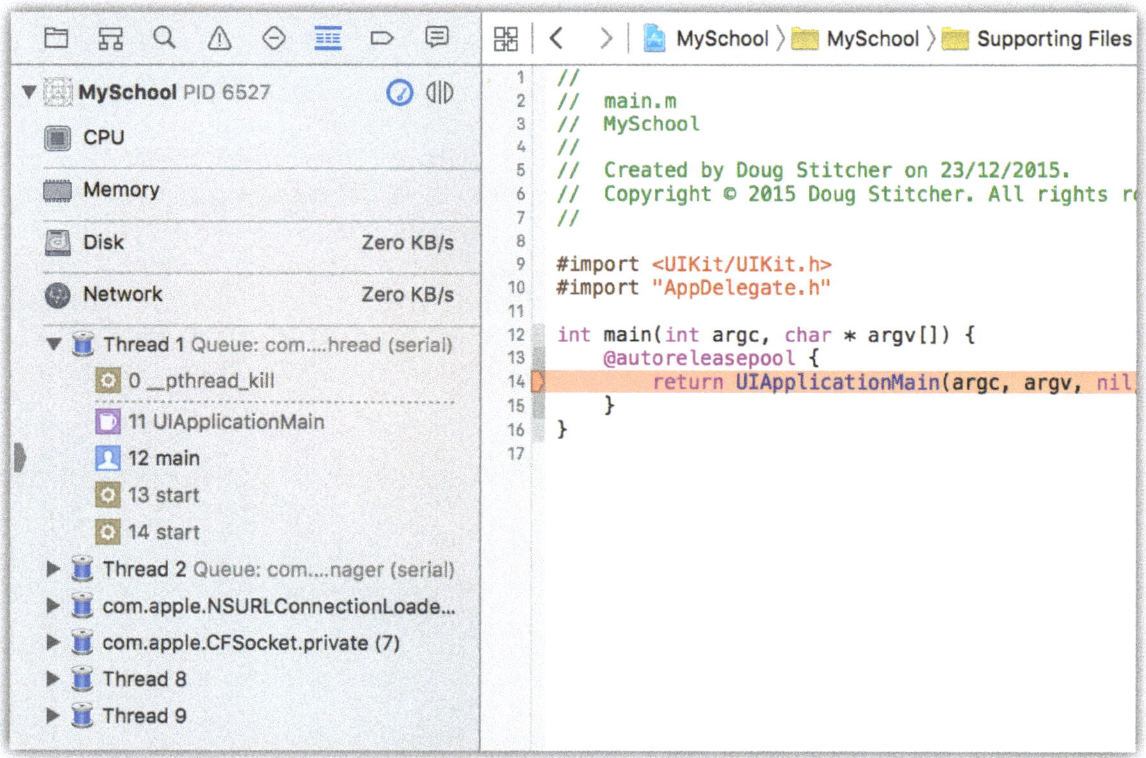

6.075

We're not quite ready to understand this screen so let's change the *Navigator* pane back to our list of *files* and *groups*.

On the top bar above the Navigator pane, there is a row of eight buttons:

6.076

Press the first one, which is the icon of a folder, and the *Navigator* pane will revert back to the layout with our files and folders.

Re-select our *FeedViewController.m* file. It's time to add the code for our *Back* and *Refresh* buttons.

First, let's do the *Back* code. This is going to be an *IBAction*. That is, code that runs when a button is pressed, in this case, the *Back* button.

Scroll to the bottom of the file and add this code just before the *@end* code:

```
- (IBAction)back:(id)sender{
    [self dismissViewControllerAnimated:YES completion:nil];
}
```

6.077

This code gets rid of the *RSS Feed* screen. Notice the *YES*. This means I want the transition to be animated. If I change that to *NO*, the screen will disappear, leaving the home screen visible. Remember, when we loaded the *RSS Feed* screen we *presented* it on top of the home screen.

Last bit now, we need to add code to refresh the feed. You can safely miss this bit out but I'll put it in so that the app is complete.

Put this code underneath the *Back* method:

```
- (IBAction)refreshfeed:(id)sender
{
    //clear the array
    [items removeAllObjects];

    //fill the array with the new feed items
    items = [[NSMutableArray alloc] init];
    [feedParser parse];

    //send them to the table
    [myTableView reloadData];
}
```

6.078

There's a little bit more here but I've added a few comments to explain it.

Here is the full code:

```
#import "NewsDetailViewController.h" // <------ THIS ONE :)
#import "FeedViewController.h"
#import "NSString+HTML.h"
#import "asyncimageview.h"
#import "UIImageView+WebCache.h"

@implementation FeedViewController

- (void)viewDidLoad{

    [super viewDidLoad];

    NSString *rssfeed = @"https://townfieldprimary.wordpress.com/feed/";
    formatter = [[NSDateFormatter alloc] init];
    [formatter setDateStyle:NSDateFormatterMediumStyle];
    items = [[NSMutableArray alloc] init];
    myTableView.userInteractionEnabled = NO;
    feedParser = [[MWFeedParser alloc] initWithFeedURL:rssfeed];
    feedParser.delegate = self;
    feedParser.feedParseType = ParseTypeFull;
    feedParser.connectionType = ConnectionTypeAsynchronously;
    [feedParser parse];

}

- (void)feedParserDidStart:(MWFeedParser *)parser {
    //while it's parsing the feed this will display the info it gets
    //you can add any code here that want to run whilst the parser is running
    NSLog(@"Started Parsing: %@", parser.url);


}

- (void)feedParser:(MWFeedParser *)parser didParseFeedInfo:(MWFeedInfo *)info {
    NSLog(@"Parsed Feed Info: "%@"", info.title);

}

- (void)feedParser:(MWFeedParser *)parser didParseFeedItem:(MWFeedItem *)item {
    //this checks that there is something in the feed. If there isn't the array
    // items remains empty - this will stop it crashing if there are no feed items
    NSLog(@"Parsed Feed Item: "%@"", item.title);
    if (item) [items addObject:item];
}

- (void)feedParserDidFinish:(MWFeedParser *)parser {
    //this is called when the parsing is all done
    NSLog(@"Finished Parsing");
    didFinish = YES;
    //allow the user to use the table again:
    myTableView.userInteractionEnabled = YES;
    [myTableView reloadData];
}

- (void)feedParser:(MWFeedParser *)parser didFailWithError:(NSError *)error {

    //Here is our error part - really important or Apple will reject the app.

    NSLog(@"Finished Parsing With Error: %@", error);

    UIAlertController *alert = [UIAlertController
                                alertControllerWithTitle:@"Error"
                                message:@"Cannot load the News Items. Please check you are connected to the internet."
                                preferredStyle:UIAlertControllerStyleAlert];

    UIAlertAction *ok = [UIAlertAction
                         actionWithTitle:@"OK"
                         style:UIAlertActionStyleDefault
                         handler:^(UIAlertAction * action)
                         {
                             [alert dismissViewControllerAnimated:YES completion:nil];

                         }];

    [alert addAction:ok];
    [self presentViewController:alert animated:YES completion:nil];

    [items removeAllObjects];
    myTableView.userInteractionEnabled = YES;
    [myTableView reloadData];
}



- (NSInteger)numberOfSectionsInTableView:(UITableView *)tableView {
    return 1;
}


- (NSInteger)tableView:(UITableView *)tableView numberOfRowsInSection:(NSInteger)section {
```

image is continued on the next page

```
    //Here, I check if there are more than 20 news items. If there are, I limit the display to 20
    // this is for performance but you can change this to suit.
    if (items.count > 20) {
        return 20;
    } else {
    //if there's less than 20 items, just display them all
    return items.count;}
}

- (CGFloat)tableView:(UITableView *)tableView heightForRowAtIndexPath:(NSIndexPath *)indexPath
{

        return 90;

}


- (UITableViewCell *)tableView:(UITableView *)tableView cellForRowAtIndexPath:(NSIndexPath *)indexPath {


    static NSString *CellIdentifier = @"Cell";

    UITableViewCell *cell = [tableView dequeueReusableCellWithIdentifier:CellIdentifier];

    //within the table we have four user interface items:
    UIImageView *mainImage; //this is the thumbnail image from the feed
    UILabel *mytitleLabel; // this is the headline of our news item
    UILabel *mysummaryLabel; // this is a summary of the content of the news item
    UILabel *mydateLabel; // this is the label that will display the date of the news item

    if (cell == nil) {
        cell = [[UITableViewCell alloc] initWithStyle:UITableViewCellStyleDefault reuseIdentifier:CellIdentifier];
    }

    cell.accessoryType = UITableViewCellAccessoryDisclosureIndicator;


        //set up the title of the news item label
        mytitleLabel = (UILabel*)[cell viewWithTag:300]; //tag stops the label being overwritten with other text

        if(!mytitleLabel){

            // set the size and position of the label
            mytitleLabel = [[UILabel alloc] initWithFrame:CGRectMake(80, -10, 210, 60)];
            // set its font
            mytitleLabel.font = [UIFont systemFontOfSize:14];
            // keep background colour clear so you can see the background image
            mytitleLabel.backgroundColor = [UIColor clearColor];
            //set the colour of the text
            mytitleLabel.textColor = [UIColor blackColor];;
            //set the number of lines - this will effect how big you need your cells. setting at 0 will give you
                unlimited lines!!
            mytitleLabel.numberOfLines = 1;
            mytitleLabel.tag = 300;

            //add the title label to the cell
            [cell.contentView addSubview:mytitleLabel];
        }


        mysummaryLabel = (UILabel*)[cell viewWithTag:400];

        if(!mysummaryLabel){
            mysummaryLabel = [[UILabel alloc] initWithFrame:CGRectMake(80, 0, 210, 95)];
            mysummaryLabel.backgroundColor = [UIColor clearColor];
            mysummaryLabel.font = [UIFont systemFontOfSize:10];
            mysummaryLabel.textColor = [UIColor blackColor];
            mysummaryLabel.numberOfLines = 2;
            mysummaryLabel.tag = 400;
            [cell.contentView addSubview:mysummaryLabel];

        }


        mydateLabel = (UILabel*)[cell viewWithTag:500];

        if(!mydateLabel){
            mydateLabel = [[UILabel alloc] initWithFrame:CGRectMake(80, 0, 320, 155)];

            mydateLabel.backgroundColor = [UIColor clearColor];
            mydateLabel.font = [UIFont systemFontOfSize:10];
            mydateLabel.textColor = [UIColor lightGrayColor];
            mydateLabel.font = [UIFont boldSystemFontOfSize:9];
            mydateLabel.tag = 500;

            [cell.contentView addSubview:mydateLabel];

        }


        mainImage = (UIImageView *)[cell viewWithTag:200];

        if(!mainImage){
            mainImage = [[UIImageView alloc] initWithFrame:CGRectMake(8,5,62,62)];
            mainImage.contentMode = UIViewContentModeScaleAspectFit;
            mainImage.tag = 200;

            [cell.contentView addSubview:mainImage]; }

        cell.backgroundColor = [UIColor whiteColor];
```

image is continued on the next page

```
    MWFeedItem *item = [items objectAtIndex:indexPath.row];
    //first we check that there is info to fill the cells with! This stops it crashing if there's nothing to display!
    if (item) {

        //Strip the html from the rss feed of its html tags - we don't need those
        NSString *itemTitle = item.title ? [[[item.title stringByStrippingTags]          'stringByStrippingTags' is deprecated
            stringByRemovingNewLinesAndWhitespace] stringByDecodingHTMLEntities] : @"[No Title]";
        NSString *itemSummary = item.summary ? [[[item.summary stringByStrippingTags]    'stringByStrippingTags' is deprecated
            stringByRemovingNewLinesAndWhitespace] stringByDecodingHTMLEntities] : @"[No Summary]";
        NSString *dateText = [formatter stringFromDate:item.date];

        //put the text into the cells
        mytitleLabel.text = itemTitle;
        mysummaryLabel.text = itemSummary;
        mydateLabel.text = dateText;

        //add a spinner beneath the images so if they're taking a while to load, it is clear something is happening
        UIActivityIndicatorView *spinner = [[UIActivityIndicatorView alloc] initWithFrame:CGRectMake(30,30,20,20)];
        spinner.activityIndicatorViewStyle = UIActivityIndicatorViewStyleWhite;
        [cell.backgroundView addSubview:spinner];
        [spinner startAnimating];

        NSString *imageLink = item.content;
        NSRange textRange;
        textRange =[imageLink rangeOfString:@"src"];

        if(textRange.location != NSNotFound)
        {

            NSString *imageName = [[imageLink componentsSeparatedByString:@"src=\""] objectAtIndex:1];
            imageName = [[imageName componentsSeparatedByString:@"\""] objectAtIndex:0];
            [mainImage setImageWithURL:[NSURL URLWithString:imageName]];

        } else {
            mainImage.image = [UIImage imageNamed:@"schoolicon.png"];
        }

    }

    return cell;
}

- (void)tableView:(UITableView *)tableView didSelectRowAtIndexPath:(NSIndexPath *)indexPath {

    //first make sure you can only select a cell if there is any news there. If there isn't, don't let the user select a
        cell
    while (items.count <1){
        tableView.allowsSelection = false;
    }


    //Store the information from the news item we selected in a variable called 'item'
    MWFeedItem *item = [items objectAtIndex:indexPath.row];

    //Store the date of the news item so we can display it on the next screen
    [[NSUserDefaults standardUserDefaults] setObject:[formatter stringFromDate:item.date] forKey:@"dateString"];

    //Get the name of the storyboard so it doesn't matter if we're using an iPhone 4 or an iPhone 5
    UIStoryboard *storyBoard = self.storyboard;

    //Load the News Detail screen from our storyboard (we haven't created it yet!)
    NewsDetailViewController *vc = (NewsDetailViewController *)[storyBoard
        instantiateViewControllerWithIdentifier:@"NewsDetail"];
    vc.item = (MWFeedItem *)[items objectAtIndex:indexPath.row];
    [self presentViewController:vc animated:YES completion:nil];

    // Deselect the table so when we go back none of the stories will be selected
    [myTableView deselectRowAtIndexPath:indexPath animated:YES];

}

- (IBAction)back:(id)sender{
    [self dismissViewControllerAnimated:YES completion:nil];
}

- (IBAction)refreshfeed:(id)sender
{
    //clear the array
    [items removeAllObjects];

    //fill the array with the new feed items
    items = [[NSMutableArray alloc] init];
    [feedParser parse];

    //send them to the table
    [myTableView reloadData];
}


@end
```

6.code2

Now we just need to add the two buttons and link them to the code. So go back to *Main.storyboard*.

Find a *UIButton* in the *Object Library*:

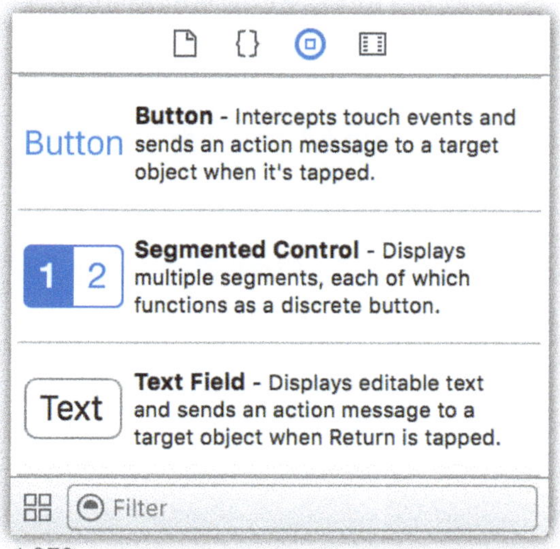

6.079

Now drag two buttons to the *RSS Feed* screen, one to the top left and one to the top right like this:

6.080

At the moment, they are in the default blue colour and both say 'Button' so let's change the first one. Select the one on the left and then look at the *Attributes* inspector on the *Utilities* pane:

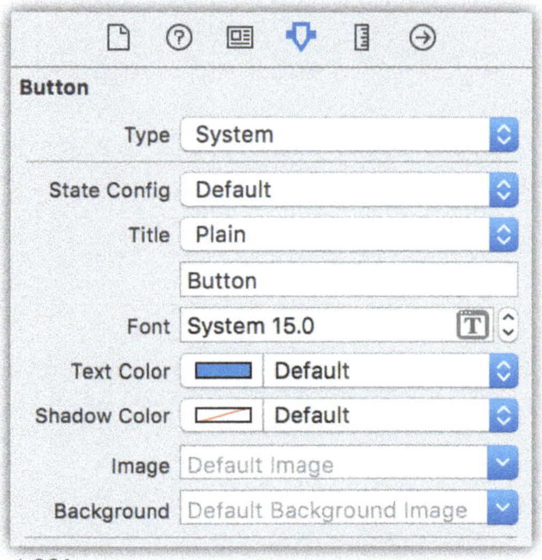

6.081

Underneath *Title*, where it says 'Button' change the text to 'Back'. Change the colour to a colour that suits your app. I'm going to change mine to a gold colour:

6.082

You could make an image for your button instead and set it using the *Image* option in the *Attributes inspector* as you did for the buttons on the home screen. But to speed things up, I'm going to create text buttons. I'm sure your class would enjoy designing some more buttons!

Repeat the process for the button on the right, change the text to 'Refresh'. You will need to make the button slightly wider to accommodate the longer word:

6.083

The last thing we need to do on this screen is link our two buttons to the code. To do that, two-finger drag from the *Back* button to the yellow circle with a square in it:

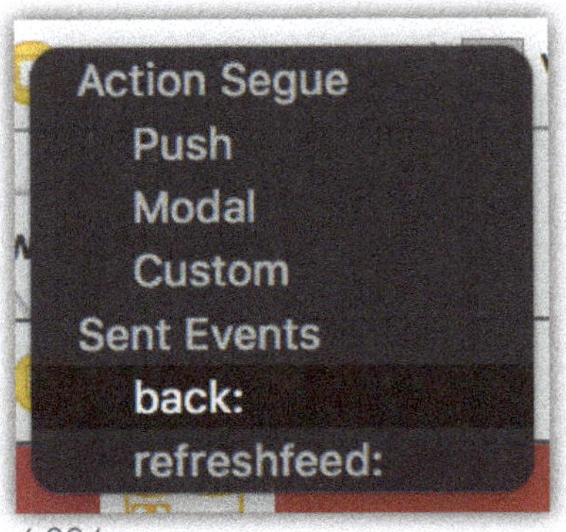

6.084

Select *back*: and the box will vanish. Repeat the process with the *Refresh* button and select *refreshfeed:*.

Now run the app and check that our two new buttons work. The *Back* button should take you back to the home screen and the *Refresh* button will reload your feed. The best way to test the *Refresh* button is to add a new post to your feed using *WordPress* and then press the Refresh button to make sure the app picks it up.

Our *RSS Feed* screen is complete.

All that's left to do now is make the screen for the *News Detail View* and add the code. Let's get started.

You should already be in *Main.storyboard*, but if you're not, select it from the *Navigator* pane.

Find a bit of space to the right of the *RSS Feed* screen and drag a new *View Controller* object from the *Object Library*:

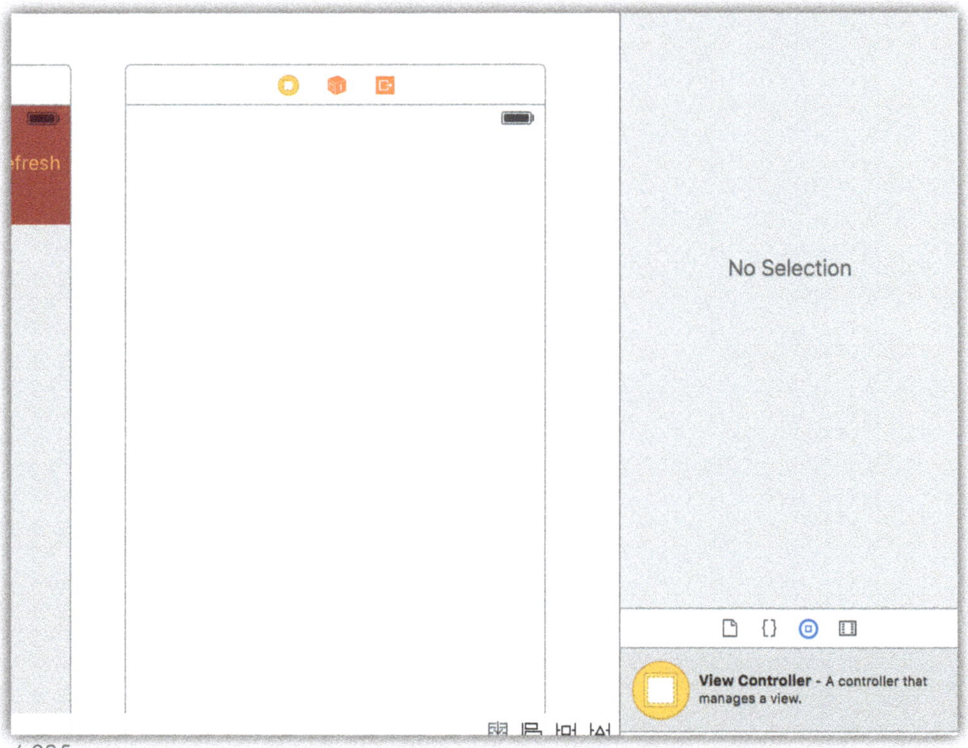

6.085

We need to link it to our *NewsDetailViewController* class. Select the yellow circle with the white square at the top of the *view controller* then, in the *Utilities* pane, select the third button from the left:

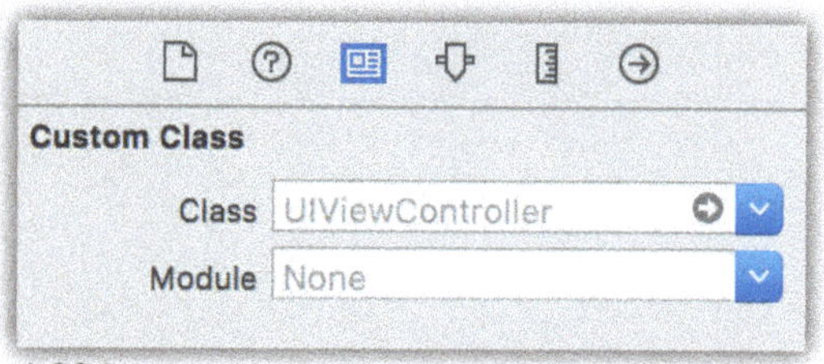

6.086

In the text field next to *Class*, type 'NewsDetailViewController', it should autocomplete. Then select the *Attributes* button, fourth one from the left, as you'll be mostly working within the *Attributes* section of the *Utilities* pane.

You may also need to turn *Autolayout* off. Do this by selecting the first button on the left that looks like a piece of paper and scroll down to uncheck the Autolayout box.

We need to copy our header image so select it on one of your other screens and press *Cmd* and 'C' to copy it. Go back to your new screen, *News Detail View Controller*, and press anywhere on the white screen. Press *Cmd* and 'V' to paste it. Then position it in the top corner. You can use the *ruler* button to set the x and y positions exactly:

6.087

You also need to copy the *Back* button, although the link to the code won't be copied so we will have to do that again later. When copying the button, it's a good idea to look on the *ruler* tab to see what the x and y positions are so that the button is in the same position on every screen. In my case, my button is positioned at 5x, 28y:

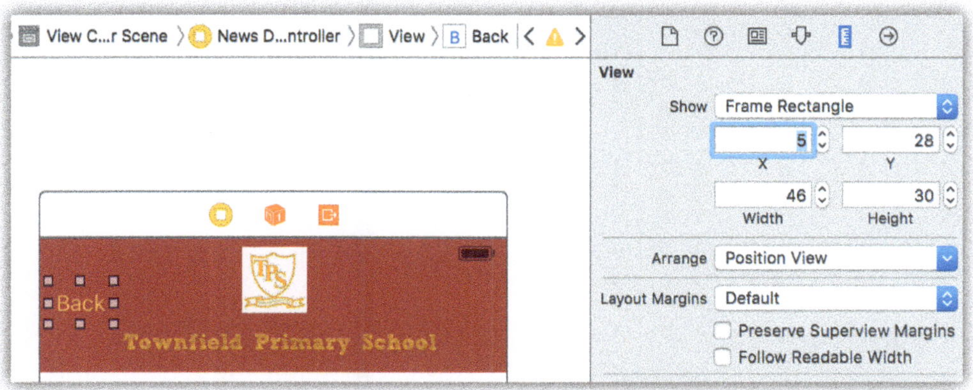

6.088

We've still got a few objects to add to this screen. It's going to display the full news story so we have to plan for the fact that we don't know how long each news story will be. To cope with that, we're going to put all of our *user interface* elements inside an object called a *UIScrollView*. This is a view that the user can scroll up and down and that we can code to get bigger if necessary depending on the size of the story.

Go to the Object Library and locate the Scroll View object:

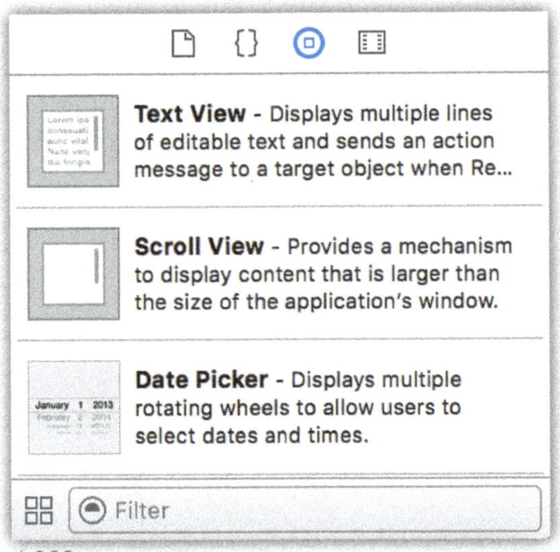

6.089

Drag the Scroll View on to the *News Detail View Controller* and fill the space below the header:

6.090

We are going to have to use our NewsDetailViewController.h file to tell Xcode about all the elements we are going to add, but let's use a neat little trick to do this. Look at the top right of Xcode:

6.091

See the interlinking circles? Press that button.

The *Editor* pane will split into two parts. On the left, you will see the *storyboard* file and on the right, you will see the *NewsDetailViewController.h* file:

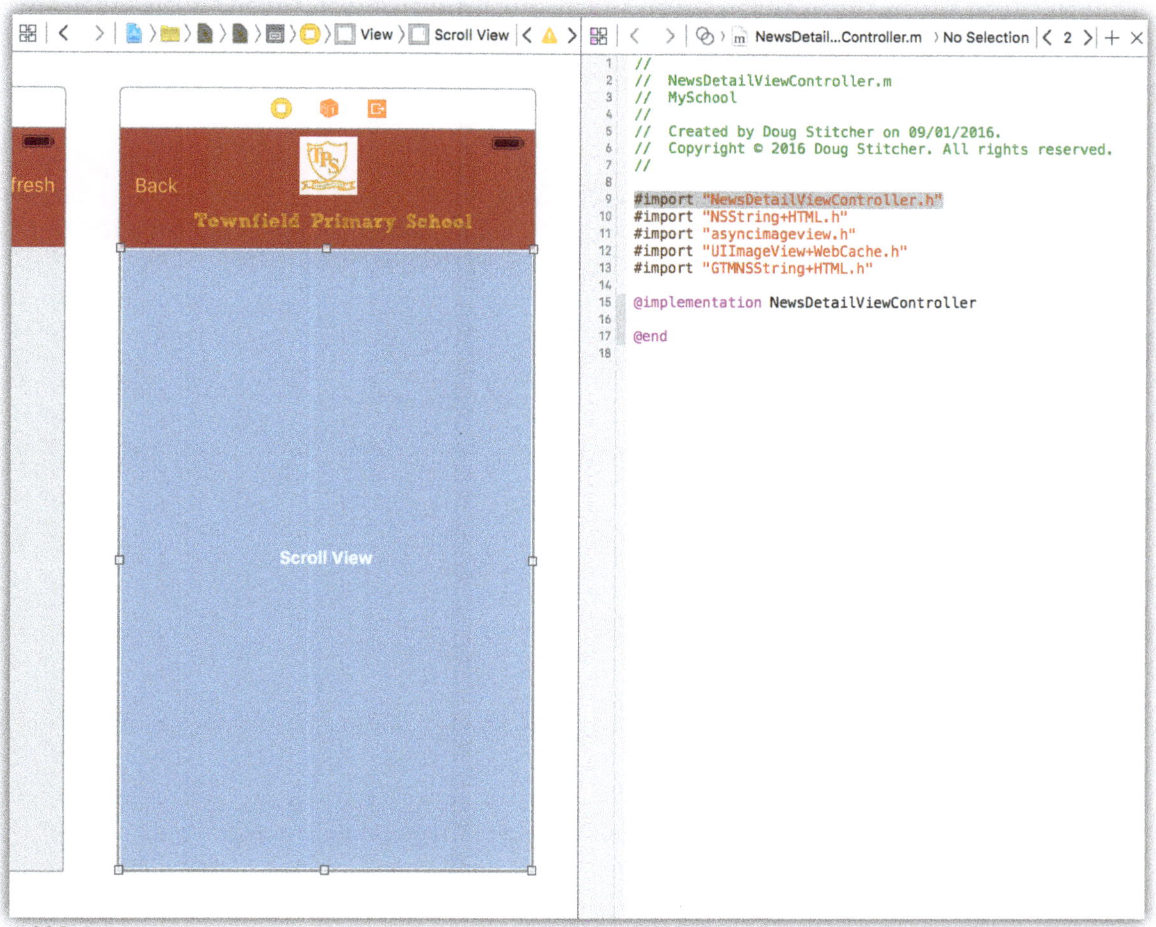

6.092

Xcode might show you the .m file instead. We don't want this so look at the top of the new file that's just opened to the right:

6.093

If you can see the above, then you are looking at the .m file instead. Don't panic. Click on *NewsDetail.Controller.m*:

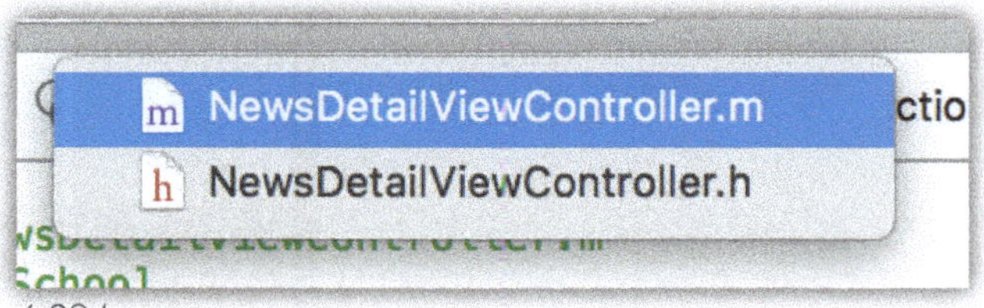

6.094

Select the .h file. That will make sure that you're looking at the right file.

To avoid getting stuck in this mode, and to go back to the full screen *Editor* pane, press the button to the left of the interlinking circles.

Before we can do any magic here, I need you to add swirly brackets to *NewsDetailViewController.h* like this:

```
@interface NewsDetailViewController : UIViewController {

}
```

6.095

Next I want you to two-finger drag from the *Scroll View* you've added to in-between the swirly brackets. Let go of the mouse and you should see this pop up (but this will only work if you release the mouse between the swirly brackets):

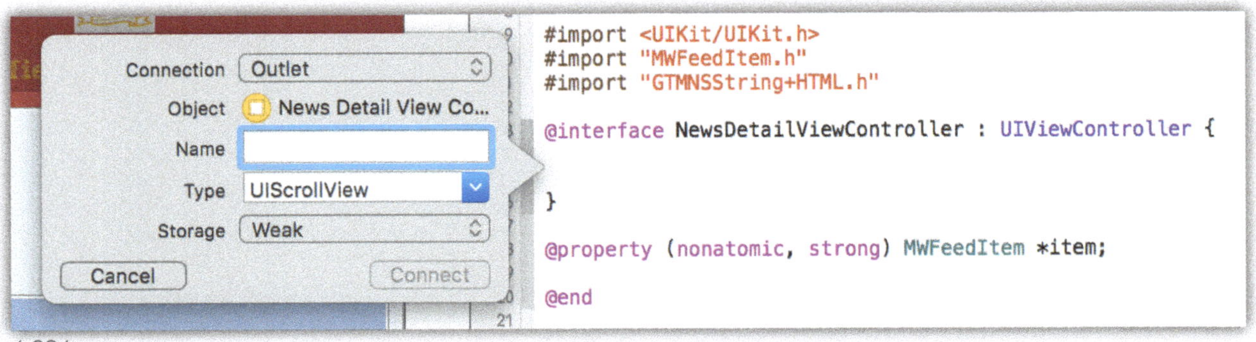

6.096

In the box that says *Name*, enter the name 'myScrollView', press *Connect* and watch what happens:

```
@interface NewsDetailViewController : UIViewController {

    __weak IBOutlet UIScrollView *myScrollView;

}
```

6.097

Xcode has magically added the code we need to define our *User Interface* object. It saves us adding an object, going back to the code and defining it and then repeating it.

We're going to use this procedure to add the other elements we need to this screen. We need to add the following items:

- A *UILabel* to display the title of the news story.
- A *UIImageView* to display a large version of the image from our news story.
- A *UILabel* to display the date of the news story.
- A *UITextView* to display the text of the news story.

Let's do them in order. Drag a *UILabel* from the *Object Library* into the *Scroll View* we just added. Place it near the top:

6.098

I need you to resize this label. The news story title could be very long so we need to make sure the label is big enough to hold it. Aim for something like this:

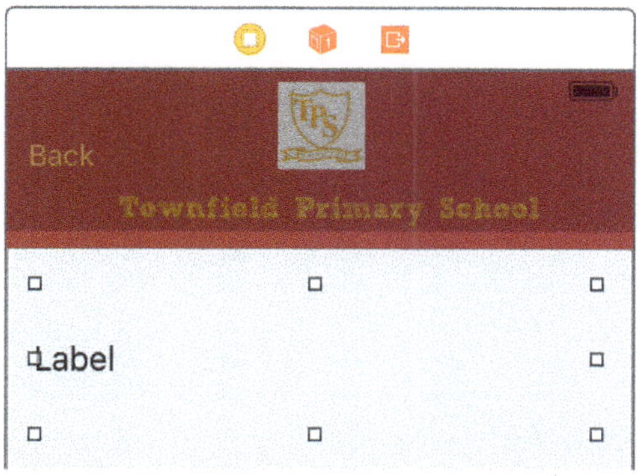

6.099

Then head over the *Utilities* pane and select the *Attributes* tab. Change the font and colour to suit your school but then you also need to do this:

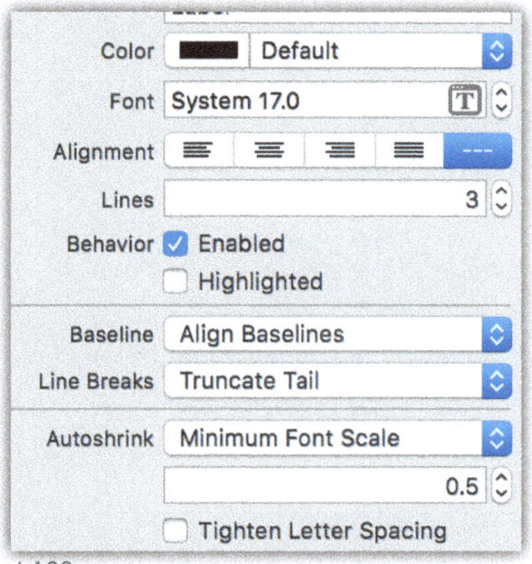

6.100

Set the number of lines to 3. That means that if the title is really long, it will display on up to three lines.

You also need to change the value in *Autoshrink* to *Minimum Font Scale* and then set it at 0.5.

This will auto shrink the text by up to 50 per cent.

Last step, let's declare this label in our .h file. Remember how to do this? Two-finger drag from the label to in-between the swirly brackets. Try to put it under the code for the *Scroll View*:

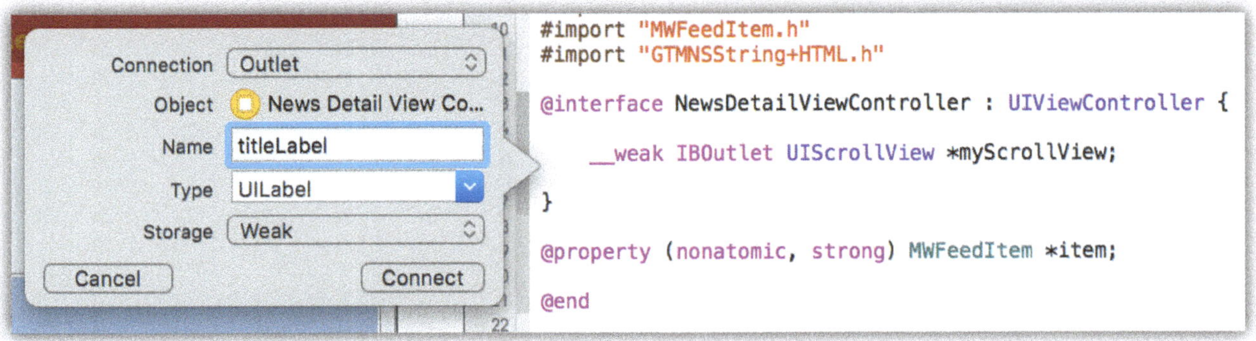

6.101

It should now look like this:

```
@interface NewsDetailViewController : UIViewController {

    __weak IBOutlet UIScrollView *myScrollView;
    __weak IBOutlet UILabel *titleLabel;

}
```

6.102

Next, let's add the *UIImageView* to display the main image from the news story. Drag an Image from the *Object Library* to the *News Detail View Controller*:

Make sure that the *Image View* doesn't overlap the bounds of the title label. Then nip over to the *Attributes* inspector in the *Utilities* pane and change *Mode* value from *Scale to Fill* to *Aspect Fit*.

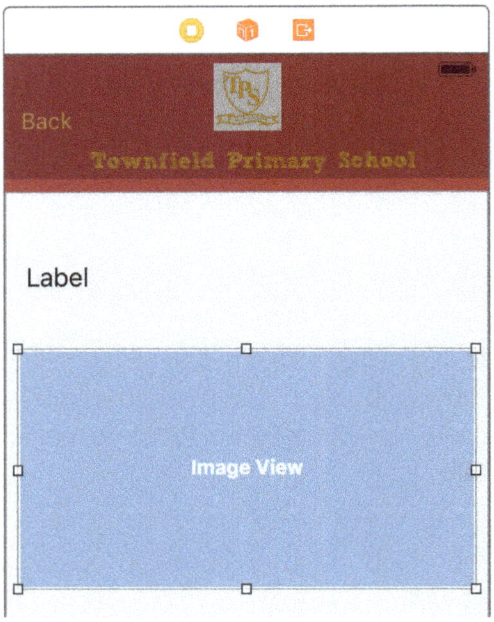

6.103

It should look like this:

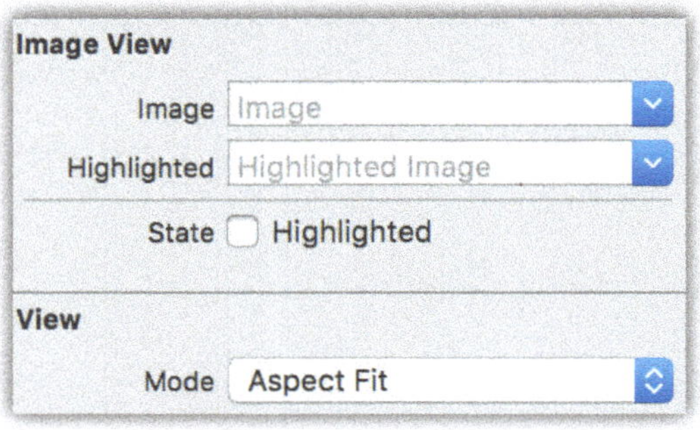

6.104

Next, link the *Image View* to the .h file by two-finger dragging: Stick it below the *titleLabel* declaration.

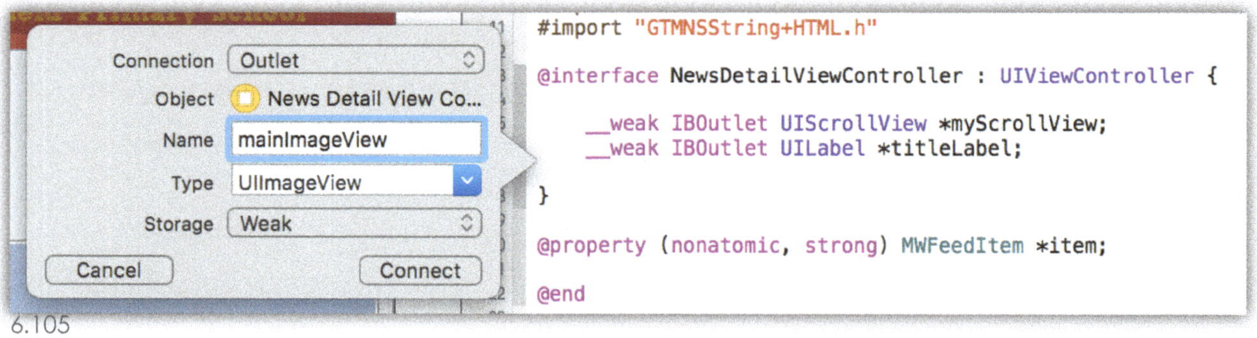

6.105

So the .h file should now look like this:

```
@interface NewsDetailViewController : UIViewController {

    __weak IBOutlet UIScrollView *myScrollView;
    __weak IBOutlet UILabel *titleLabel;
    __weak IBOutlet UIImageView *mainImageView;

}
```

6.106

We need to add the label to hold the date. Drag a *UILabel* to below the right of the *Image View*. Set its colour to be a light grey and make it wide enough to hold '31 Dec 2016'. Then two-finger drag to the .h file. Call your label 'dateLabel'.

This is what it should like like:

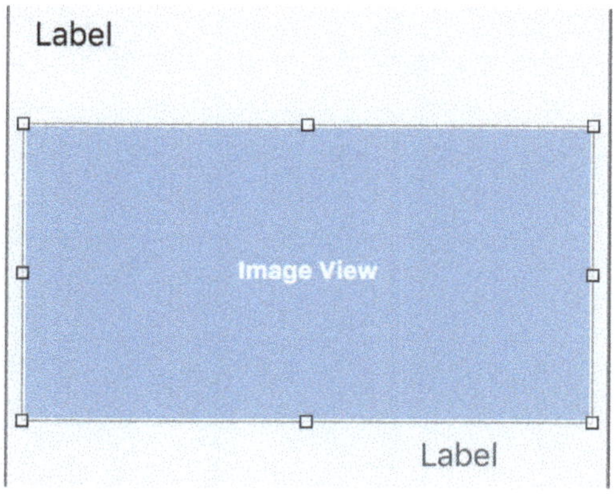

6.107

The last object to add is a *UITextView*. We haven't added one of these before but it's the same process. A UITextView holds multiple lines of text and lets the user scroll through the lines of text so we can hold a lot more text than will fit on the screen.

Find the UITextView in the *Object Library*:

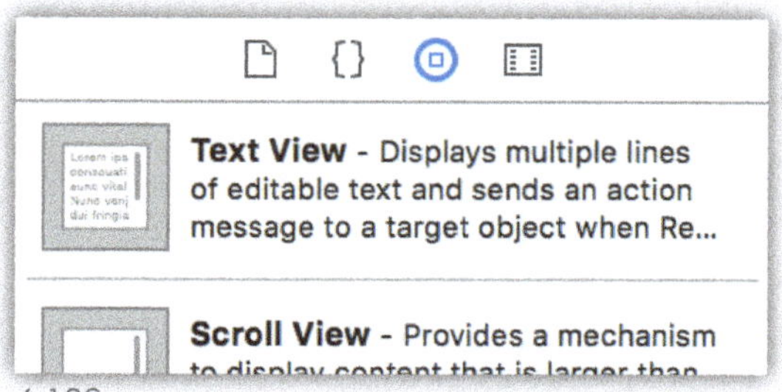

6.108

Drag it into the *Scroll View* just below the date label:

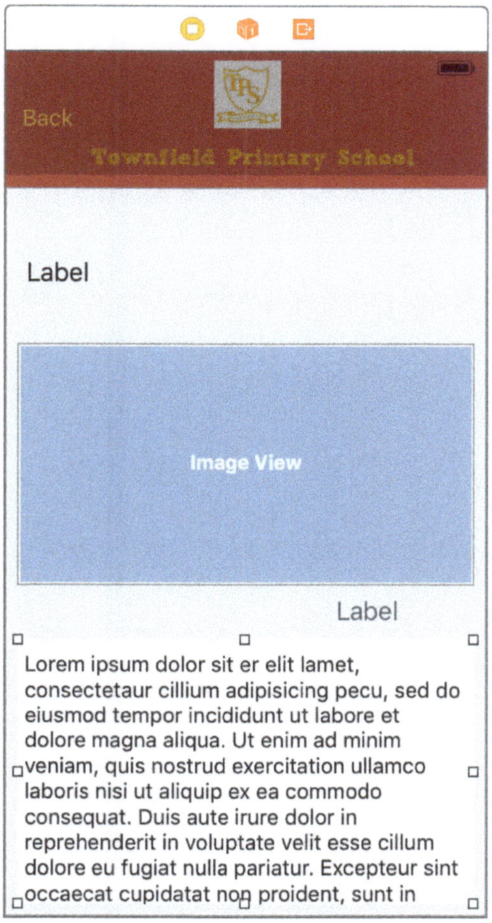

6.109

Head to the *Attributes* in the *Utility* pane and uncheck the box that says *Editable* in the *Behavior* section.

Finally, two-finger drag from the *Text View* to the .h file:

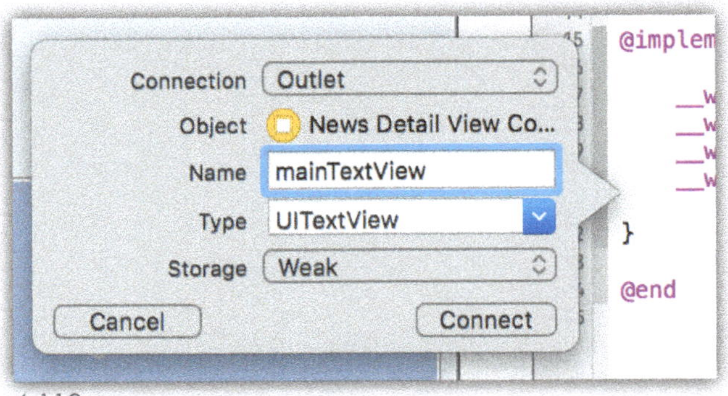

6.110

Name it 'mainTextView'.

Your final code should look like this:

```
@interface NewsDetailViewController : UIViewController {

    __weak IBOutlet UIScrollView *myScrollView;
    __weak IBOutlet UILabel *titleLabel;
    __weak IBOutlet UIImageView *mainImageView;
    __weak IBOutlet UILabel *dateLabel;
    __weak IBOutlet UITextView *mainTextView;

}
```

6.111

You've just added five user interface elements to your screen and to your header file. And you've learned a nice little trick to speed it up.

This bit is done so you can press that button next to the interlinking circles to come out of the split-screen mode:

6.112

The *Editor* pane should revert to displaying your *storyboard* file.

You might have noticed we didn't add the *Back* button to the header file. This is because we don't need to tell that button to do anything other than go back when it's pressed. If I wanted to change the text of the button for some reason, then I would have needed to reference it.

Our next task is to add the code to make our *News Detail View Controller* display the news story in full.

Go over to *NewsDetailViewController.m*.

Before we add our *viewDidLoad* method, we need to add one line of code underneath *@implementation*:

```
@implementation NewsDetailViewController
@synthesize item;
```

6.113

Add the line beginning with *@synthesize*. I won't explain it for now but we need it here.

We're ready to write our *viewDidLoad* method. It's pretty long because it does nearly everything we need on this screen. Once we've written it, we're nearly there.

First, add this:

```
- (void)viewDidLoad {

    [super viewDidLoad];

}
```

6.114

This declares our *viewDidLoad* method. All the code we will add goes after the *[super viewDidLoad];* line.

The next thing we want is for the app to search for the large image so it can display it in that big *Image View* we added. This is much the same code we added in *FeedViewController*. Add this below *[super viewDidLoad]*:

```
NSString *imageLink = item.content;

NSRange textRange;
textRange =[imageLink rangeOfString:@"src"];
if(textRange.location != NSNotFound)
{
    NSString *imageName = [[imageLink componentsSeparatedByString:@"src=\""] objectAtIndex:1];
    imageName = [[imageName componentsSeparatedByString:@"\""] objectAtIndex:0];
    [mainImageView setImageWithURL:[NSURL URLWithString:imageName]];

} else {
    mainImageView.image = [UIImage imageNamed:@"schoolicon.png"];

}
```

6.115

As before, it just looks through the news item for an image. If it finds one, it displays it on the screen.

Directly underneath, add this code:

```
titleLabel.font = [UIFont boldSystemFontOfSize:25];
mainTextView.font = [UIFont systemFontOfSize:20];
dateLabel.font = [UIFont systemFontOfSize:12];
dateLabel.text = [[NSUserDefaults standardUserDefaults] objectForKey:@"dateString"];
```

6.116

This sets the font size for our three *labels* and populates the date label with the date we saved on the previous screen when the user selected it.

Now add this:

```
NSString *itemTitle = item.title ? [[[item.title stringByStrippingTags] stringByRemovingNewLinesAndWhitespace]
    stringByDecodingHTMLEntities] : @"[No Title]";

//set the title label to be the text from the feed
titleLabel.text = itemTitle;

NSString *itemContent = item.content ? [[[item.content  stringByDecodingHTMLEntities]
    stringByReplacingOccurrencesOfString:@"</p>" withString:@"\n"  ] stringByReplacingOccurrencesOfString:@"<p>"
    withString:@"" ] : @"[No Title]";
NSString *newItemContent = itemContent ? [itemContent stringByStrippingTags] : @"[No Text To Display ]";

//set the text view to be the story from the feed
mainTextView.text = newItemContent;
```

6.117

The above code goes through the news story and removes any *HTML* and gibberish, and makes it readable in our app.

We then use that information to set the text of our *titleLabel* to be the title from the feed and the text of our *Text View* to be the story in the feed.

Directly underneath, add this:

```
CGRect frame;
frame = mainTextView.frame;
frame.size.height = [mainTextView contentSize].height;
CGSize textViewSize = [mainTextView sizeThatFits:CGSizeMake(mainTextView.frame.size.width, FLT_MAX)];
frame.size = textViewSize;
float d = frame.size.height + 280;
[myScrollView setContentSize:(CGSizeMake(myScrollView.frame.size.width, d))];
mainTextView.frame = frame;
```

6.118

Don't worry about this block of code. It makes sure that our *Scroll View* and *Text View* correctly resize depending on the content.

That's your *viewDidLoad* method done.

We have one final thing to do before we can test it and add the code for our *Back* button. Go back to *Main.storyboard* and find the *News Detail View Controller*.

Press the yellow circle with the square in it at the top of the View Controller:

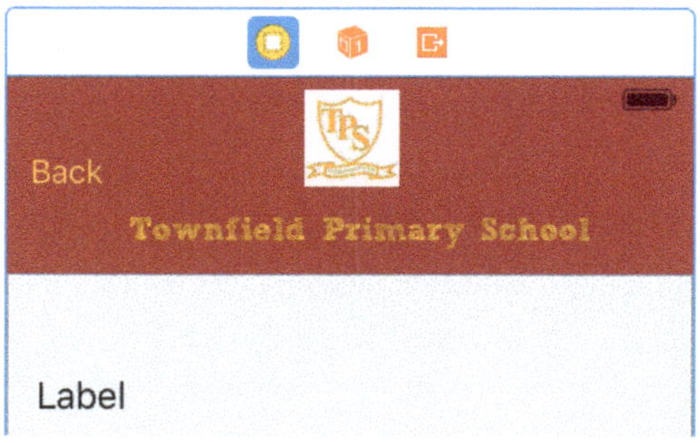

6.119

Now go to the *Utilities* pane and select the third button from the left:

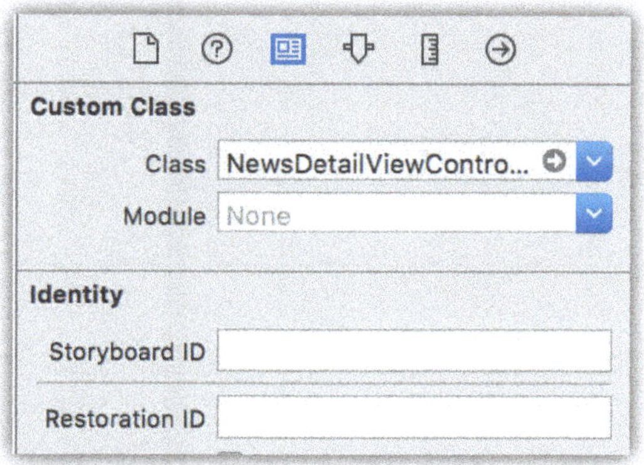

6.120

In the third text box down, *Storyboard ID*, enter the text 'NewsDetail'. This is how our app will find this screen; by its ID. Make sure you press *return* and then press *Cmd* and 'S' to save it.

It's time to test. Press that *Play* button and test the app.

Press *Latest News* and then select the first news story. You should see a variant of this screen:

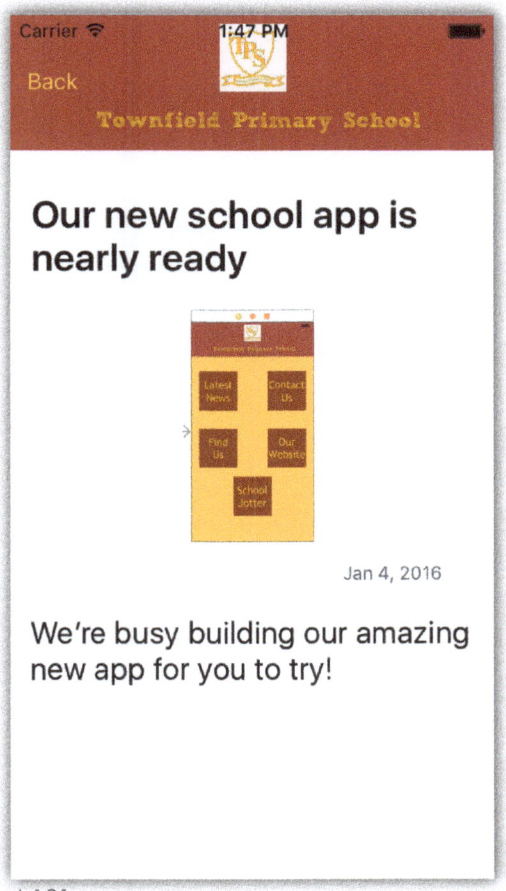

6.121

Of course, our *Back* button doesn't work. Let's add that code and then we have finished this screen of our app and, indeed, this very long chapter!

Go back to *NewsDetailViewController.m* and put the following *IBAction* method underneath your *viewDidLoad* method. Useful tip: it's the same code we used to go back on *FeedViewController* so why not copy and paste it?

```
- (IBAction)back:(id)sender{
    [self dismissViewControllerAnimated:YES completion:nil];
}
```

6.122

Finally, go back to *Main.storyboard* and find the *Back* button on the *News Detail View Controller*:

6.123

Hopefully, you remember what to do. Two-finger drag from the *Back* button to the yellow circle with the square in it.

When the pop-up box appears, select *back*:

6.124

You should be able to run the app again and this time, you can navigate fully between all the screens you've created.

If you've got this far, you have persevered and accomplished something that you may never have thought you'd be able to do.

And the good news is that of all the elements of our app, this is the hardest part as it has the most parts to it.

What's next?

In Chapter 7, we will be making the *Contact Us* screen. This is considerably easier than the screens that we've just built. We will be working with the *UIMessage framework* which will let us send an email directly from the app to our school email address and we will be learning how to access the Phone app so we can make a call directly from the app.

But for now, bask in your own glory. Show your colleagues. You have just created an app that can read and display an RSS Feed.

Great job!

http://www.alanpeat.com/build-an-app/Chapter6

CHAPTER SEVEN
CREATING THE CONTACT US SCREEN

Time to make the Contact Us screen. This one is a bit easier.

Let's have a quick look at what we're doing here:

7.01

We're going to need two buttons: one for calling and one for emailing. We'll then link them to a couple of *IBActions* that do those two things.

Before you start, I suggest you make yourself a couple of buttons at 100 x 100 in the same theme as the ones on your home screen. Again, here is a perfect opportunity for your pupils to experiment with design but I would emphasise here that from a design perspective, consistency is key. We don't suddenly want blue buttons if we've had maroon buttons throughout. I won't go through how to do that again but, if you get stuck, just refer back to earlier in the book when we used an online image editor to knock up some buttons. I've called mine 'callUsBtn.png' and 'emailUsBtn.png'. I suggest you use the same naming convention so my instructions make sense.

Once they're made, drag them into the supporting files group on the *Navigator* pane:

7.02

We need to add a new .h and .m file, or a new *class*. We've done this a few times but I'll talk you through it.

Select *NewsDetailViewController.m*. Two-finger click and select *New File*. Press *Next* on the pop-up box and then name this class 'ContactUsViewController'. Press *Next* again and then press *Create*. If you need a visual reminder of how we do this, go back to when we added *NewsDetailViewController*.

If you've done it correctly, you should see this:

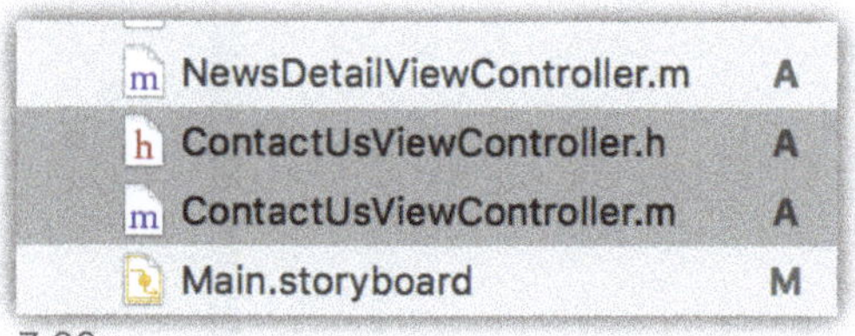

7.03

Next, let's design the *user interface*. Go to *Main.storyboard*. Create a bit of space underneath your *Feed View Controller* by scrolling around in the *Editor* pane:

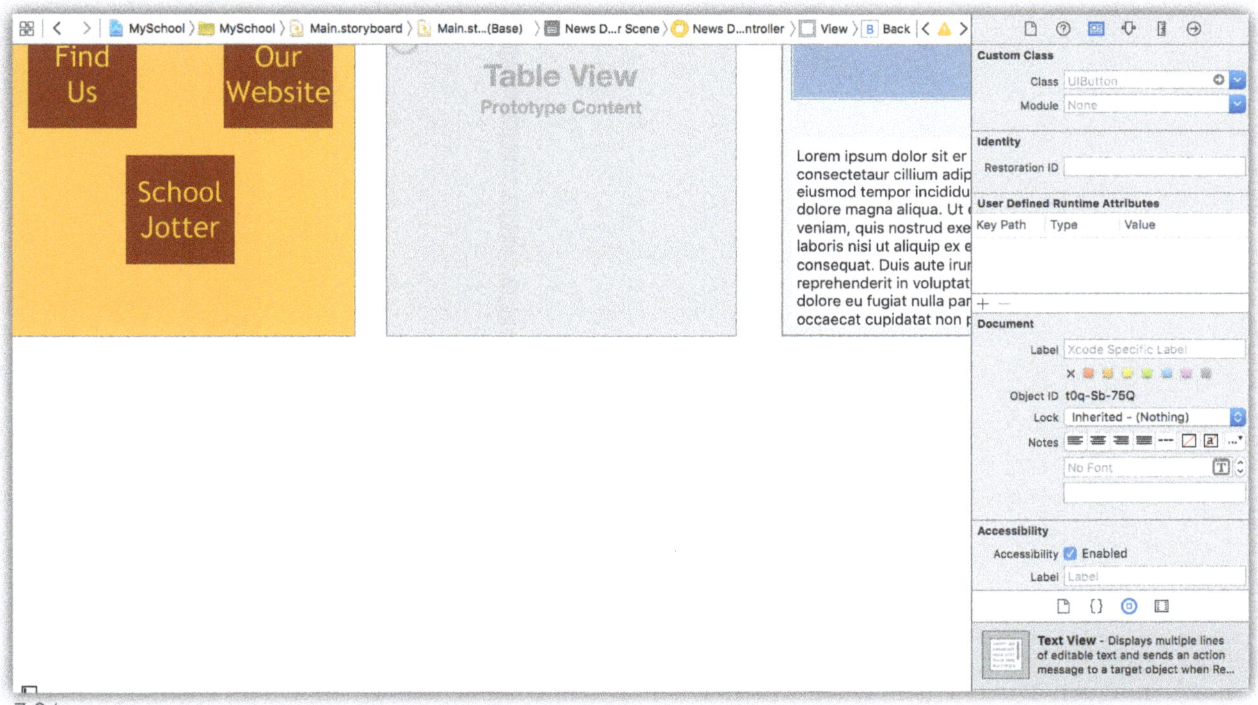

7.04

Now drag a new View Controller from the Object Library in to the Editor pane:

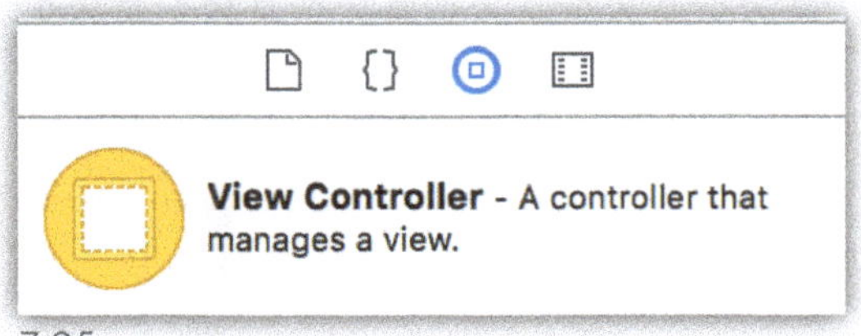

7.05

You should have a new View Controller in your storyboard, move it down so it is on its own:

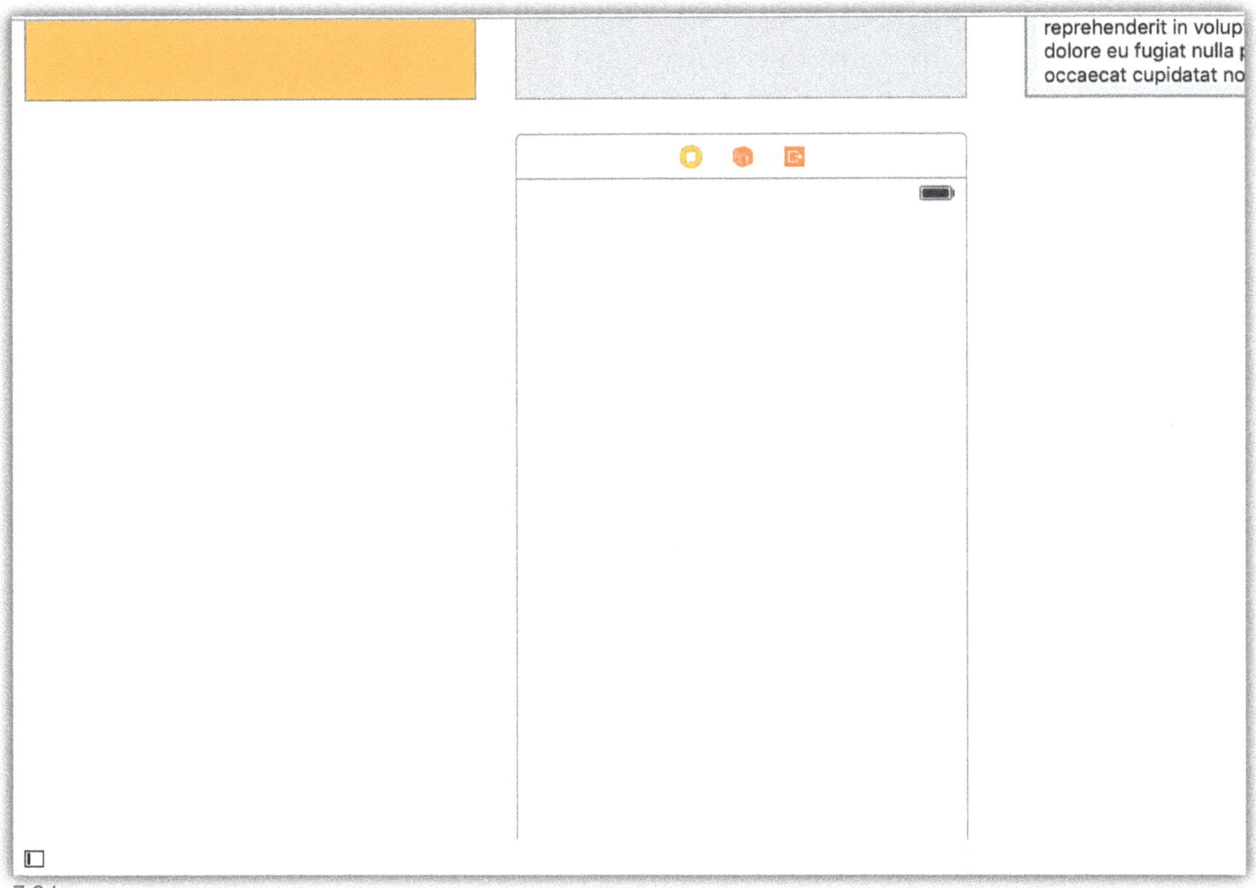

7.06

Select the yellow circle with the square in it. We need to link this View Controller to our *ContactUsViewController* class. Go over to the *Utilities* pane and press the third button from the left. This opens the *Identity inspector*.

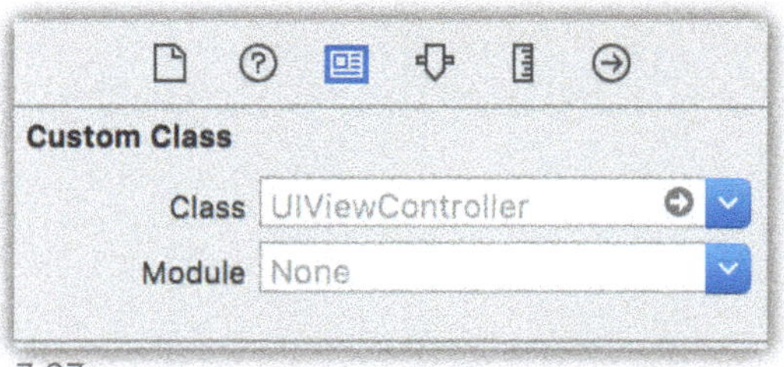

7.07

In the *Class* box, type 'ContactUsViewController'. It should autocomplete.

The next job is to copy our header and *Back* button over to this View Controller so go back to either your Feed View Controller or your News Detail View control and press *Cmd* and 'C' to copy the header image. Paste it into place on Contact Us View Controller and repeat with the *Back* button. Remember to make sure the button is in the exact position by using the *Ruler* button in the *Utilities* pane to open the *Size inspector*.

7.08

Next, we need to add two buttons, so drag them from the *Objects Library* on to the *View Controller*:

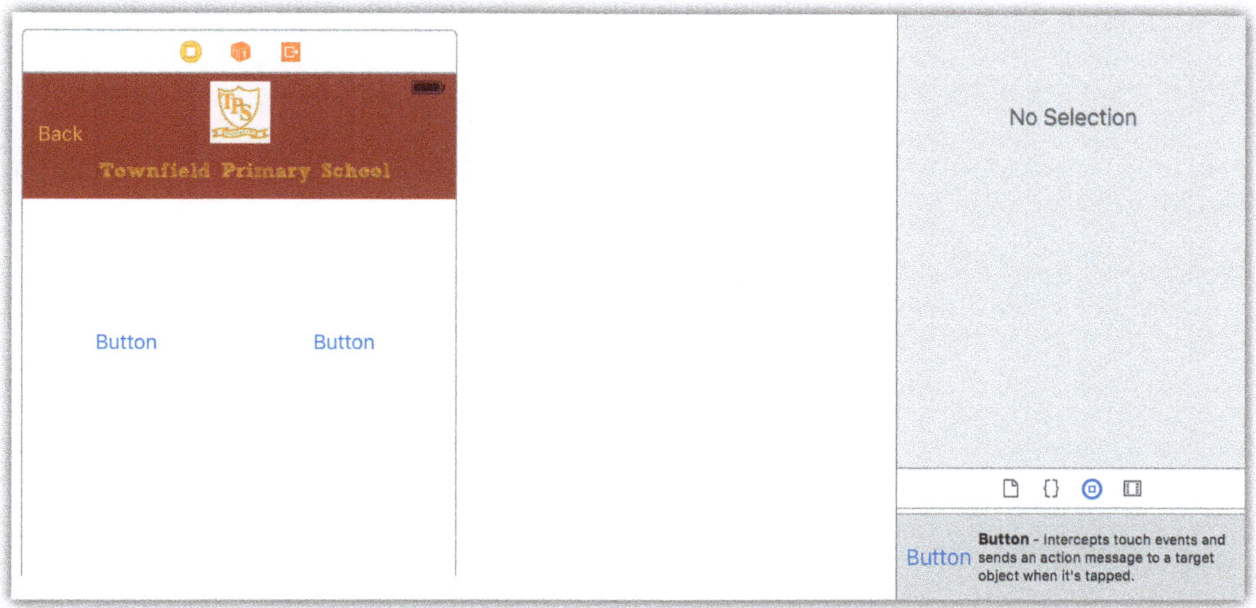

7.09

Select the button on the left. Then press the shield button in the Utilities pane to open the *Attributes* inspector.

Under *Title* delete the word 'Button' and next to *Image*, start to type the name of your *Call Us* button and it should autocomplete. Press *return* and your button should change.

Repeat this to change the title of the other button to *Email Us*.

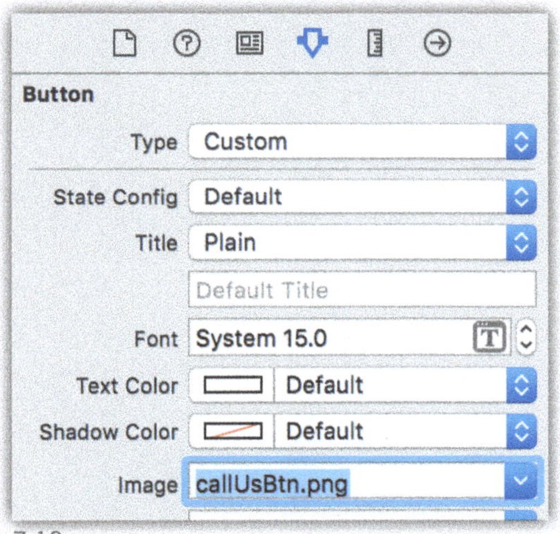

7.10

If all has gone well, your screen should now look like this:

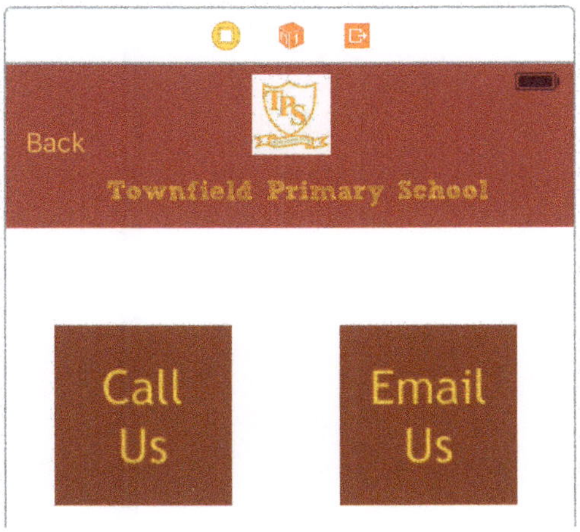

7.11

Now we need to add the code to make those two buttons do the things we want them to.

One key thing we have to do to send emails from our app is add something called a *Framework*. I've talked about these before. They are files that *Xcode* doesn't automatically include in apps (to save space), so you have to choose to add them.

We need to add the *MessageUI* Framework to our app so that it can handle the code to send emails.

We haven't done this yet so this procedure is new. The first thing I'd like you to do is select your project in the *Navigator* pane. This is the blue icon at the top of the list of files:

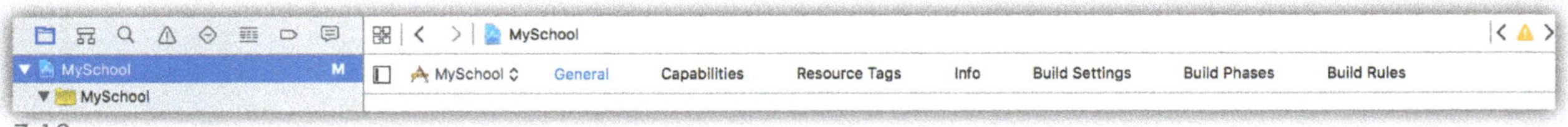

7.12

The *Editor* pane will change and you'll see a new menu appear at the top of it. I'd like you to select *Build Phases*. This the second button from the right.

You'll then see the *Editor* pane change to this:

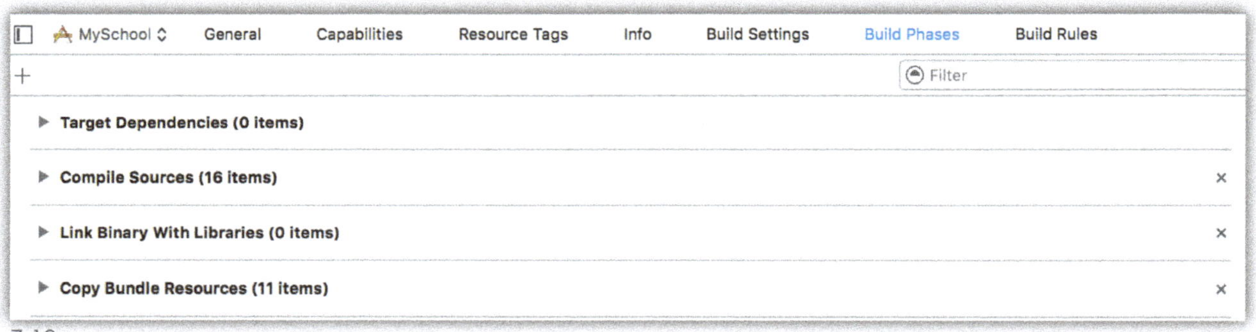

7.13

Click on the small arrow next to Link Binary With Libraries. This will expand the screen:

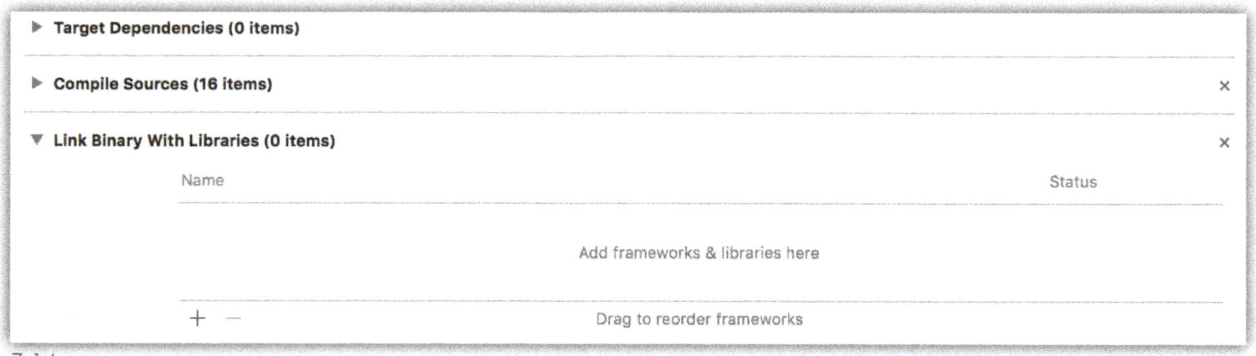

7.14

At the bottom of this section, you'll see a plus and minus sign. Press the '+' sign. A pop-up menu will appear:

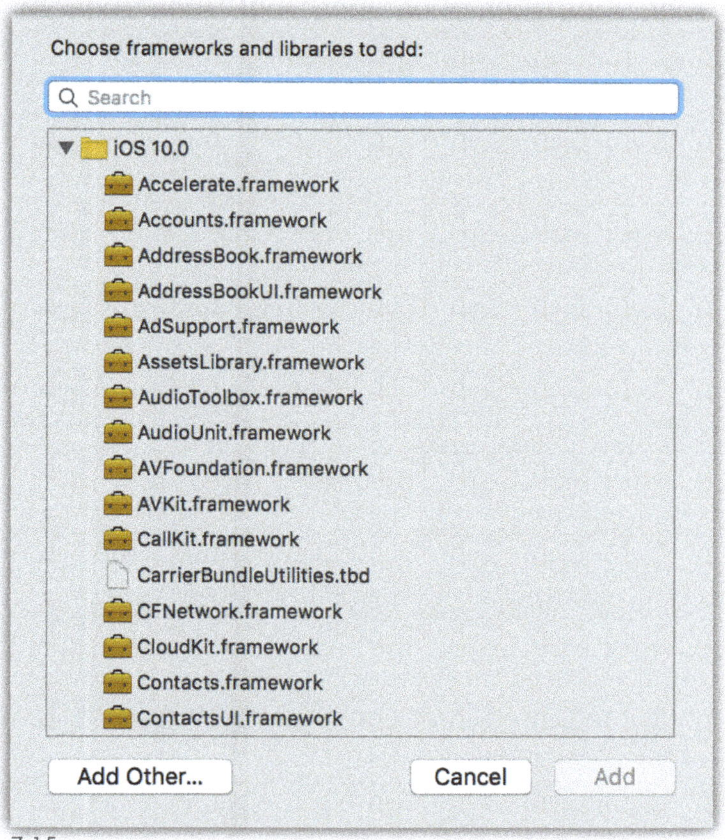

7.15

In the search bar at the top, type 'Message'. Most of the frameworks will disappear and you'll be left with just a couple.

Select the one called *MessageUI.framework* and then press the blue *Add* button.

And that's it. You've added the framework to your project. So let's get on with adding the code to make use of it.

In the *Navigator* pane, select *ContactUsViewController.h*.

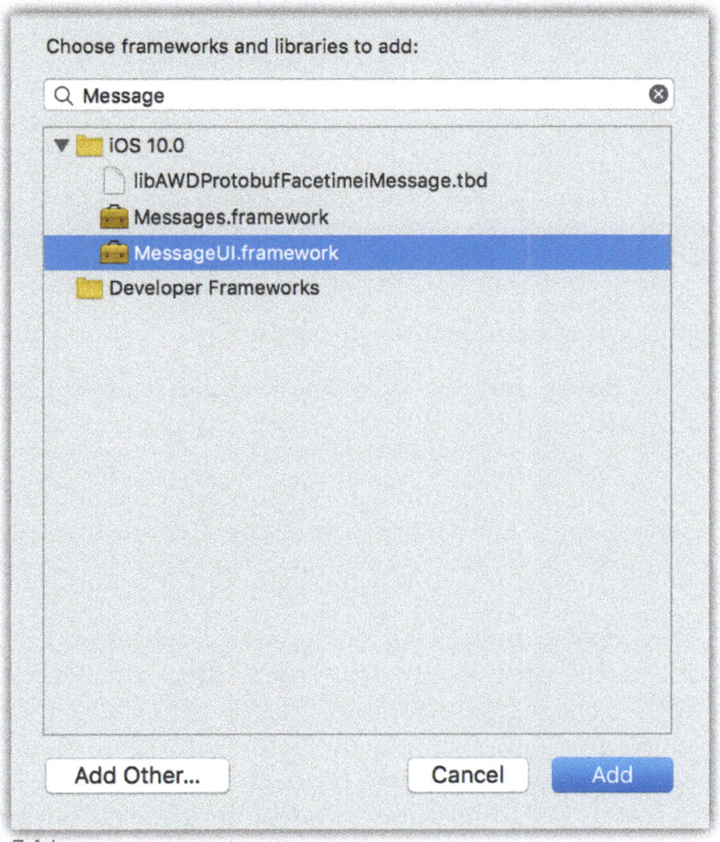

7.16

The first thing to add is a file we're going to import from the framework we've just added:

```
#import <UIKit/UIKit.h>
#import <MessageUI/MessageUI.h>

@interface ContactUsViewController : UIViewController

@end
```

7.17

Finally, we need to add a bit of code at the end of the *@interface* line:

```
@interface ContactUsViewController : UIViewController <MFMailComposeViewControllerDelegate,
    MFMessageComposeViewControllerDelegate>

@end
```

7.18

This time, we don't need any swirly brackets as we're not declaring anything in our .h file on this screen.

It's time to add the code to *ContactUsViewController.m*, so open up the file.

Let's add our *viewDidLoad* method first. Add this underneath the *@implementation* line:

```
- (void)viewDidLoad
{
    [super viewDidLoad];
}
```

7.19

Next, let's add the code to phone your school. This will be an *IBAction* method as it will be called when you press the *Call Us* button:

```
- (IBAction)callSchool:(id)sender{

    [[UIApplication sharedApplication] openURL:[NSURL URLWithString:@"+44151111111"]];
}
```

7.20

Obviously, you'll need to change the number. Notice the format of the number. We add the code for the UK (+44) and drop the '0' from the area code.

A word of warning, this code will run when you press the *Call Us* button so it will instantly open the phone app and dial. Best practice would be to provide the user with a confirmation box, so they can cancel calling if they'd prefer.

Also, if you were building an app for an iPad, you'd need to handle the fact iPads can't make calls. But as our app is just for phones, we don't need to worry.

Regardless, we do need to add the code to send an email. I've put comments this to help you understand it a bit better:

```
- (IBAction)sendMail:(id)sender{

    //start the email composer
    MFMailComposeViewController *picker = [[MFMailComposeViewController alloc] init];
    picker.mailComposeDelegate = self;

    //set the subject of the email
    [picker setSubject:@"Contact from Townfield Primary School's app"];

    //set the recipient of the email
    NSArray *toRecipients = [NSArray arrayWithObject:@"schooloffice@townfieldprimaryschool.sch.uk"];
    [picker setToRecipients:toRecipients];

    //show the email composer to the user
    [self presentViewController:picker animated:YES completion:nil];


}
```

7.21

You will need to change the strings in red to match your own school's details. We then need to add a bit of code to deal with errors, for example if the user's internet fails and the email isn't sent.

Add this *method* directly below the *sendMail* method:

```
- (void)mailComposeController:(MFMailComposeViewController*)controller didFinishWithResult:(MFMailComposeResult)result
    error:(NSError*)error
{
    if(error) {

        UIAlertController *alert = [UIAlertController
                                    alertControllerWithTitle:@"Error"
                                    message:@"Unable to send your email. Please try again later."
                                    preferredStyle:UIAlertControllerStyleAlert];

        UIAlertAction *ok = [UIAlertAction
                             actionWithTitle:@"OK"
                             style:UIAlertActionStyleDefault
                             handler:^(UIAlertAction * action)
                             {
                                 [alert dismissViewControllerAnimated:YES completion:nil];
                                 [self dismissViewControllerAnimated:YES completion:nil];

                             }];

        [alert addAction:ok];
         [self presentViewController:alert animated:YES completion:nil];


    }
    [self dismissViewControllerAnimated:YES completion:nil];
    return;
}
```

7.22

You can probably get the gist of this code. If there's an error, a pop-up tells the user. If not, the email sends and the email composer disappears.

Let's add the code to go back and then we can link the actions to our buttons and test it.

So, under the last method, add the following code:

```
- (IBAction)back:(id)sender{
    [self dismissViewControllerAnimated:YES completion:nil];
}
```

7.23

Go back to the *Main.storyboard* file and find your *Contact Us View Controller*.

Two-finger drag from the Back button to the yellow circle with the white square and select back:. Do the same with the *Call Us* button and select *callSchool*: and then repeat with the *Email Us* button and select *sendMail*:.

Finally, two-finger press anywhere that isn't touching a *View Controller* in the *Editor* pane. You should see this menu:

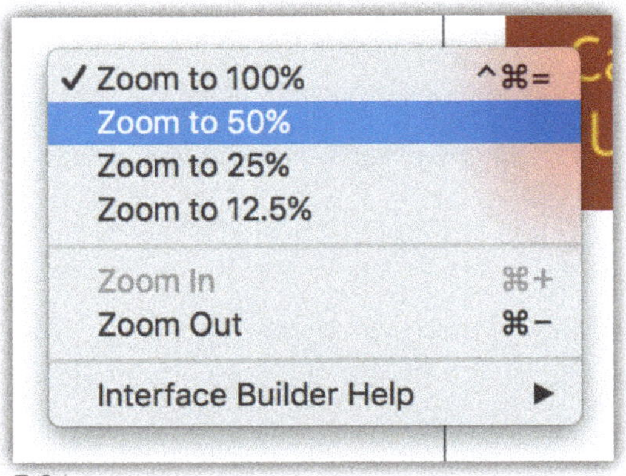

7.24

Select *Zoom to 50%* and you will be able to see all of your screens so far:

7.25

Go to the *Contact Us* button on your home screen – but don't click it – and two-finger drag from the button to your *Contact Us View Controller*.

You should see this pop-up:

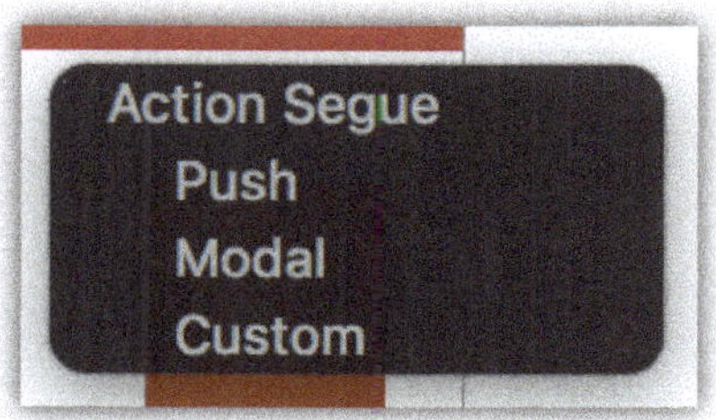

7.26

Choose *Modal*. The box will disappear.

You're ready to test your app. Go ahead and press the *Play* button. Go to the *Contact Us* screen and test out the features.

You'll notice you can't test the phoning feature. The simulator won't let you, but it should let you test the email feature.

You may find that the email composer flashes up and goes off again. Don't worry, this isn't your fault, it's a bug in *Xcode*. You'll know if you're seeing the bug as you'll see this error message:

7.27

Just press *Ignore* and don't worry about it. When we test it on a device, it will be fine.

Next up, we'll be making our *Find Us* screen which adds a map to show your school's location.

You'll need your school's postcode for the next chapter.

http://www.alanpeat.com/build-an-app/Chapter7

CHAPTER EIGHT
CREATING THE FIND US SCREEN

It's time to add our map. This is reasonably straight-forward but we're going to use a little bit of third-party code.

Go to **http://tinyurl.com/mapkitfiles** and download the two files (*DisplayMap.h* and *DisplayMap.m*) or download the one zip folder. Again, it's a good idea to get these files downloaded prior to asking the children to repeat these steps. It will speed the development up a great deal!

Once you've got them on your computer, drag them to your *Xcode* project beneath *ContactUsViewController.m* in the *Navigator* pane. Make sure you tick the *Copy items if needed* box:

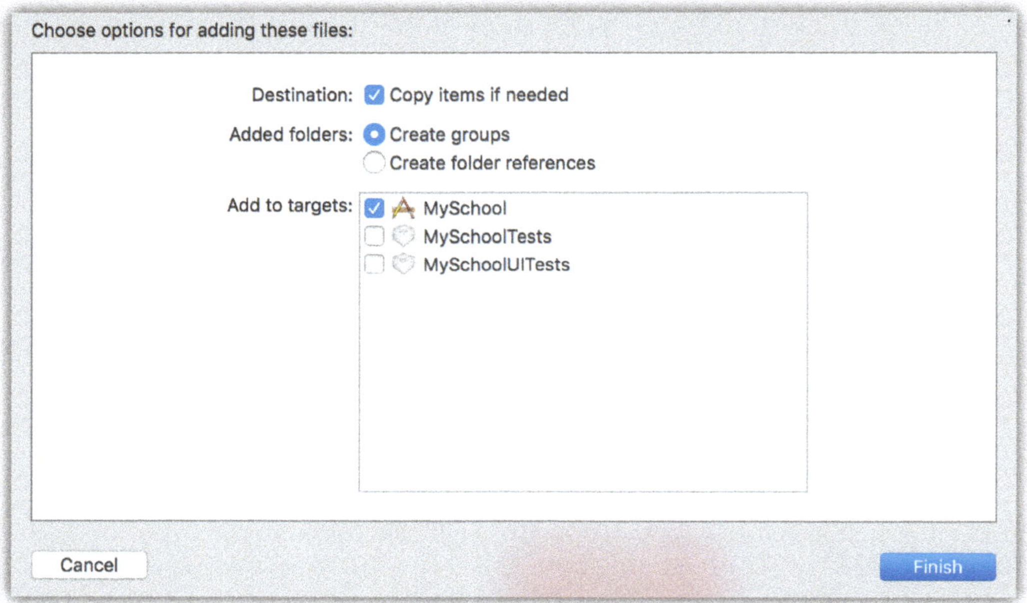

8.01

Your *Navigator* pane should look like this now:

8.02

We won't need to touch these files again, so just forget about them! But we do now need to add a new *framework*.

This is just what we did for the *MessageUI* framework.

So select your project in the *Navigator* pane. This is the blue icon at the top of the list of files:

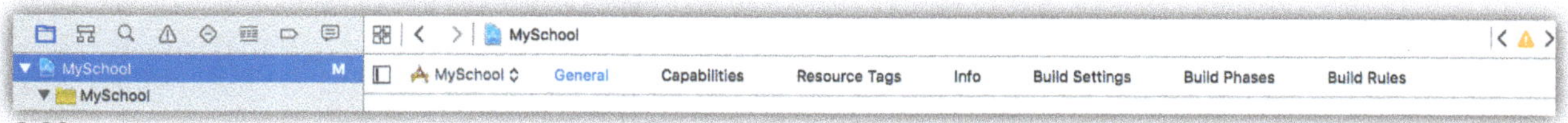

8.03

The *Editor* pane will change and you'll see that menu appear at the top of it. Select *Build Phases* – the second button from the right.

You'll then see the *Editor* pane change to this:

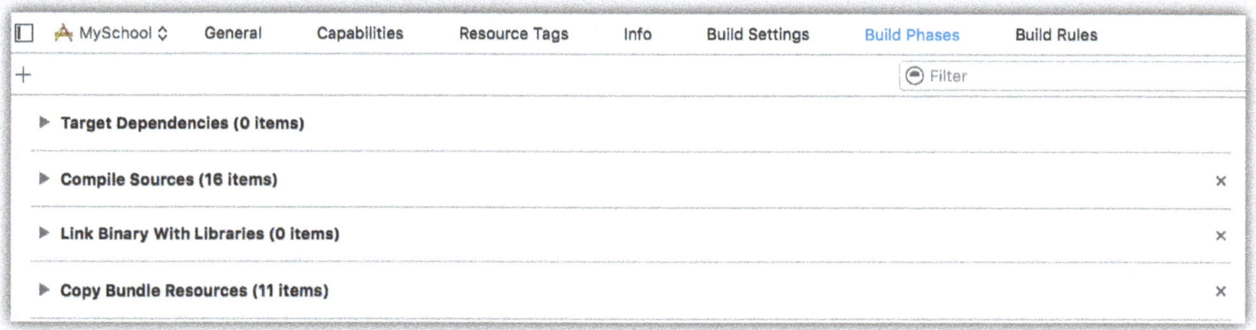

8.04

Click on the small arrow next to *Link Binary With Libraries*:

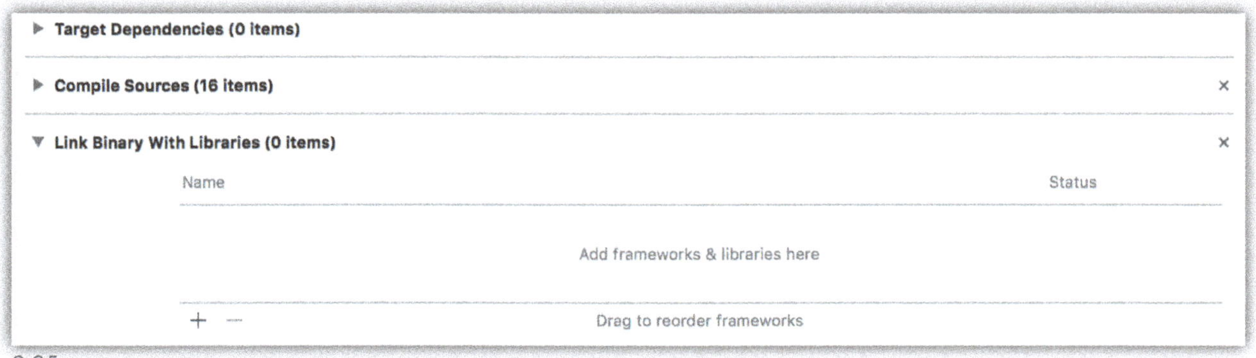

8.05

Press the '+' sign to bring up pop-up box:

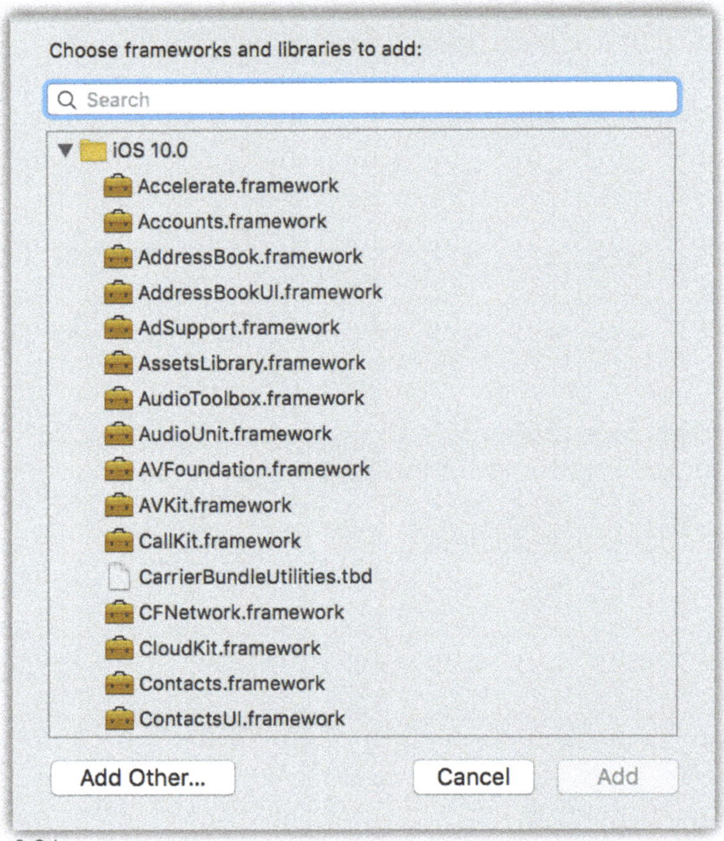

8.06

In the search bar at the top, type 'Map'. Most of the frameworks will disappear and you'll be left with the one we want.

Select the *MapKit.framework* and then press the *Add* button:

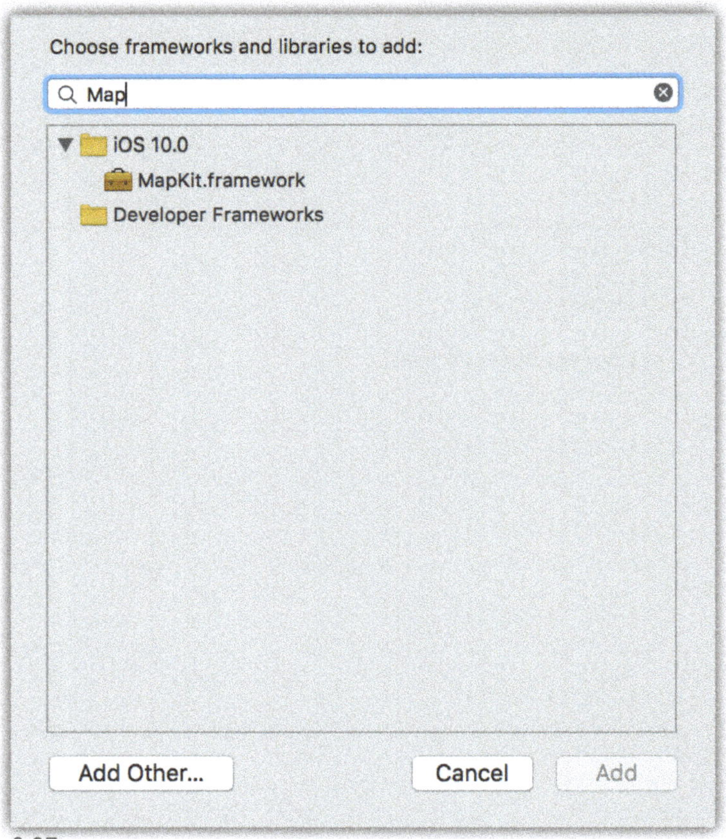

8.07

Now we need to make a new *class* to hold the code for our map. We've done this a fair few times so it should be easy.

Click on *DisplayMap.m* and then two-finger press to bring up the pop-up menu. Select *New File*, press *Next* and then enter the name for your new class: 'MapViewController'. Press *Next* again and then *Create*. Your new files should appear underneath *DisplayMap.m*:

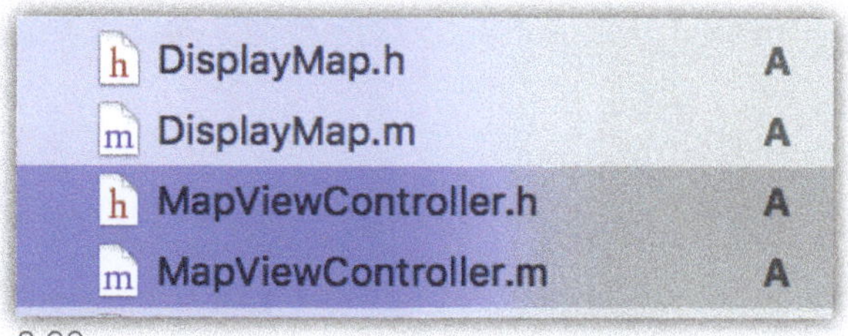

8.08

Let's build our *user interface* before we add some code.

Go to *Main.storyboard* and find some space next to *Contact Us View Controller*. Drag a new *View Controller* from the *Object Library* to the *Editor* pane and move it so that it is tidily arranged:

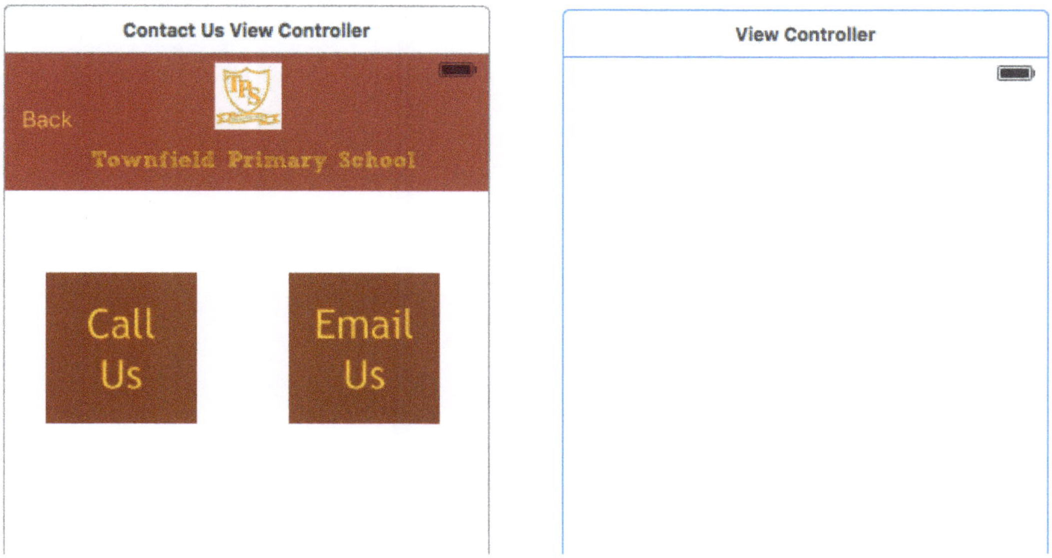

8.09

As we've done before, click on the new *View Controller* so that these buttons appear:

8.10

Select the yellow circle with the square in it. Then go to the *Utilities* pane, and select the third button from the left to open the *Identity inspector*:

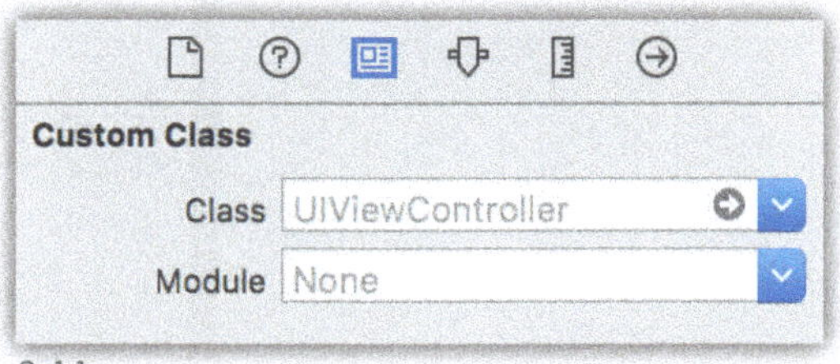

8.11

By now, you should know what to do next. In the *Class* box, type *MapViewController*. As always, it will attempt to autocomplete. Press *return*.

Next you need to copy the header image and the *Back* button from somewhere. I suggest using the *Contact Us View Controller* as it's closest.

Copy by using *Cmd* and 'C' and paste with *Cmd* and 'V':

8.12

We need to add a couple of other objects to our screen: a map and a segmented button so that we can flick between satellite view, hybrid or map view.

Find the *Map Kit View* in the *Object Library*:

8.13

Drag the Map Kit View onto your View Controller. Make it fill most of the screen, but leave a little bit of room at the bottom like this:

8.14

Then find the *Segmented Control* in the *Object Library*:

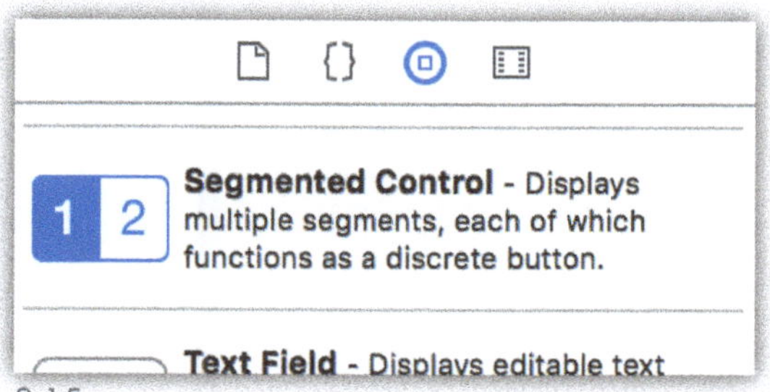

8.15

Drag this underneath your *Map Kit View*:

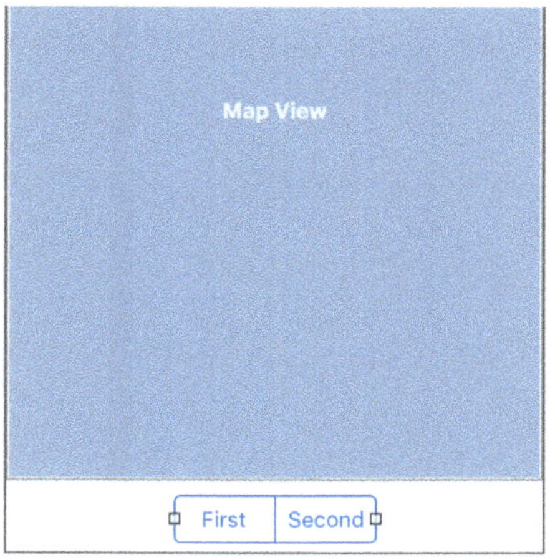

8.16

As you can see, this button has two options, but we want three. Make sure the *Segmented Control* is selected and then press the shield button in the *Utilities* pane to open up the *Attributes inspector*:

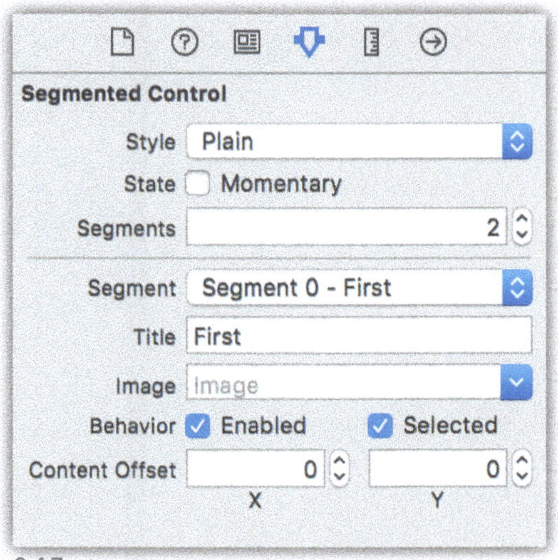

8.17

Find the box that is called *Segments*. You'll notice that it currently has a '2' in it. Change that to a '3'.

Beneath *Segments*, there is a drop-down menu called *Segment* (without the 's' on the end). Once you've changed the number of segments to '3', selecting the drop down menu of 'Segment' will look like this:

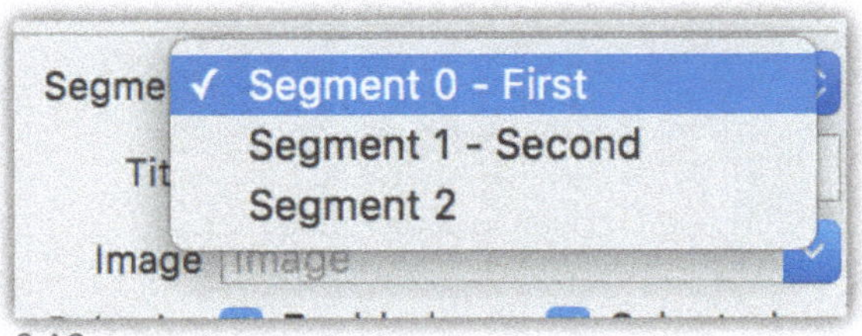

8.18

This gives you the opportunity to toggle between each segment and make changes to its properties. Note that the first segment is called 'Segment 0' and not '1'. This is because computers generally start counting from '0' instead of '1'.

Select *Segment 0* so that the drop-down menu disappears. Underneath, in the box labelled *Title*, change *First* to *Map*. Press *return*.

Repeat this process and change the *Segment 1 - Second title* to *Satellite*. Press *return*.

Finally, select *Segment 2* and add the title *Hybrid*. Press *return*.

Go back to your *Segmented Control* on your *View Controller* and make it wider so that it can accommodate the titles:

8.19

Next, we need to tell *Xcode* about our *Map View* and our *Segmented Control*, so press the two interlinking circles in the top right of *Xcode*:

8.20

Your *Editor* pane should have split into two parts. You may need to select *MapViewController.h* at the top of the right-hand side of the split pane:

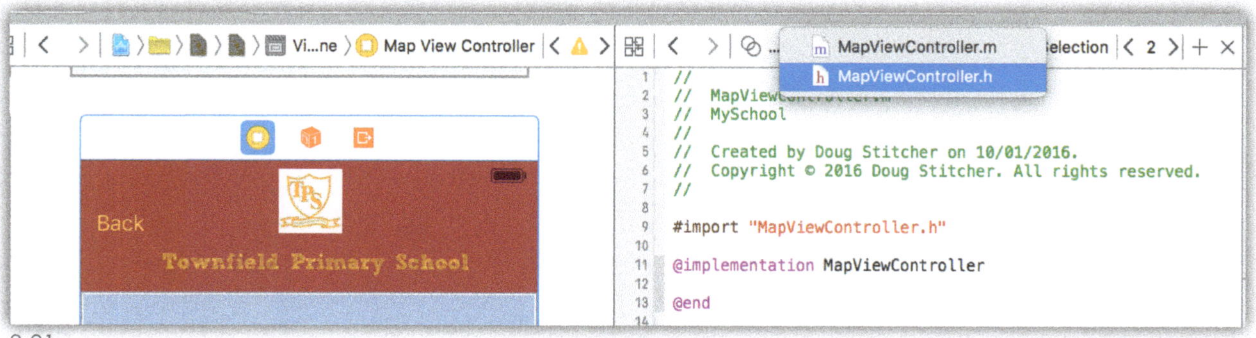

8.21

Do make sure that the .h file on the right-hand side is the right file. You can be sure it is the .h file by checking this line:

```
@interface MapViewController : UIViewController
```

8.22

If the purple writing says '@interface', it is your .h file - if it says *@implementation*, it is your .m file.

In the .h file add the following code:

```
#import <UIKit/UIKit.h>
#import <MapKit/MapKit.h>

@class DisplayMap;

@interface MapViewController : UIViewController <MKMapViewDelegate> {

}

@end
```

8.23

Your code won't all fit on the lines like mine does but don't worry. Type it as you see it. It doesn't do anything other than set our screen up for using the features of the *Map Framework*.

Now, we're going to add our two *user interface* items; the *Map View* and the *Segmented Control* in the same way we did earlier.

Go to the *Map View* and two-finger drag it in-between the swirly brackets in the .h file to the right: call it 'mapView':

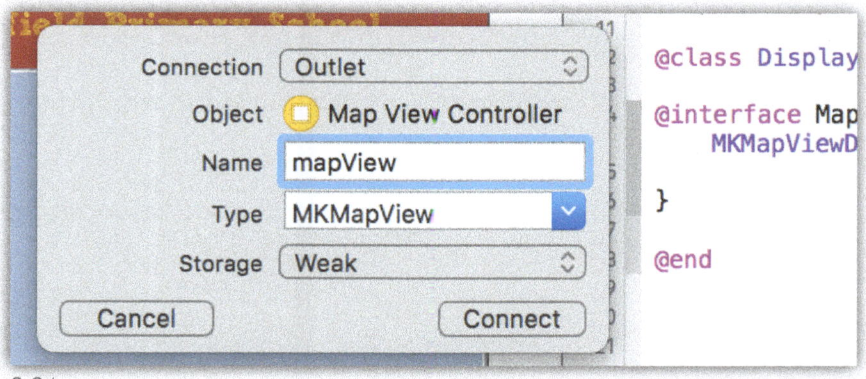

8.24

The code should look like this:

```
@interface MapViewController : UIViewController <
    MKMapViewDelegate> {

    __weak IBOutlet MKMapView *mapView;
    __weak IBOutlet UISegmentedControl *mapTypeBtn;
}
```

8.25

For the time being, we're done with editing our user *interface* so press the button to the left of the interlinking circles:

8.26

That will exit the split-screen mode (actually known as the *Assistant editor*) but your storyboard will still be visible. So select *MapViewContoller.m* from the *Navigator* pane and we can get on with editing our code.

There's not too much code to add here. Start by importing the *DisplayMap* files you downloaded earlier. Add this line to the top of the file:

```
#import "MapViewController.h"
#import "DisplayMap.h"
```

8.27

Now add our *viewDidLoad* method. Put this between the *@implementation* line and *@ end*:

```
- (void)viewDidLoad {
    [super viewDidLoad];
    self.title = @"Find Us";
    [mapView setMapType:MKMapTypeStandard];
    [mapView setZoomEnabled:YES];
    [mapView setScrollEnabled:YES];
    MKCoordinateRegion region = { {0.0, 0.0 }, { 0.0, 0.0 } };

    //set the co-ordinates of your school:
    region.center.latitude = 00.00;
    region.center.longitude =  00.00;

    region.span.longitudeDelta = 0.01f;
    region.span.latitudeDelta = 0.01f;
    [mapView setRegion:region animated:YES];

    [mapView setDelegate:self];

    DisplayMap *ann = [[DisplayMap alloc] init];

    //set the titles of the labels
    ann.title = @"Your School Name";
    ann.subtitle = @"School Lane, School Town SC40 0LS";
    ann.coordinate = region.center;
    [mapView addAnnotation:ann];
    [mapView selectAnnotation:ann animated:YES];
}
```

8.30

The preceding code starts up the map and sets the longitude and latitude information required to show your school.

Find the lines *region.center.latitude = 00.00;* and *region.center.longitude = 00.00;'* We need to add our co-ordinates there.

To do this, go to **http://www.latlong.net/** and enter your school postcode:

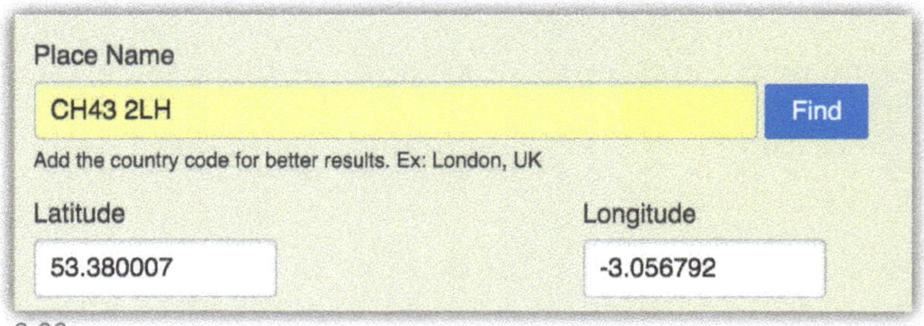

8.28

You may wish to obtain these figures for your students before you begin this coding with them.

Copy and paste those figures under the *Latitude* and *Longitude* boxes into your code. For example, if you were adding my school, those two lines would look like this:

```
//set the co-ordinates of your school:
region.center.latitude = 53.380007;
region.center.longitude =  -3.056792;
```

8.29

The only other change you will need to make to your *viewDidLoad* method is to add your school name and address to replace the red code that says '*Your School Name* and *School Lane, School Town SC40 0LS*' with your information.

Let's add the code to control our *Segmented Control*. This is an *IBAction*, so we will need to link it up. Add this beneath your *viewDidLoad* method:

```
- (IBAction)changeType:(id)sender{
    if(mapTypeBtn.selectedSegmentIndex==0){
        mapView.mapType=MKMapTypeStandard;
    }
    else if (mapTypeBtn.selectedSegmentIndex==1){
        mapView.mapType=MKMapTypeSatellite;
    }
    else if (mapTypeBtn.selectedSegmentIndex==2){
        mapView.mapType=MKMapTypeHybrid;
    }
}
```

8.31

As you can probably tell, this code loads the right type of map after we press the *Segmented Control*.

Lastly, we need to add another *back* method. You can either copy and paste it from one of your other classes or copy it directly from below:

```
- (IBAction)back:(id)sender{
    [self dismissViewControllerAnimated:YES completion:nil];
}
```

8.32

Next we need to head back to *Main.storyboard* and go to our *Map View Controller*:

8.33

Two-finger drag from your *Back* button to the yellow circle with the square in it. You should be used to this by now. In the pop-up box that appears, select *back*:

Repeat with the *Segmented Control* and select *changeType*:

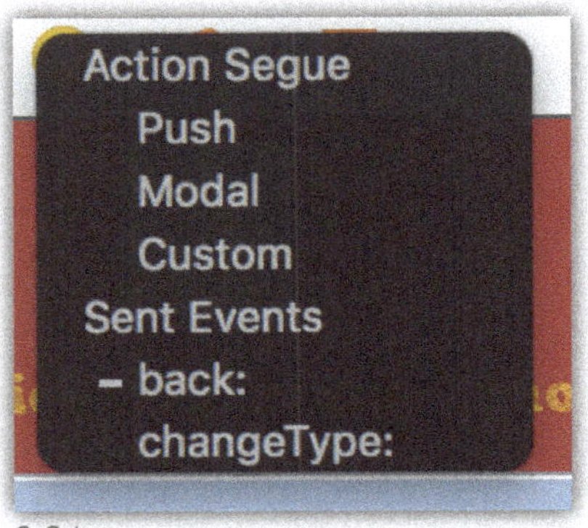

8.34

Last thing to do is link our *Find Us* button on the home screen to this *View Controller*. Zoom out by two-finger clicking anywhere on the *Editor* pane away from the view controllers, and select *Zoom* to 50%.

You should be able to two-finger drag – without clicking on the button first – from the *Find Us* button to the *Map View Controller*:

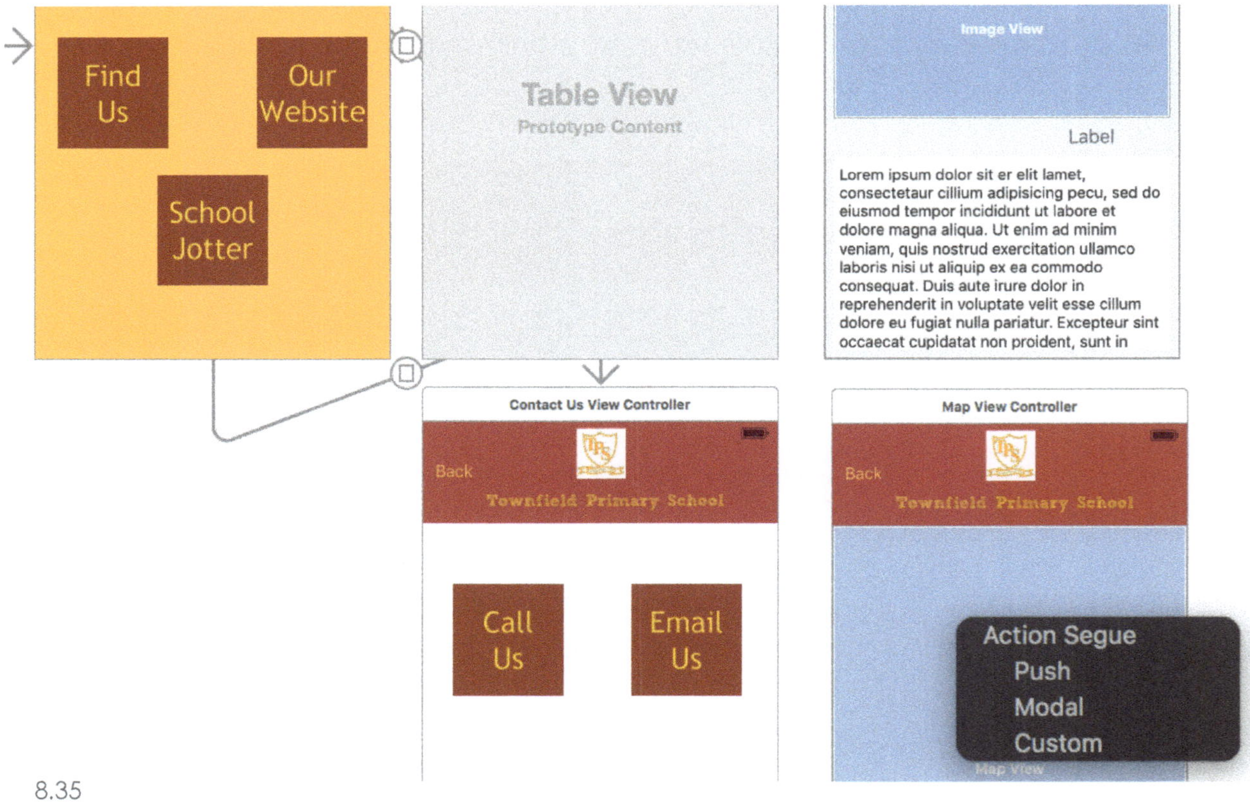

8.35

Select *Modal*. The pop-up will disappear and we're ready to test the app.

Press our favourite *Play* button. If all has gone to plan, you should be able to press the *Find*

Us button on the app and load a map that shows your school. Try out the *Segmented Control* to make sure it works and then test your *Back* button. If any of the buttons don't work, go back the storyboard and check you've linked them correctly with the *IBAction* methods.

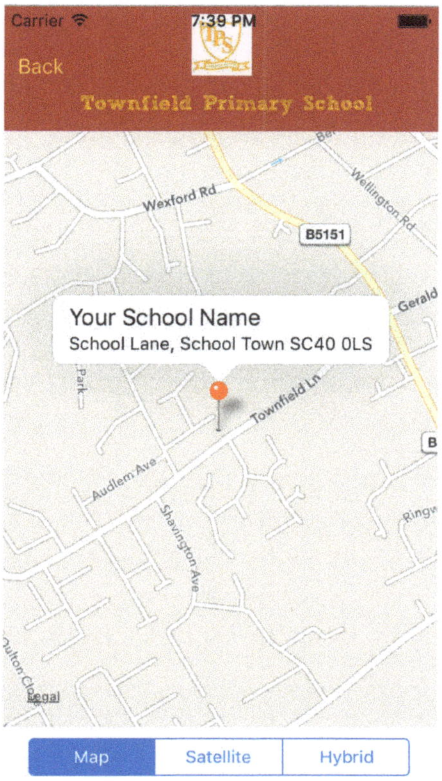

8.36

You have successfully added a map view to your app. Hopefully, you'll have found that it's getting easier as we go.

By now, your students should be getting used to the model, emulate approach that you will need to adopt to get them to reproduce the steps involved.

Next up, we need to add a screen to display our school website.

http://www.alanpeat.com/build-an-app/Chapter8

CHAPTER NINE
CREATING THE 'OUR WEBSITE' SCREEN

So far you've had to work hard building difficult screens and adding many lines of complicated code. The good news is that in this chapter we will be letting third-party code to do a lot of the work.

We're going to use the freely available code from **https://github.com/TransitApp/SVWebViewController** by Sam Vermette. You can download the files you need from there directly but to make things easier, I've put everything you need in a *Dropbox* folder at **http://tinyurl.com/webViewFiles**. Once again, get these files downloaded and share with the students before starting to model it.

Go there and download the *zip file* to your computer. Double-click it to unpack it. You should see this:

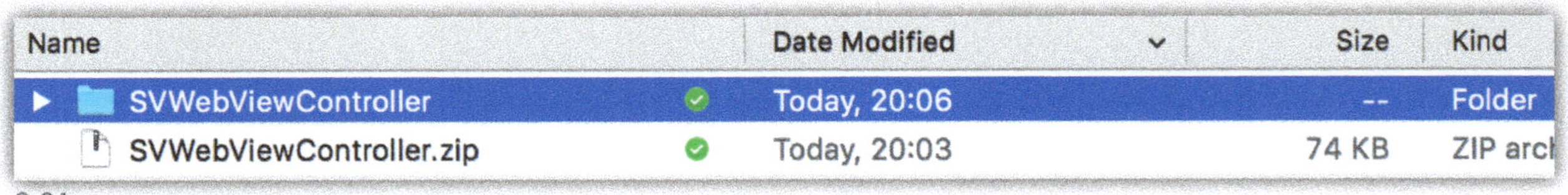

9.01

It's the blue folder called *SVWebViewController* that we want to add to our *Xcode* project, so drag the whole folder to your *Navigator* pane above the file *AppDelegate.h*. Be careful not to put it in the *RSS Feed Reader* group. You should see this:

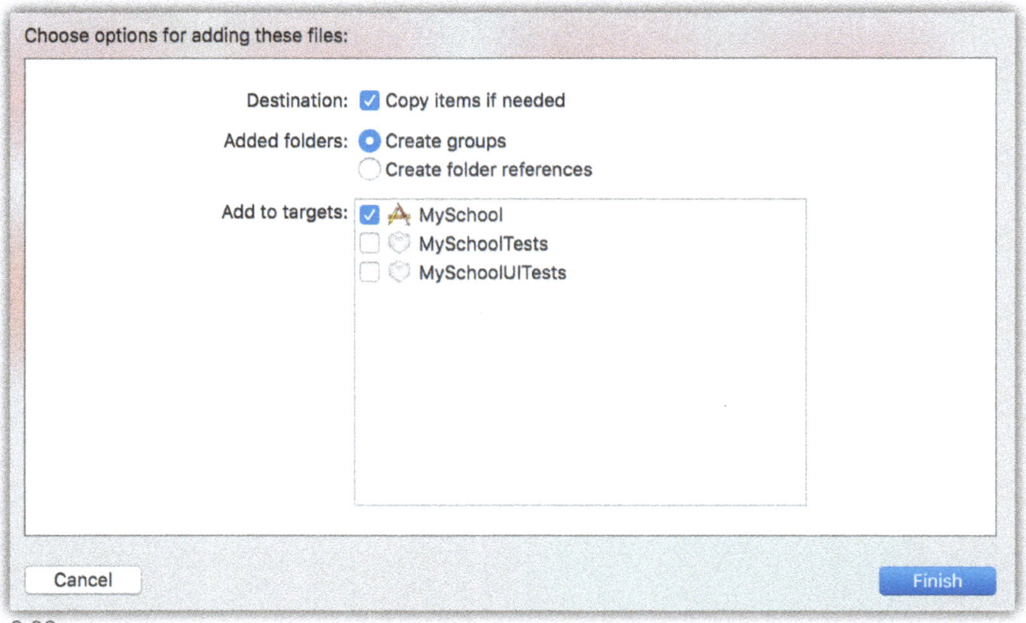

9.02

Make sure you tick the *Copy items if needed* option and that *Create groups* is also checked. Press *Finish* and the folder should appear as a group in the *Navigator* pane:

9.03

Next up, we need to go to a file we haven't really touched in a long time: *ViewController.m*. Head over there and add this line to the top of the code:

```
#import "ViewController.h"
#import "SVModalWebViewController.h"
```

9.04

Our third-party code brings up a screen that loads a website. This is useful as it saves us lots of time adding buttons and code. But it doesn't work properly with our storyboard. So far, every screen we load we have joined by dragging from the button to the appropriate *View Controller*. But we can't do that with this one.

Instead, we're going to add an *IBAction* method to *ViewController.m* that we will link to our *Our Website* button.

Here's the code:

```
- (IBAction)loadWebsite:(id)sender {
    SVModalWebViewController *webViewController = [[SVModalWebViewController alloc] initWithAddress:@"http://
        www.townfieldprimaryschool.co.uk/"];
    [self presentViewController:webViewController animated:YES completion:NULL];
}
```

9.05

All this does is load the *Web View Controller* that was kindly provided for free by Sam Vermette.

Last thing to do is to link this *IBAction* method to our *Our Website* button. Go to *Main.storyboard* and find the home screen:

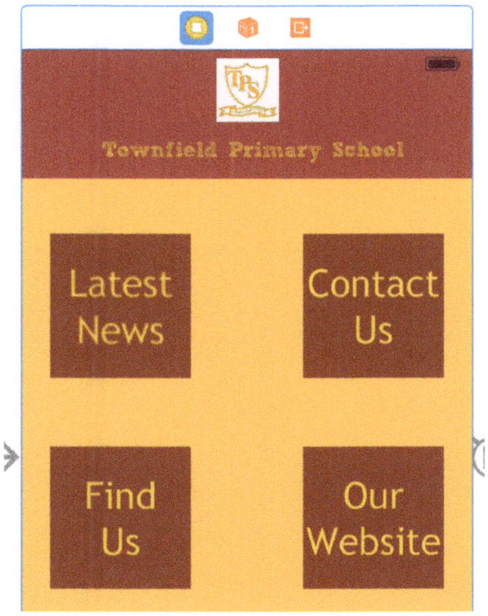

9.06

Two-finger drag from the *Our Website* button to the (you guessed it) yellow circle with the white square. On the pop-up menu, select *loadWebsite*:

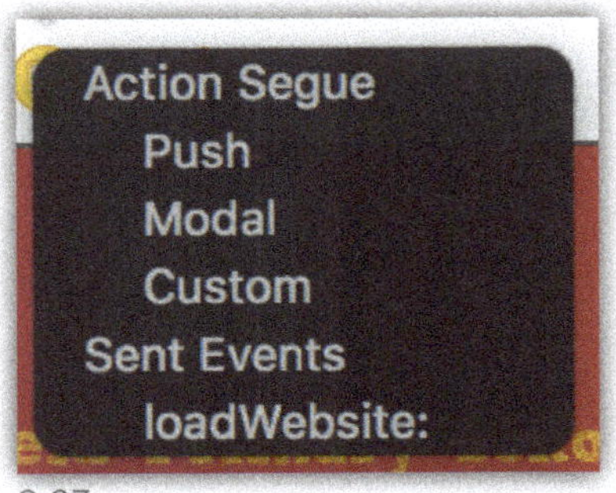

9.07

The black box will disappear and you're ready to test it.

Go ahead and press the *Play* button.

Make sure you press the *Our Website* button. The *Web View* will load perfectly but it doesn't matter how long you wait, the website won't load.

Go back to *Xcode* and have a look at the debugger:

```
2016-01-11 20:26:20.132 MySchool[18361:7763862] App Transport
Security has blocked a cleartext HTTP (http://) resource load
since it is insecure. Temporary exceptions can be configured
via your app's Info.plist file.
```

9.08

Basically, as a security measure our app is preventing us from loading a website.

So there is one last thing to do. Go to the *Navigator* pane and find a file called *Info.plist*:

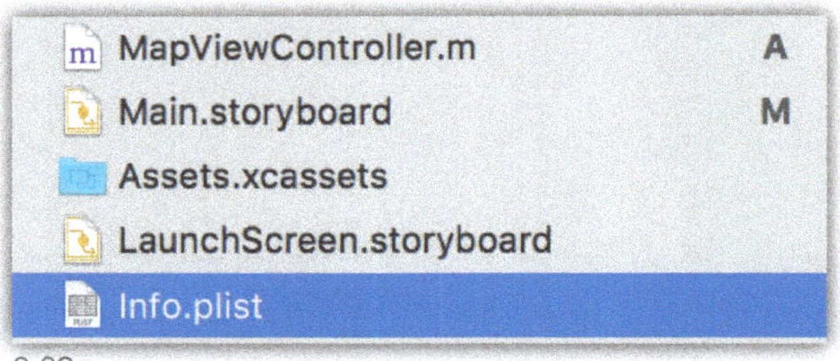

9.09

Select it and it will open in the *Editor* pane. We will use this file later on before we submit our app to the App Store and I'll talk about it a bit more then. For now, all you need to know is that this file is used for settings for our app, like its version number and the name to display on the device under the icon.

Two-finger click in the empty space under the rows of information in the *Editor* pane:

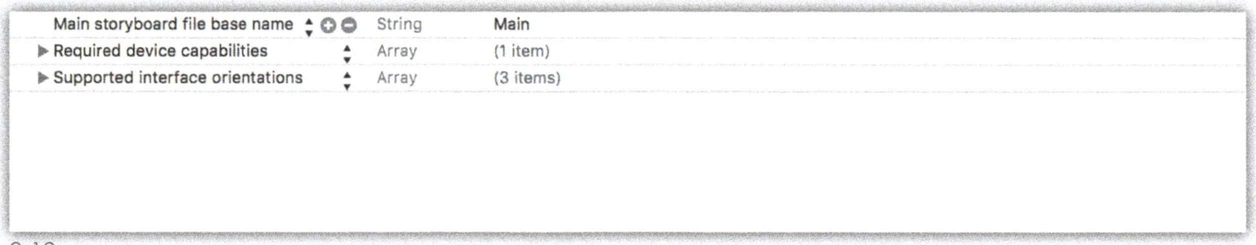

9.10

This pop-up menu should appear:

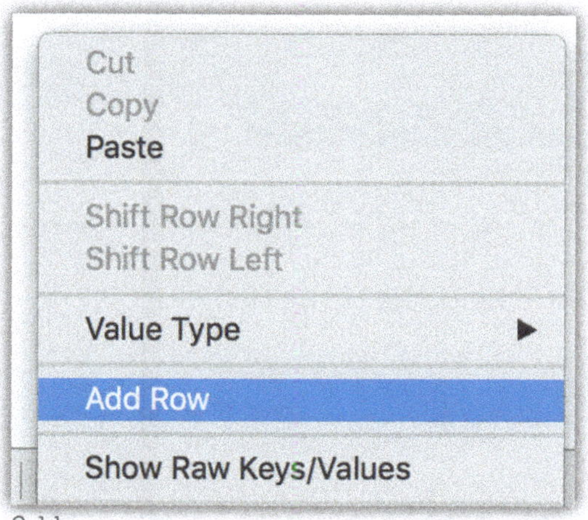

9.11

Select *Add Row* and a scary looking drop-down menu will appear:

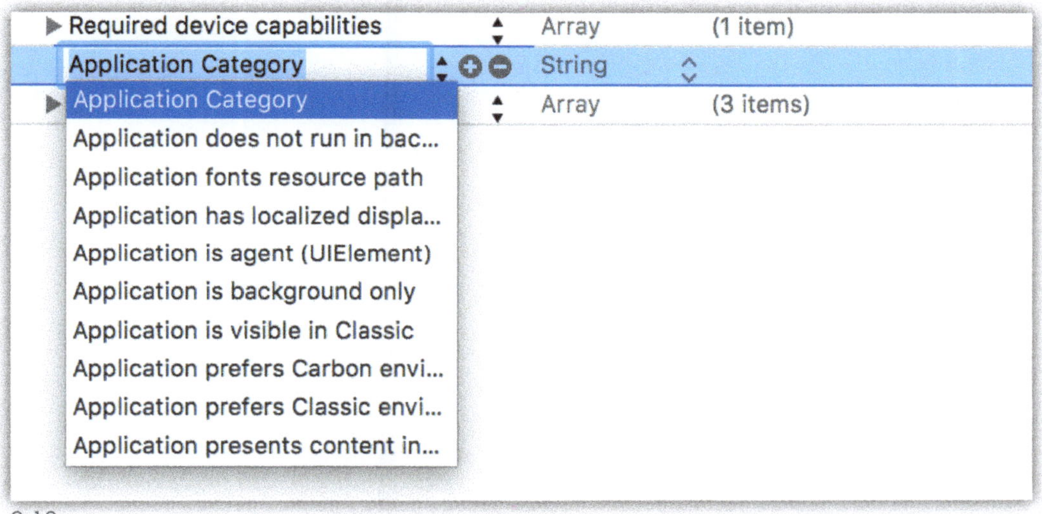

9.12

In the text box, type *App Transport* and the box should autocomplete to say *App Transport Security Settings* – make sure you use the capital letters. Press *return*.

You'll see a new row added to your *Info.plist* file:

9.13

Make sure that *App Transport Security Settings* is selected. It should be highlighted in blue:

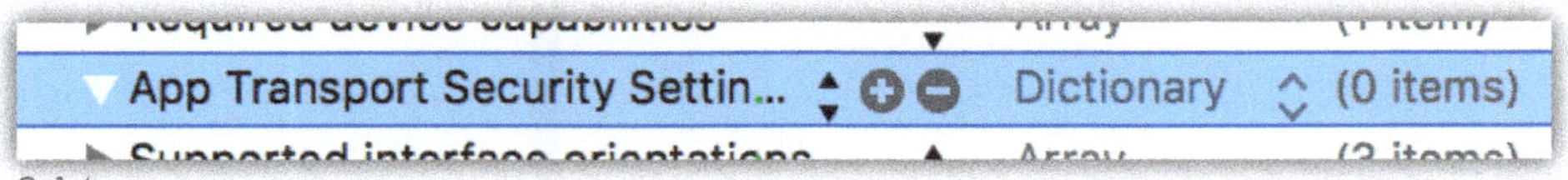

9.14

Press the '+' sign in a circle. This menu will appear:

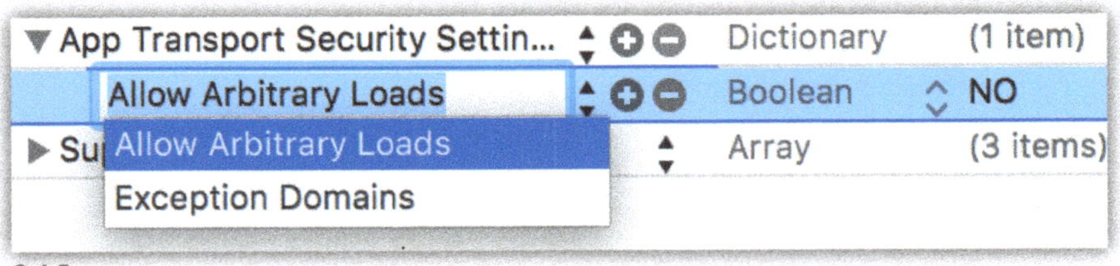

9.15

Select *Allow Arbitrary Loads* so the rows look like this:

9.16

Next, press on the little arrows to the far right of the word *NO* and select *YES* from the drop-down menu:

9.17

What you've done is given the app permission to load websites. So press *Cmd* and 'S' to save your *Info.plist* file and now it's time to test the app.

Press the magic and glorious *Play* button.

And there you should have it.

9.18

One fully functional website screen. And it really didn't take very long. I don't want you thinking we cheated. We didn't. We did something lots of developers do all the time. We took some freely available code and utilised it to speed up our app development.

Now we have one screen left to create: our *School Jotter* page.

In the next chapter, I will talk you through it. We will need to add some third-party code but we will also need to design our *user interface*.

http://www.alanpeat.com/build-an-app/Chapter9

CHAPTER TEN
CREATING THE SCHOOL JOTTER

I haven't really mentioned the *School Jotter* so far beyond the fact that its main purpose is to get our app through the Apple App Approval process.

What this essentially means is that you don't need to add this section but, if you don't, there is a possibility that those nice folks at Apple might reject your app. To be fair, there's always that possibility whether you add this screen or not.

However, as a general rule, Apple are slightly more lenient towards schools publishing their own apps. At this point, I would explain the Apple Review process to the children and how Apple run a tight ship. You may even want to show them the Apple Review Guidelines to demonstrate some of the strict rules. You'll need to remember to only show the appropriate ones to the pupils!

Just to be on the safe side in terms of Apple's review process, let's add this extra feature. It's fun.

When we planned out our app earlier in the book, we didn't plan this page so let's have a look at what we're aiming for.

Here is a screenshot of the final screen:

10.001

It's a simple note-taking feature. It allows the user to draw on the screen as well as type notes, save them and send them to someone in an email.

If you look at the top, we have a bar containing seven buttons: a *Done* button, three colours to choose from, an *Undo* button, a *Clear* button and a camera button to save the image that you draw.

On the bottom bar, we have a *Take Notes* button. That's the pencil on paper image. We also have an arrow, which the user will press to send their notes via email, and a *Save Notes* button.

In order to create this screen, I'm going to need you to add four files of mine and I'll also give you the images you will need for the button and the background.

Once again, I'd get these files downloaded before modelling this process to the children.

All the files we need are at **http://tinyurl.com/SchoolJotter** so head over there. What you'll see will vary depending upon whether you are signed in to *Dropbox* or not. But either way, you will see the list of files.

You can either download them individually, by right-clicking on them one at a time and choosing *Download*, or you can download the zip file and get them all in one go. That's the easier method so go ahead and download this file:

10.002

Once you have the file saved on your computer, double click it. This will automatically unpack the zip file and you'll see the folder in your *Downloads* folder:

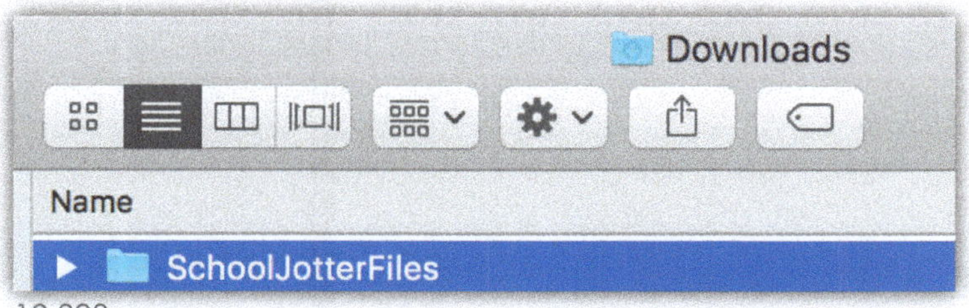

10.003

Open the folder to reveal the files:

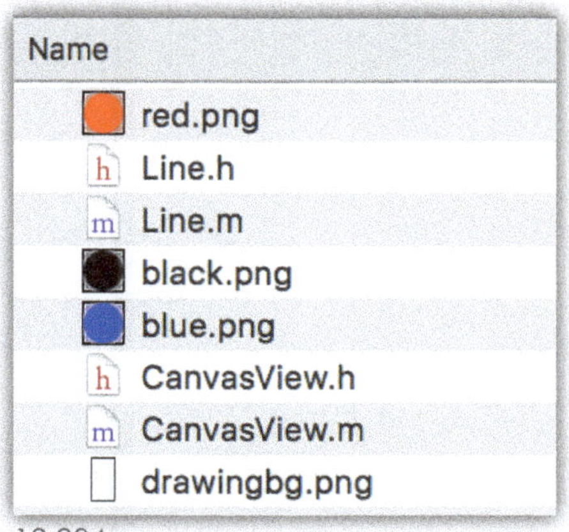

10.004

Look closely at the file names. Anything ending in *.png* is an image and then the other files are header and implementation files.

We need to import all eight files into *Xcode*. But the images need to go in the *Supporting Files* folder and the .h and .m files need to go beneath *MapViewController.m*.

Start with the images. We're going to select them all together. To do this, click on one of the files ending with *.png*, then, keeping your finger on the *Cmd* key on your keyboard, select the other three:

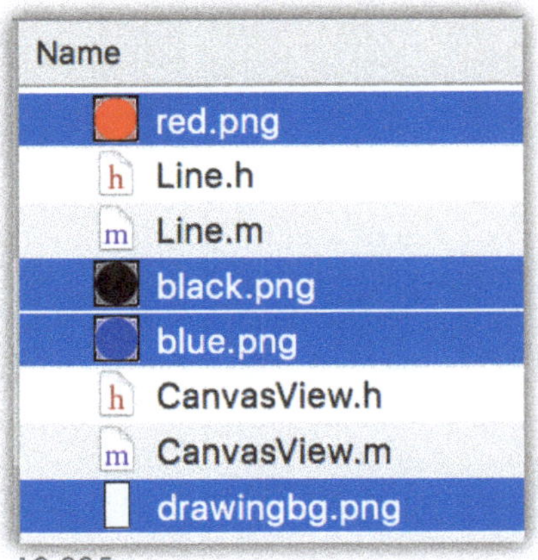

10.005

Click and drag from any of the selected files to the *Supporting Files* group in *Xcode*:

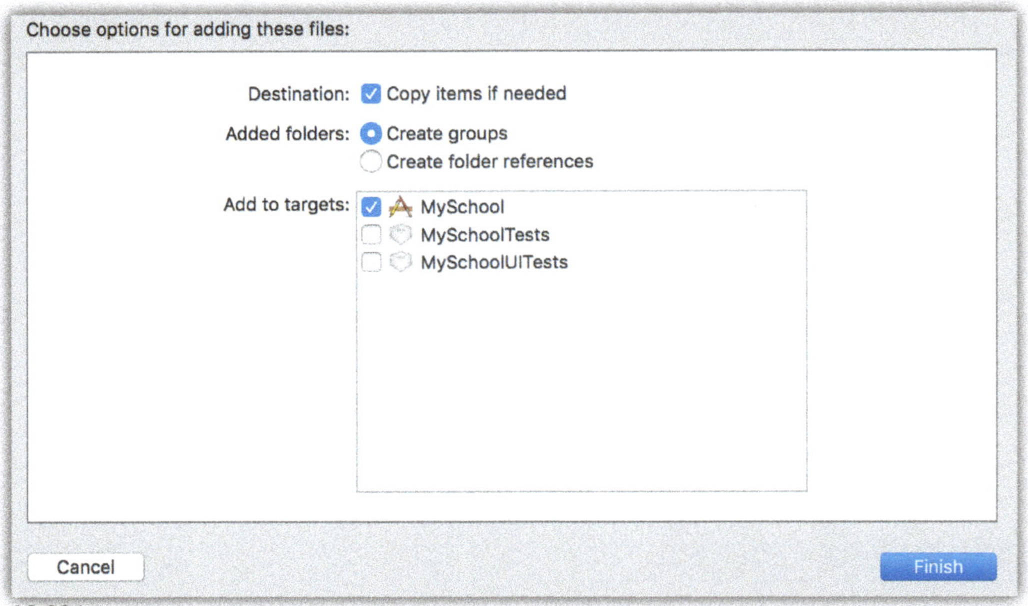

10.006

Make sure the usual boxes are selected and ticked and press Finish. The Navigator pane should look like this:

10.007

Remember, your icons may be different if you use a different image editor to me.

Repeat the selection process – clicking while holding down the *Cmd* key – to select the two .h files and two .m files.

Drag these to underneath *MapViewController.m*:

That's the fiddly bit done.

10.008

The four files of code you've added (*Line.h, Line.m, CanvasView.h and CanvasView.m*) help us to create a screen where the user can draw.

We need to add some *frameworks* to our app. They're frameworks that contain code to help us draw and there are three to add.

Firstly, select your project in the *Navigator* pane. It's the top item with a blue icon and your project name:

10.009

Then it's a case of repeating what we did earlier when we added the other frameworks:

The *Editor* pane will change to this: select *Build Phases*:

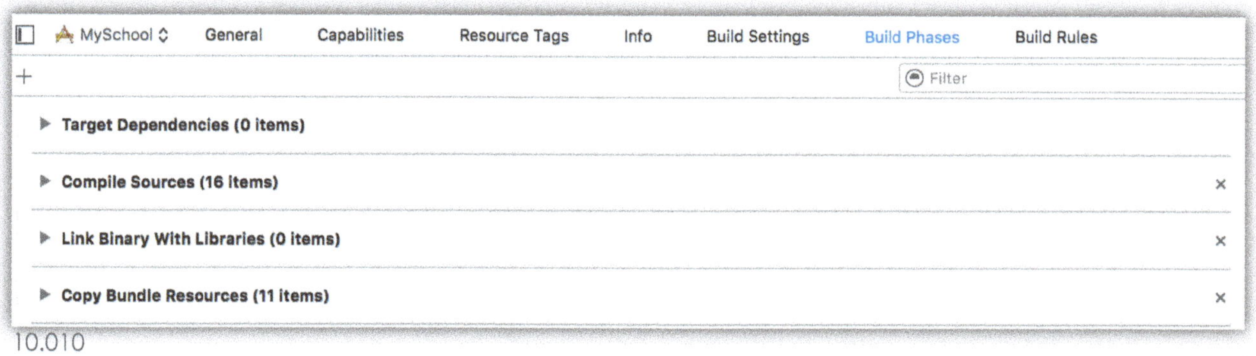

10.010

Click on the small arrow next to *Link Binary With Libraries*:

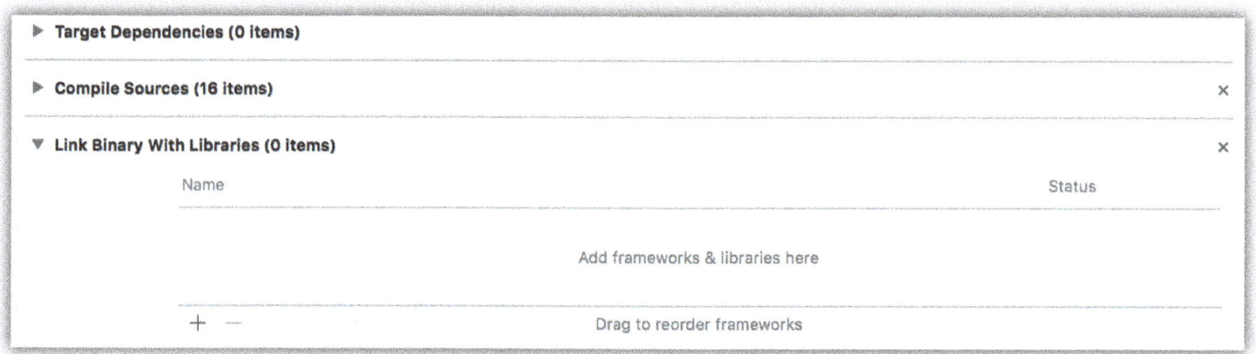

10.011

Press the '+' sign to bring up the pop-up box:

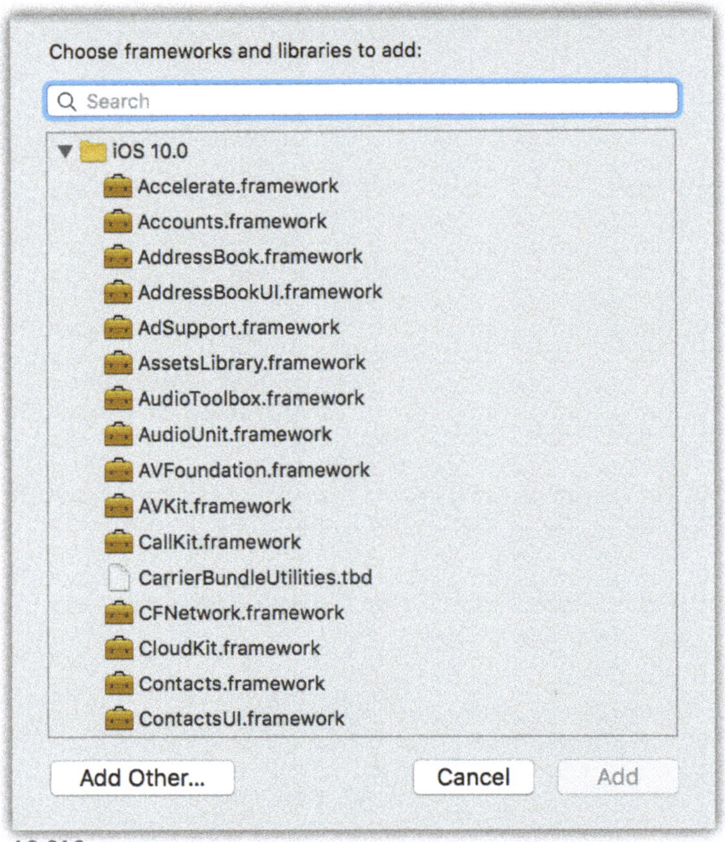

10.012

Type 'CoreGraphics' into the search box, select the CoreGraphics framework and press Add:

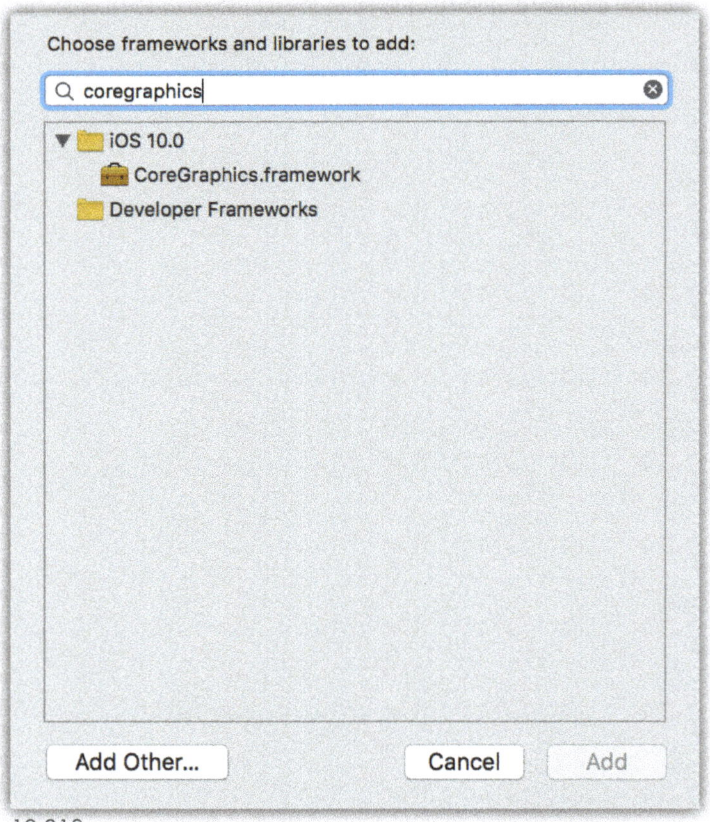

10.013

Repeat this process to add the following two frameworks:

- *QuartzCore.framework*
- *Foundation.framework*

At the top of your *Navigator* pane, you should see all of the *frameworks* we've added so far, including the *MessageUI* and *MapKit* ones we added earlier:

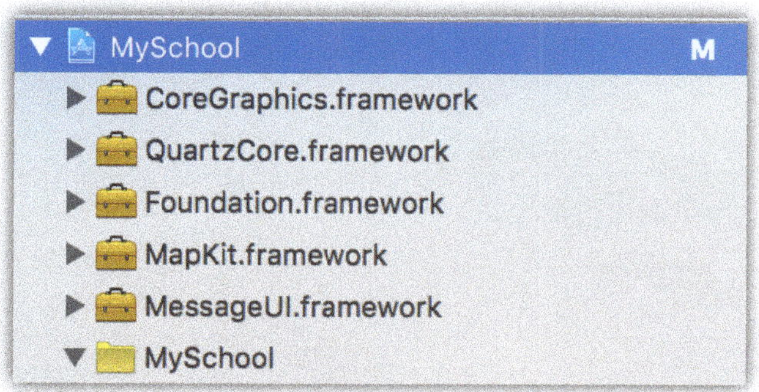

10.014

The final step in this process is to create the screen I showed you at the start of this chapter and write its code.

If you remember, the first thing we need to do when creating a new screen is add a new file. In the *Navigator* pane, select *CanvasView.m* and two-finger press.

Select *New File*, press *Next*. Then on the next screen, call your new screen 'JotterViewController', press *Next* again and then press *Create*. Your new files should appear beneath *CanvasView.m*:

10.015

Now, and for the last time, we need to add our View Controller to our storyboard. Select Main.storyboard from the Navigator pane. Scroll around the storyboard so that you've created a bit of space below the Contact Us View Controller:

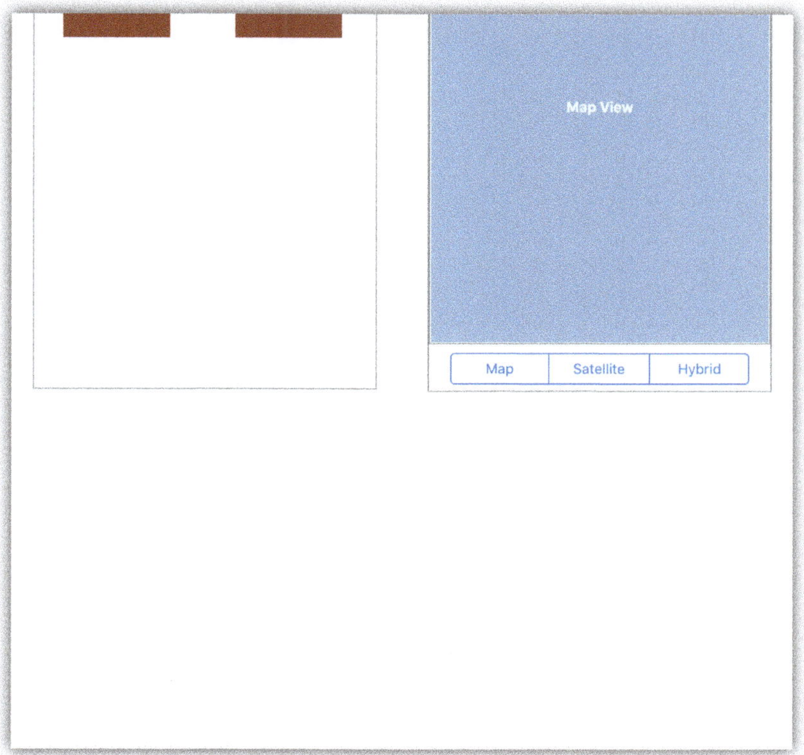

10.016

From the *Objects Library*, drag a *View Controller* underneath:

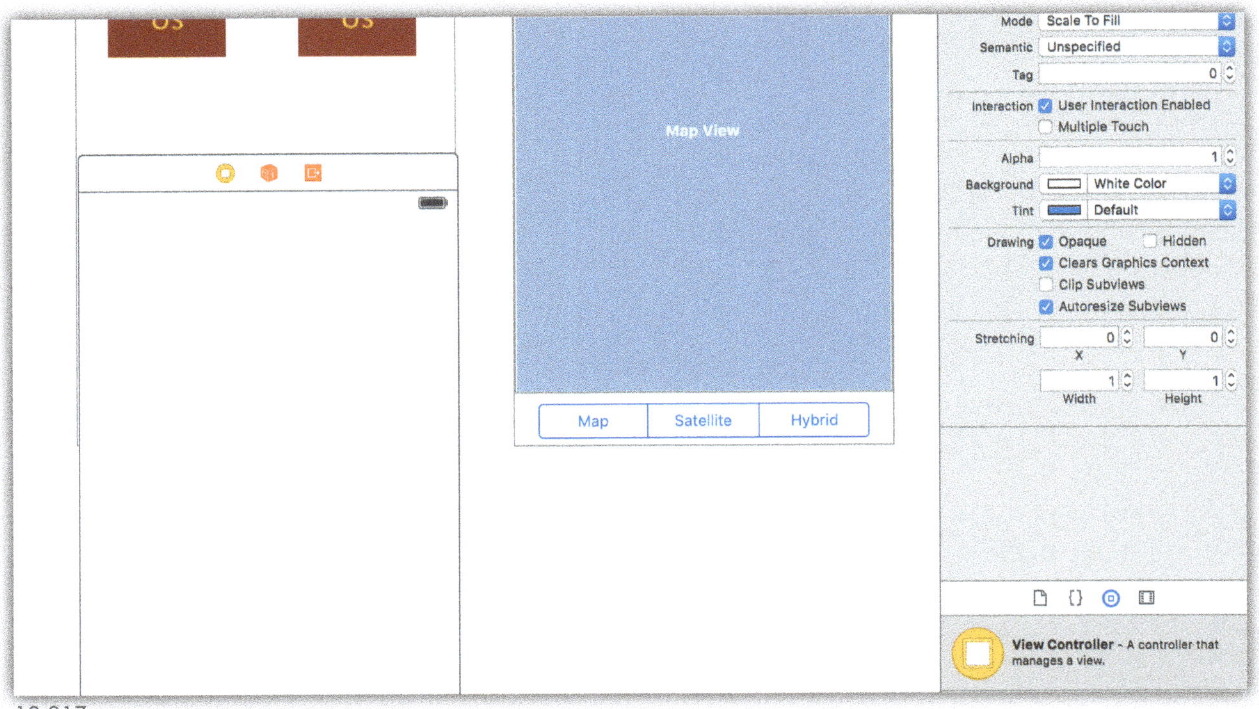

10.017

You'll have to put it so it partially covers the *Contact Us View Controller* and then move it down a bit so you're looking at your new *View Controller* on its own:

10.018

As we've done all the way through the book, we need to associate the *View Controller* with *JotterViewController* so select the yellow circle with the square in it. Then go to the *Utilities* pane, and select the third button from the left to open the *Identity inspector*:

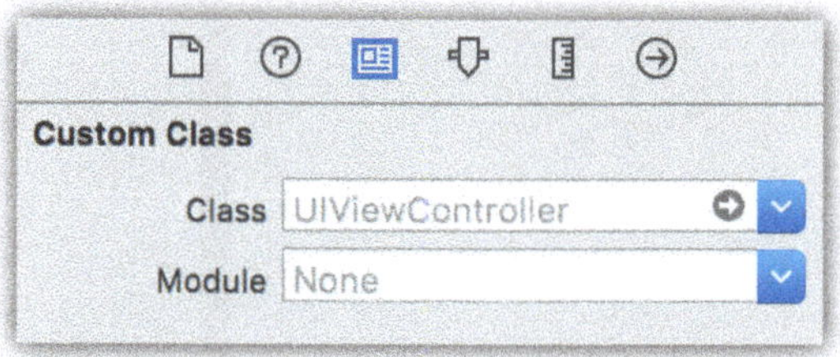

10.019

In the *Class* box, type *JotterViewController*. As usual, it will attempt to autocomplete. Press *return*.

We're ready to start building. Out of all of our screens, this one has the most *user interface* elements so we'll add them one at a time and by the time we're finished, it will all make perfect sense.

We need to add some of them to our header file too. So press the two interlinking circles in the top right of *Xcode*:

10.020

Your *Editor* pane should now have split into two parts. You may need to select *Jotter* at the top of the right-hand side of the split pane:

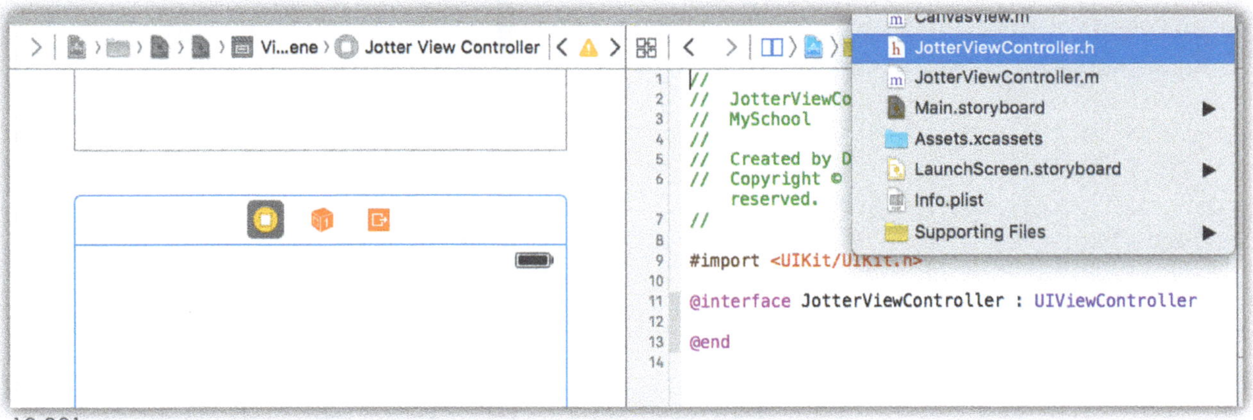

10.021

Again, please make sure it's the .h file and not the .m file.

Let's get adding stuff. First of all, I'd like you to add an *Image View* so find the Image View in the *Object Library*:

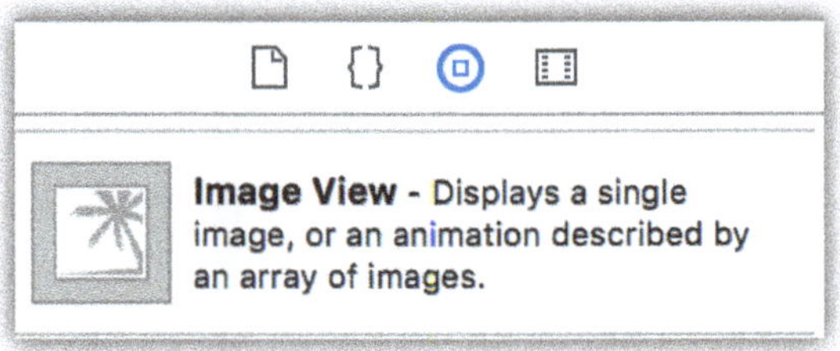

10.022

Make it fill the whole *View Controller*, leaving a small gap at either end:

10.023

With the *Image View* still selected, go over to the *Utilities* pane and select the shield button to open up the *Attributes inspector*. We need to type 'drawingbg.png' into the *Image* text box and change the *Mode* from *Scale to Fill* to *Aspect Fit*:

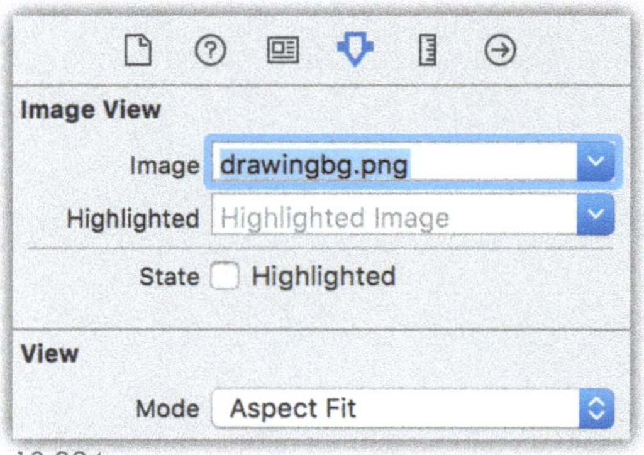

10.024

Your *Image View* should look like an A4 pad (which I spent a whole 10 minutes making). You can, of course, change that image to anything you want.

Because our *Image View* isn't going to change throughout the life of our app running, we don't need to declare it in the header file.

We're going to add our buttons to the top of the screen. This is the layout we're going to try to achieve:

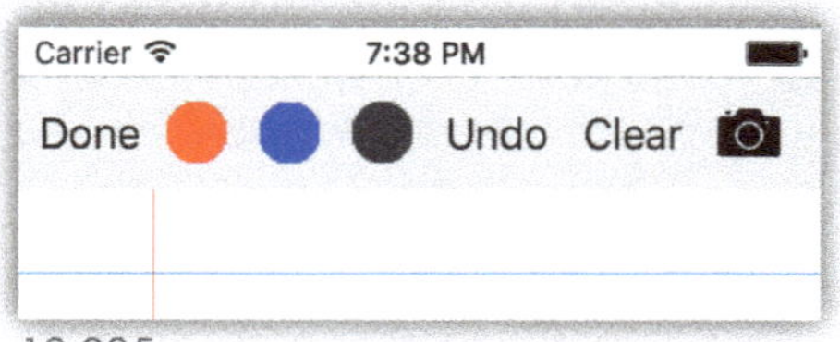

10.025

You can probably see a light grey box behind the buttons. This a *Toolbar* and they're used a lot in apps.

They're handy because the buttons we add will all be in one place but they're also a bit fiddly because you can't just move the buttons around freely within the *Toolbar*. You'll see what I mean in a minute.

Let's add the *Toolbar*. Head to the *Object Library* and find this:

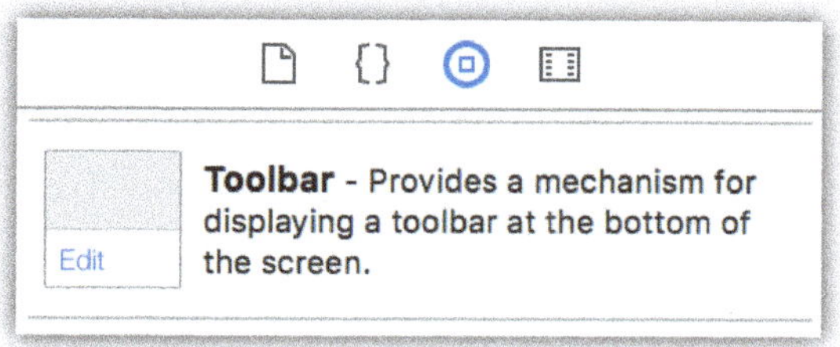

10.026

Drag from here to the top of your screen:

10.027

You might need to resize your *Image View* to make sure there is room for the *Toolbar* at the top.

You'll notice that there is already a button on our *Toolbar*. It's called *Item* but we're going to change that. Click on the button then head over to the *Utilities* pane and check that the *Attributes inspector* is selected.

You should see these options:

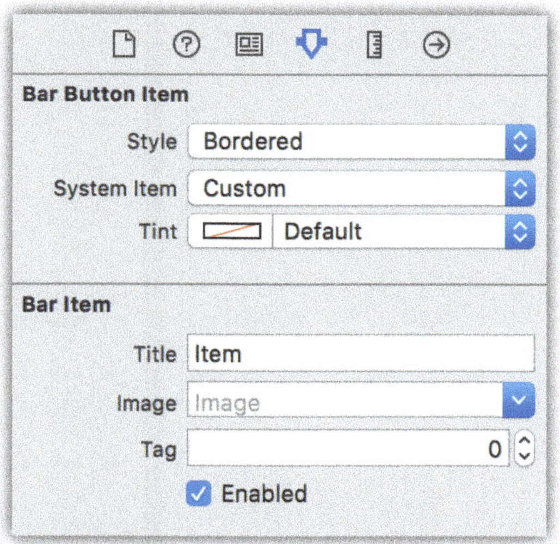

10.028

If you press on the word *Custom*, a drop-down menu will appear. Select *Done* from the menu:

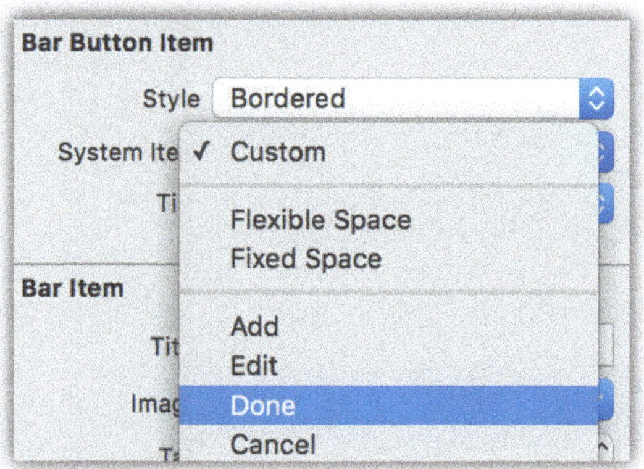

10.029

And with a sprinkle of Apple magic, the first button in your *Toolbar* will look like this:

10.030

Next, let's add our first colour-picking button: the red one. In the *Object Library*, beneath *Toolbar*, you'll see a *Bar Button Item*, drag this next to your *Done* button:

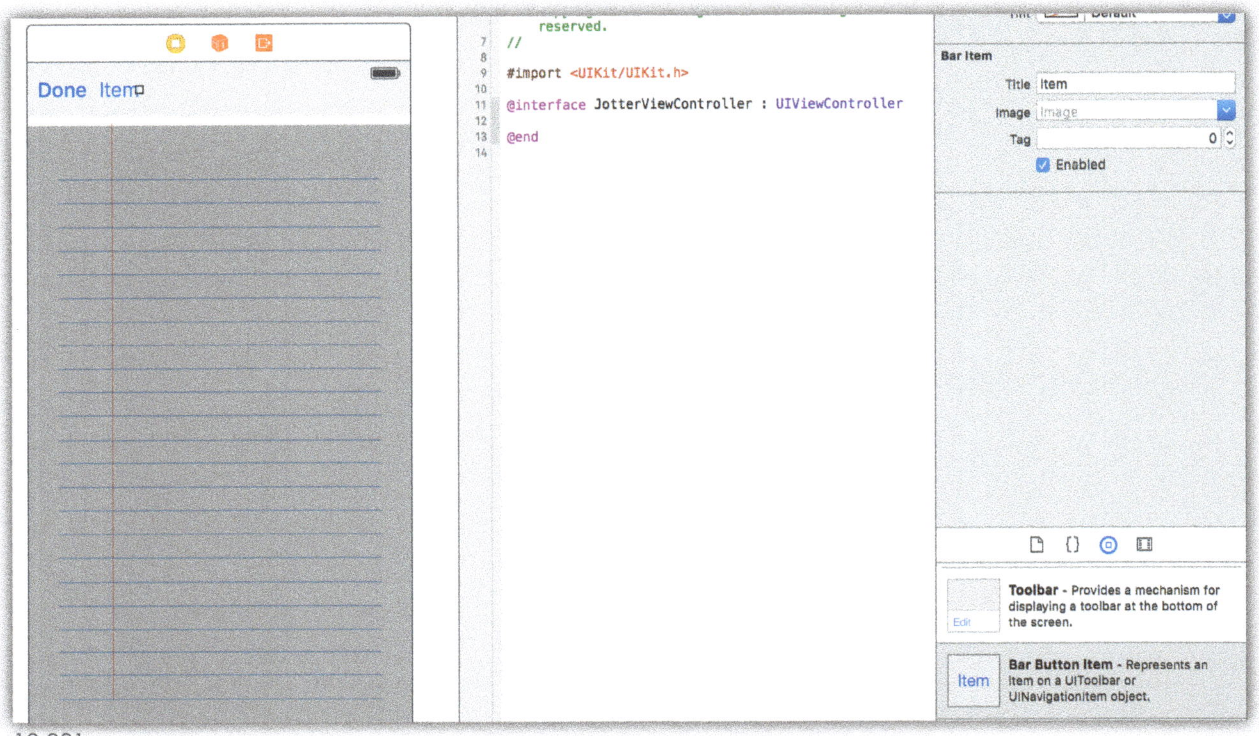

10.031

Select your new button, currently called *Item* by clicking on it in the *Toolbar*. Look in the *Attributes inspector* in the *Utilities* pane:

There are a few things to change here.

Firstly, press next to *Tint* to bring up the colour palettes. Remember, pressing *Other...* brings up the crayons. Select a red colour.

Next, clear the *Title* field by deleting *Item*.

Finally, click in the text box next to *Image* and type *red.png*.

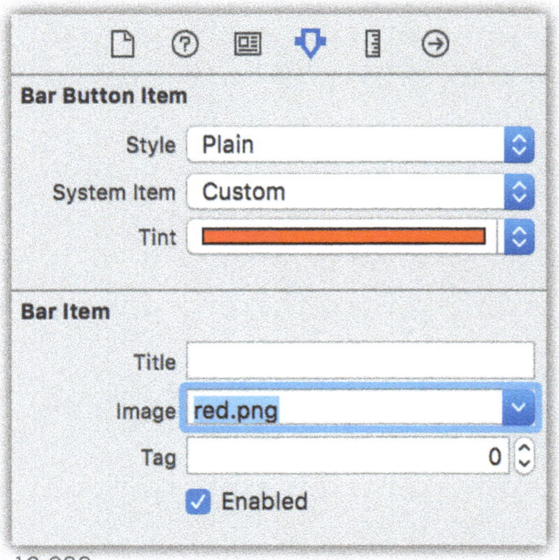

10.032

Your *Toolbar* should look like this:

10.033

Add the next two colours by repeating this procedure:

- Drag a *Bar Button Item* next to your previous button.
- Change the colour in the *Attributes inspector*.
- Remove the *Title*.
- Type in the name of the image.

By the time you're done, your *Toolbar* should look like this:

10.034

If it doesn't, go back through the previous pages and check that you followed each step.

We also need to add our *Undo* and *Clear* buttons. It's the same process but we don't need to change the colour – of course, you can if you want – and we don't need to add an image.

But what we do need to do is change the title from *Item* to *Undo* and *Clear* respectively.

Start by dragging your *Bar Button* Item and then go to the *Attributes inspector* to make the changes you need:

10.035

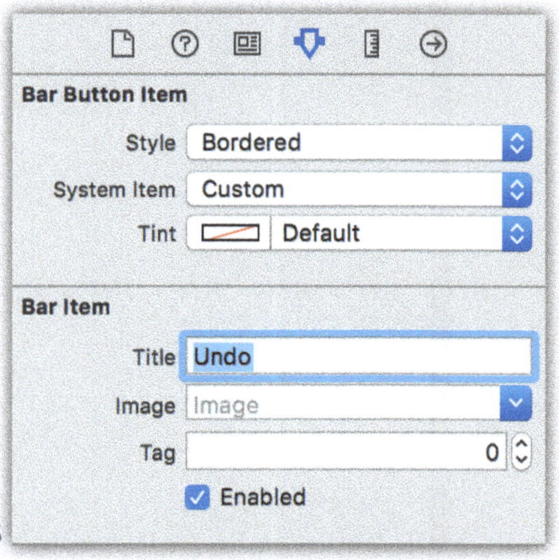

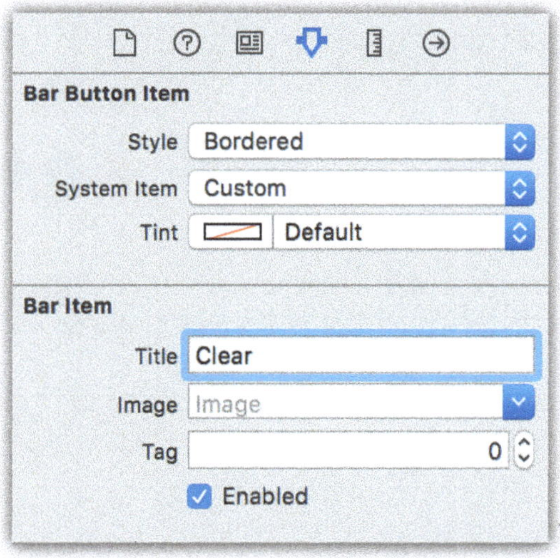

10.036

Only one more button to go on this Toolbar.

Drag another Bar Button Item to the Toolbar, next to the Clear button:

10.037

Select it by clicking on it. Then, in the *Attributes inspector*, click on the word *Custom* and select *Camera* from the drop-down menu:

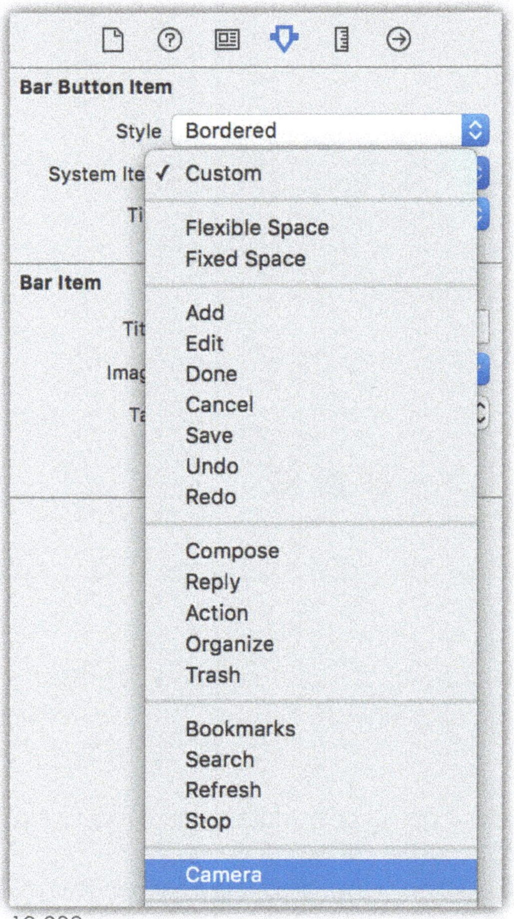

10.038

That's all you need to do. And your *Toolbar* should look like this:

10.039

If you don't like the blue colour of the text, feel free to change it by clicking on the button and changing the colour in the *Attributes inspector*.

You may have noticed that we haven't done that thing where we drag items from the *user interface* to the .h file. This is because we don't need to reference any of these so we can leave them as they are.

Our next step is to add our bottom *Toolbar*:

10.040

This one only has three buttons, but you'll notice that they are spread out. To accomplish this, we will need to add something called a *Fixed Space Bar Button Item* between each button.

To do this, drag a *Toolbar* to the bottom of the *View Controller*. You may need to resize the background *Image View* to make sure everything fits okay:

10.041

Select Item. Go to the *Attributes inspector* and click on *Custom* to bring up the drop-down menu and select *Compose*:

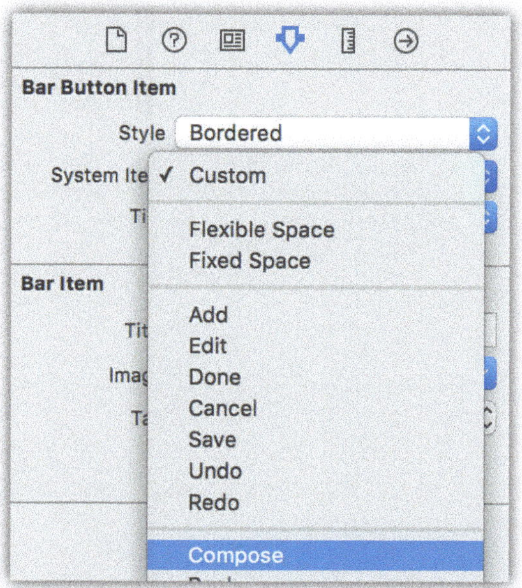

10.042

Your button will change to match mine:

10.043

We're going to add our space. Scroll down to the bottom of the *Object Library*:

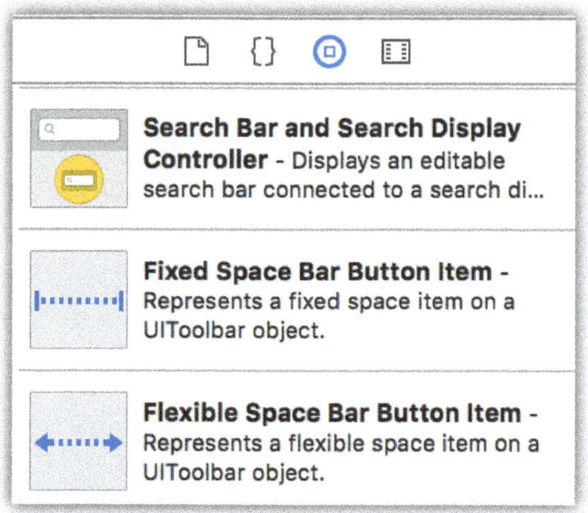

10.044

We want the *Fixed Space Bar Button Item* as opposed to the *Flexible Space* one. This is because we won't change how big our spaces are mid-app. Drag it next to the paper and pen button on your new Toolbar.

It should look like this:

10.045

If you click on the tiny little square to the right of the *Fixed Space Bar Button Item*, you can drag to the right to make it bigger or to the left to make it smaller.

I'm happy with the space it represents as is, so I'm going to drag a new *Bar Button Item* next to the *Fixed Space Bar Button Item*:

10.046

Select the button in the *Toolbar* and go to the *Attributes inspector* in the *Utilities* pane. Click on the *Custom* text to bring up the drop-down menu and select *Reply*. You could also use *Action*. It's up to you, it's your app:

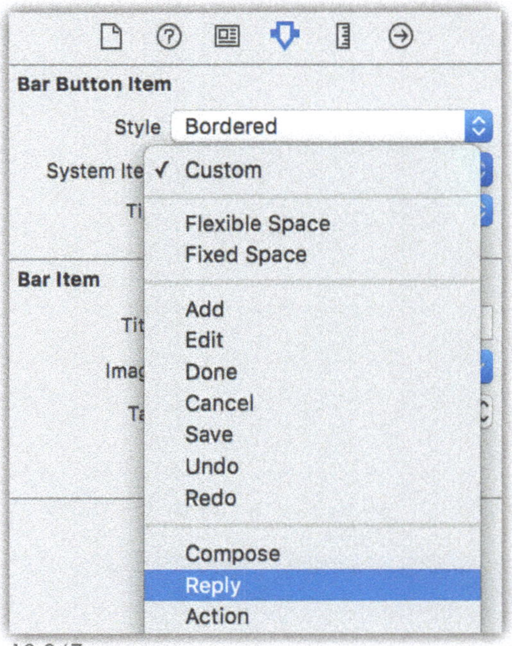

10.047

Your *Toolbar* should now look like this:

10.048

Drag another *Fixed Space Bar Button Item* to the *Toolbar* and stretch it by dragging from the small square so it looks like this:

10.049

In the Attributes inspector, change the title to Save Notes:

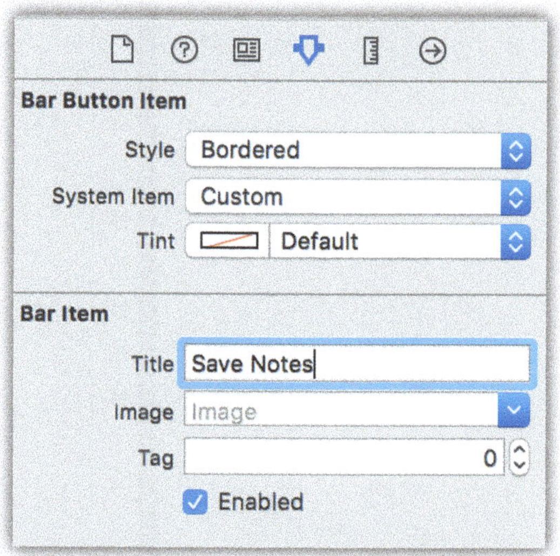

10.050

Your finished bottom *Toolbar* should look like this:

10.051

We've got an awful lot of buttons here and they're all going to be linked to an *IBAction* soon but for now, we need to finish off building the user interface.

Remember I said this screen will let you take notes? To do this, we need to add a *Text View* to our screen. Find the *Text View* in the *Object Library* and then drag it to your *View Controller* so it's placed like this:

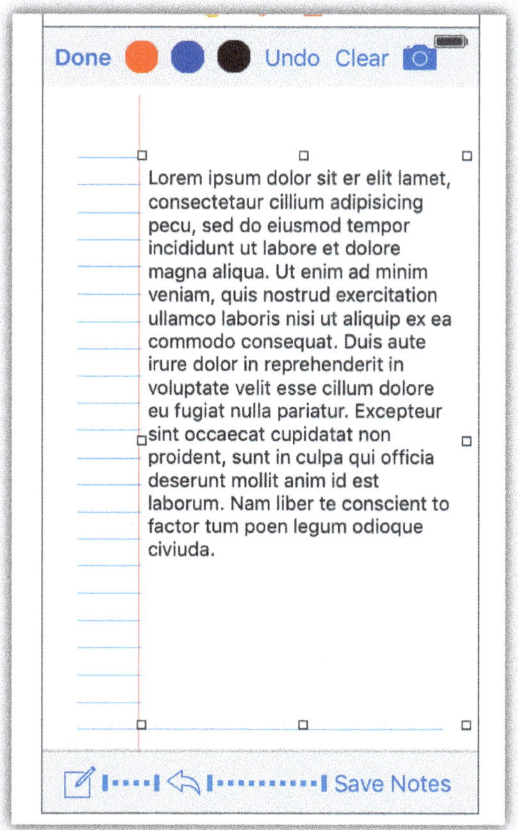

10.052

Notice how the white background of the *Text View* hides our image of the paper? We need to sort that out, so look in the *Attributes inspector*. Scroll down until you find the section headed *View* in bold font:

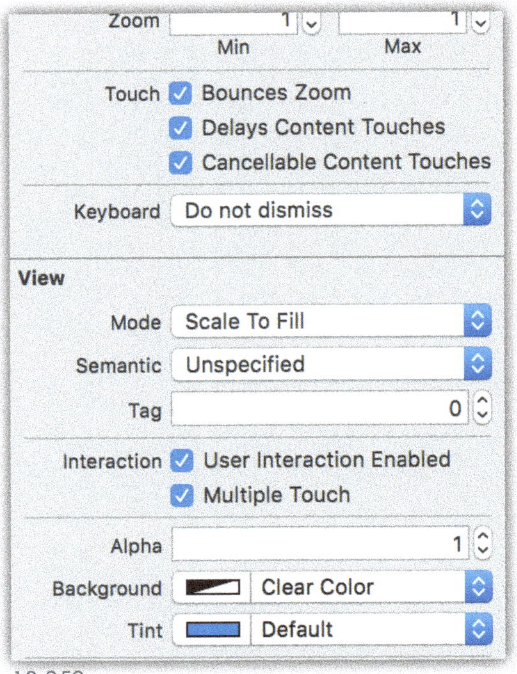

10.053

Find the *Background* option and click on it. Change it from *White* to *Clear Color*. You should now be able to see the paper through the *Text View*.

Scroll back up in the *Attributes inspector* and select all the latin 'gibberish' text:

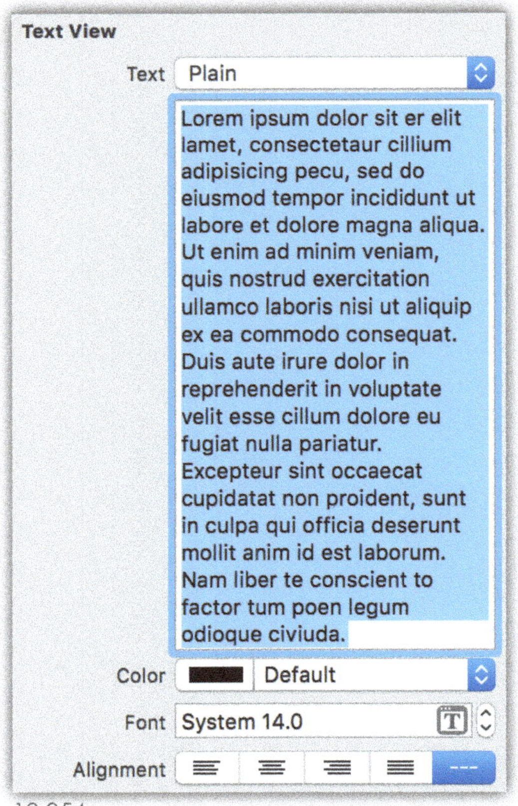

10.054

With that all selected, press the backspace button on your keyboard to delete it all. We want our *Text View* to be empty before we start.

This *Text View* needs to be declared in our .h file – which should still be open alongside your *Storyboard*. Add the following code to your .h file:

```
#import <UIKit/UIKit.h>
#import "CanvasView.h"
#import <QuartzCore/QuartzCore.h>
#import <MessageUI/MessageUI.h>

@interface JotterViewController : UIViewController <
    UITextViewDelegate> {

}

@end
```

10.055

Just a note, because there isn't much room, the file is narrower than usual so the lines of code continue underneath. There is no space between '<' and *UITextViewDelegate*.

This adds the files we need from the *frameworks* we added. It tells it we're using a *Text View* and adds the swirly brackets!

Now, two-finger drag from your *Text View* in the *storyboard* to between the swirly brackets in the .h file. Call it 'myTextView':

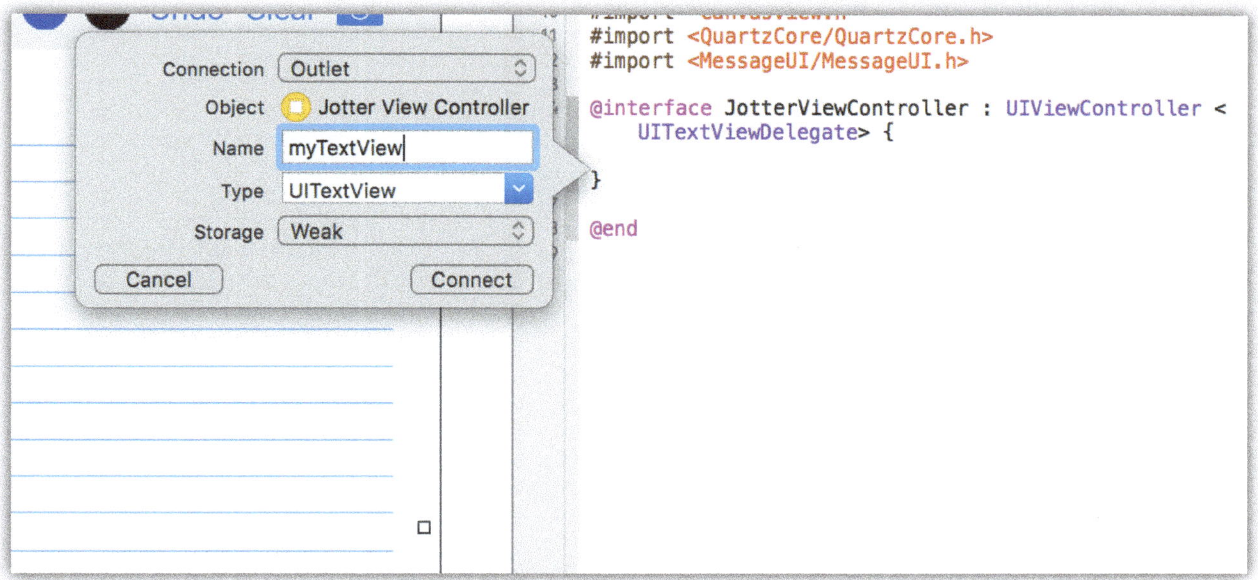

10.056

The code should look like this:

```
@interface JotterViewController : UIViewController <
    UITextViewDelegate> {

    __weak IBOutlet UITextView *myTextView;
}
```

10.057

We need to add the space that the user can draw in. To do this, we are going to add an object called a *View* – not a *View Controller*. Find it in the *Object Library*:

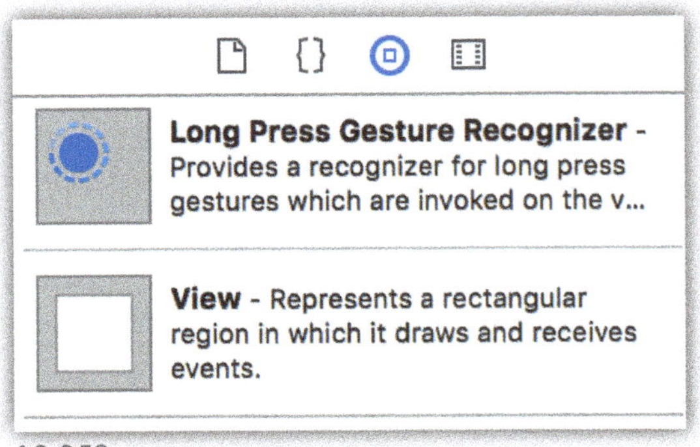

10.058

Drag the View to your View Controller and make it fill the space between the Toolbars, but don't let it overlap them:

10.059

The more observant of you will notice that again, the view is white and so obscures our background image.

Go to the Attributes inspector:

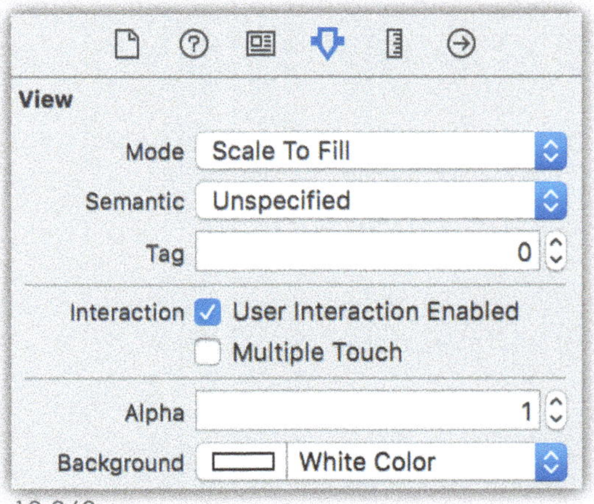

10.060

Click on White Color and change it to Clear Color. Your recently added View should be beautifully transparent.

We have to do something a bit complicated now. Although this is a *View*, we want it to be a special *View*. It will be our *Canvas View*. This isn't a real thing. You can't add one willy nilly to any app. But remember earlier when we added two files called *CanvasView.h* and *CanvasView.m*? These files turned a normal *View* into a special view that our user can draw on and we named it *CanvasView*.

However, we do need to tell *Xcode* that this *View* we added is a *CanvasView*.

With the *View* selected, press the third button from the left in the *Utilities* pane to open up the *Identity inspector*:

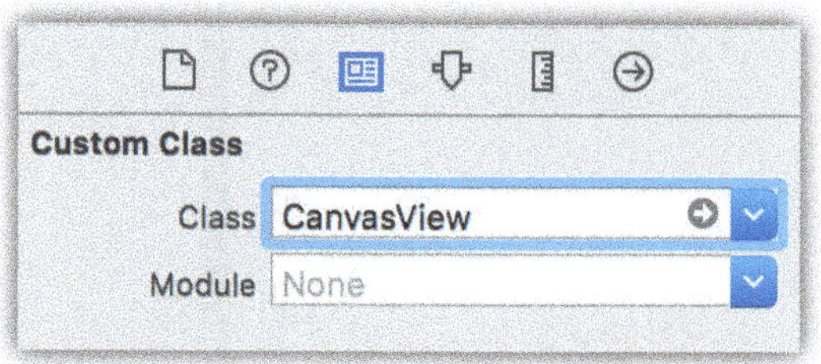

10.061

In the *Class* box, type 'CanvasView' as you can see above. It will autocomplete once you type the 'C'.

Once you've done that, I suggest you press the shield button – fourth from the left – to re-open the *Attributes inspector*.

Now, two-finger drag from the *View* to the .h file:

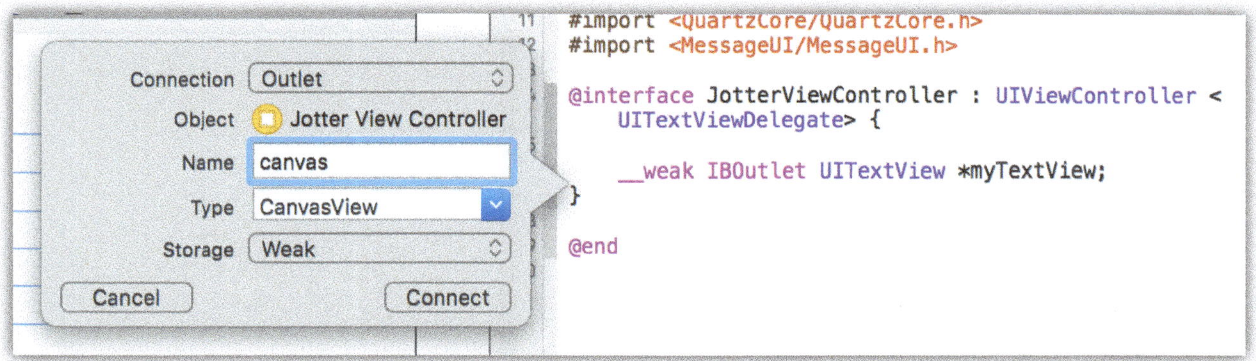

10.062

Type 'canvas' in the *Name* box and make sure it goes underneath the *myTextView* code. It should look like this:

```
@interface JotterViewController : UIViewController <
    UITextViewDelegate> {

    __weak IBOutlet UITextView *myTextView;
    __weak IBOutlet CanvasView *canvas;
}
```
10.063

There's one more item to add to our screen. Find a *Button* in the *Object Library* and drag it to the screen. Size it to fill everything apart from the bottom *Toolbar*:

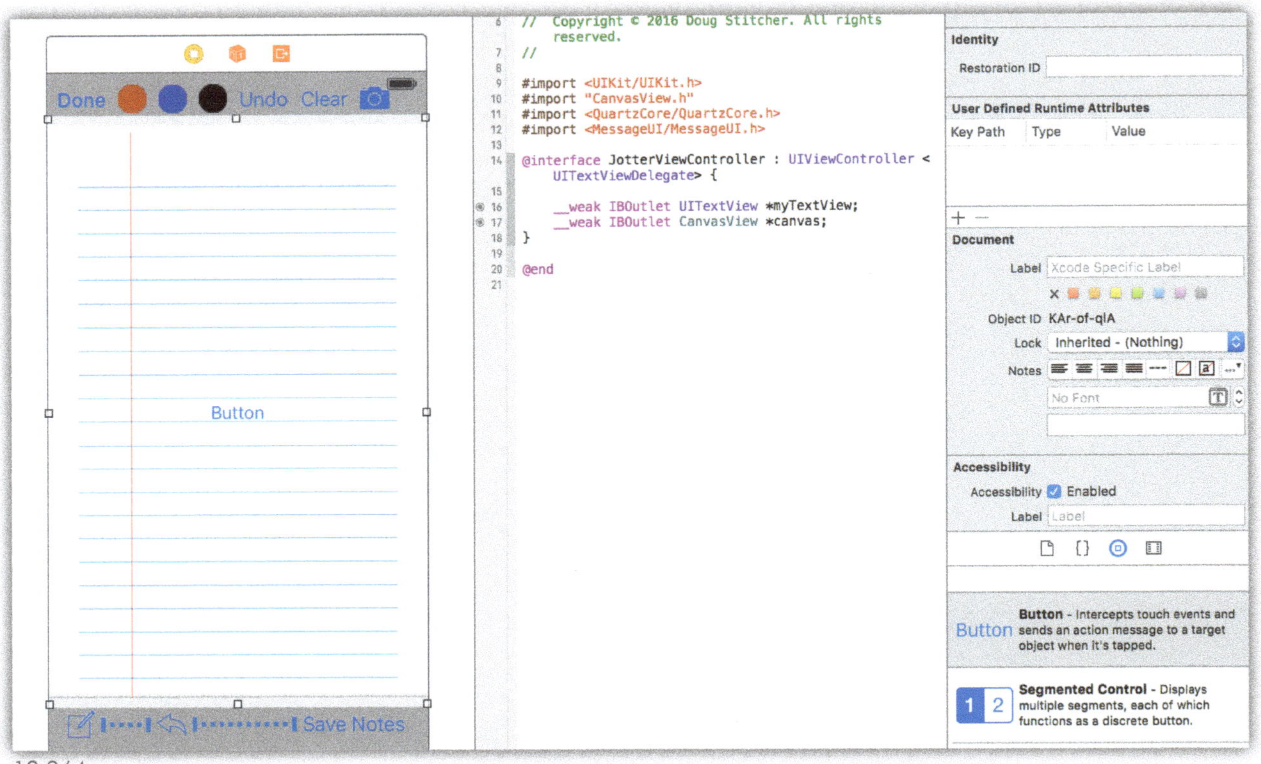

10.064

Open the *Attributes inspector* and delete the word 'Button' in the title section.

Now, two-finger drag from the button to the .h file underneath where you declared the *CanvasView* and call it 'secretButton':

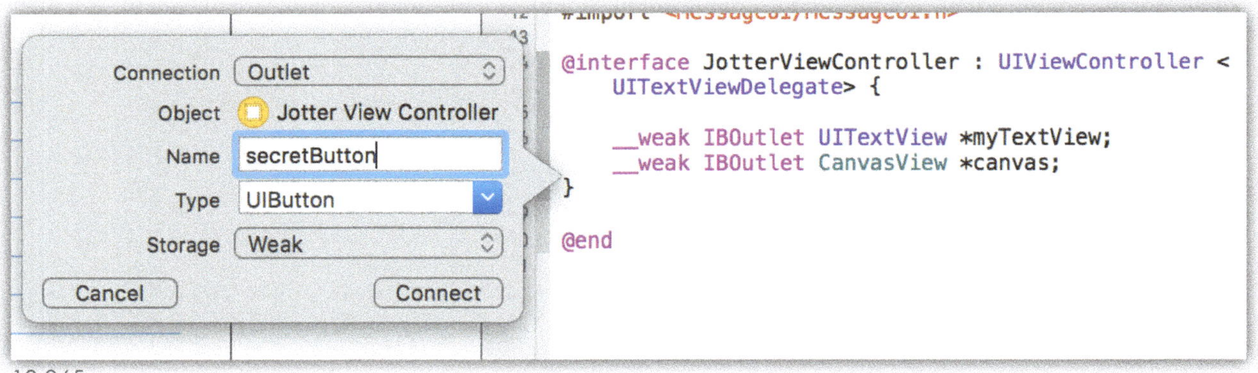

10.065

The final code should look like this:

```
@interface JotterViewController : UIViewController <
    UITextViewDelegate> {

    __weak IBOutlet UITextView *myTextView;
    __weak IBOutlet CanvasView *canvas;
    __weak IBOutlet UIButton *secretButton;
}
```

10.066

There's another thing to do here. When you added the big button, it actually went INSIDE the *CanvasView*. We need this button on the top of all of our objects.

You may already be able to see this part of the *Editor* pane, but if you can't, look for this button to the bottom left of the *pane*:

10.067

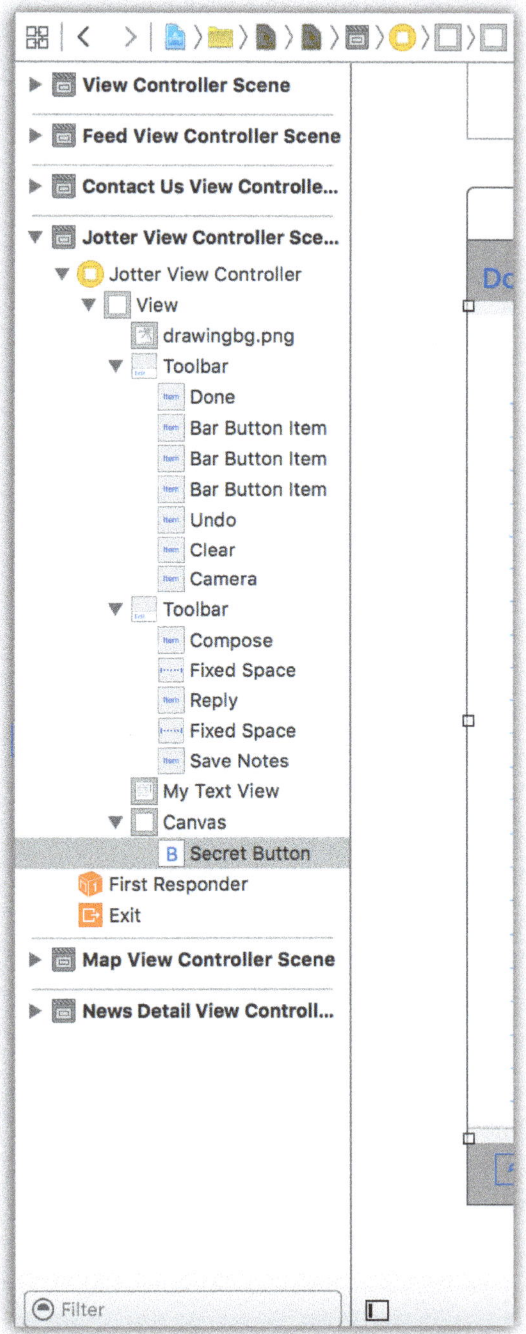

10.068

Press it, and a new side-bar, pictured left, will appear. This side-bar may have already been visible, in which case pressing that button will make it disappear. Use the button to toggle between seeing the side-bar and hiding it.

Here, you can see all the objects you have added and the *Secret Button* should be selected.

You can see that the button is inside the *Canvas*. We need to move it out of the Canvas.

To do this, drag the Secret Button object up so a blue line appears between *My Text View* and *Canvas*.

Let go of the mouse and the *Secret Button* will be between the two:

10.069

The last thing you need to do is move the *Secret Button* to the top. To do this, select *Canvas*, drag it above *Secret Button* but below *My Text View*.

It should look like this:

10.070

You've now arranged your objects. Everything is in the right place. We will come back to our *storyboard* when we've finished the coding to link our buttons to the *IBActions* we are about to write.

First of all, you need to exit the split-screen view. Look to the top-right of *Xcode* and select the button with the lines on:

10.071

The split-screen will disappear and you'll be left looking at the *storyboard* file. Select *JotterViewController.h* as there are still a few bits of code we need to add.

Your .h file should look like this:

```
#import <UIKit/UIKit.h>
#import "CanvasView.h"
#import <QuartzCore/QuartzCore.h>
#import <MessageUI/MessageUI.h>

@interface JotterViewController : UIViewController <UITextViewDelegate> {

    __weak IBOutlet UITextView *myTextView;
    __weak IBOutlet CanvasView *canvas;
    __weak IBOutlet UIButton *secretButton;
}

@end
```

10.072

There's not a lot left to add here but for a few lines between the '<' and '>' so put your cursor after *UITextViewDelegate* and put a comma. Change the line to look like this:

```
@interface JotterViewController : UIViewController <UITextViewDelegate, MFMessageComposeViewControllerDelegate,
    MFMailComposeViewControllerDelegate> {
```

10.073

All we're doing here is telling the file that in the *School Jotter*, we will be using the *framework* that lets us send messages. In our case, we'll be sending emails but I've also prepared it to send text messages, though we won't be using that feature.

There's one more line to add, underneath the swirly brackets:

```
    __weak IBOutlet UIButton *secretButton;
}

@property (nonatomic, retain) IBOutlet CanvasView *canvas;

@end
```

10.074

We're done in the .h file, so open up *JotterViewController.m*. The first thing we need to do is add a bit of code under the *@implementation* line:

```
#import "JotterViewController.h"

@implementation JotterViewController
@synthesize canvas;

@end
```

10.075

Now let's add our first *method*, our *viewDidLoad* code:

```
- (void)viewDidLoad {
    [super viewDidLoad];

    //hide our secret button - you'll see what that's for in a little while!
    secretButton.hidden = TRUE;

    myTextView.delegate = self;

    //Now, check for any saved notes:
    if  (![[NSUserDefaults standardUserDefaults] stringForKey:@"notes"]){
        //There's none there so we don't need to load any
    } else {
        //We've found some saved ones, so let's put them into the Text View
        myTextView.text = [[NSUserDefaults standardUserDefaults] stringForKey:@"notes"];
    }

    //Set the position of the canvas for drawing based on whether we're on a 3.5 or 4 inch screen
        CGSize result = [[UIScreen mainScreen] bounds].size;
        if(result.height == 480)
        { // iPhone 4
            CanvasView *newCanvas = [[CanvasView alloc] initWithFrame:CGRectMake(0, 64, 320, 380)];
            self.canvas = newCanvas;
        }
        else {
            //iPhone 5
            CanvasView *newCanvas = [[CanvasView alloc] initWithFrame:CGRectMake(0, 64, 320, 450)];
            self.canvas = newCanvas;

        }

    //Set the line that we draw with to black with a width of 5.0
    self.canvas.currentLine.lineColor = [UIColor blackColor];
    self.canvas.currentLine.lineWidth = 5.0;
    self.canvas.currentLine.opacity = 1.0;

    //Add our canvas
    [self.view addSubview:canvas];
}
```

10.076

This code sets up our *School Jotter* screen and hides the *Secret Button* – I'll tell you what that's for later.

Then we load the text that the user has previously saved using *NSUserDefaults*, like we did early on when we saved the user's name.

Next, we size our canvas, that's the view that the user will draw on, depending upon the size of the screen they are using.

Finally, we set some properties to start drawing with.

Now to add *methods*. The next few are *IBActions*. As we add them, try to think which button they will be attached to. Put these two methods underneath your *viewDidLoad*:

```
- (IBAction)beginTyping:(id)sender{
    [myTextView becomeFirstResponder];
    secretButton.hidden = FALSE;
    [self.view bringSubviewToFront:secretButton];
}

- (IBAction)quitTyping:(id)sender{
    [myTextView resignFirstResponder];
    secretButton.hidden = TRUE;
}
```

10.077

Have you worked out what the *Secret Button* is for yet? When we are typing, we put an invisible button over the *Text View*. When we want to stop typing, we press anywhere on the *Text View* and in doing so, we press the invisible button. This will then call the *quitTyping* method and make the keyboard disappear – that's what *resignFirstResponder* does.

Next method. This one saves our notes so we can load them again at a later point:

```
- (IBAction)saveTyping:(id)sender{
    //save the notes
    [[NSUserDefaults standardUserDefaults] setObject:myTextView.text forKey:@"notes"];

    //tell the user we have saved notes
    UIAlertController *alert = [UIAlertController
                                alertControllerWithTitle:@"Your text notes have been saved"
                                message:@"To save your jottings, you must take a picture of the screen by pressing the
                                    camera icon."
                                preferredStyle:UIAlertControllerStyleAlert];

    UIAlertAction *ok = [UIAlertAction
                         actionWithTitle:@"OK"
                         style:UIAlertActionStyleDefault
                         handler:^(UIAlertAction * action)
                         {
                             [alert dismissViewControllerAnimated:YES completion:nil];

                         }];

    [alert addAction:ok];
    [self presentViewController:alert animated:YES completion:nil];
}
```

10.078

This code saves our notes and tells the user that that is what we have done. This isn't the first time we've used *UIAlertViewController* to present a pop-up box. They're useful as a way of telling the user what is going on.

Now we need to add the code to send our notes, and any image we draw, by email. Put this code underneath the *saveTyping* method:

```
- (IBAction)openMail:(id)sender
{
    if ([MFMailComposeViewController canSendMail])
    {
        MFMailComposeViewController *mailer = [[MFMailComposeViewController alloc] init];
        mailer.mailComposeDelegate = self;
        [mailer setSubject:@"My School Jotter Notes"];
        UIGraphicsBeginImageContext(self.view.bounds.size);
        [self.view.layer renderInContext:UIGraphicsGetCurrentContext()];
        UIImage *viewImage = UIGraphicsGetImageFromCurrentImageContext();
        UIGraphicsEndImageContext();
        NSData *imageData = UIImagePNGRepresentation(viewImage);
        [mailer addAttachmentData:imageData mimeType:@"image/png" fileName:@"School Jotter Notes"];
        NSString *emailBody = myTextView.text;
        [mailer setMessageBody:emailBody isHTML:NO];
        [self presentViewController:mailer animated:YES completion:nil];


    }
    else
    {
        UIAlertController *alert = [UIAlertController
                                    alertControllerWithTitle:@"Unable to Send Mail"
                                    message:@"Your device doesn't support emailing or you have not set up any email
                                        accounts."
                                    preferredStyle:UIAlertControllerStyleAlert];

        UIAlertAction *ok = [UIAlertAction
                             actionWithTitle:@"OK"
                             style:UIAlertActionStyleDefault
                             handler:^(UIAlertAction * action)
                             {
                                 [alert dismissViewControllerAnimated:YES completion:nil];

                             }];

        [alert addAction:ok];
        [self presentViewController:alert animated:YES completion:nil];


    }
}
```

10.079

It's quite a big *method*. Let's go through what it does.

It checks that the user can send emails from their device. If they can, we set the email subject as 'My School Jotter Notes' but you can change this if you want.

From the line *UIGraphicsBeginImageContext* to the line *UIGraphicsEndImageContext*, we take a photo of the user's drawing and put it in the email as an attachment.

We then set the body text of the email to be the contents of the *Text View* so that the email contains both the typed notes and the image, if they drew one. Finally, we present the email composer.

If their device isn't capable of sending an email, we use a *UIAlertController* to tell the user this.

The next piece of code, you can copy and paste from your *ContactUsViewController.m* file. It's the code for handling if there's an error sending the email. We've added this before so either copy and paste it or type it again:

```
- (void)mailComposeController:(MFMailComposeViewController*)controller didFinishWithResult:(MFMailComposeResult)result
    error:(NSError*)error
{
    if(error) {

        UIAlertController *alert = [UIAlertController
                                    alertControllerWithTitle:@"Error"
                                    message:@"Unable to send your email. Please try again later."
                                    preferredStyle:UIAlertControllerStyleAlert];

        UIAlertAction *ok = [UIAlertAction
                             actionWithTitle:@"OK"
                             style:UIAlertActionStyleDefault
                             handler:^(UIAlertAction * action)
                             {
                                 [alert dismissViewControllerAnimated:YES completion:nil];
                                 [self dismissViewControllerAnimated:YES completion:nil];

                             }];

        [alert addAction:ok];
         [self presentViewController:alert animated:YES completion:nil];


    }
    [self dismissViewControllerAnimated:YES completion:nil];
    return;
}
```

10.080

We also need to add the *methods* for changing the colour of the pen that we are drawing with. Add these three methods underneath the last one:

```
-(IBAction)redLine:(id)sender {

    self.canvas.currentLine.lineColor = [UIColor redColor];
    self.canvas.currentLine.lineWidth = 5.0;
    self.canvas.currentLine.opacity = 1.0;
}
-(IBAction)blueLine:(id)sender{

    self.canvas.currentLine.lineColor = [UIColor colorWithRed:0.0235 green:0.4824 blue:1 alpha:1.0];
    self.canvas.currentLine.lineWidth = 5.0;
    self.canvas.currentLine.opacity = 1.0;

}
-(IBAction)blackLine:(id)sender{

    self.canvas.currentLine.lineColor = [UIColor blackColor];
    self.canvas.currentLine.lineWidth = 5.0;
    self.canvas.currentLine.opacity = 1.0;

}
```

10.081

Each of these *IBActions* sets the colour of the line. If you look at the code for the *blueLine*, I've set the colour in a different way. This is because the standard *UIColor blueColor* isn't the right shade. Instead, I've set it using decimal values of red, green and blue.

It might look complicated but if you have experience of working with different colours on a computer, you might well have seen something similar before.

Next we need to add the code to *Undo* the previously drawn line and one to *Clear* all the lines we draw. Copy these two *methods* underneath the ones for setting the colour:

```
-(IBAction)undoLine:(id)sender{
    if ([self.canvas.lines count] > 0) {
        [self.canvas.lines removeLastObject];
        [self.canvas setNeedsDisplay];
    }
}

-(IBAction)clearLines:(id)sender{
    if ([self.canvas.lines count] > 0) {
        int c = [self.canvas.lines count];
        for (int d=0;d<c;d++)
        {
        [self.canvas.lines removeLastObject];
            [self.canvas setNeedsDisplay];}
    }
}
```

10.082

What this code does is quite clever. It counts the lines you draw, where one line is anything you draw before lifting your finger. Then in the *Undo* code, it deletes the last line you drew. The *Clear* code deletes the last line you drew and then repeats this until all the lines have gone. To do this, the code uses something called a *loop*. Loops are very important in coding. They are a way of doing something over and over again. For a more detailed explanation, have a look at **http://whatis.techtarget.com/definition/loop**.

A small aside: the line in *clearLines'* - *'int c = [self.canvas.lines count];* will throw up a yellow warning. You can safely ignore this for our purposes.

Only two more methods to go and one of them you should know well; the *Back* method. You can copy this from one of our other screens or type it out again. Put it under the *clearLines* method:

```
- (IBAction)back:(id)sender{
    [self dismissViewControllerAnimated:YES completion:nil];
}
```

10.083

Last *method* now; this one is for the *Camera* button. It needs to be able to take a screenshot and save it to the *camera roll*. Here's the code:

```
-(IBAction)captureScreen:(id)sender{

    UIGraphicsBeginImageContext(self.view.bounds.size);
    [self.view.layer renderInContext:UIGraphicsGetCurrentContext()];
    UIImage *viewImage = UIGraphicsGetImageFromCurrentImageContext();
    UIGraphicsEndImageContext();
    UIImageWriteToSavedPhotosAlbum(viewImage, nil, nil, nil);

    UIAlertController *alert = [UIAlertController
                                alertControllerWithTitle:@"Jottings Saved"
                                message:@"Your jottings have been saved to the camera roll."
                                preferredStyle:UIAlertControllerStyleAlert];

    UIAlertAction *ok = [UIAlertAction
                         actionWithTitle:@"OK"
                         style:UIAlertActionStyleDefault
                         handler:^(UIAlertAction * action)
                         {
                             [alert dismissViewControllerAnimated:YES completion:nil];
                             [self dismissViewControllerAnimated:YES completion:nil];

                         }];

    [alert addAction:ok];
    [self presentViewController:alert animated:YES completion:nil];
}
```

10.084

You might recognise the *UIGraphicsBeginImageContext* code. We used it in the email code to take a screenshot. That's what we're doing here. Only this time, instead of putting the result, the image, into the email, we add it to the *camera library* using the code *UIImageWriteToSavedPhotosAlbum*.

And that's it. You'll be delighted – and relieved – to hear that's all the code we will need for our school app.

The last thing we have to do is link all our *IBActions* up to our buttons. So open up Main.storyboard:

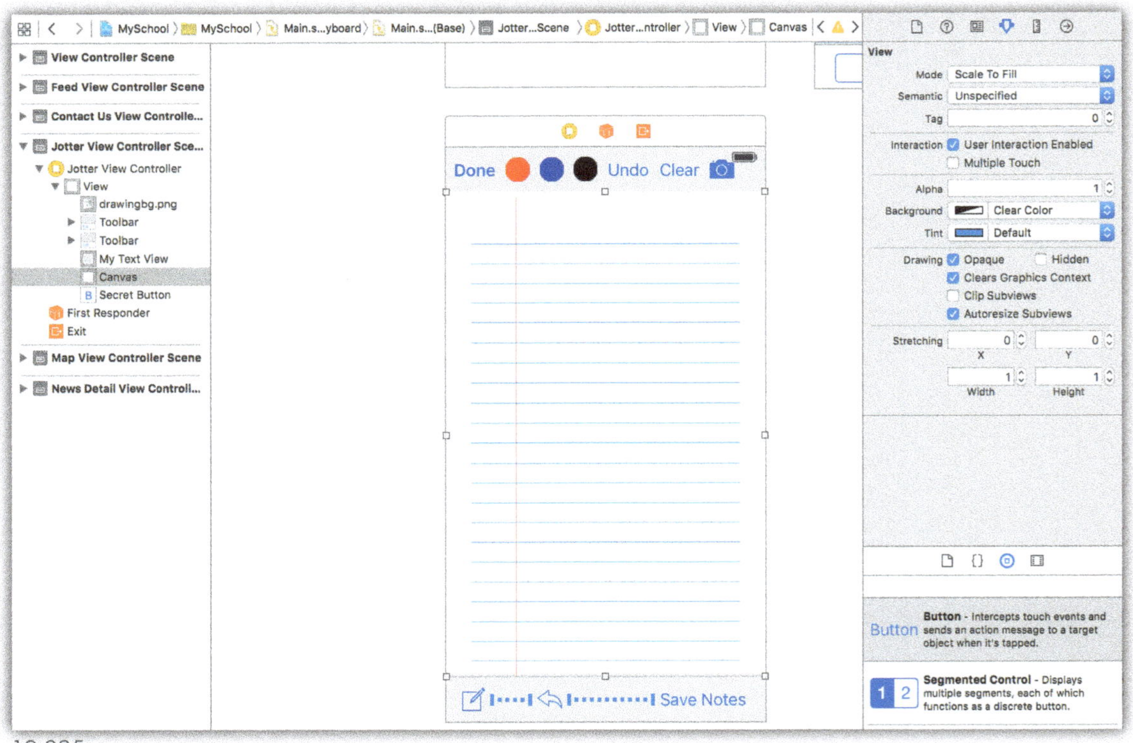

10.085

You might notice that I still have the sidebar open to the left of my *View Controller*. I deliberately didn't tell you to close it earlier as we are going to use it as an alternative method of adding our *IBActions* to our buttons.

Unlike our other screens, here we have objects on top of each other. This will make it hard to do our two-finger drag to the yellow circle with the square in it.

Take a closer look at the sidebar:

At the top, you will notice the yellow circle again. So we can drag from our items in the list to that yellow circle.

The only problem is that at the moment, you can't see all the objects. This is because our two *Toolbars* are currently compacted to save space. So click on the little arrows next to them. This will expand the *Toolbars* and you'll be able to see all of the buttons on them.

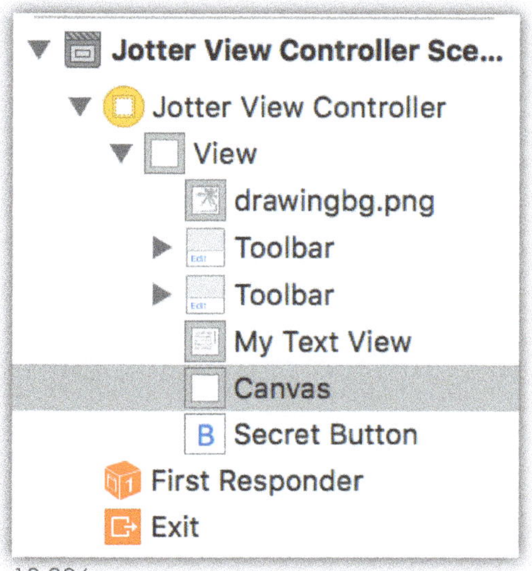

10.086

With the *Toolbars* expanded, the sidebar should look like this:

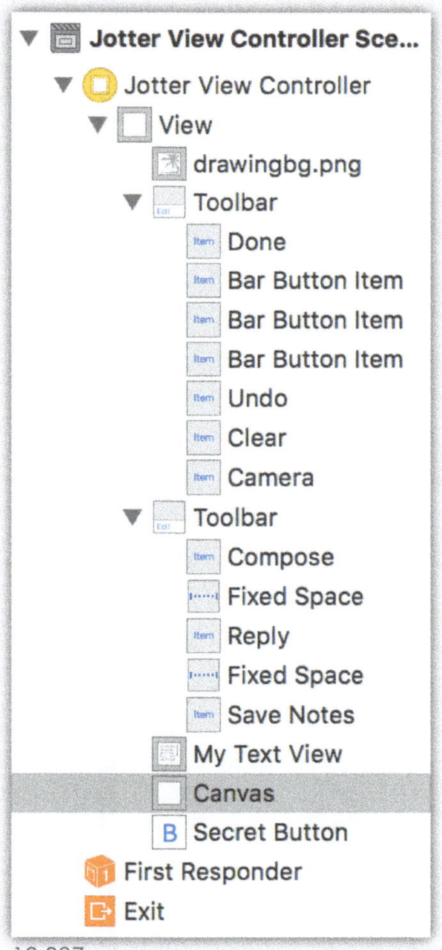

10.087

Now *Xcode* helps us out here. It tries to tell us what everything is. You can see, for example, our *Done* button as the first item under the first *Toolbar*. However, this isn't always possible. Under the *Done* button there are three *Bar Button Items* – these are our colours – but you don't know which is which. Select one and keep an eye on the *View Controller* to the right:

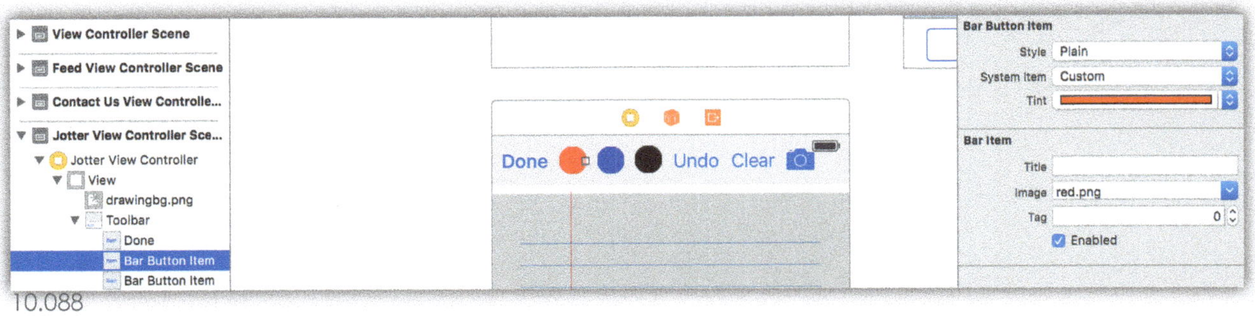

10.088

Look where the handle (the little square) appeared – on top of the red button. Look at the *Attributes inspector* and you can see this is the button that you made red. Now you know which button we have selected.

Knowing this, you can identify all of the objects. Go through each one in the list and watch it become selected on the *View Controller*.

Therefore, let's add our first *IBAction*. Two-finger drag from *Done* in the sidebar to the yellow circle:

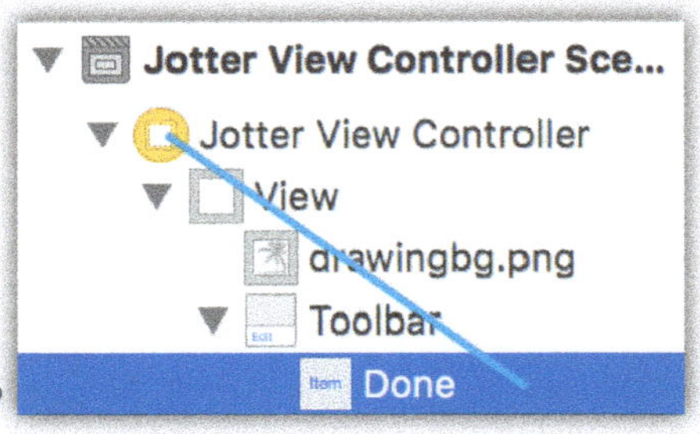

10.089

The usual black pop-up box will appear, only this time it's much bigger, as we have a lot more *IBActions*:

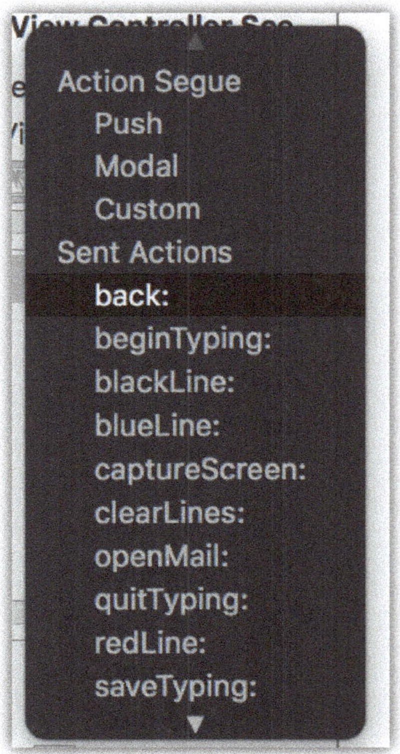

10.090

Select *back:* as our *Done* button will call the code to go back.

Repeat the process with the *Bar Button Item* under *Done*. Check that it's the red button and two-finger drag to the yellow circle.

Select the method *redLine:* from the pop-up box. Repeat this with the other two *Bar Button Items* by dragging from the yellow circle and selecting the correct colour method for their colour.

At this point, you should be up to the Undo button:

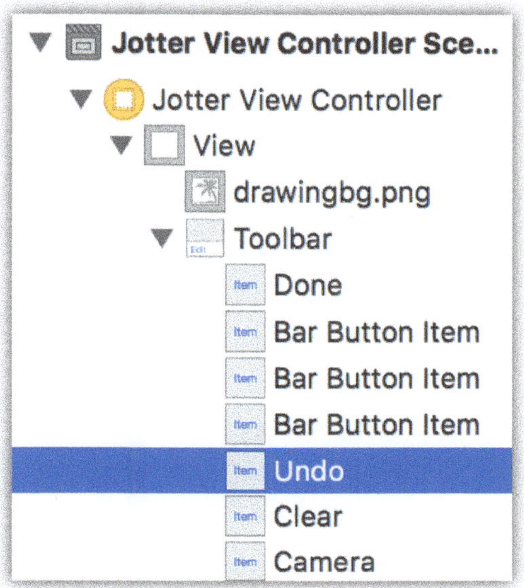

10.091

Two-finger drag to the yellow circle. We're looking for the *undoLine:* method:

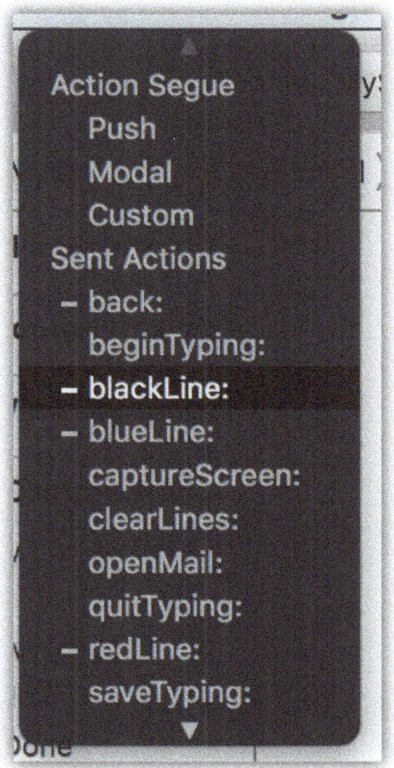

10.092

At first glance it doesn't appear to be there but by pressing the arrow under the *saveTyping:* method the *undoLine:* method becomes visible:

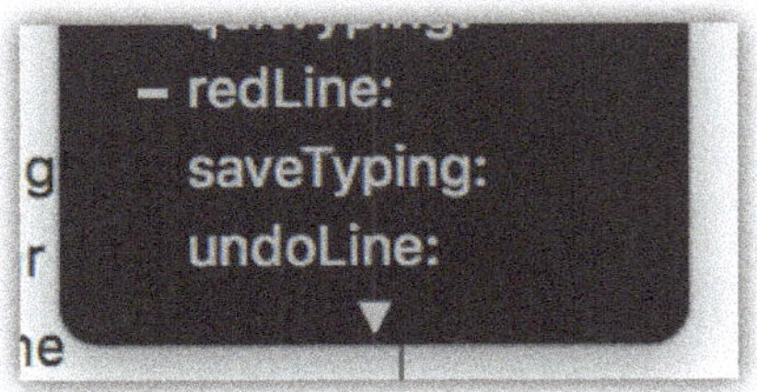

10.093

Select it and the black box will disappear.

That is the only *method* you'll need to scroll down to find but it's handy to know about it in case you ever write code with lots of *IBActions*.

Repeat the process for the *Clear* button and select the method *clearLines:*

Then select the *Camera* button and two-finger drag to the yellow circle. Link it to the *captureScreen:* method.

That's the first *Toolbar* fully linked up!

Let's look at the second Toolbar:

Here we can ignore the *Fixed Space* items. There are two of them.

Link the following buttons to these methods:

Compose **link to** *beginTyping*

Reply **link to** *openMail*

Save Notes **link to** *saveTyping*

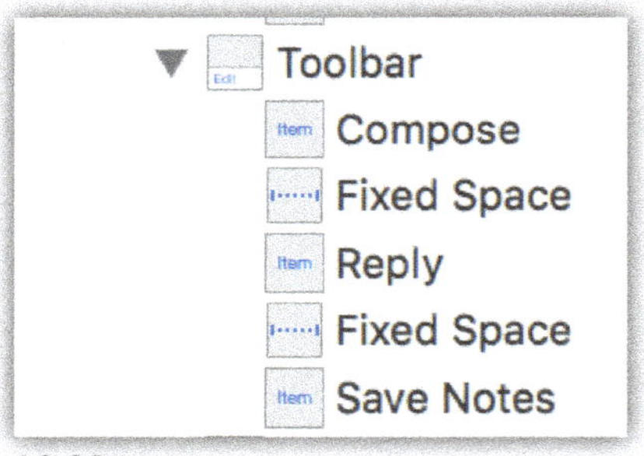

10.094

One last method to add. Go to your *Secret Button*:

10.095

Two-finger drag from the *Secret Button* the yellow circle and select *quitTyping:*

That's it. You've finished the *School Jotter* screen, but there is one thing left to do before you can test it.

We need to link the *School Jotter* button on the home screen of our app to the *Jotter View Controller*, so find a space in your *storyboard* and two-finger click to bring up the menu:

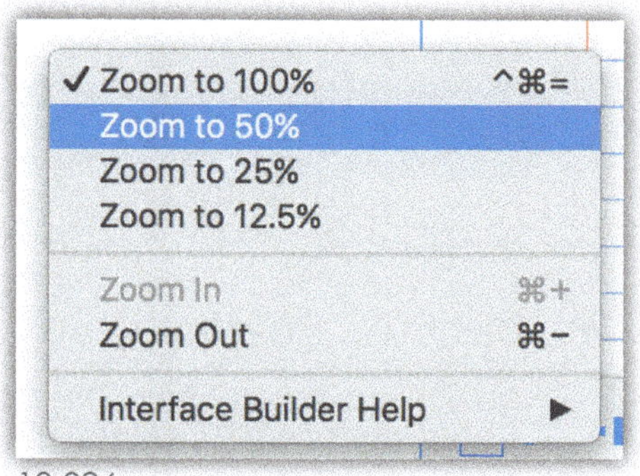

10.096

Select *Zoom to 50%*:

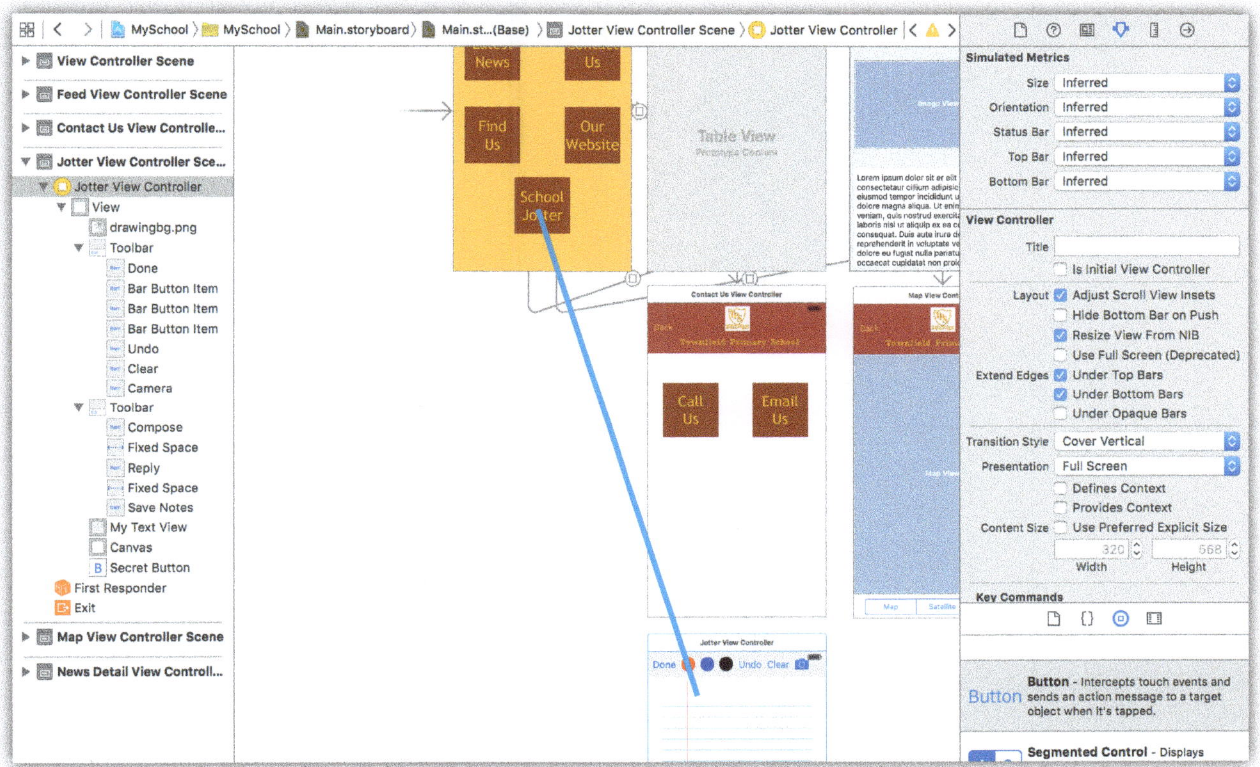

10.097

Two-finger drag from the *School Jotter* button to *Jotter View Controller* and select *Modal* from the black pop-up menu.

Finally, I need you to go back to *JotterViewController.h*.

We have to make one tiny edit to the code that is there:

```
__weak IBOutlet UITextView *myTextView;
__weak IBOutlet CanvasView *canvas;
__weak IBOutlet UIButton *secretButton;
```

10.098

This code was automatically generated when we dragged from our *user interface* items into the .h file.

On the line about *CanvasView*, could you please delete *_weak* so that the code looks like this:

```
__weak IBOutlet UITextView *myTextView;
IBOutlet CanvasView *canvas;
__weak IBOutlet UIButton *secretButton;
```

10.099

You are now ready to test your *School Jotter* feature. Press the *Play* button.

You should be able to draw, make notes, save them, email them, change the colour, go back – everything!

10.100

While you're in the simulator, go back and test all the buttons. The whole thing should work. You have just built your own school app.

We haven't focused on the meaning of the code, instead, we've got to grips with *Xcode* and the procedures involved.

By doing lots of things time and time again, you should be getting used to the way apps are built. And knowing this is the hardest part. You can always Google the code bit. But learning how to put it all together is the tricky bit.

We're not quite finished. We have built our app for iPhone 5 but Apple state that all iPhone apps must support iPhone 4, with the 3.5 inch screen.

This will only involve some minor tweaking and adding a few lines of code in one of our files.

http://www.alanpeat.com/build-an-app/Chapter10

CHAPTER ELEVEN ADAPTING OUR STORYBOARD FOR iPHONE 4

If you cast your mind back to the beginning of this book – before I taught you how to make an app – we talked about different screen sizes.

So far, we've built our app for the 4 inch screen, which covers iPhone 5, iPhone 5S, the newer iPod touches and will work on iPhone 6, iPhone 6s, iPhone 6 Plus, iPhone 6s Plus and the most recent devices announced in September 2016.

The only iPhone size our app won't work on is the 3.5 inch screen. This covers iPhone 3, iPhone 4 and iPhone 4S, as well as some older iPod touch models.

As we are going to make our app work only on iOS 8.0 and above, this will rule out older devices but it could still run on the iPhone 4 and iPhone 4S.

Earlier we also talked about *Auto Layout* and that is what we should use to make our app work on multiple devices. However, fully covering *Auto Layout* to the point where we could use it for this purpose would take way too many pages of this book.

So instead, we're going to make another storyboard for the 3.5 inch screen.

Don't panic, it's pretty easy. We are going to copy our 4 inch storyboard, the one you've spent hours developing with me, and make a few changes so that it works perfectly on iPhone 4. Although this is quite easy to do, it will be difficult to model to the pupils. I'd suggest doing one screen at a time with them and taking it quite slowly.

We won't have to link any buttons to *IBActions* – all that will be copied over. And most of our screens will only require a little tinkering to make them work.

When we've finished doing this, we need to add a little bit of code to tell the app which storyboard to use depending on the size of the screen of the device it is on.

First of all, select *Main.storyboard* in the *Navigator* pane and two-finger press it:

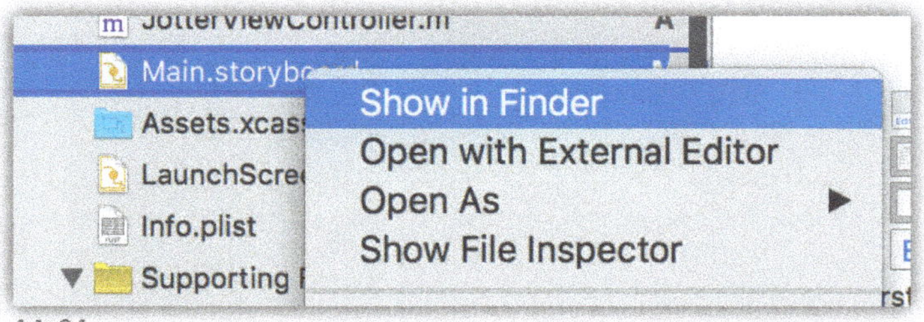

11.01

From the menu that appears, select Show in Finder so that the file opens up in a new

Finder window.

You should then see something like this:

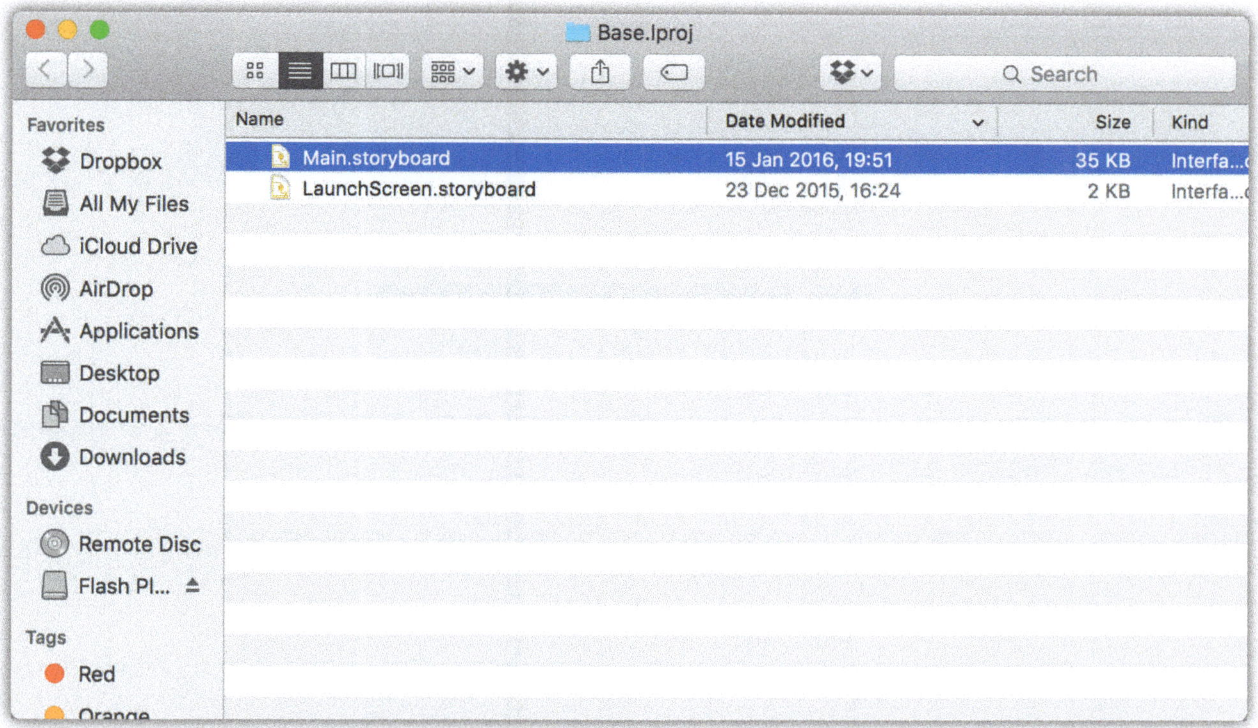

11.02

Two-finger press on *Main.storyboard* and select *Duplicate* from the pop-up menu:

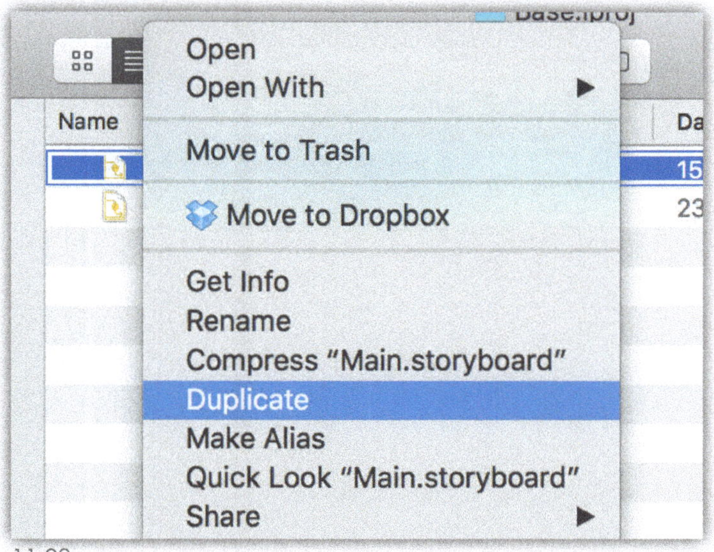

11.03

This will put a copy of your storyboard file above your original file:

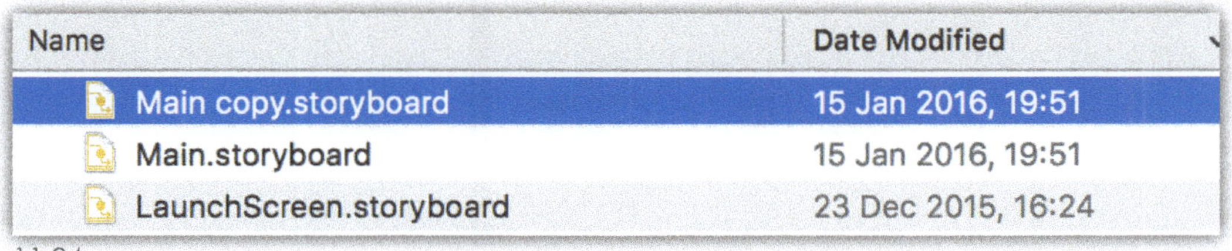

11.04

The file is called *Main copy.storyboard*. This isn't much good to us, so click once on the file name and it will become editable so you can change it:

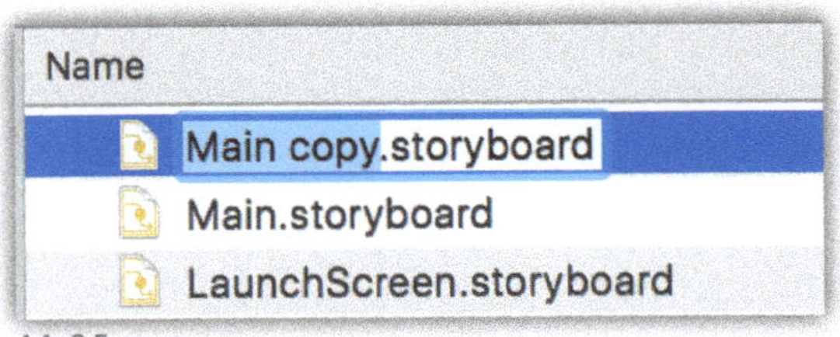

11.05

Replace *Main copy'* with *MainiPhone4* so that it looks like this:

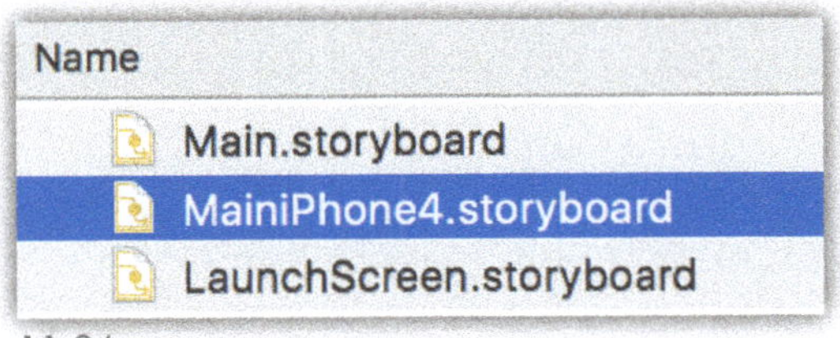

11.06

Mine has dropped below the original file, but whether or not yours does that will depend on how your files are organised in Finder.

Next, drag the *MainiPhone4.storyboard* file from the *Finder* window into *Xcode*, just below *Main.storyboard* in the *Navigator* pane. Make sure you have the usual boxes ticked when you import the file:

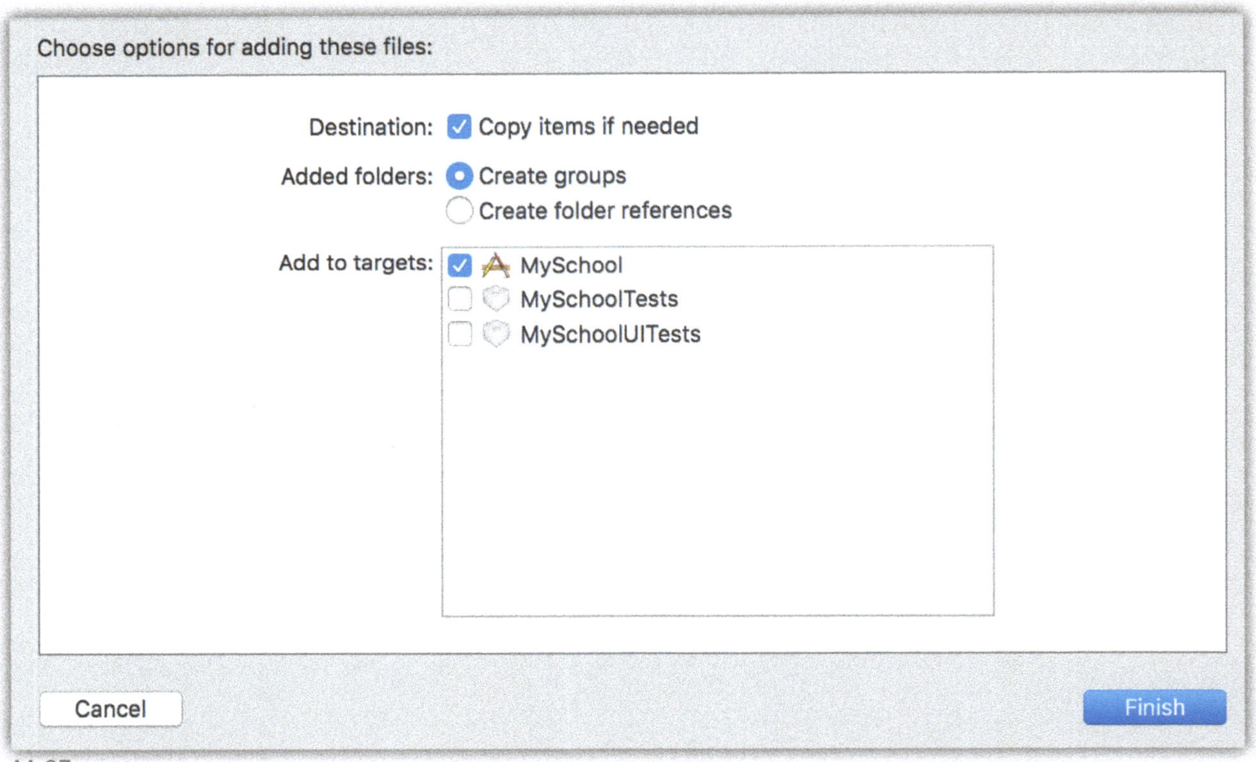

11.07

If you've done it right, your *Navigator* pane should look like this:

11.08

Click on your new *MainiPhone4.storyboard* file and have a look in the *Editor* pane:

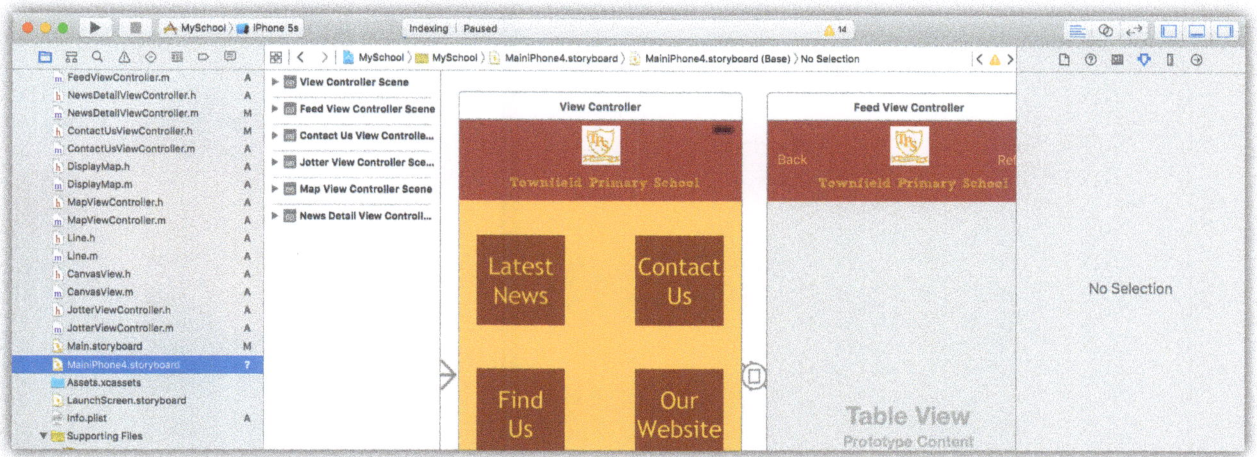

11.09

It should look like your *Main.storyboard* file.

We need to change things to fit the iPhone 4. In Xcode 8, this is much easier than in previous versions. With your *MainiPhone4.storyboard* open, select the 'View As iPhone SE' option at the bottom of the Editor Pane:

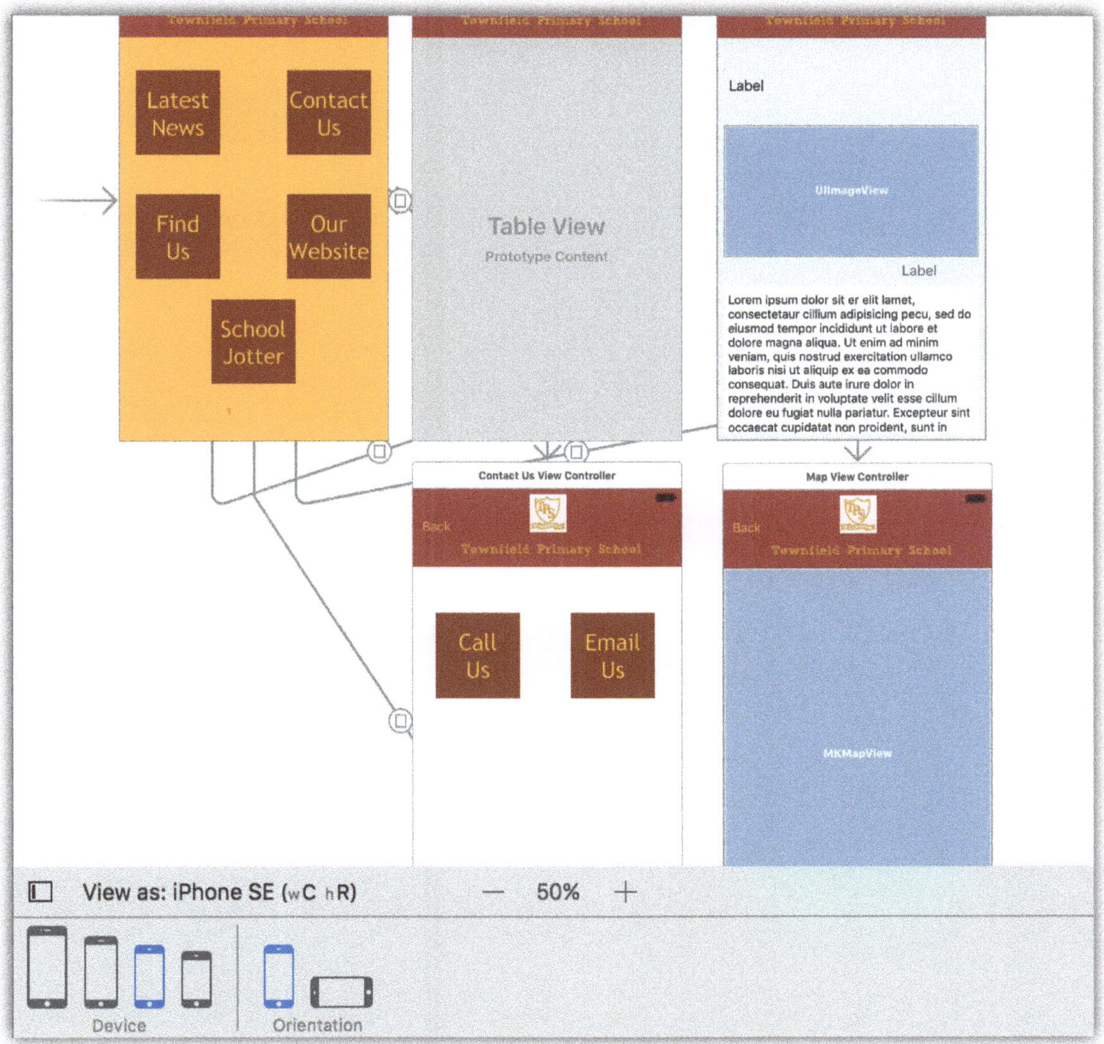

11.10

Now, choose the smallest screen size - the iPhone 4:

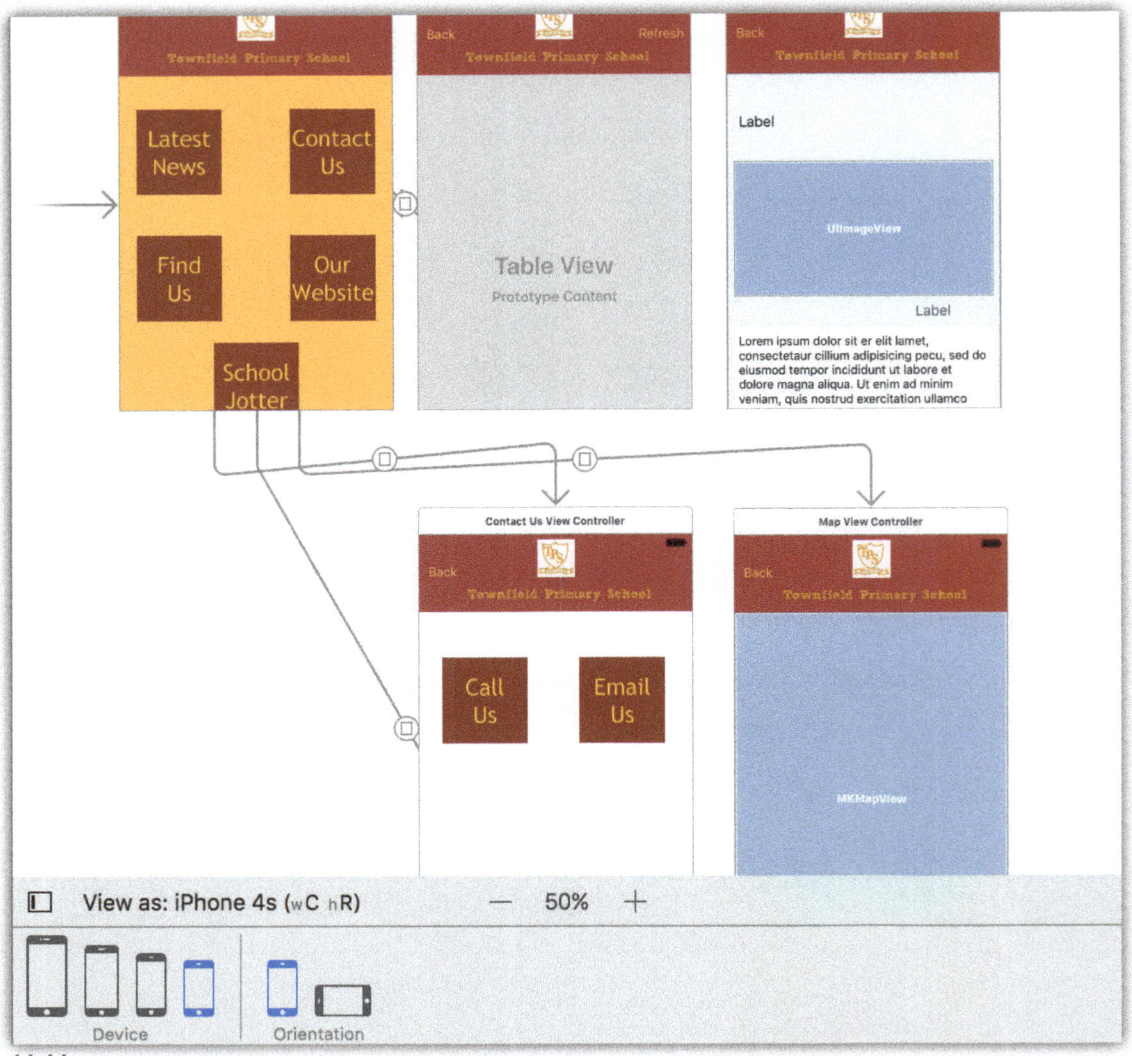

11.11

As if by magic, all of your screen sizes will change to show you what your screens will look like on Apple's smallest devices.

We now need to alter the layout slightly of each screen to make sure all our buttons and content are visible on the smaller devices. Let's start with the home screen:

Depending on where you placed your buttons, you may not even have to do anything here.

Here's mine:

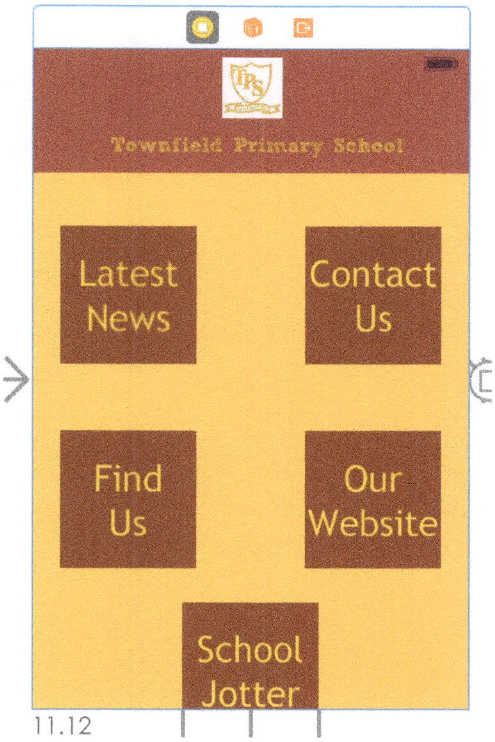

11.12

You can see that my *School Jotter* button goes off the screen slightly. All you need to do is move the buttons. Select them one at a time and use the arrow buttons on your keyboard to nudge them around the screen until you're happy. You can also use the mouse to drag them around:

11.13

That's it for this screen. The buttons are all visible and I've played around with them to try to keep the spacing even.

Let's go on to the next screen.

Find Feed View Controller in the storyboard:

All we need to do is resize our *Table View* so that it isn't so long it goes off the screen.

As it stands, it would work but there would be some news items that would never scroll into view so we're going to make it shorter.

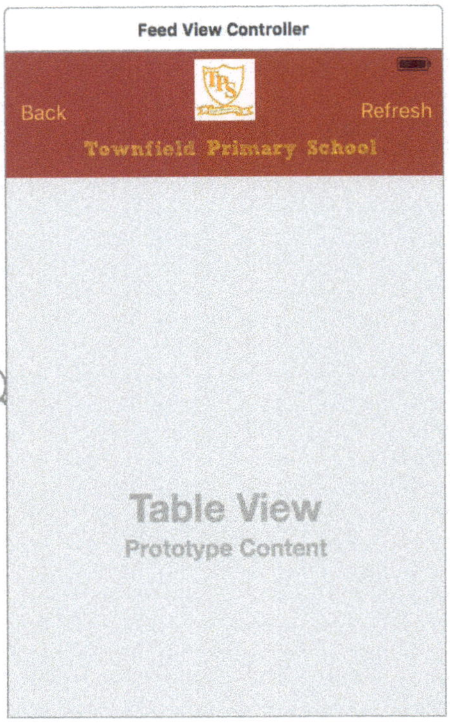

11.14

Click on the *Table View* to select it. You should see little white squares (handles) appear around it:

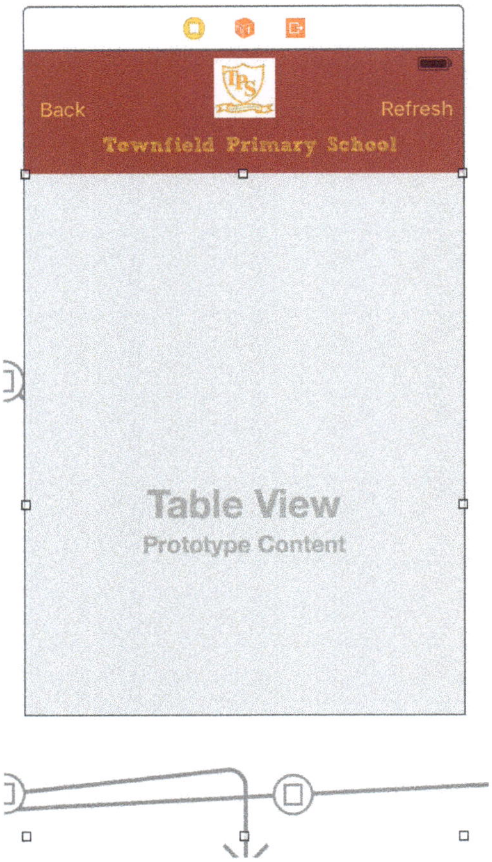

11.15

About two centimetres below the *View Controller* there are three of those little white squares. These are on the bottom of our *Table View*.

All we have to do is click on any one of those bottom three handles and drag up to the bottom of the *View Controller*.

Your *Table View* is the correct height to fit in the gap between our header image and the bottom of the screen.

And that's all that's required on *Feed View Controller*.

11.16

But let's do a tricky one now. Click on the *News Detail View Controller*:

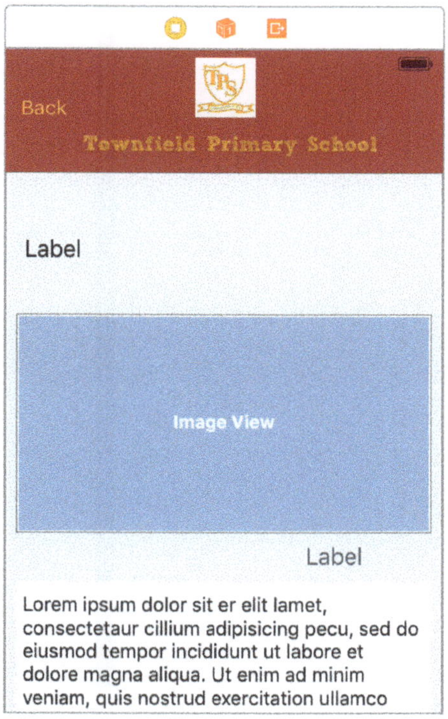

11.17

So let's have a look at what is required.

We could do with moving the *Label,* where the headline goes, up a bit. We need to move the *Image View* up a bit, the *date label* up a bit, the *Text View* up a bit – and it will need to be made shorter. We will also need to resize the *Scroll View* so it doesn't go off the screen.

Start with the Scroll View. You can easily select this by pressing to the far left of the date label:

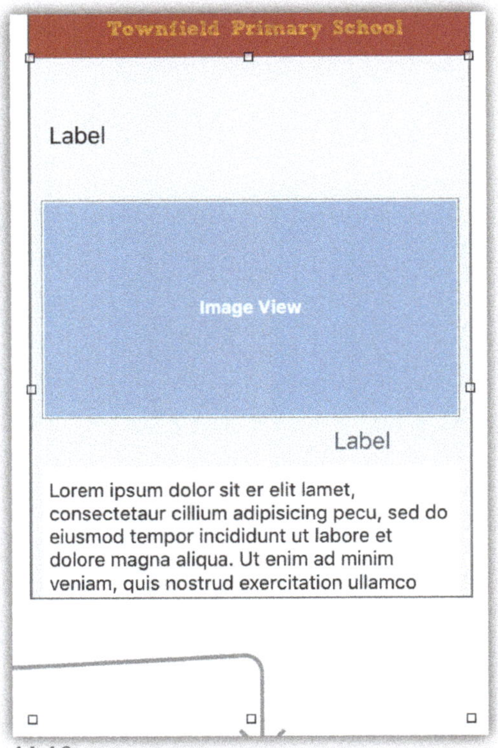

11.18

Just as with our Table View on the previous screen, drag up the handles from the bottom and bring them in line with the base of the View Controller:

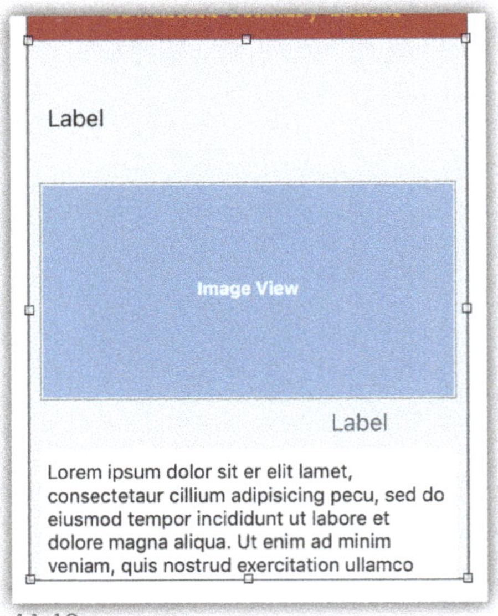

11.19

Next, working from the top down, select the *Label* we use for the news headline:

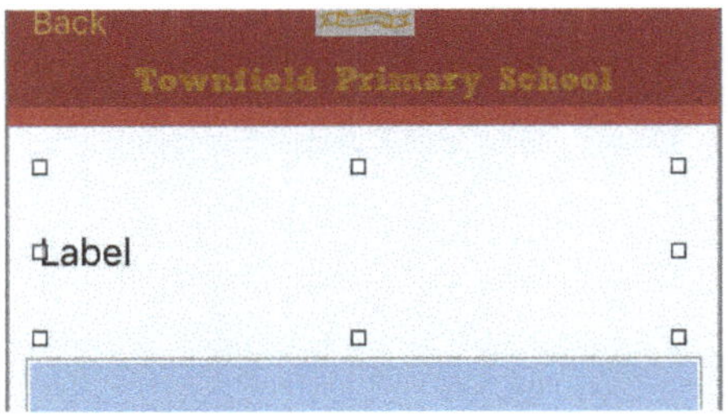

11.20

There's not a great deal of room here so using the arrows on your keyboard, nudge the *Label* up so the top three handles are just touching the bottom of your header image:

11.21

That's about as much as you can do, but you can nudge up the *Image View* by selecting it and using the arrow keys to move it up slightly like this:

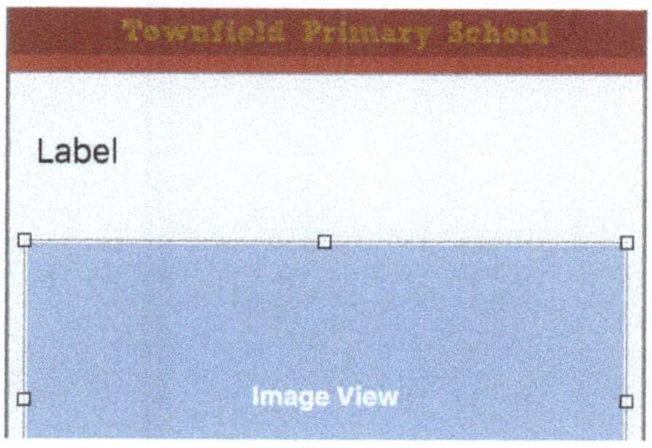

11.22

Take care not to let the *Image View* overlap the headline *Label*. You can check this by clicking back on the *Label* and seeing whether the bottom handles of it are over the *Image View* or not.

Your screen should look like this:

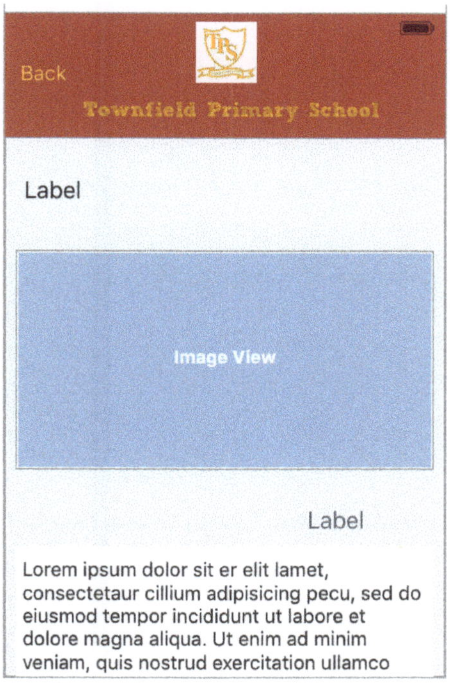

11.23

Select the date *Label* and nudge it up a bit so that it's just below the *Image View*:

11.24

The last thing to do is sort out the *Text View* that our main text goes into. There are two things to do here. We need to drag it up a bit and also we need to resize it so it doesn't go off the bottom of the screen. Select the *Text View*:

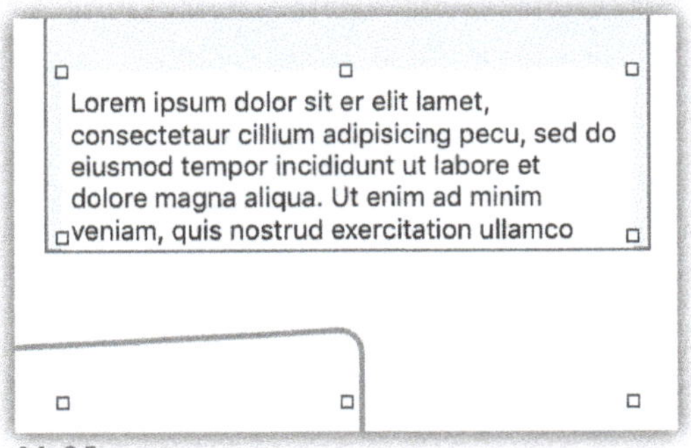

11.25

Use the arrow keys on your keyboard to nudge it up so it is just below the date *Label*.

It should look like this:

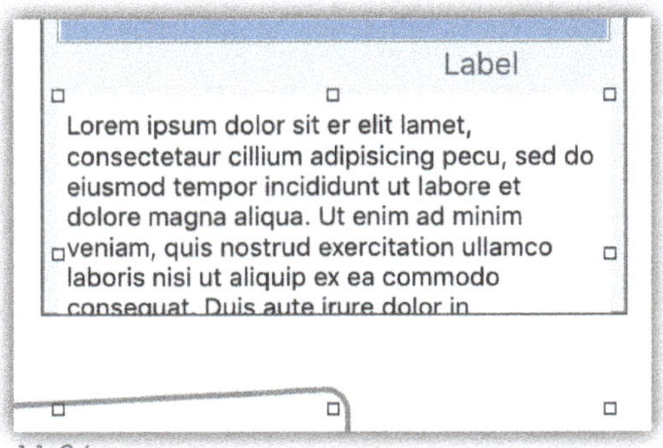

11.26

Finally, select one of the bottom handles – the ones that are off the bottom of the *View Controller* – and drag up to resize the *Text View* so that it doesn't go off the screen:

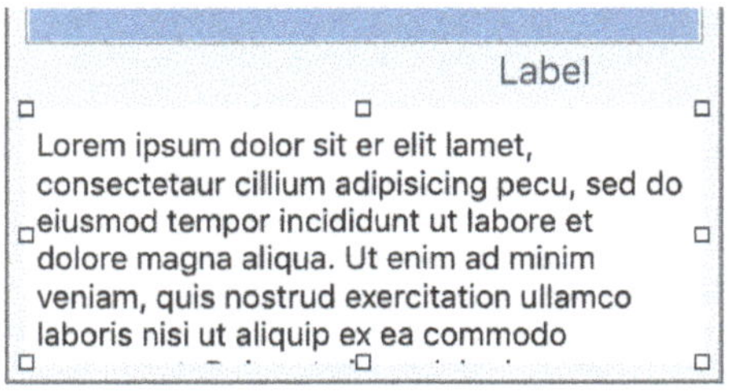

11.27

The *News Detail View Controller* is now ready for the iPhone 4.

Next up, find *Contact Us View Controller*:

Notice anything? It's fine just the way it is. We don't need to do anything to this screen unless you placed your buttons considerably lower than mine.

If you did, just nudge them up a bit.

You may wish to centre them but really, there's nothing to do here.

11.28

Only two screens left. Go to *Map View Controller*:

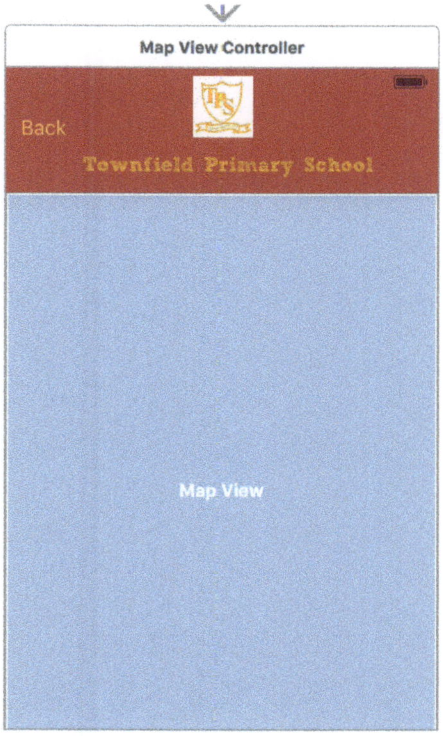

11.29

Two things to do here: resize the *Map View* so it isn't off the bottom of the screen and then move up our *Segmented Control* (that's the button that flicks between the satellite and map views).

Select the *Map View*:

11.30

As with the others, drag up from the bottom handles, but remember to drag it a little bit higher to leave room for the *Segmented Control*.

Your *Map View Controller* should look like this:

11.31

But we have a problem. Where has our *Segmented Control* gone? You've probably worked out that it is below the visible screen but, as we can't see any of it, we're going to have to find it somewhere else.

Do you remember the sidebar in the *Editor* pane which we used to move objects in the *School Jotter* around? That's a handy way of locating our objects. Make sure the sidebar is activated by pressing the button in the bottom left-hand corner of the *Editor* pane:

11.32

On the sidebar, locate *Map View Controller* and double-click it to expand it and reveal all of the objects. It may already be expanded:

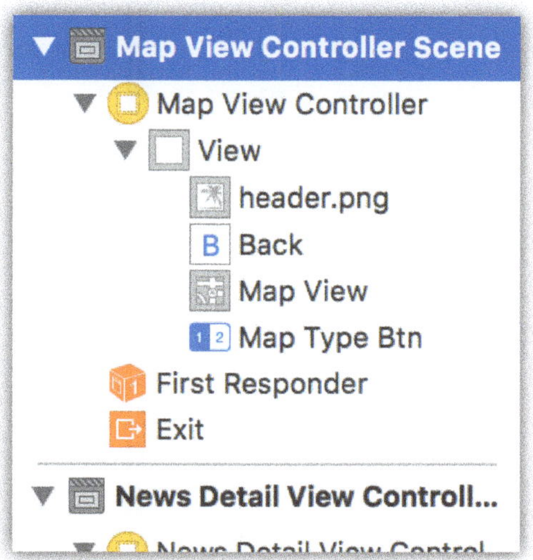

11.33

If you look through the list of objects, just under *Map View* you should be able to spot *Map Type Btn*. That's what we called our *Segmented Control*. Click on it and, as you do, keep an eye on the *Map View Controller* screen in the right-hand side of the *Editor* pane:

11.34

Below the *View Controller*, you will see two handles. The reason you can only see two and not nine as in the other objects is because you can't change the height of a *Segmented Control*.

Carefully click on one of the small squares. A rectangle where the *Segmented Control* is will briefly flash. Now you can use the arrow keys on your keyboard to move it up until it appears on the screen:

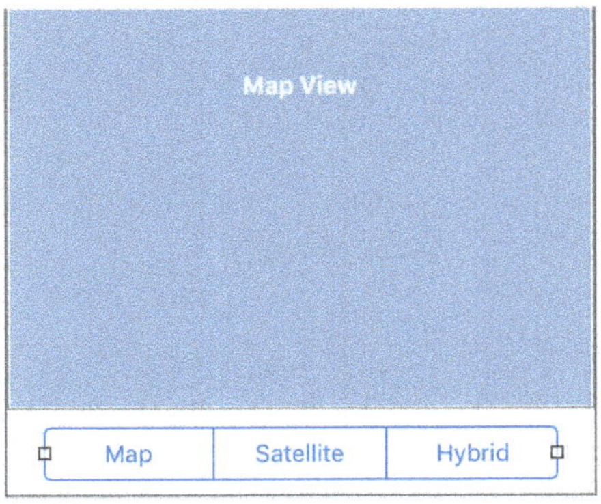

11.35

There you go. The *Map View Controller* is now fully iPhone 4 compatible.

That leaves one screen to go; the *School Jotter*. Find it on your *storyboard* file and have a look at what needs to be done.

Here it is:

11.36

It's a bit harder to see here as we have lots of invisible objects, so I'll help you out. We're missing the top *Toolbar*, so we'll need to bring that down. Our *Text View* (for typing notes) is slightly too long, so we'll need to resize that. We also need to resize the *Canvas*. Apart from that, there's not a lot to do.

First find the *Toolbar*. It's the same method we used for finding the *Segmented Control*. Go to the sidebar and locate *Jotter View Controller*:

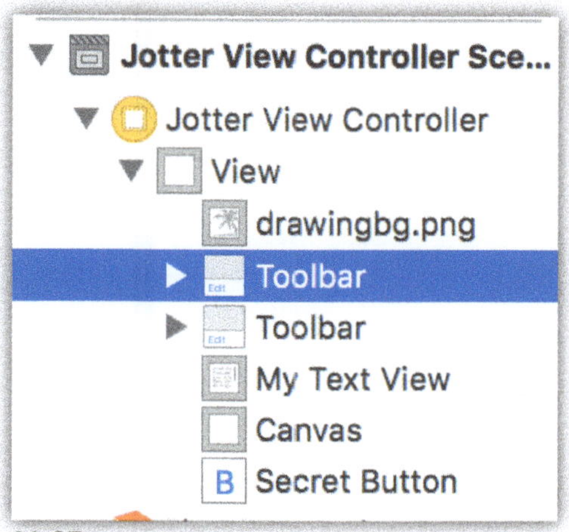

11.37

Click on the top *Toolbar*. It should be the first *Toolbar* in the list – but it might not be – so press it and check.

If two handles appear at the top of the *View Controller*, you've got the right one:

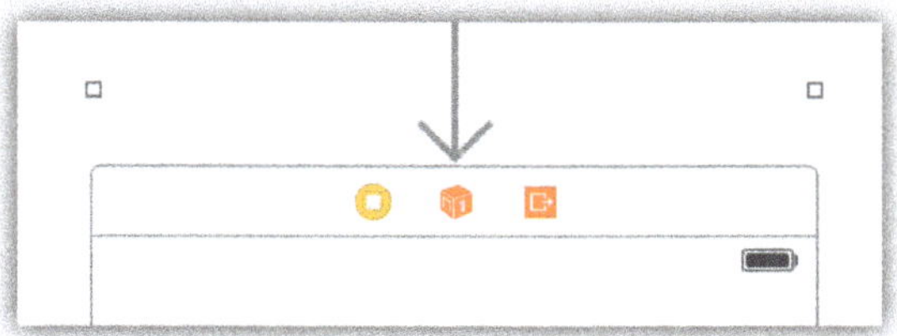
11.38

As before, if you press one of the handles, a rectangle will flash and you can nudge it down using your arrow keys until the Toolbar appears at the top of the screen. Move it into position:

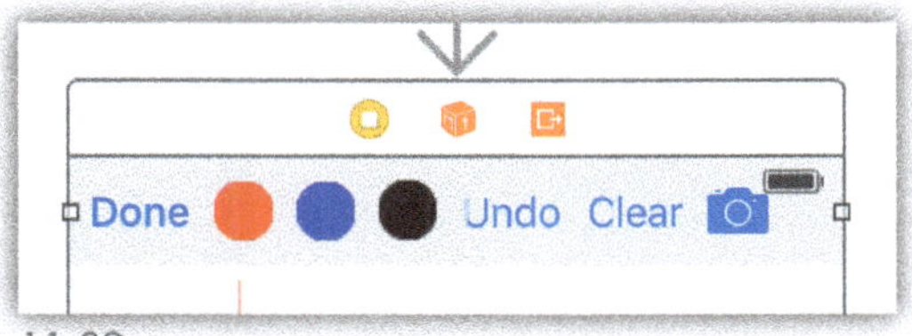

11.39

Now, in the sidebar, locate the *Text View*:

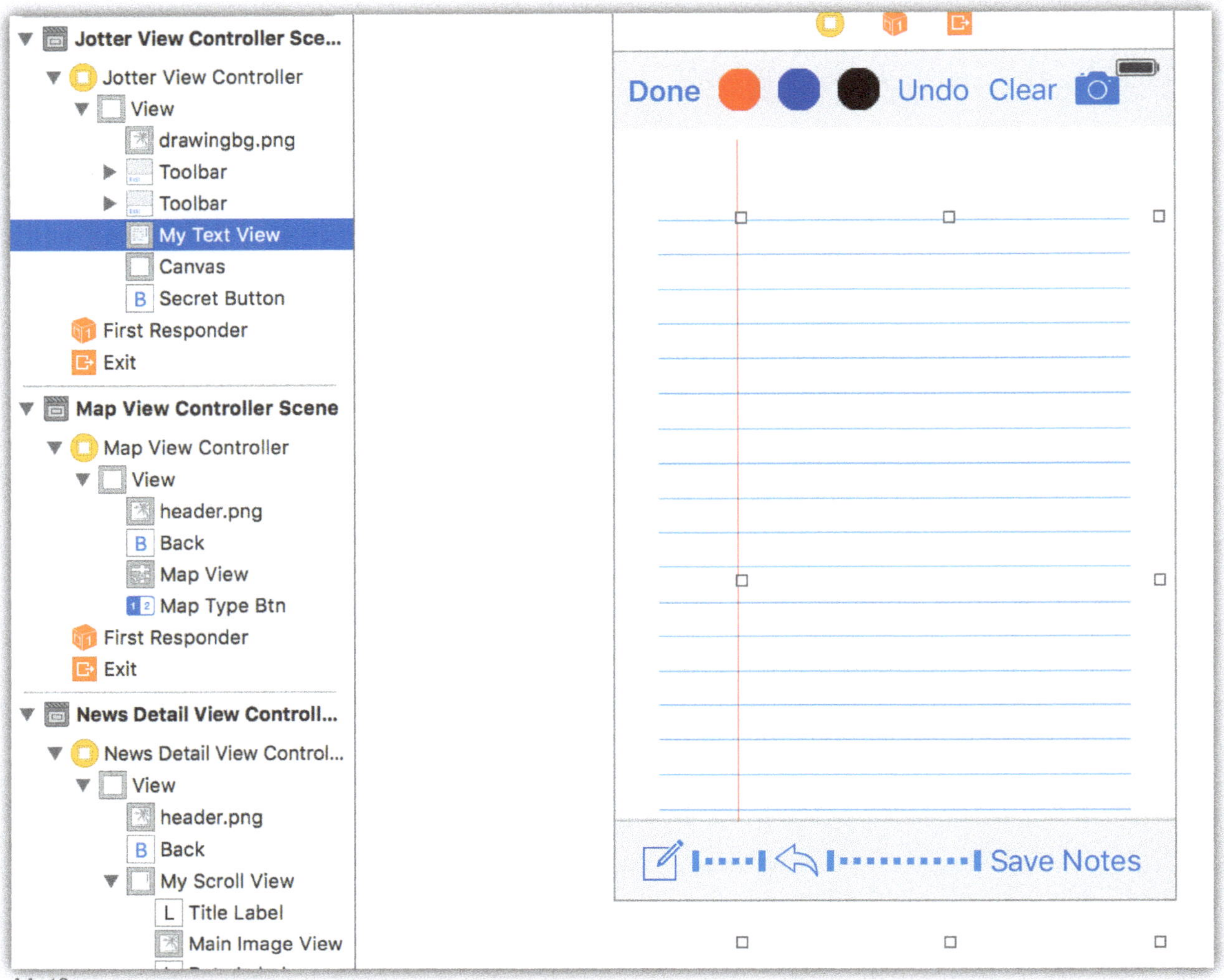

11.40

As before, drag from the handles below the *Text View* and resize it so it comes just above the bottom *Toolbar*.

The screen should look like this:

11.41

Finally, select the Canvas from the sidebar:

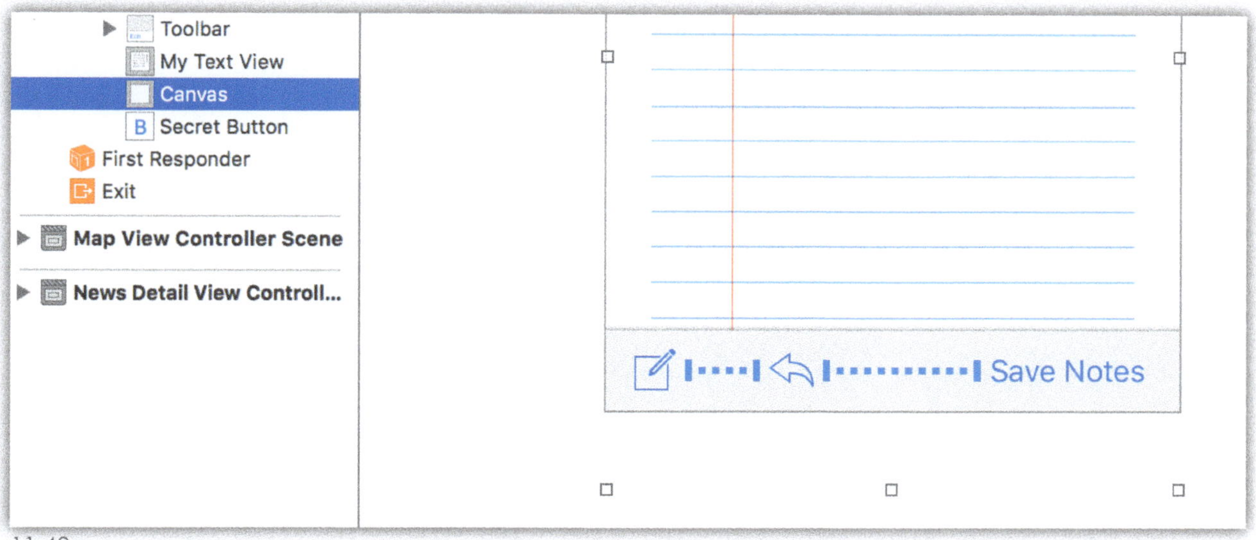

11.42

Drag from the bottom handles until the *Canvas* is just above the bottom *Toolbar*.

All of your screens are now iPhone 4 ready. All that's left to do is tell the app that is what we've done.

To do this, we're going to add a little bit of code. In the *Navigator* pane, find *AppDelegate.m*. Change the first *method, application didFinishLaunchingWithOptions*, in the file to this:

```
@implementation AppDelegate

- (BOOL)application:(UIApplication *)application didFinishLaunchingWithOptions:(NSDictionary *)launchOptions {
    // Override point for customization after application launch.

    CGSize iOSDeviceScreenSize = [[UIScreen mainScreen] bounds].size;

    if (iOSDeviceScreenSize.height == 480)
    {
        // Instantiate a new storyboard object using the storyboard file named Storyboard_iPhone35
        UIStoryboard *iPhone35Storyboard = [UIStoryboard storyboardWithName:@"MainiPhone4" bundle:nil];

        // Instantiate the initial view controller object from the storyboard
        UIViewController *initialViewController = [iPhone35Storyboard instantiateInitialViewController];

        // Instantiate a UIWindow object and initialize it with the screen size of the iOS device
        self.window = [[UIWindow alloc] initWithFrame:[[UIScreen mainScreen] bounds]];

        // Set the initial view controller to be the root view controller of the window object
        self.window.rootViewController  = initialViewController;

        // Set the window object to be the key window and show it
        [self.window makeKeyAndVisible];
    } else {
        UIStoryboard *iPhone4Storyboard = [UIStoryboard storyboardWithName:@"Main" bundle:nil];
        UIViewController *initialViewController = [iPhone4Storyboard instantiateInitialViewController];
        self.window = [[UIWindow alloc] initWithFrame:[[UIScreen mainScreen] bounds]];
        self.window.rootViewController  = initialViewController;
        [self.window makeKeyAndVisible];
    }
    return YES;
}
```
11.43

One more thing to do.

In the *Navigator* pane, go to the top item, the one with blue project icon:

11.44

Then press the *General* button that appears to the right.

You will see this screen:

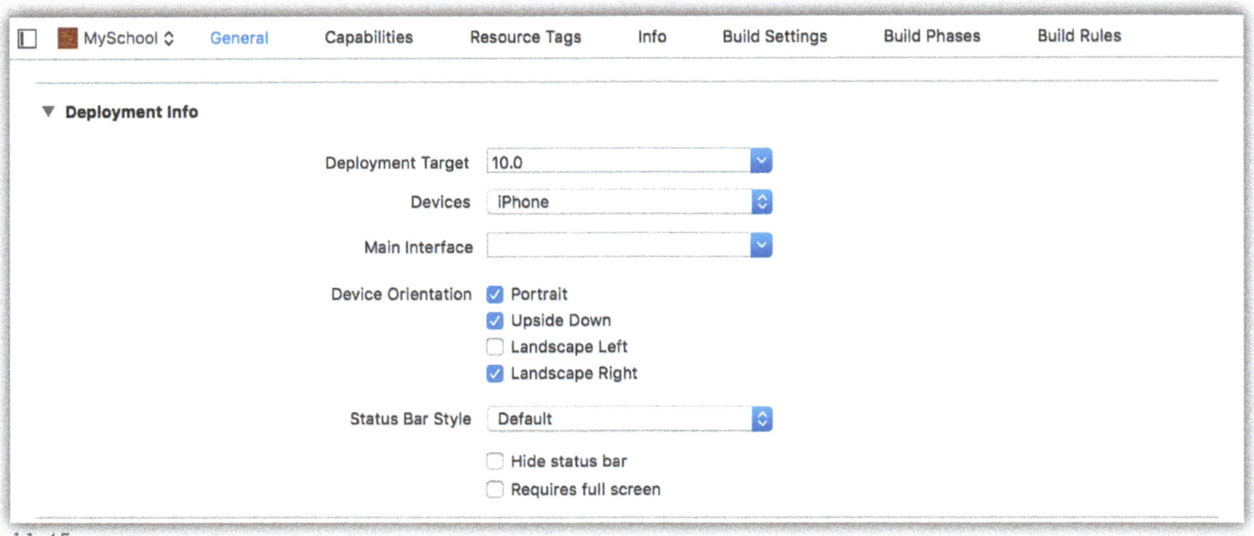

11.45

We will make a few changes here.

In the section headed *Deployment Info*, make sure *Deployment Target* says '8.0' by clicking and selecting from the drop-down menu.

Then, check that *Devices* is set to *iPhone*.

Go to *Main Interface* and delete the word 'Main'.

Next, on *Device Orientation*, leave *Portrait* checked, but also select *Upside Down*. Then deselect *Landscape Left* and *Landscape Right*.

Finally, tick the two boxes next to *Hide status bar* and *Requires full screen*.

The final screen should look like this:

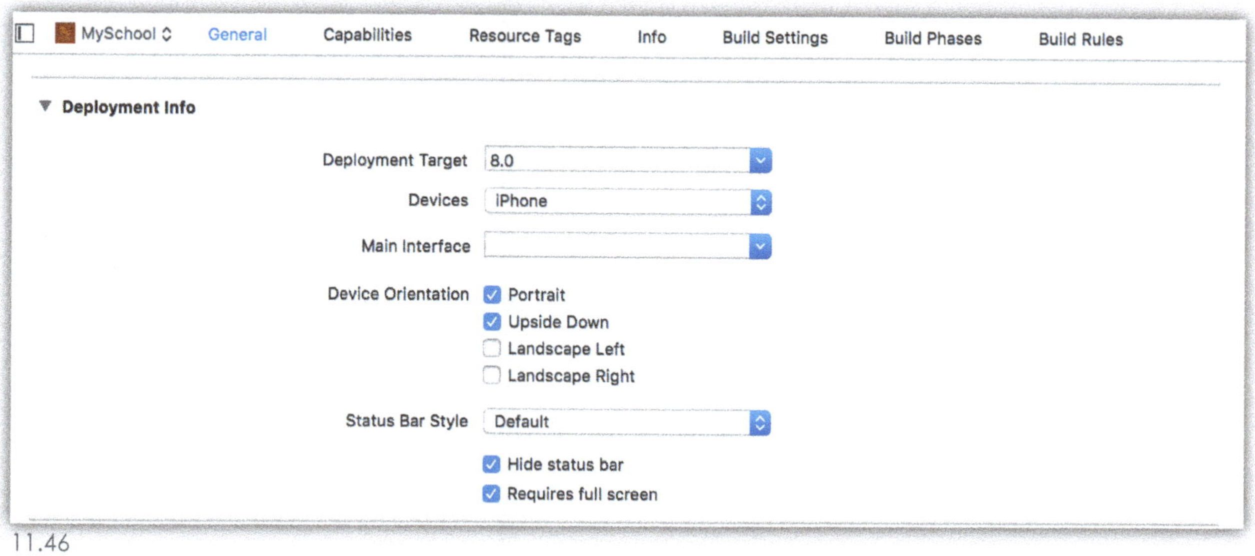

11.46

You are ready to test the app on the iPhone 4 simulator. Go to the top of *Xcode*:

11.47

Click on the name of the iPhone type on which you last ran the simulator and this menu will appear (if you cannot see an iPhone 4 in the list, you may not have set your Deployment Target to iOS 8.0 - iPhone 4's cannot run iOS 10 so will not appear if the Deployment Target is set to iOS 10):

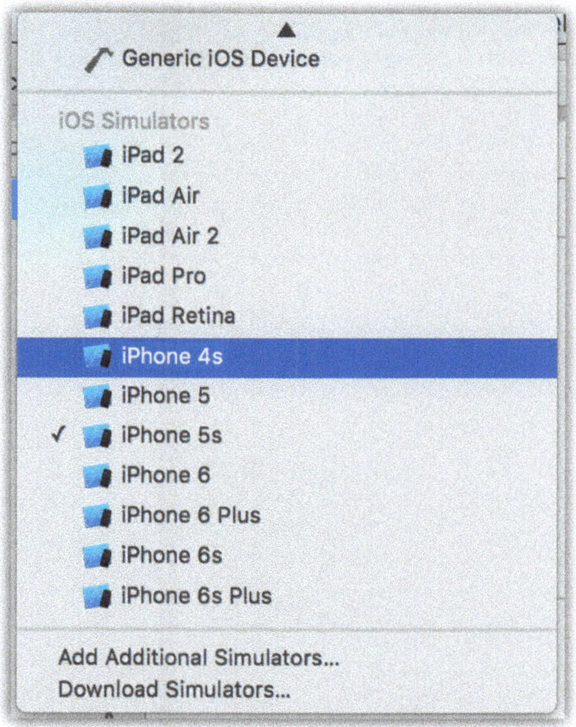

11.48

Select *iPhone 4s* and press the *Play* button. The simulator should open with a 3.5 inch screen:

11.49

You have finished your app. It works on two screen sizes and does enough that we should be able to get it into the App Store.

We still have a few things left to do. I will talk you through the process of adding an icon that will appear on the home screen of the device, adding a launch screen – the screen that shows for a second or two when you start an app – and setting the name.

Once we've done that, I will walk you through the app submission process. In order to submit an app to the App Store, you will need an Apple Developer Account, which costs £79 per year.

Don't feel like you have to get one now! But I will describe the process so that when you are ready, you have everything you need to submit your app.

http://www.alanpeat.com/build-an-app/Chapter11

CHAPTER TWELVE
THE FINISHING TOUCHES

You've done the hard bit – you've built your app. Now we're on to fine-tuning our app for the App Store.

In this chapter, we will learn how to:

- Create an icon in all the appropriate sizes.
- Create a launch screen for iPhone 4 and iPhone 5.
- Hide the status bar at the top of the iPhone – the one that shows the time and signal strength etc.
- Change the display name – the name that appears underneath the icon on the device home screen.

There's no code here but there is a fair amount of image manipulation involved which means the children in your class can once again be actively involved in a lot of the process.

If you need to refresh your memory on how to create images, go back to Chapter 3 and look at the section on using *iPiccy*. I'm not going to go over how to create images again, but instead we will focus on what we do with the images after we've created them.

Also you may be using your own favourite image editor, such as Fireworks. That's fine.

Creating the Icon

This is the image that will be displayed on the home screen of the device. Here are the rules:

- The image must be 1024 x 1024 pixels (a big square).
- Apple automatically create the round corners, so we need to stay away from the corners or our image will look weird.
- We can't use any transparency – so I recommend you save your image as a *jpg* file rather than a *PNG*.
- Text doesn't work very well – you're better off using your school logo.

In your prefered image editor, create a 1024 x 1024 image with your school logo on it. Here's mine (not to scale):

12.01

Save it somewhere you'll remember and call it 'icon.jpg'.

In order to put this icon into *Xcode*, we have to create lots of different versions of it. This is because Apple display the icon for your app in lots of different places and in lots of different sizes.

Luckily, there's a free app we can download to make this a lot easier.

Open up the *Mac App Store* by selecting this icon from the *dock*:

12.02

In the search bar, type *Prepo*:

12.03

Download the first app that comes up in the search: *Prepo*:

12.04

Let it install. Once it has finished, open it up:

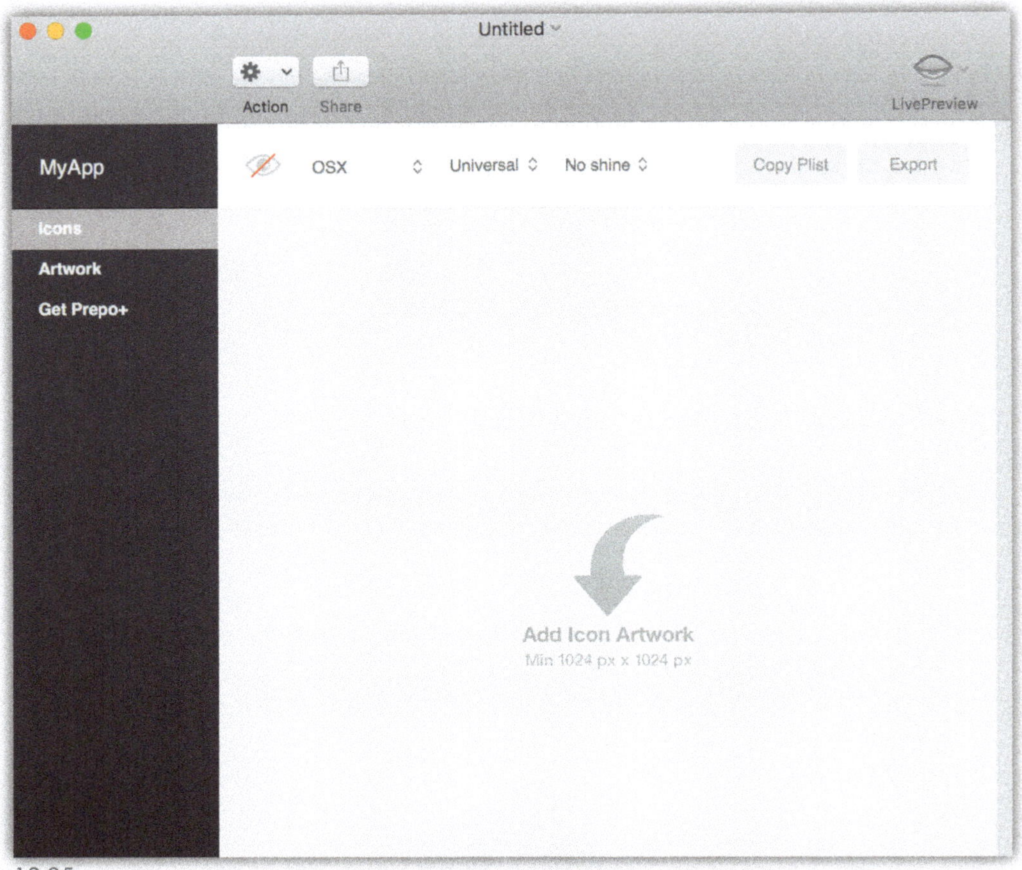

12.05

Drag the icon that you created earlier to the big space in the middle of the screen where it says *Add Icon Artwork*, then sit back and watch the magic happen...

You should see your icon automatically resized like this:

12.06

See the big *Export* button at the top? Press it.

A *Finder* window will appear. Choose where you want to save your icons – I suggest the desktop – and press the *New Folder* button and call your folder *App Icons*:

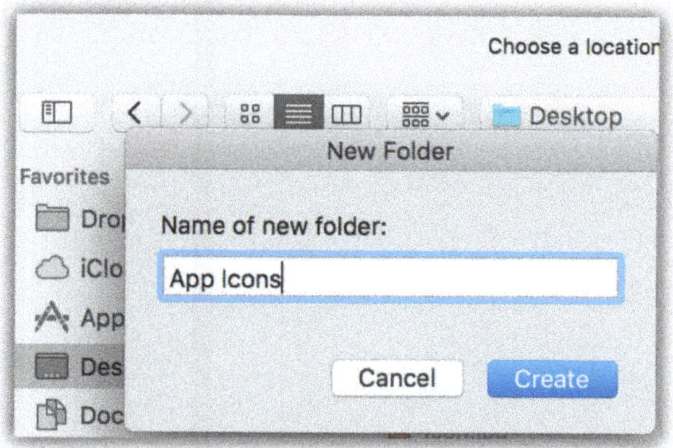

12.07

Press the blue *Create* button. You'll then see your empty *App Icons* folder. Press *Choose* in the bottom right and all your icons will be saved nicely.

Now we need to add our icons to our app. This is a case of dragging and dropping but we need to be careful about where we drag them to.

So, go back to *Xcode* and select your project, that's the top icon in the *Navigator* pane:

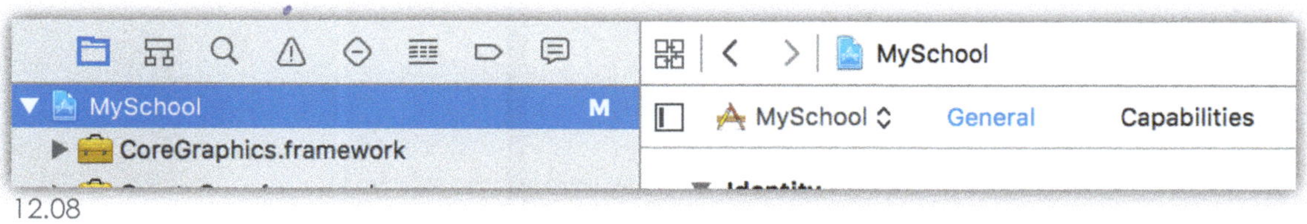

12.08

Make sure *General* is selected from the menu bar in the *Editor* pane.

Scroll down in the *Editor* pane until you see this section:

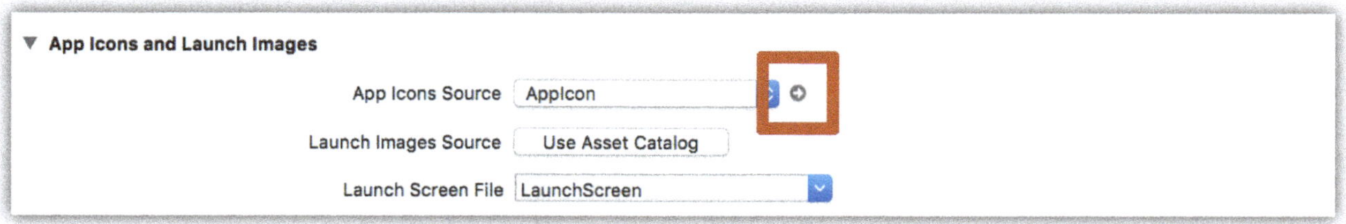

12.09

Press the little grey and white arrow next to the *AppIcon* drop-down menu. The *Editor* pane will change to show this screen:

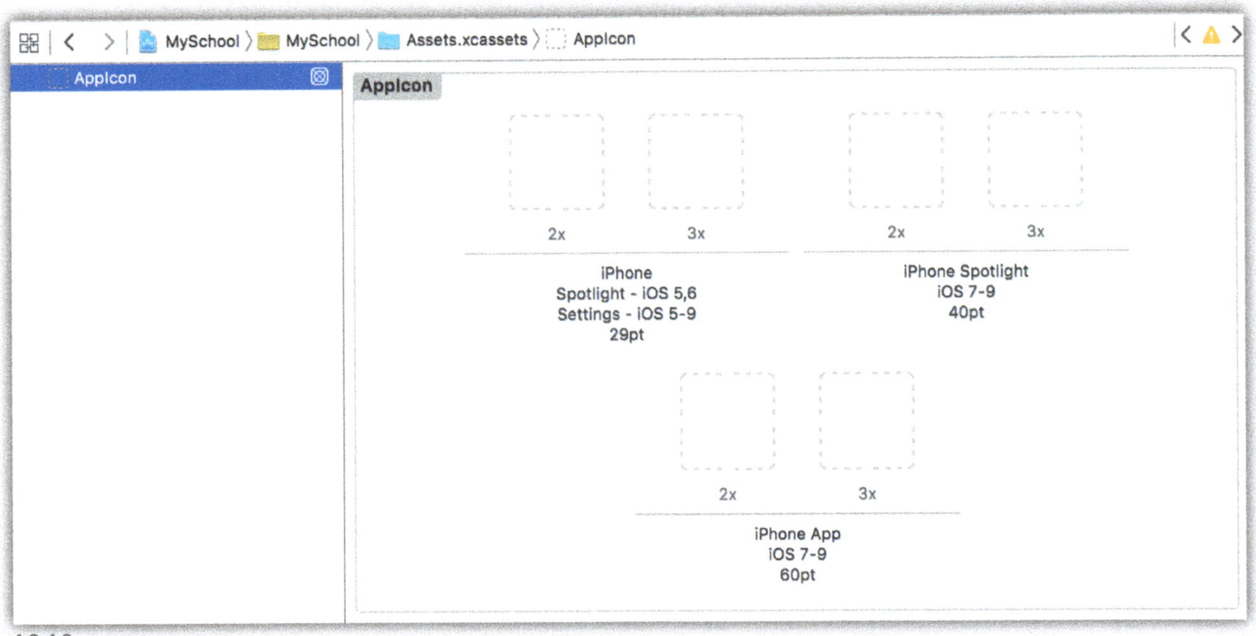

12.10

As you can see, we need six icons. Each one has the size at the bottom: 29pt, 40pt and 60pt. But beneath each square, we have a 'x2' or a 'x3'. So, looking at the top left box, it wants a 29 x 29 pixel icon but at a 'x2' resolution – so what it really wants is a 58 x 58 pixel icon.

Let's look at the icons in our *App Icons* folder that you created:

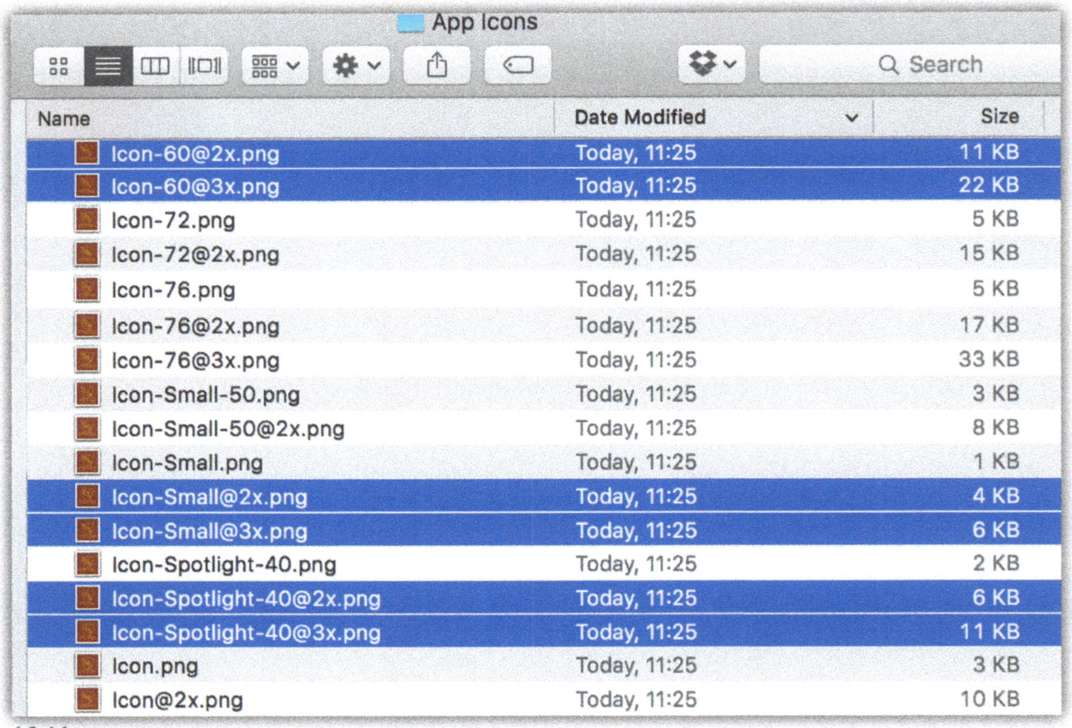

12.11

There are way more icons than we need, so I've highlighted the ones you will need to use. The only tricky one is the 29 pixel one. For some reason, *Prepo* doesn't call it *Icon-29* as it does with the others. Instead, it calls it *Icon-Small*.

We need to drag these icons to *Xcode*. Unfortunately, you have to do this one at a time and instead of dragging to the *Navigator* pane as we've done in the past, you'll have to drag the icon to the empty square in the *Editor* pane that corresponds with the correct icon:

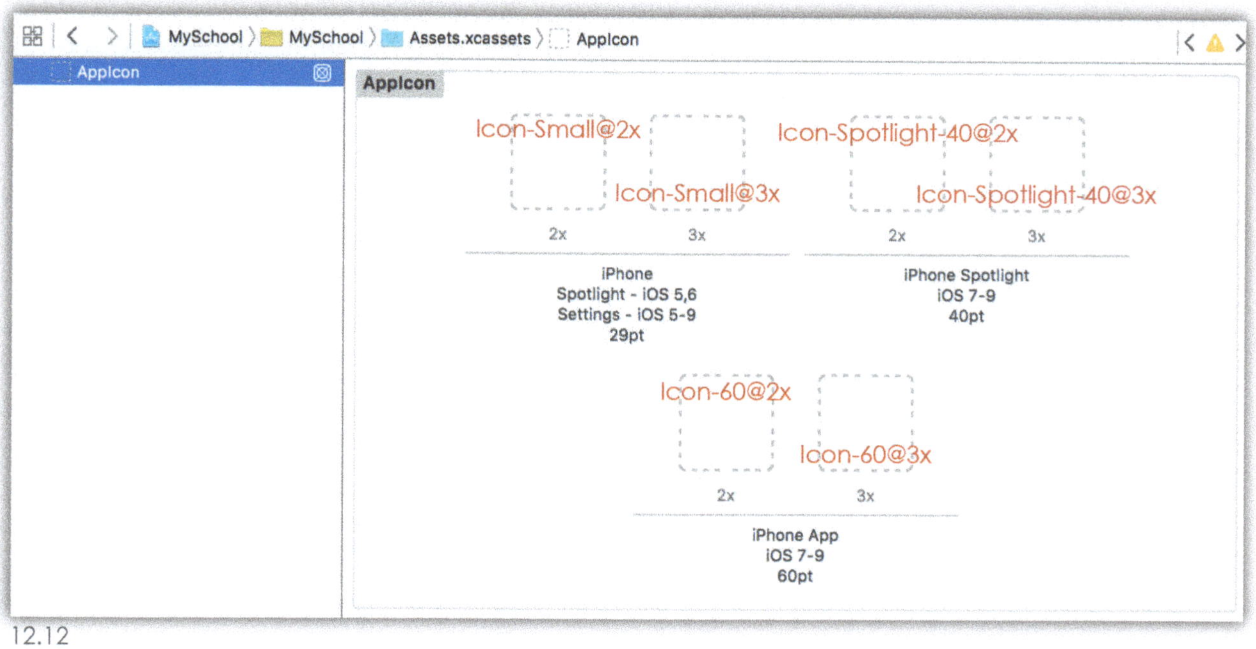

12.12

To help you know which image to drag where, I've labelled the above diagram in red with the file names.

So go ahead and drag the icons to the correct places.

If you've done it right, it should look like this:

12.13

And that is all you need to do. You've now added your icons to your app.

Launch Images

The launch image process is very similar. We are going to make two images that will display briefly when your app loads.

We need to make two different launch images: one for a 3.5 inch screen and one for a 4 inch screen.

The dimensions you need are as follows:

3.5 inch: 640 x 960 pixels
4 inch: 640 x 1136 pixels

I normally make the 4 inch one and then change the image size. It's a bit quicker but you might want to get some pupils to make the 3.5 inch one and some to make the 4 inch one.

Here are mine:

12.14

12.15

You can see the only real difference is the height.

For ease of reference, I've saved them to my Desktop and called them *iPhone4Launch.png* and *iPhone5Launch.png*.

With my images made, I need to set them to appear, so head back over to *Xcode*.

You should still be under the *General* tab in the *Editor* pane. If you're not, select the project at the top of the *Navigator* pane and then *General* from the menu in the *Editor* pane:

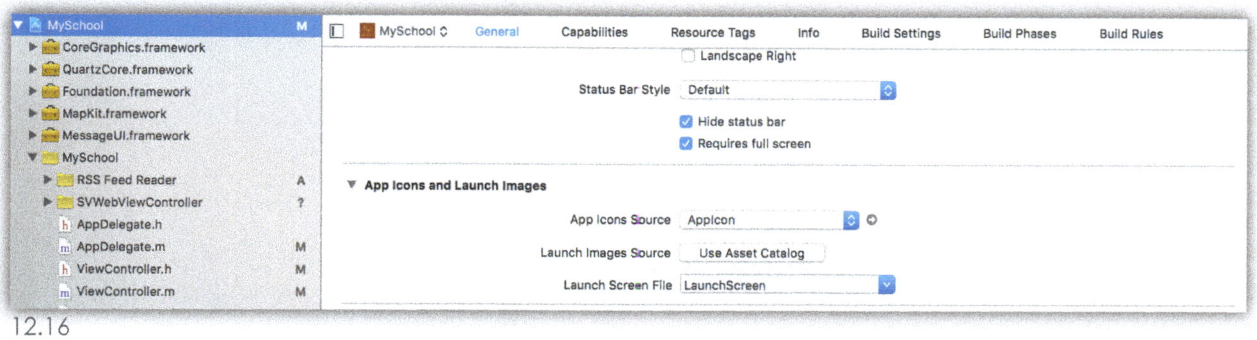

12.16

As before, scroll down to the *App icons and Launch Images* section.

Next to *Launch Image Source*, press *Use Asset Catalog*.

You'll see this pop-up:

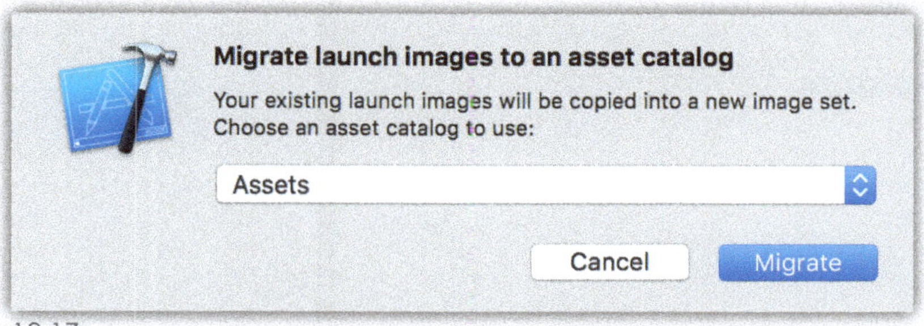

12.17

Press *Migrate*.

You'll notice that next to *Launch Image Source*, a box has appeared saying *LaunchImage* and a small arrow has appeared to the right:

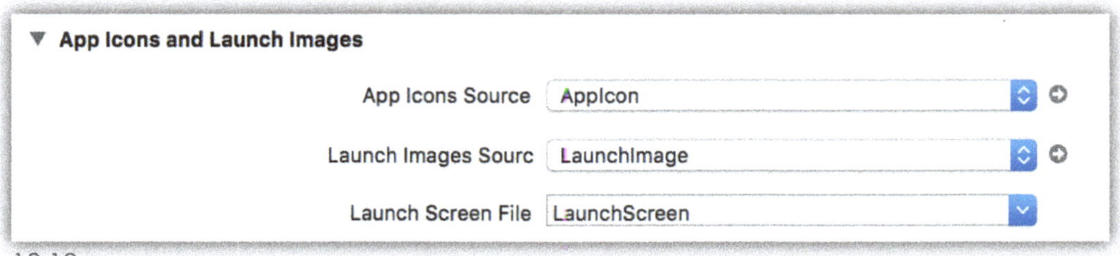

12.18

Press the small grey and white arrow next to *LaunchImage*.

You'll see this:

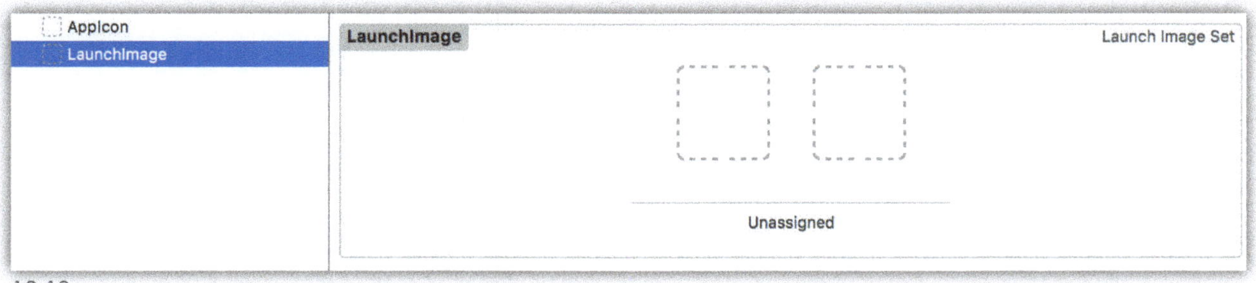

12.19

Two-finger press on *LaunchImage* in the left sidebar:

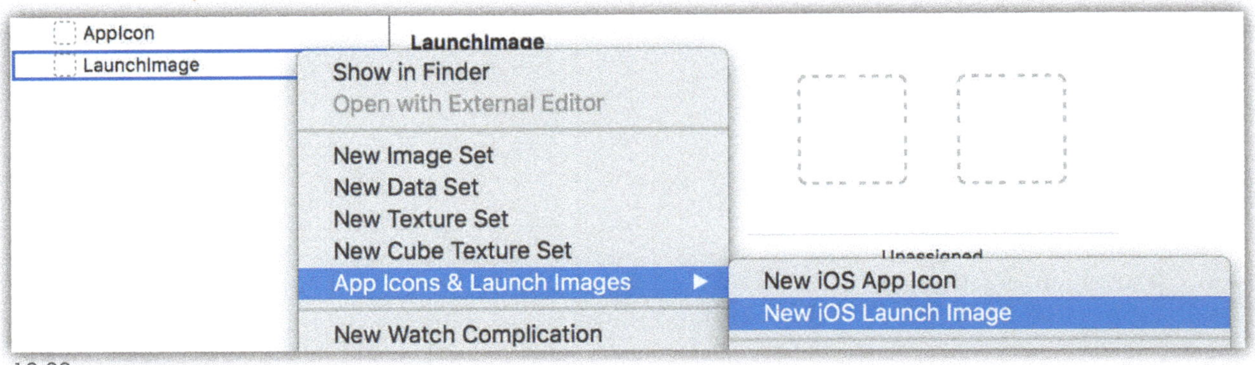

12.20

Select *App Icons & Launch Images* and then *New iOS Launch Image*. The screen will change to this:

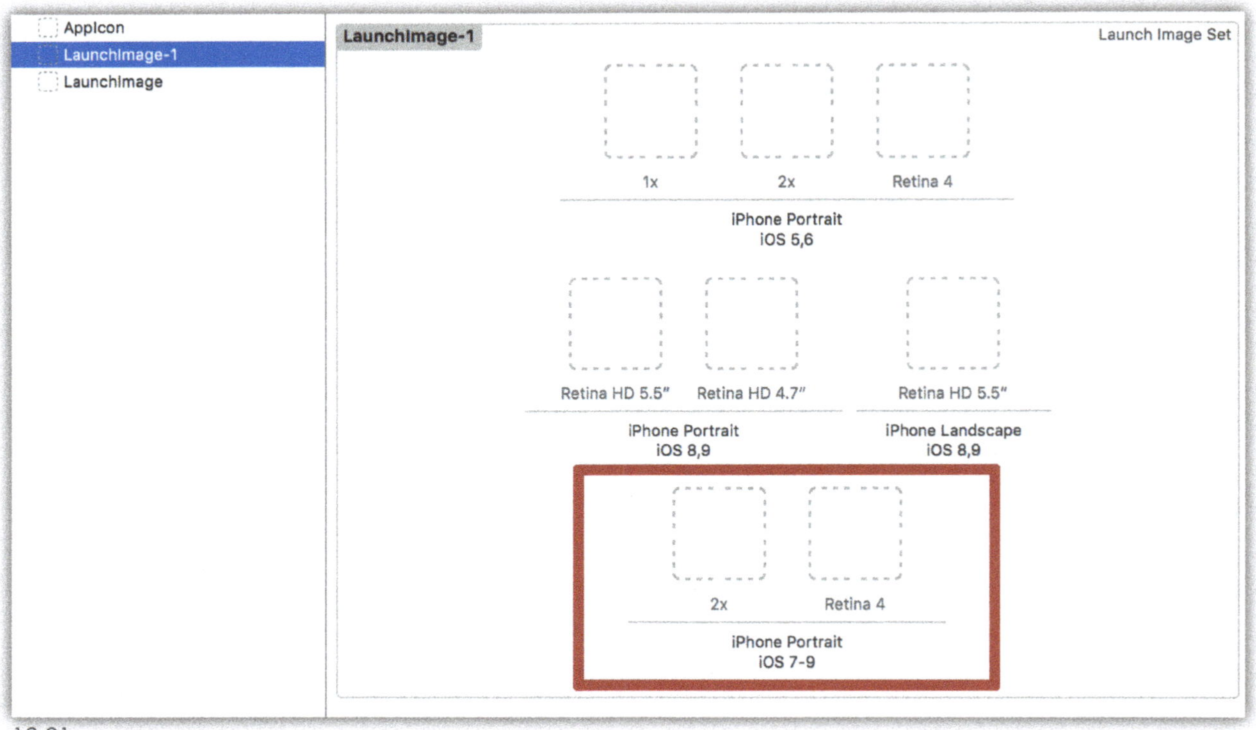

12.21

It looks like we need loads of launch images. We don't. We only need the two we just made, because we are not making our app for devices running iOS 5 or 6 (that's the bottom three spaces) and we're not making it specifically for iPhone 6 or iPhone 6 Plus (that's the top three spaces).

So drag your iPhone 4 launch image to the box in the bottom row which has '2x' written underneath it and drag the iPhone 5 launch image to the box in the bottom row which has 'Retina 4' written underneath it.

Mine look like icons because my background is white. If yours is a colour, they will look like miniature versions of your images.

Next click on your *project* icon in the *Navigator* pane to go back to the *General* page in the *Editor* pane:

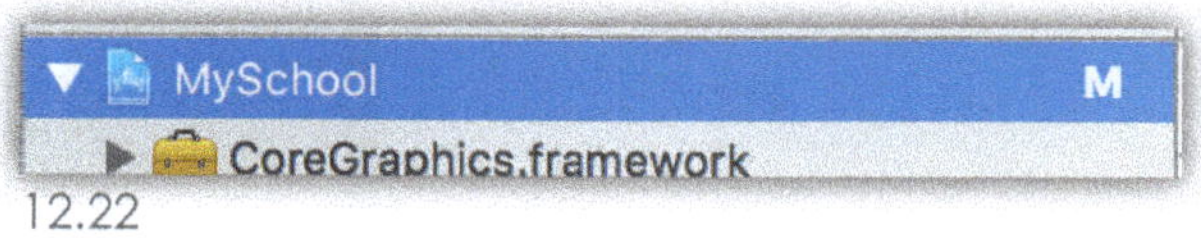

12.22

Then scroll down to the *App Icons and Launch Images* section:

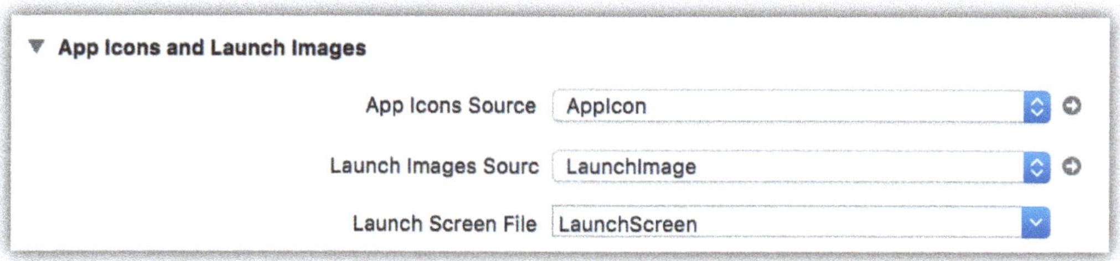

12.23

Select *LaunchImage* to bring up the drop-down menu and select *LaunchImage-1*.

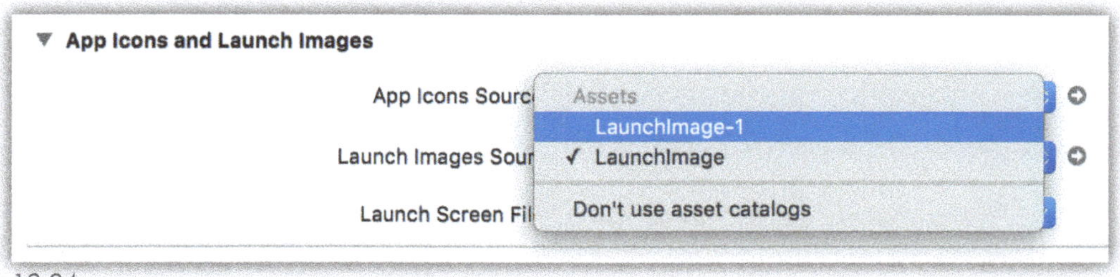

12.24

Finally, where it says *Launch Screen File* delete the words *LaunchScreen*, press *return* and save by pressing *Cmd* and 'S'.

Now run your app on the iPhone 5S simulator and watch as the launch screen appears for a second or two.

Hide the Status Bar

This bit is optional. On my app, the status bar doesn't really belong:

12.25

It goes over my header image awkwardly.

So I'm going to make it go away. Go to the *Navigator* pane and locate the *Info.plist* file:

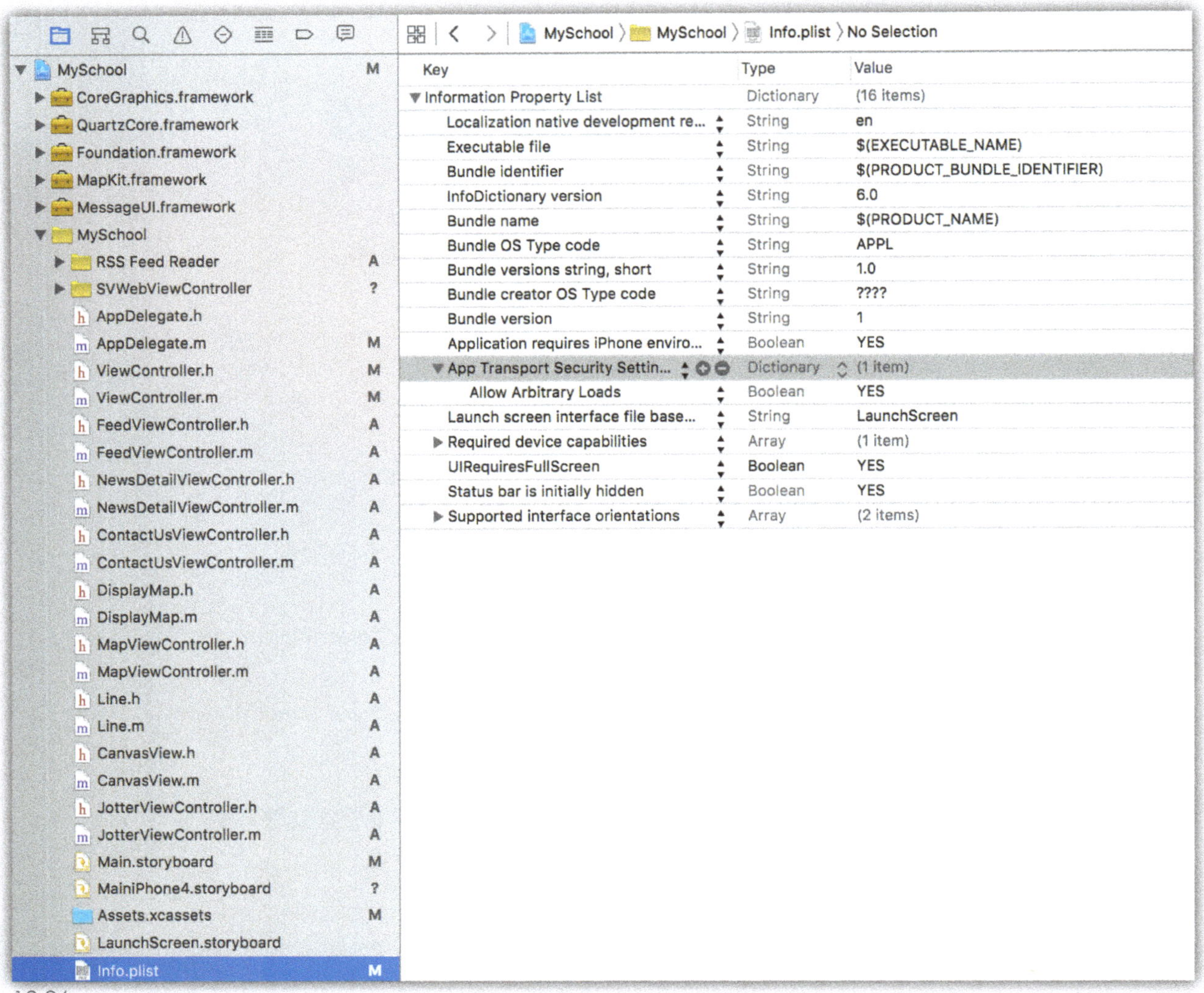

12.26

Single click anywhere in the *Editor* pane beneath the rows.

Then two-finger click and select *Add Row*:

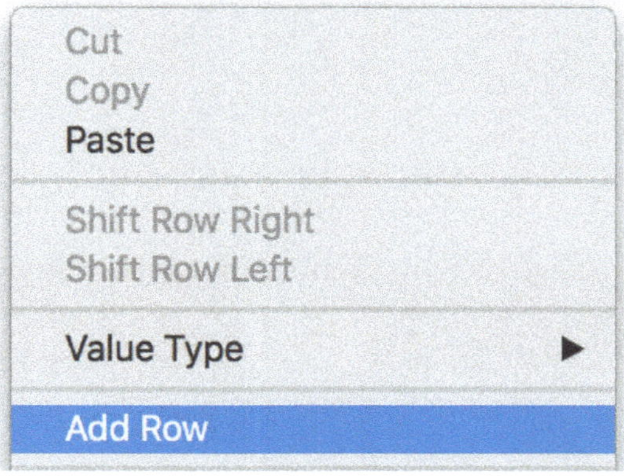

12.27

A new row will appear:

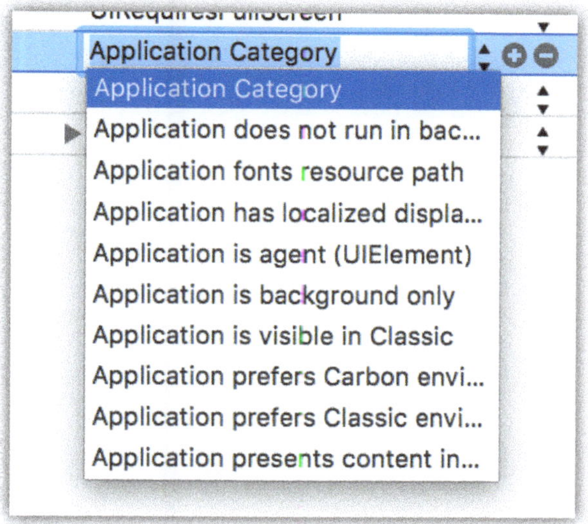

12.28

You'll be presented with a very long list of possible options - most of which you do not need to worry about.

Start typing 'View' and it will autocomplete, but remember the capital 'V' on 'View'. Press *return* and your new row will look like this:

12.29

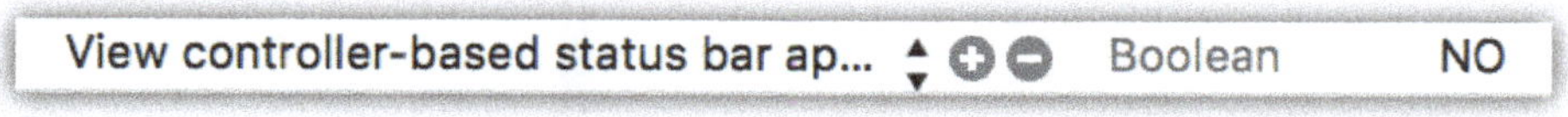

You've just told your app to hide the status bar.

Run it and see.

While we're here, we also need to delete a row. This row looks for a different launch screen and may sometimes prevent your app from showing your launch screen.

Find this row and click on it:

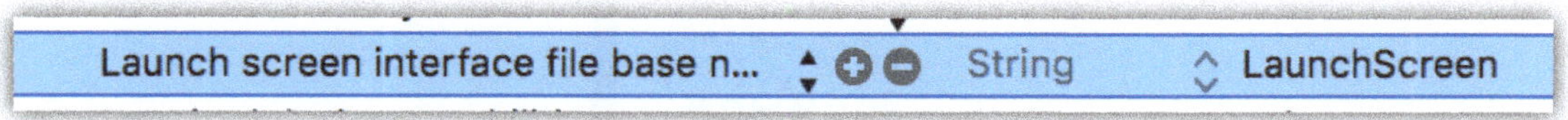

12.30

Press the *backspace* button on your keyboard and it will vanish.

Changing the Display Name

The *Display name* is the name that appears under the icon on the device.

On an iPhone, you're limited to 11 characters. Any more than this and the name will truncate like this 'Townf..l' instead of displaying 'Townfield Primary School'.

So the first thing you need to do is decide what you want to be displayed. You may need to abbreviate your school name.

Once you've decided, select your project file from the *Navigator* Pane and press the *General* tab in the *Editor* Pane. Make sure you scroll to the top of the options. You should see this:

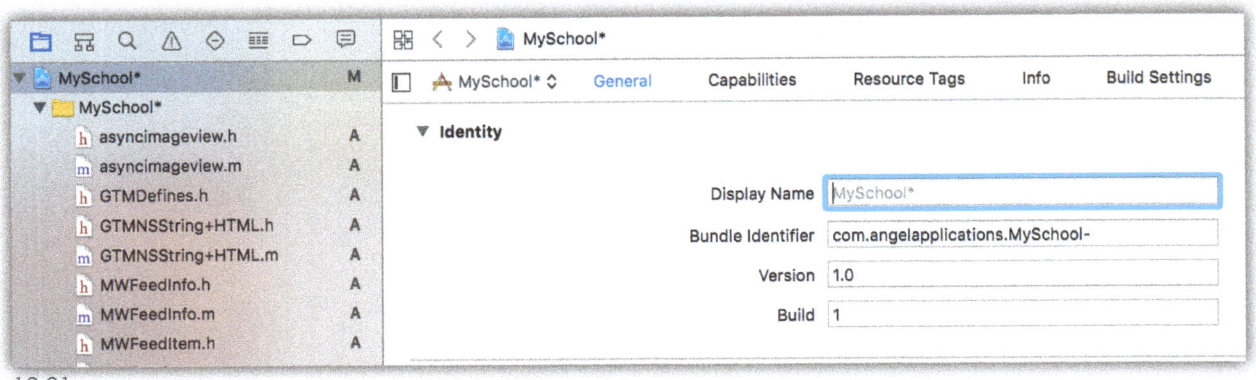

12.31

In the top box called 'Display Name', type the name you'd like to appear under that app.

Time to test…

In this chapter, you have added icons, added a launch screen, hidden the status bar and changed the display name.

In the next chapter, we will look at how to enrol as an Apple Developer and how to submit your app to Apple for review.

http://www.alanpeat.com/build-an-app/Chapter12

CHAPTER THIRTEEN
SUBMITTING TO THE APP STORE

This chapter is for you the teacher, and not really relevant for the children. The process of uploading an app to the App Store is quite complicated. It's also not really going to interest any of your students. They will have wanted to create the app and make it work! They won't care about how you get it in the App Store.

That said, I believe it's worth sharing some elements of the process with the children so that they know what happened to their app. This could be as basic as telling them that you uploaded it to the App Store Review Team for them to look at it, or if your pupils are ready for it, you could explain that the app has to be digitally signed so that another app can't pretend to be your app. I'll leave it up to you!

So here's the deal...

It's free to download *Xcode* and write an app. But to put an app in the Apple App Store, you must join the Apple Developer Programme. And this costs money – it's £79 per year at the time of writing.

The money will give you access to a secret website called *iTunes Connect* where you can publish your apps. You will also have access to the iOS Developer members' page where you can do lots of boring admin things.

If you ever stop paying the annual fee, Apple remove your apps from the App Store. In addition, if you want to charge for your apps, Apple take a 33 per cent cut.

There are a lot of steps involved in submitting an app to the App Store. Here's a brief overview of the whole process:

1. Enrol as an Apple Developer.
2. Wait 24-48 hours for Apple to grant you access.
3. Go to iOS Member page then go to the Certificates and Provisioning section and create a Distribution Certificate.
4. Download the certificate to your Mac.
5. Register the unique ID of your app.
6. Create a Distribution Provisioning Profile.
7. Download the profile.
8. Set your build settings in *Xcode*.
9. Configure all the App Store options – things like price and description.
10. Build your app.
11. Upload it to the App Store.
12. Submit the app for review by Apple.

Only steps 5-12 need to be done each time you create a different app. Steps 1-4 need to be done annually.

It looks quite daunting. But I will show you each step as we go. You won't get through this chapter in one go as you will need to wait for Apple to process your application to become an Apple Developer.

Enrol as an Apple Developer

The first thing you need to do is go to **https://developer.apple.com/programs/**

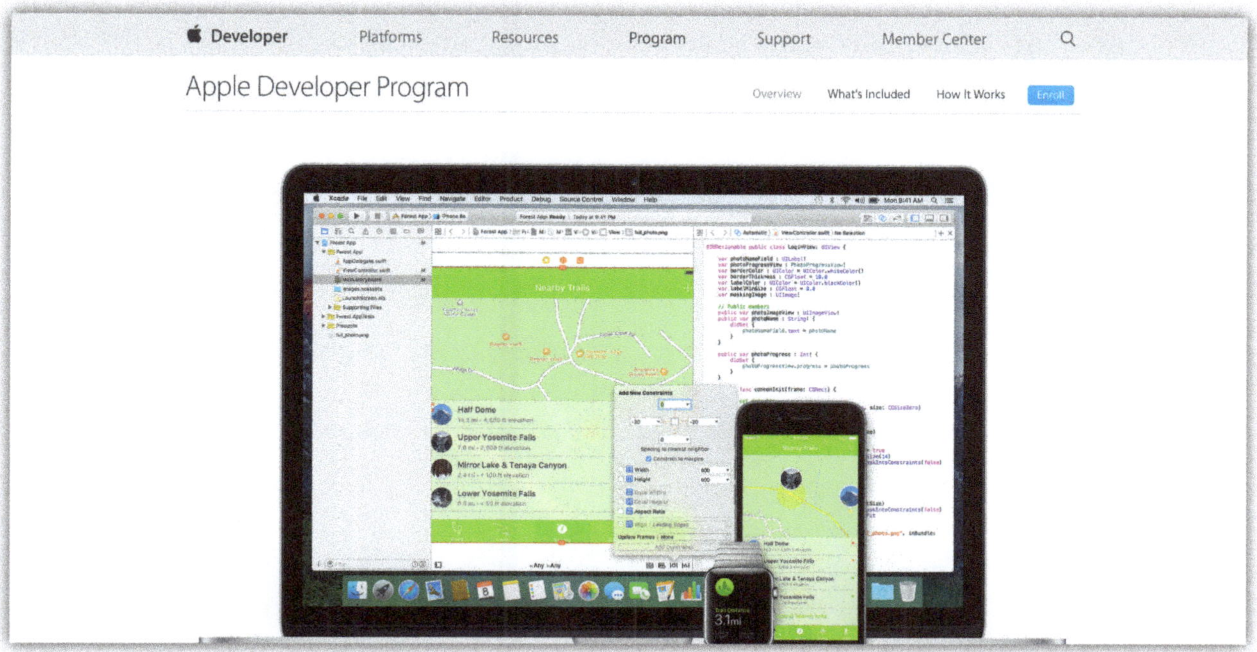

13.01

The website may change over time, but should look something like the image above. Press the blue *Enroll* button in the top right.

The next page will talk you through the two options you have for enrolling: you can either enrol as an individual or a legal entity. Enrolling as an individual is much easier. You don't need to send any proof of who you are. But enrolling as a legal entity requires proof like your company's certificate of incorporation. For schools, the best option is to enrol as an individual - usually the Head Teacher.

The only caveat here is that if you choose to enrol as an individual, your name will appear above your app in the App Store. That's why many people set up companies just to put an app in the App Store.

Scroll down and choose *Start Your Enrolment*. You'll be directed to a page prompting you for your Apple ID if you're not already signed in to an Apple account.

And then you will be presented with this legal agreement:

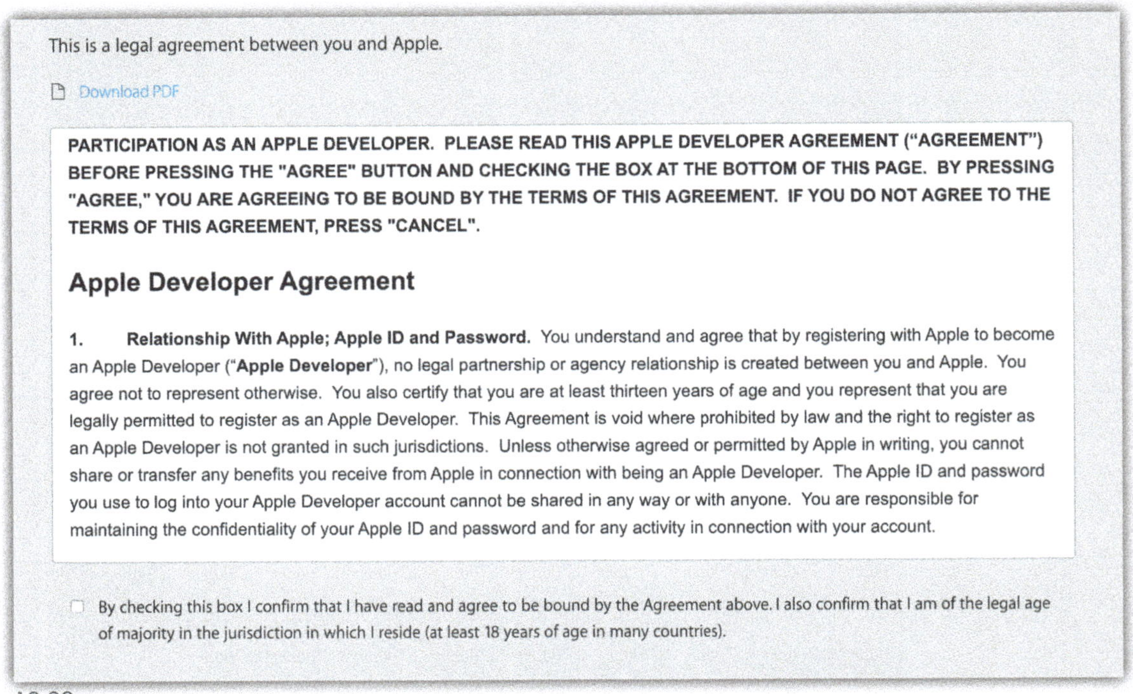

13.02

Have a read through and, if you're happy with it, tick the box and scroll down to the blue *Submit* button.

On the next page, you have to make a final decision about registering as an individual or a company:

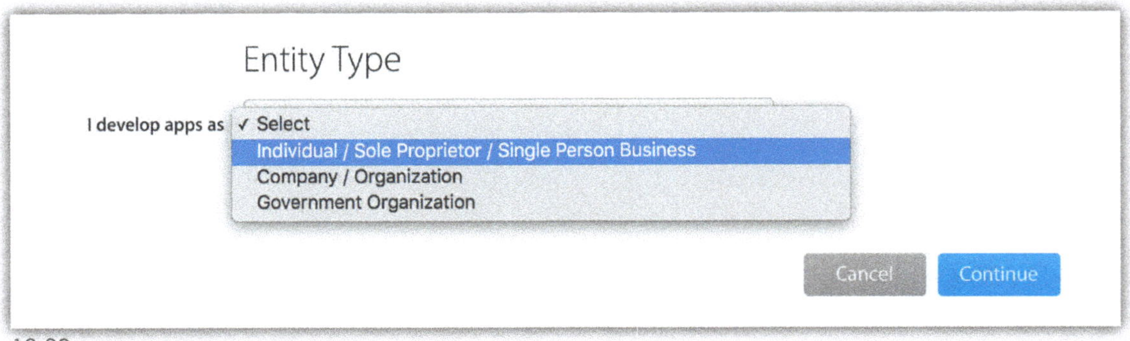

13.03

Make your choice and select *Continue*.

The next page requires you to fill out all of your contact information:

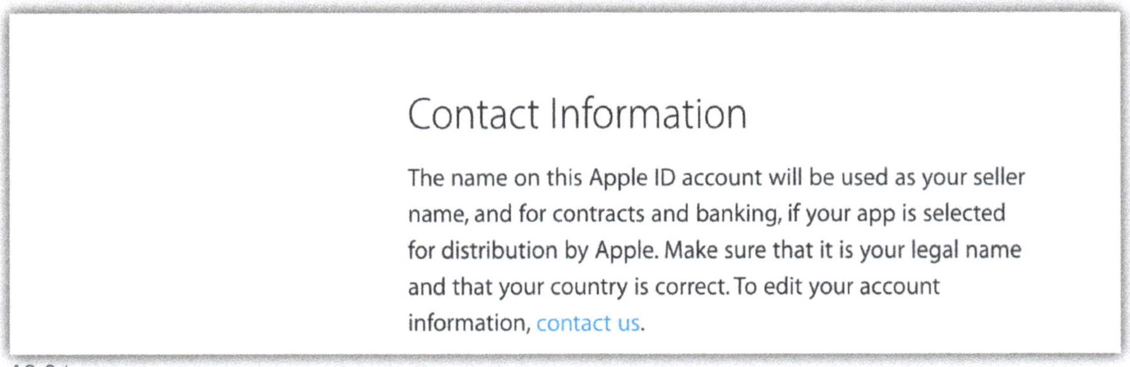

13.04

Once you've filled this in and submitted it, you will taken to a confirmation page to check your details. If it's all okay, press *Continue*. You'll see this page:

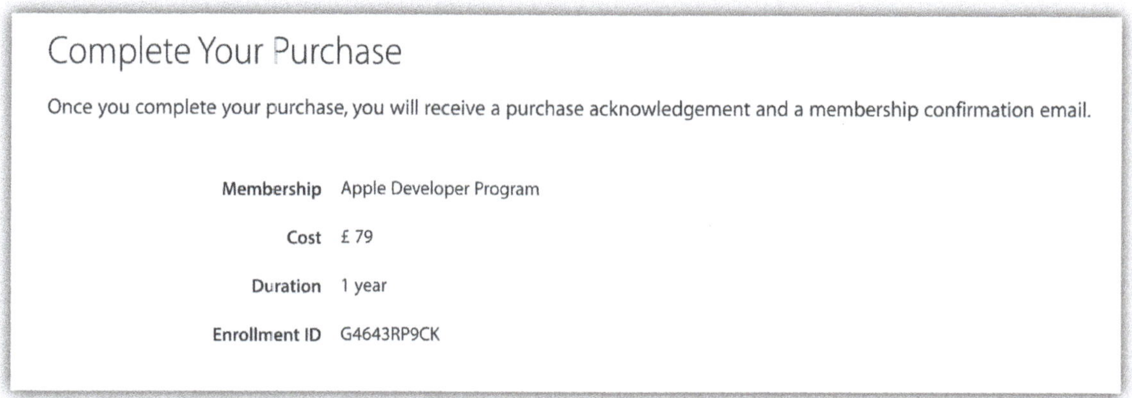

13.05

If you're happy with it all, scroll down and select the blue *Purchase* button. You'll then be prompted for payment information.

Fill it all in and complete your purchase.

You should receive an email confirming your order and, in a day or two, further emails confirming you have access to *iTunes Connect* and the iOS Developer Members' Center.

So you can't do any of the following stuff for a couple of days.

Go to iOS Member page, then go to the Certificates and Provisioning section and create a Distribution Certificate and download it to your Mac

Two days have passed and your confirmation email from Apple has arrived.

The email will give you the links you need. I'll put them here too but, remember, they won't work until Apple have given your account the go-ahead.

As an Apple Developer, the first thing we need to do is create some Certificates – these link your Apple ID to *Xcode* and then in-turn to your app.

There are a few types of certificate, but for the purpose of submitting the app, we don't need them all.

Head to this link: **https://developer.apple.com/membercenter/index.action** and log in with the Apple ID with which you set up your developer account.

You'll see this screen:

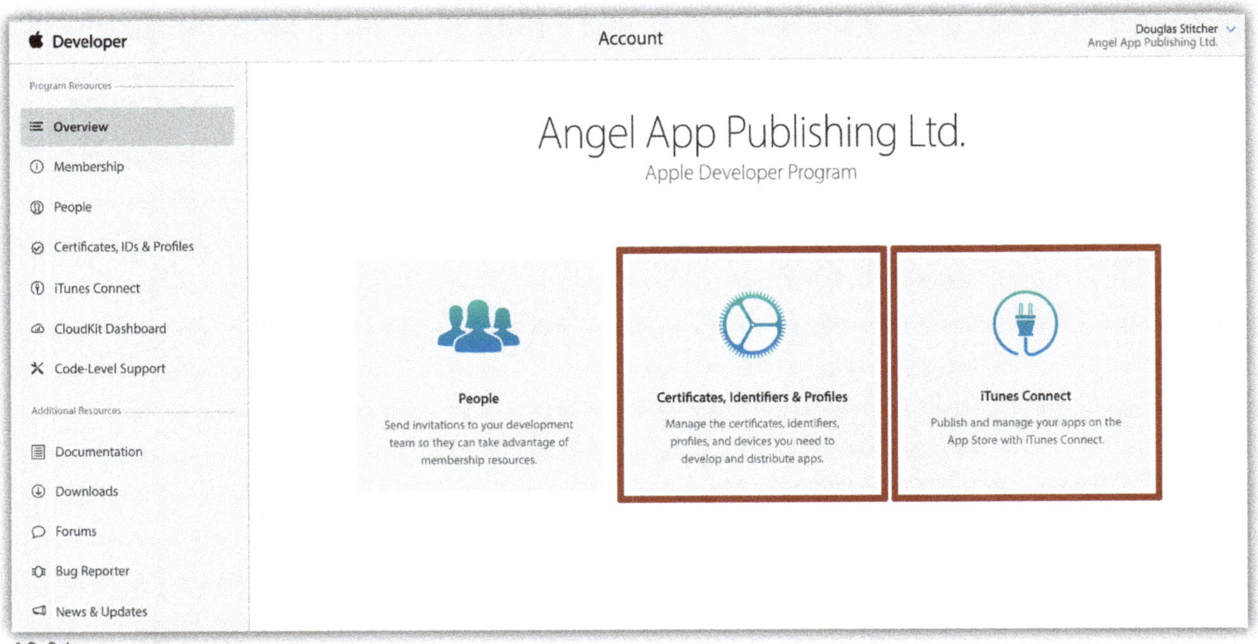

13.06

This is a bit like the hub of all your posh developer activities. From here you can access all the resources available to Apple developers, although you'll only need two links here: *Certificates, Identifiers & Profiles* and *iTunes Connect*.

The others are useful but you probably won't use them at first.

Click on the *Certificates, Identifiers & Profiles* link.

This is what you'll see next:

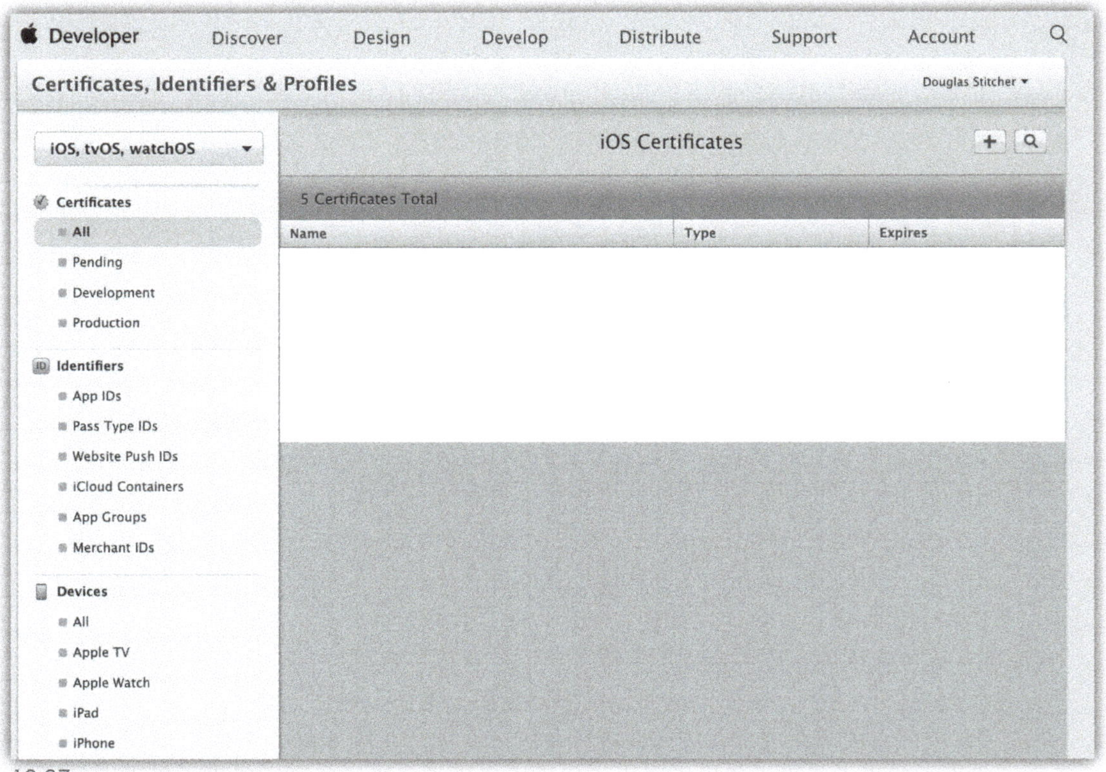

13.07

As we're starting off by creating Certificates, it makes sense to go there first so click on that link:

13.08

You won't have any certificates in the list so let's add one by pressing the '+' sign in the top right just under your name. You'll see this:

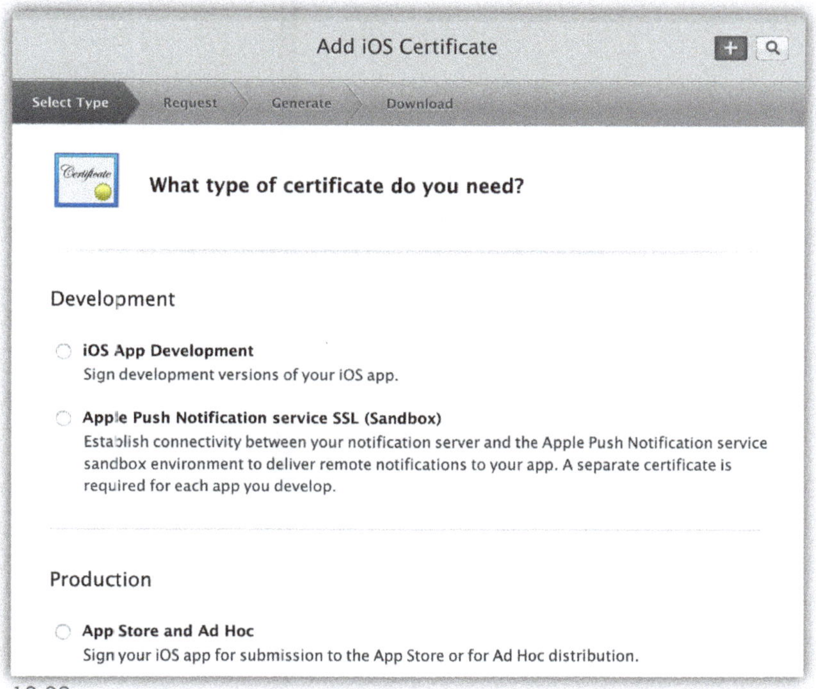

13.09

There are loads of different types of certificates and they come under two categories - Development and Production.

To submit an app to the App Store, we need a Production certificate, so select the *App Store* and *Ad Hoc* option:

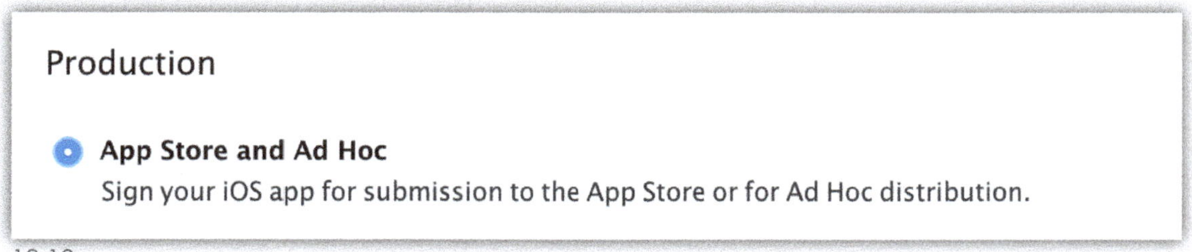

13.10

Scroll to the bottom of the page and select Continue. This will reveal this screen:

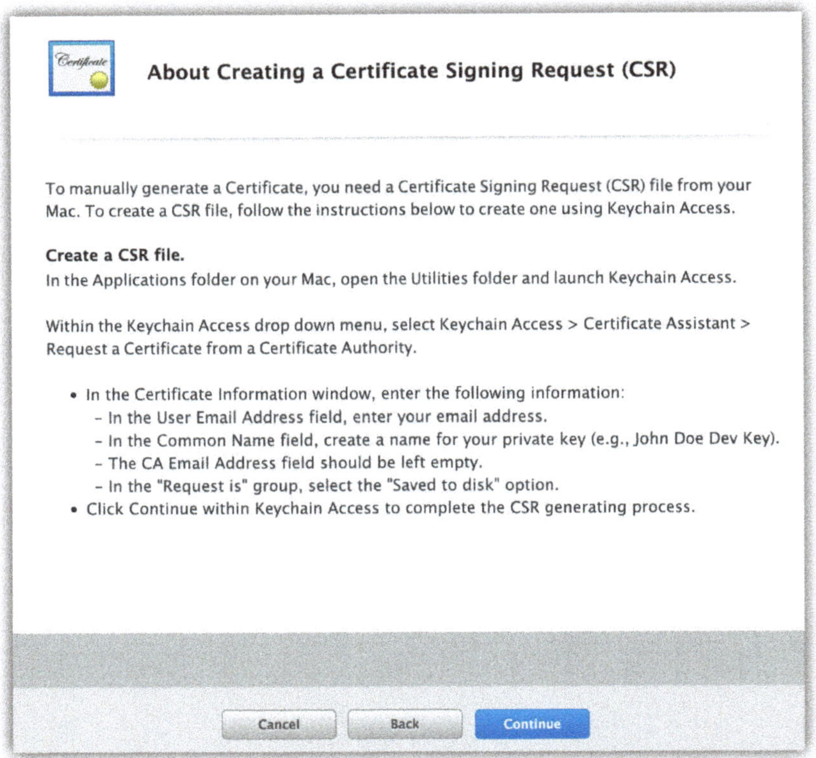

13.11

The beauty of the above screen is it does my job for me! It explains what to do. Before you get a certificate, you need to create a Certificate Signing Request or *CSR* and that's what the instructions above will let you do.

The first thing you need to do is find an app on your Mac called *Keychain Access*. To do this, go to your *Applications* folder. It's usually on the bottom right of the *Dock* next to the trash.

Inside the *Applications* folder, you will find a folder called *Utilities*:

13.12

Open this up and select the app called *Keychain Access*:

13.13

A new window will open; it will look something like this:

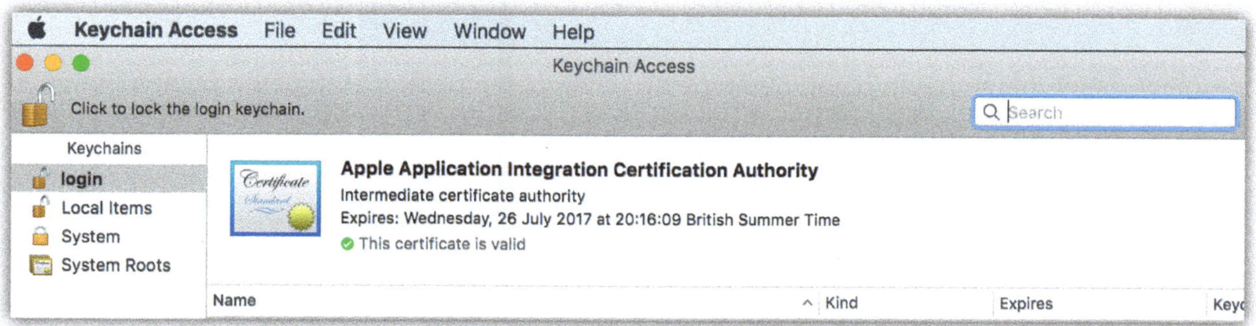

13.14

To do what we need to do here, we use the top menu bar – the one with the Apple logo on the far left. Click on the *Keychain Access* button next to the Apple logo:

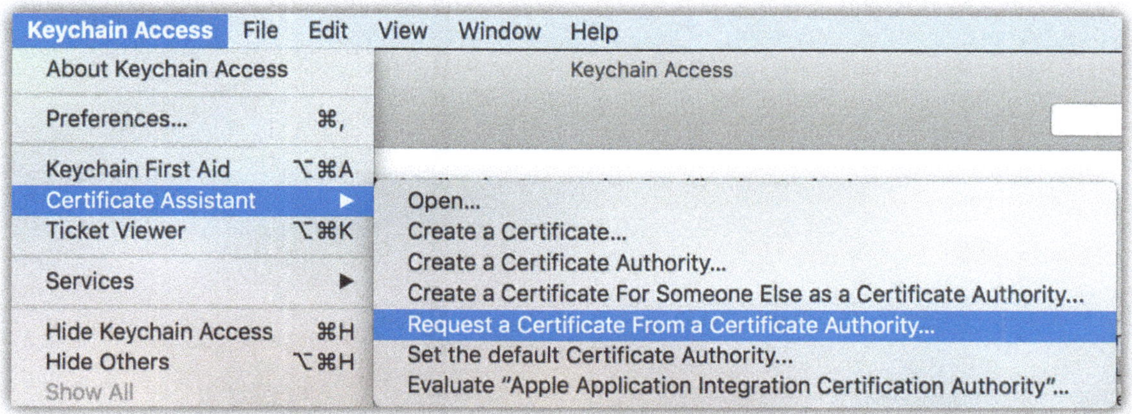

13.15

Select *Request a Certificate From a Certificate Authority*. - You'll see this screen:

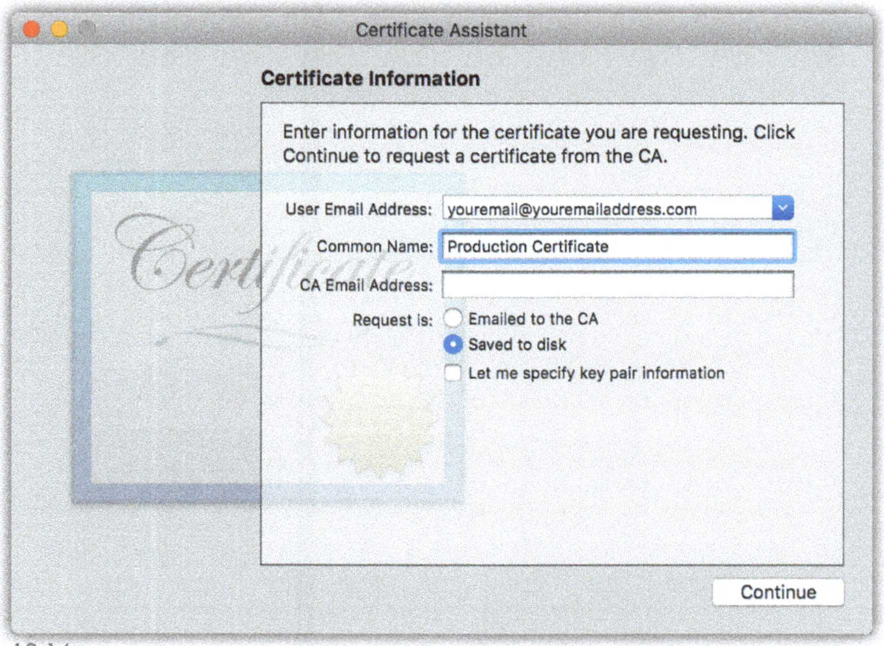

13.16

Make sure it's your email address in the top box. Change the *Common* Name to 'Production Certificate' and then check the *Saved to disk* option.

Press *Continue*. You'll then be asked to save the *CSR*. Save it to the Desktop so it's easy to find:

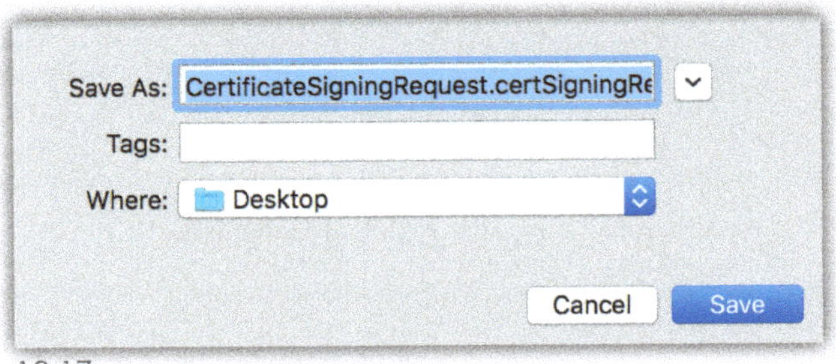

13.17

Press *Save*.

Now go back to that screen from Apple in your internet browser:

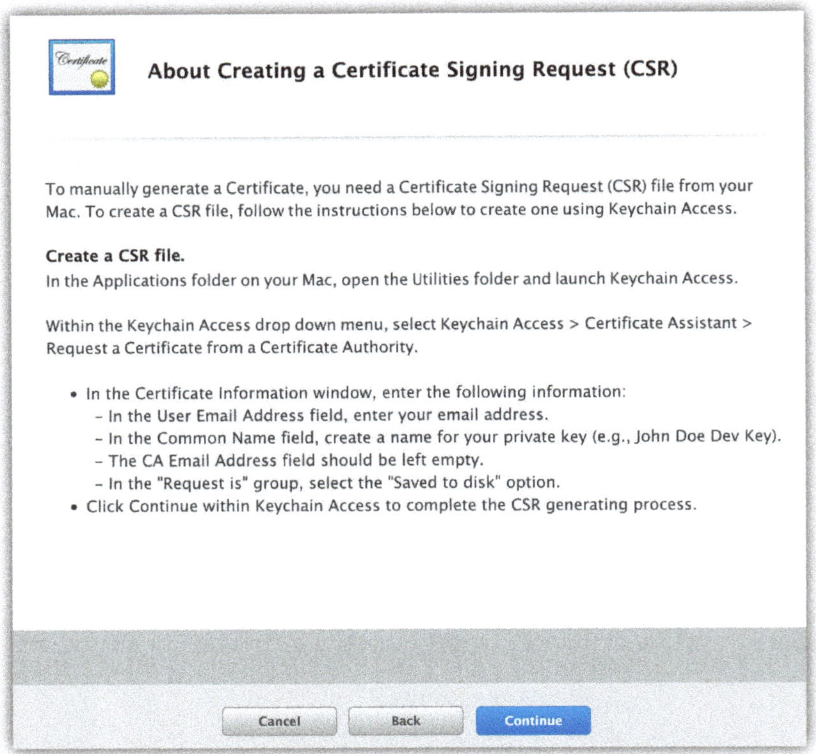

13.18

Press the *Continue* button to see this:

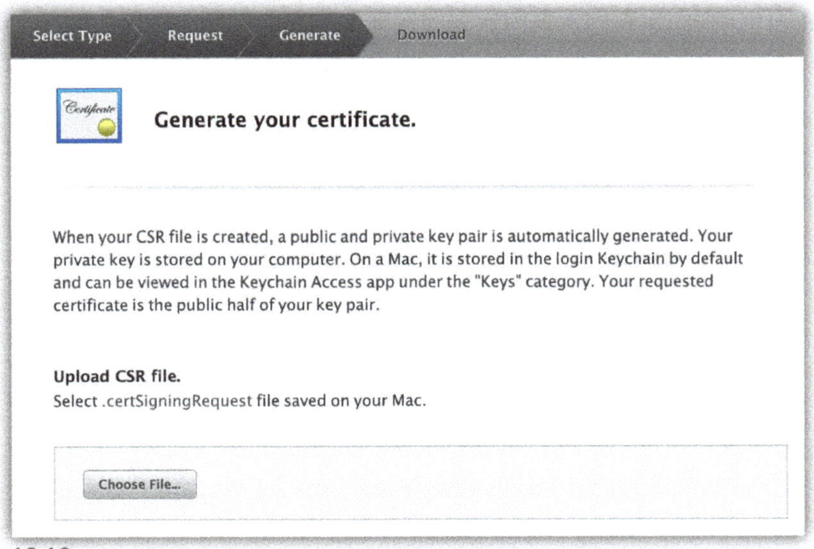

13.19

Press the *Choose File* option and locate the *CSR* file you just saved:

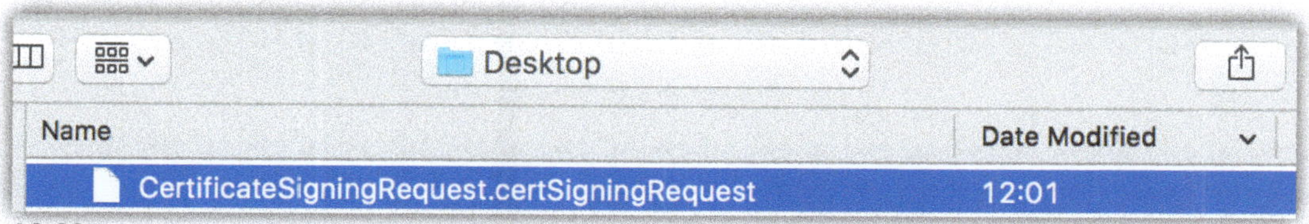

13.20

Press *Open* in the Finder window and you will then see your *CSR* appear on the webpage:

13.21

You can now press the blue *Generate* button in the bottom left.

You will then see the last page in this process:

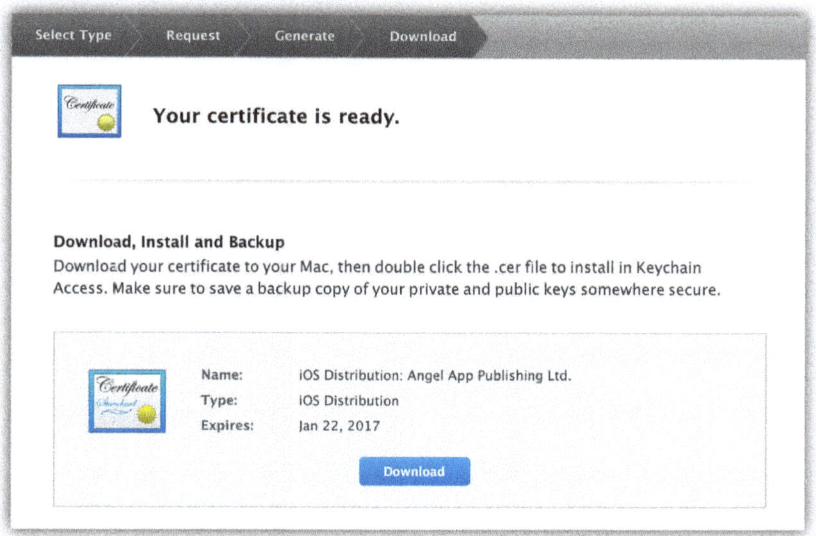

13.22

Press the blue *Download* button. The certificate will then download to your *Downloads* folder. Go to *Finder* and locate it:

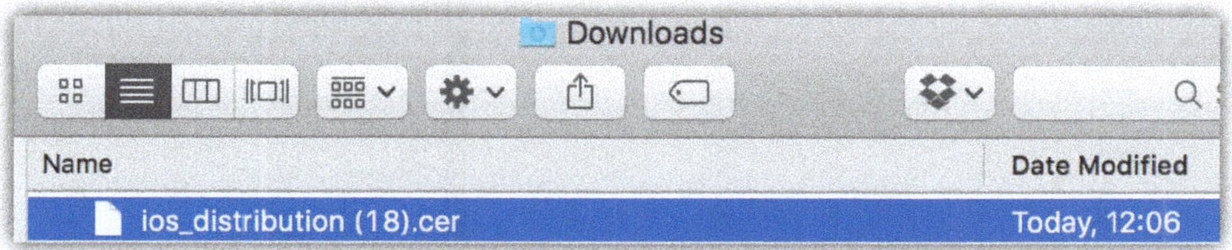

13.23

Yours probably won't have a number in brackets next to it. This will depend on how many certificates you have downloaded in the past. As this is most likely your first, there won't be any numbers there.

Double click on the file.

The *Keychain Access* app will open and the new certificate will appear in the list of certificates.

That's all you have to do here. It seems like quite a lot of hassle for something that you don't really see doing much but it has to be done.

The good news is you only need to do this once a year when you renew your Apple Developer account subscription.

Registering the unique ID of your app, creating a 'Distribution Provisioning Profile' and downloading it to your Mac

The next step is to create a *provisioning profile* for your app. This is a special file that associates your app with your permission to make apps for the App Store. You will have to do this every time you want to register a new app.

The process is easier than creating a certificate.

On the left-hand side of the *Certificates, Identifiers & Profiles* page, under the *Identifiers* heading, select *App IDs*:

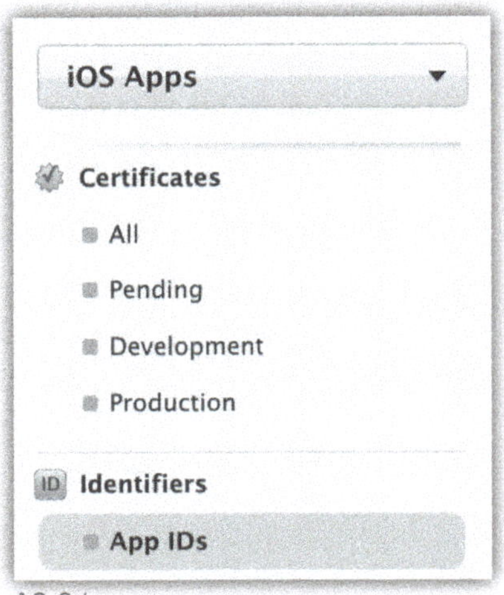

13.24

The top of the main part of the screen will change to this:

13.25

Press the '+' button.

This will bring up *Register iOS App ID* screen.

There are a few options here we need to change.

Firstly, we need to give our app a name:

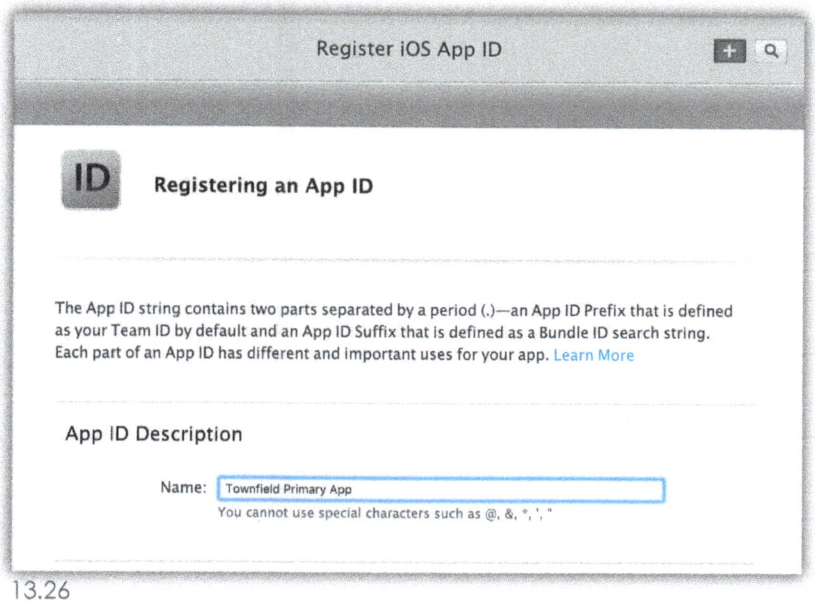

13.26

In the section called *App ID Description*, type a name for your app. It can't have any special characters in it.

Then scroll down to this section:

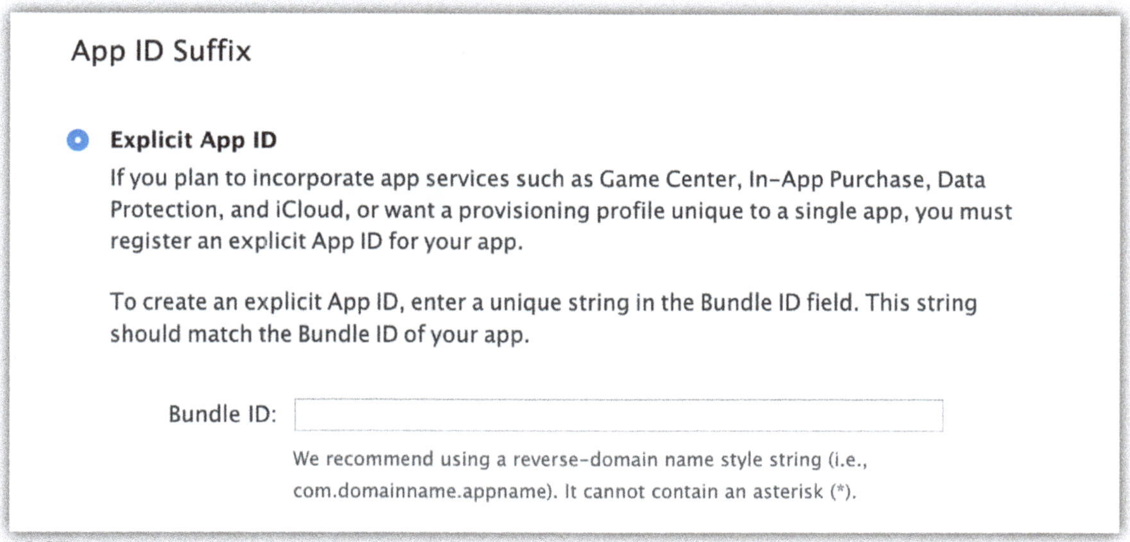

13.27

This bit is important. The *Bundle ID* is the unique ID of your app. None of the other millions of apps in the App Store can have it. But we already created it when we set up our app.

Go back to *Xcode*, and select your project at the top of the *Navigator* pane:

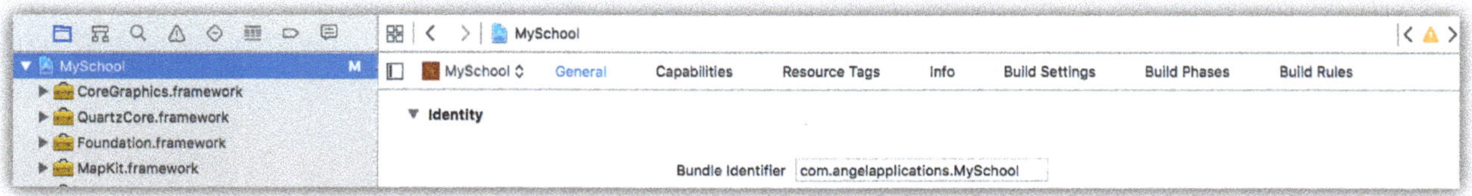

13.28

Make sure you select *General* from the menu bar in the *Editor* pane.

The first option in the *Editor* pane is the *Bundle Identifier* and this is what we need to put in the box on the webpage.

So double-click in the box to select it, copy it and go back to the webpage to paste it into the box:

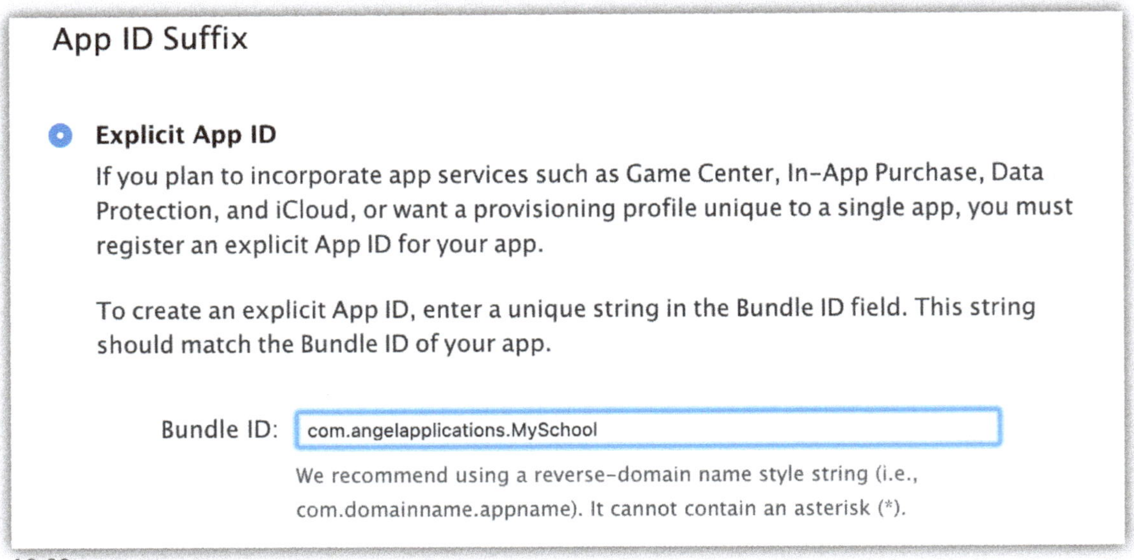

13.29

Scroll down to the bottom of the page and press the blue *Continue* button:

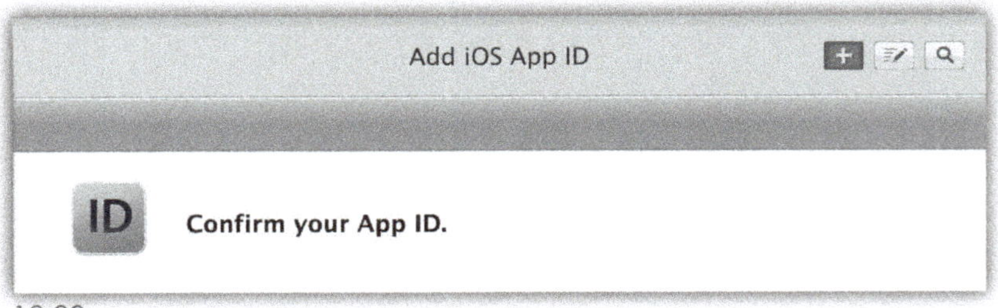

13.30

Scroll down to the bottom of the *Confirm your App ID* page and press the *Submit* button.

You've now registered your App ID.

With the app registered, we need to create this *provisioning profile* I've been going on about.

From the left-hand menu, select *Distribution* from the *Provisioning Profiles* section:

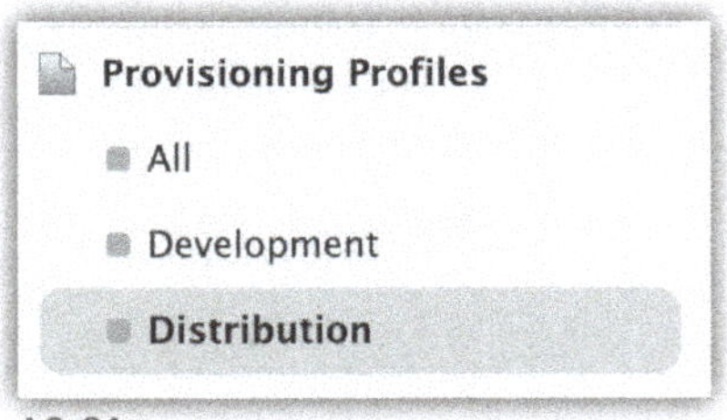

13.31

Just as before, select the '+' button from the top right:

13.32

You'll be asked what type of provisioning profile you want to create. Select App Store, which is an option underneath Distribution:

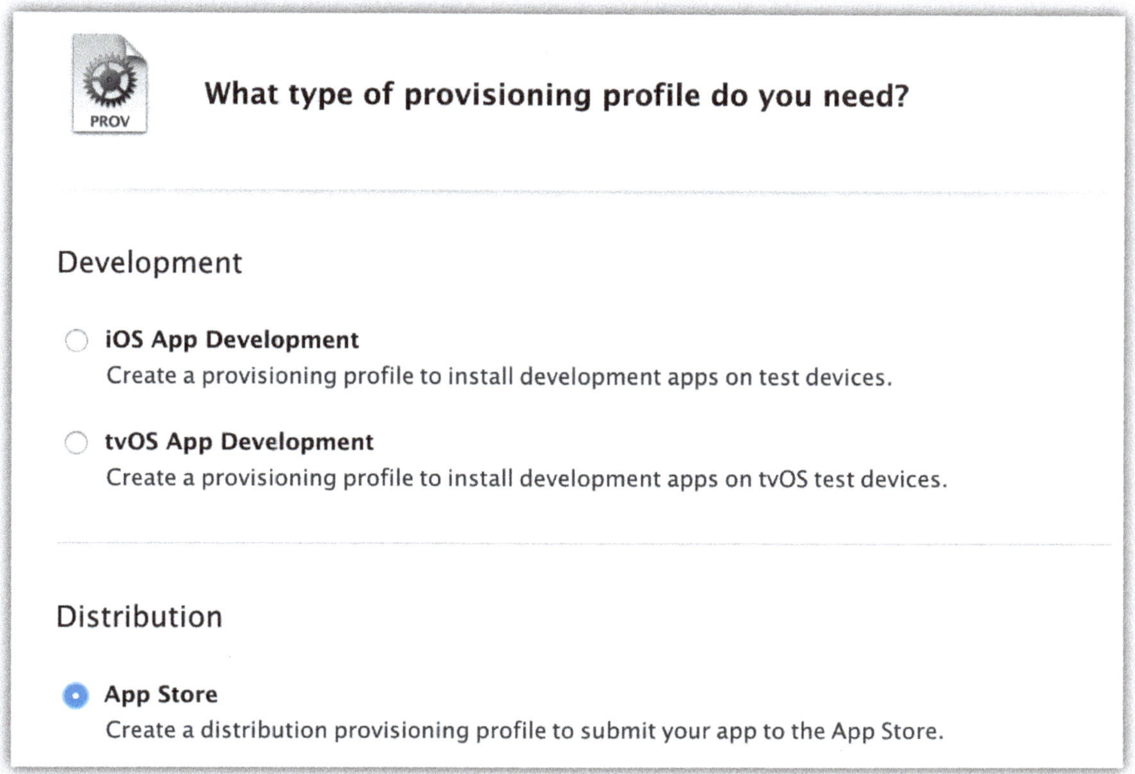

13.33

Scroll down and press the blue *Continue* button.

The next screen is the *Select App ID* screen so this is where you associate your provisioning profile with your app. Click on the drop-down menu and select your app from the options:

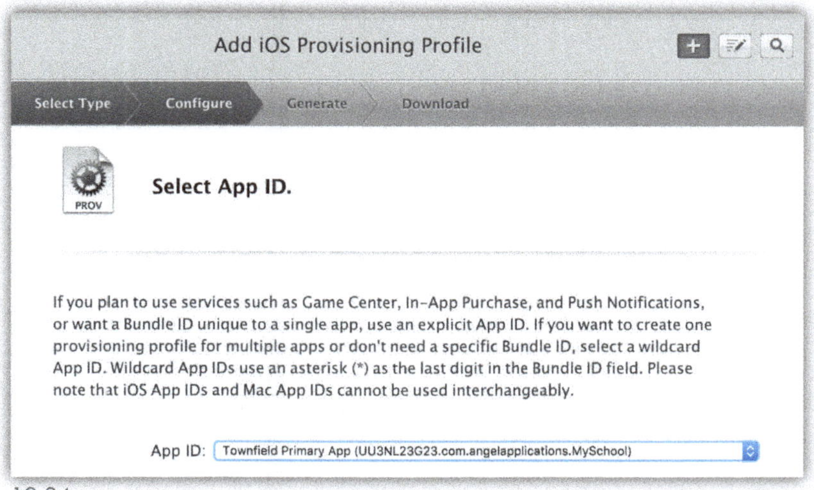

13.34

Scroll down to the bottom of the page and press *Continue*.

You'll be asked to select a certificate to include in your provisioning profile – this is the certificate we created earlier – so select it and press the *Continue* button:

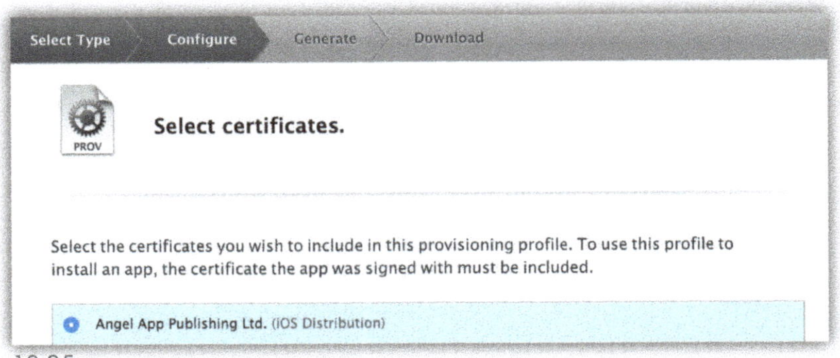

13.35

You'll be asked to name your provision profile. You can call it anything you want, but I tend to use my app name and then 'App Store' like this:

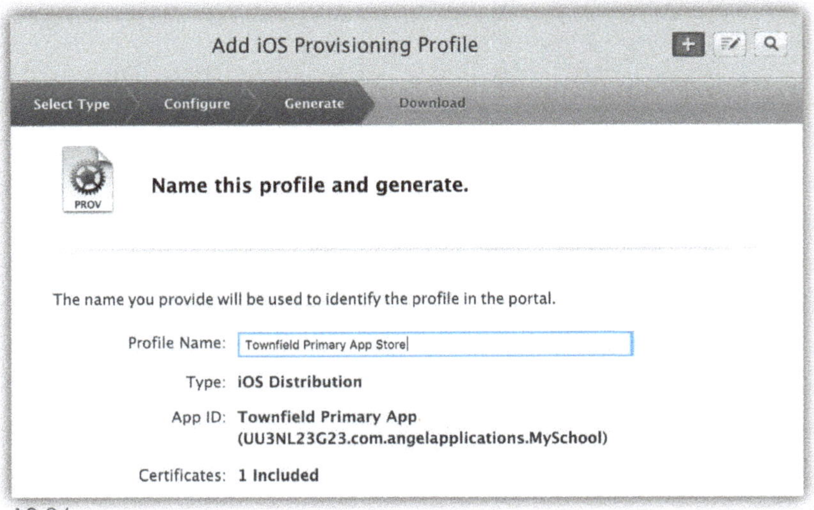

13.36

Scroll down and press the blue Generate button. This will bring up the final page:

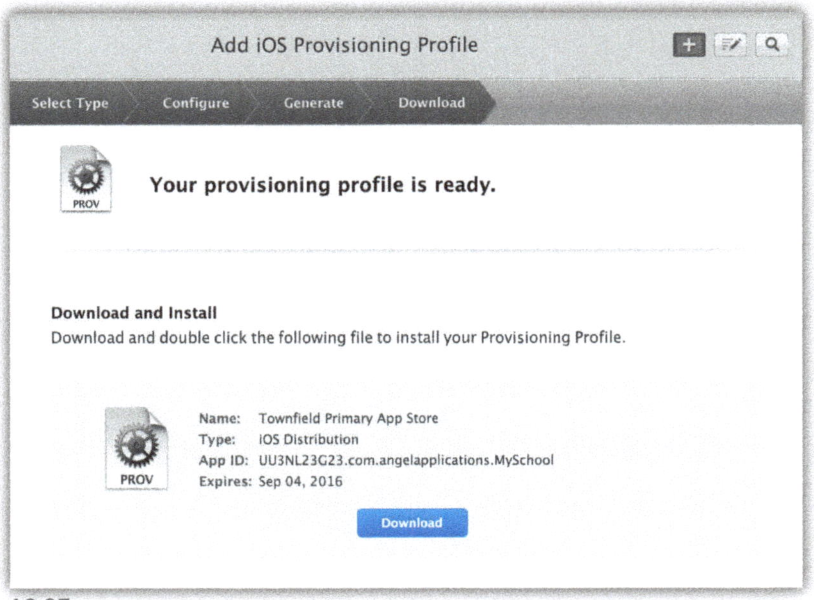

13.37

As with our certificate earlier, press the Download button. Find the file in Finder:

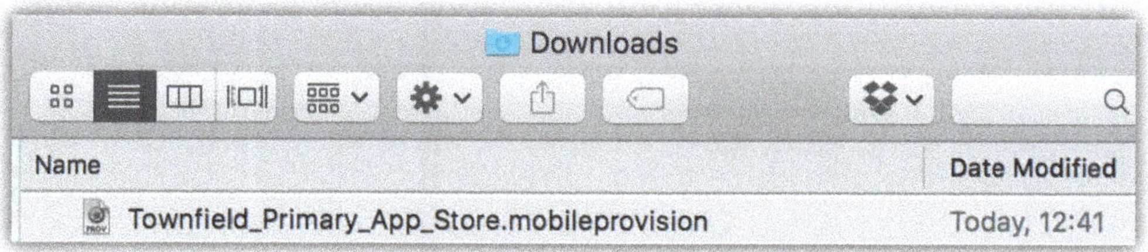

13.38

Double-click it and *Xcode* will become your main window.

That is your provisioning profile created but we need to tell *Xcode* to use it when we build our app.

Set your Build Settings in Xcode

You've created your certificate and provisioning profile but you need to link everything together in *Xcode*.

The first thing we're going to do is link your Apple ID – which is linked to your Developer account – to Xcode. So, in *Xcode*, find the top menu bar:

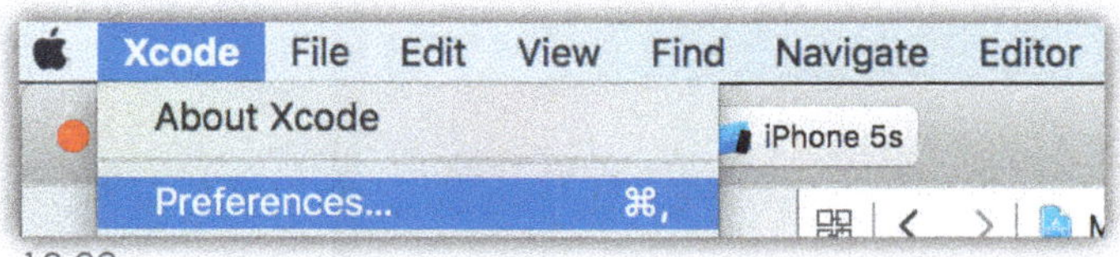

13.39

Select *Xcode* and then *Preferences*. In the window that pops up, select *Accounts*:

13.40

In the bottom left of the window, you should see these buttons:

13.41

Select the '+' symbol and choose *Add Apple ID*. Enter your Apple ID in this pop-up box:

13.42

Next, let's use our provisioning profile. Select *Build Settings* from the menu at the top of the *Editor* pane:

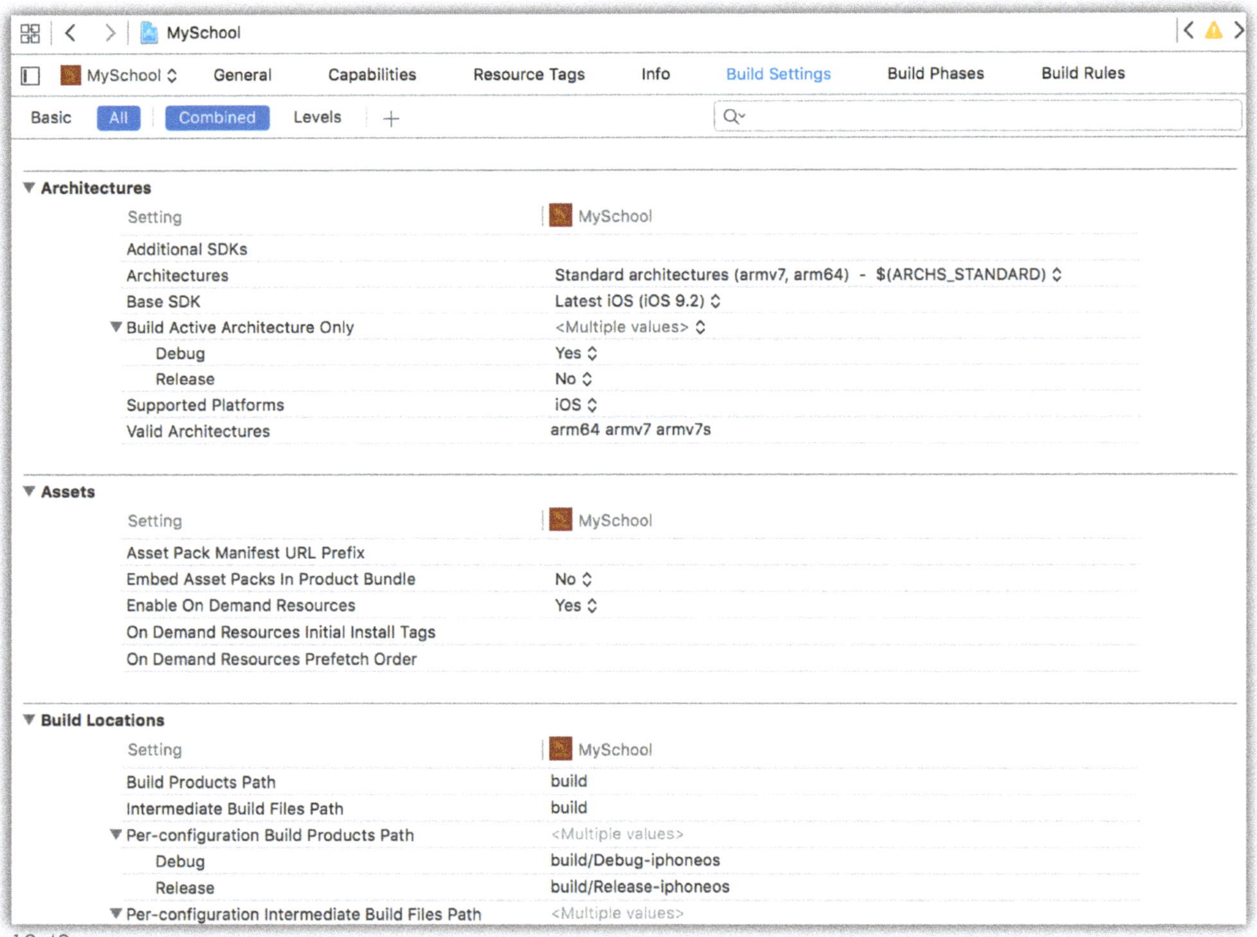

13.43

I know this is a scary looking page but we only need to make a couple of changes here.

Scroll down until you find the *Code Signing* section:

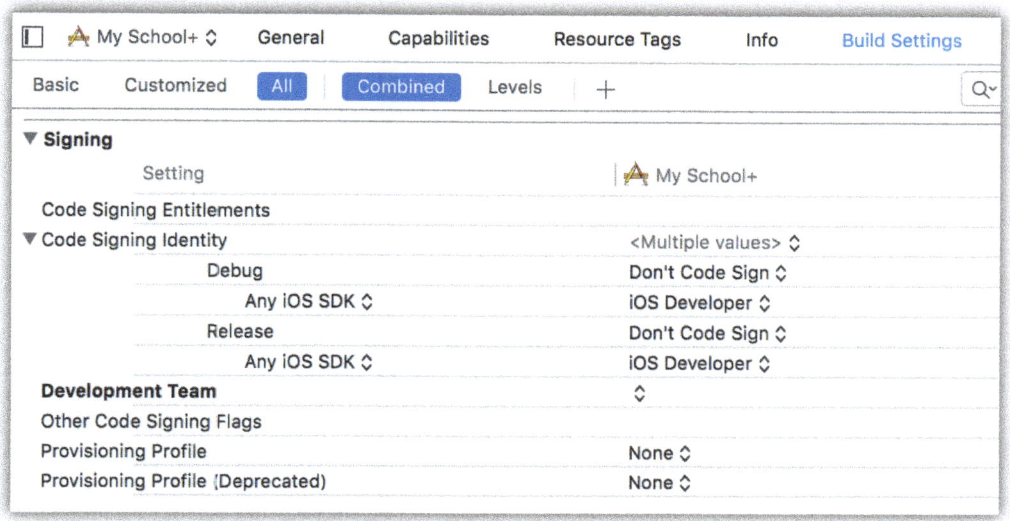

13.44

See all the options that say *iOS Developer* or *Don't Code Sign* and the empty option for *Development Team*? Select each one and change it to your Developer account, ensuring that you choose the one that is prefixed with *iPhone Distribution*. Then, where it says *None* next to *Provisioning Profile* and *Provisioning Profile (Deprecated)*, select your provisioning profile:

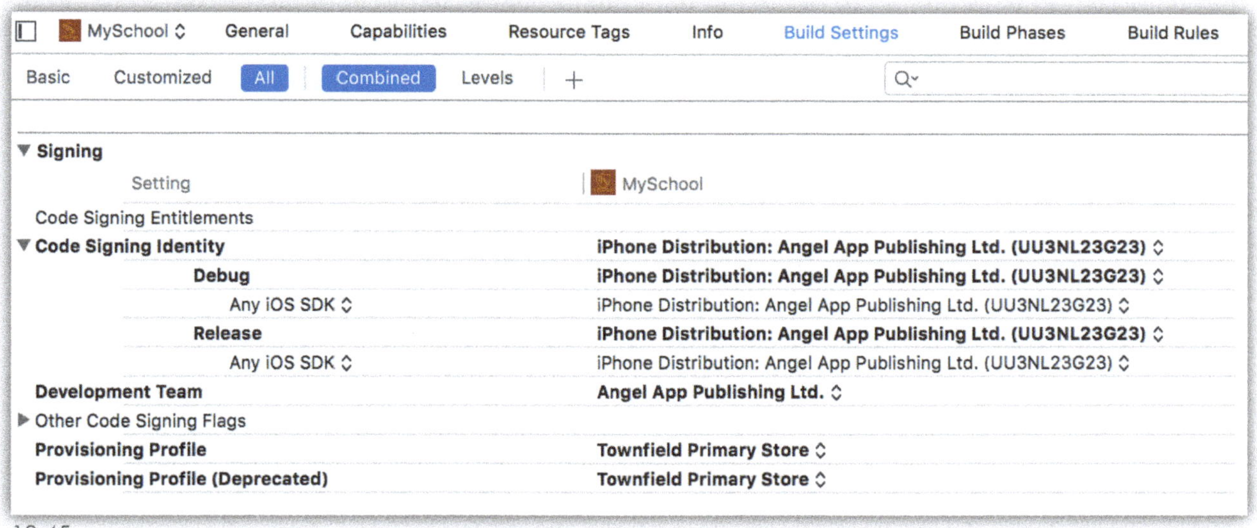

13.45

And you're done.

We only have a couple of things left to do in *Xcode*, but we'll come back here later.

Now, it's time to configure our app for sale in the App Store.

Configuring your app in iTunes Connect

You have to do all the boring certificate and provisioning profile stuff before you can add your app to *iTunes Connect*.

We've done all that. So let's head to *iTunesConnect* now at **https://itunesconnect.apple.com**:

13.46

This is where you'll find everything you need to add and manage your apps on the App Store. If you want to create a 'paid for' app – an app that makes you money – you will need to add your banking information to the *Agreements, Tax and Banking* section. But we are making a free app so the only thing we need to do is add our app.

To do this, press the first button: *My Apps*. You'll see all the apps you have built but as we haven't submitted any yet, this page will be blank. Let's fix that by adding our first app. Press the '+' sign in the top left and select *New App*:

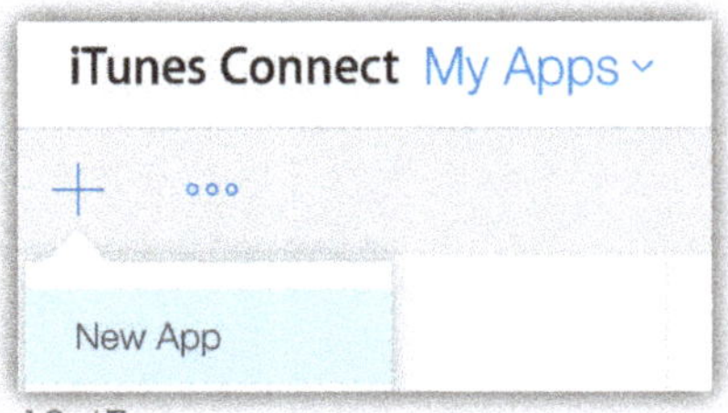

13.47

You'll see a pop-up box where you need to enter all the information about your app. Here's mine completed so you can see what you need to do:

Bear in mind, the *Name* must be unique, so you couldn't call it *Angry Birds* for example! The *SKU* is a code so that you can quickly identify your apps in your sales reports. For this app, it doesn't really matter what you put there.

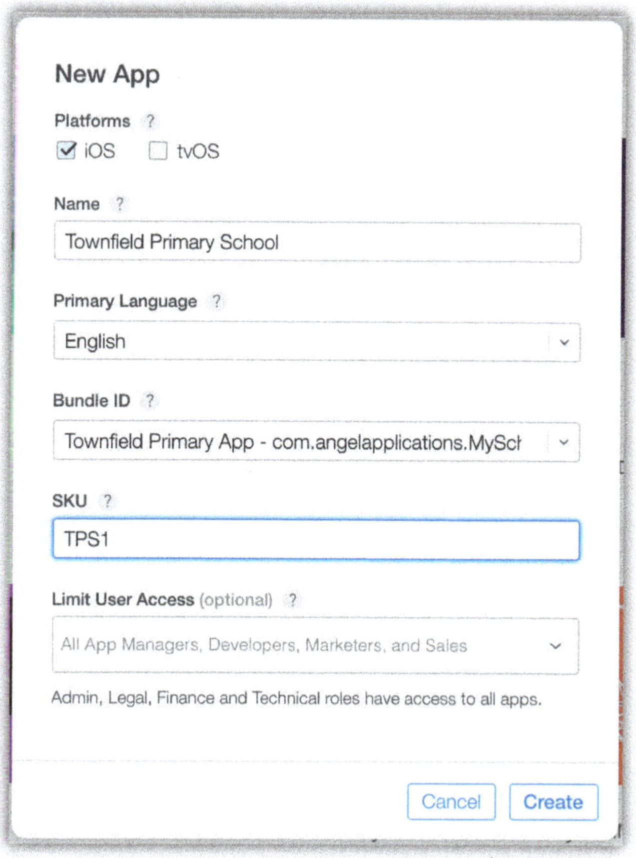

13.48

Once you're happy, press the *Create* button.

There's quite a lot we need to do here, so we'll go through each of the sections on the left-hand side together.

Let's start with *App Information* which is the section you are taken to first anyway.

There's only one thing to change here and that's the app *category* for the App Store. Click on where it says *Primary* and select *Education*:

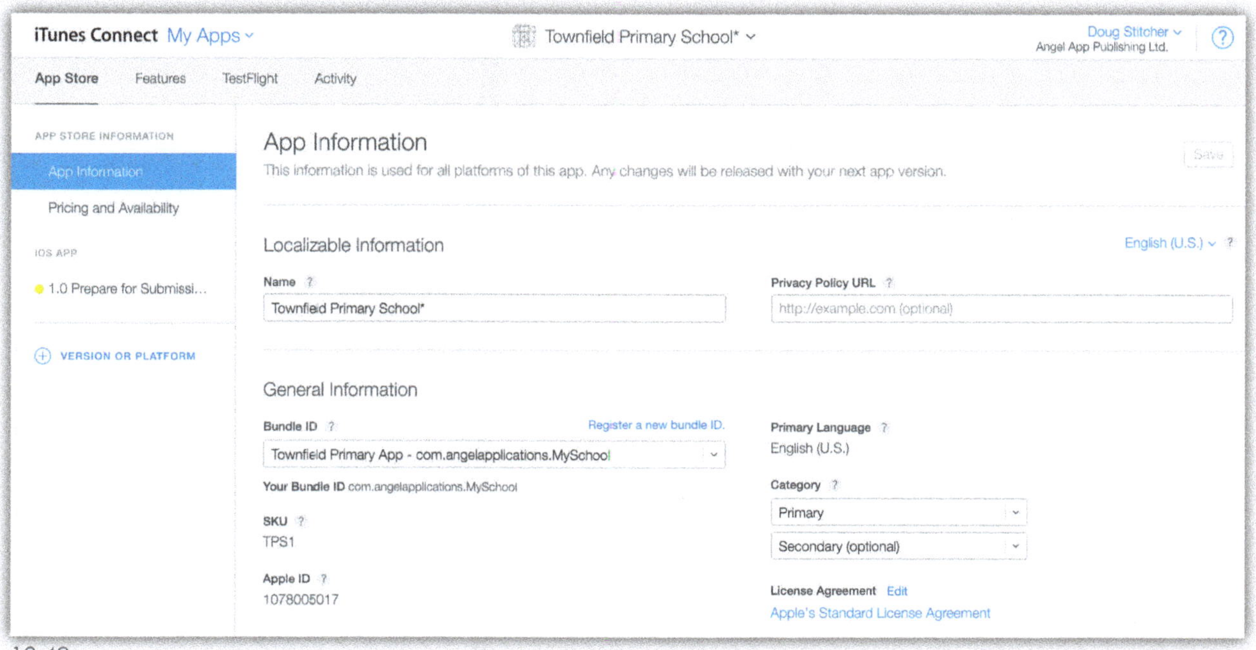

13.49

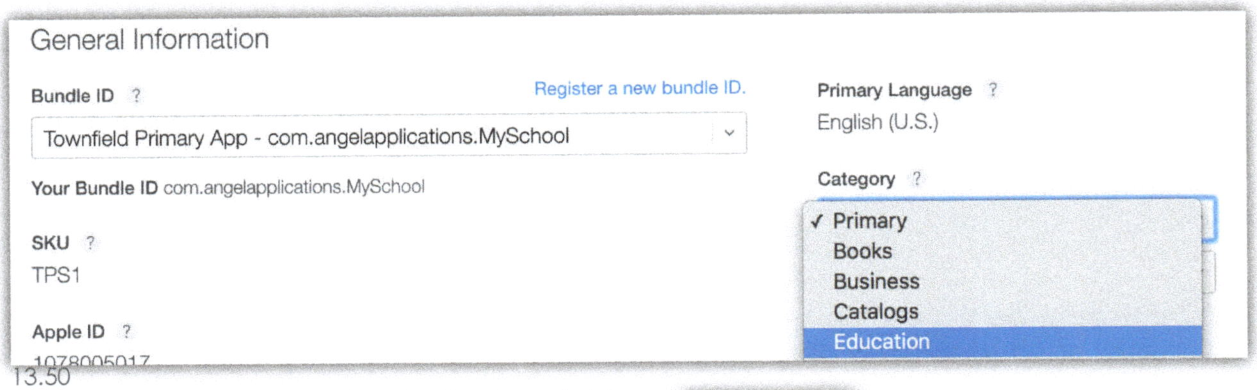

13.50

Then press the *Save* button to the top right:

13.51

Now, under *App Store Information* on the left-hand side, select *Pricing and Availability*:

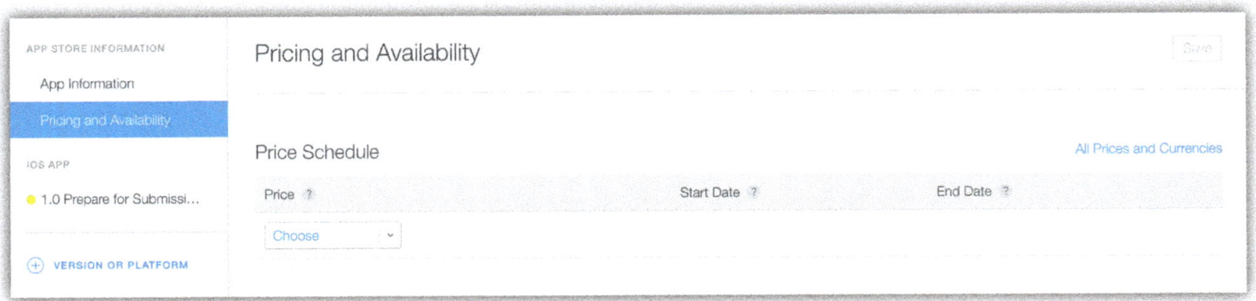

13.52

Click on where it says *Choose* under *Price* and select the first option which will set your price at free (GBP 0). Press the *Save* button.

The last, but most involved, section is where it says 1.0 *Prepare for Submission*:

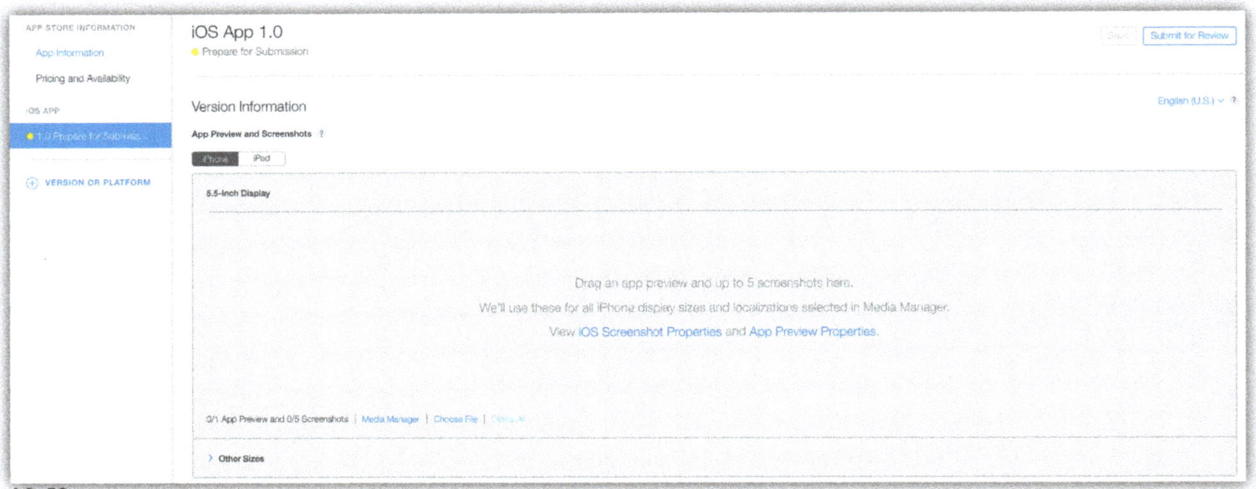

13.53

Here, we will add screenshots, a description, copyright information and loads of other stuff.

Let's have a look at the *App Video Preview and Screenshots* section. This where we upload screenshots from our app for every device our app supports. Our app only supports iPhone 3.5 inch and iPhone 4 inch. While it will work on 4.7 inch and 5.5 inch (iPhone 6 and iPhone 6 Plus) screens, we can't put screenshots from those devices in to our description as the app isn't optimised for those devices.

Before we upload any screenshots, we need to get some. To speed this up, we'll use a screenshot of our home screen on iPhone 4S and iPhone 5S but you can add up to five screenshots.

So go to *Xcode* and run your app on the iPhone 4S Simulator:

Press the *Play* button and let the app run. Click anywhere in the simulator – except on one of your buttons – and then press *Cmd* and 'S'. This will save a perfectly sized screenshot to your desktop.

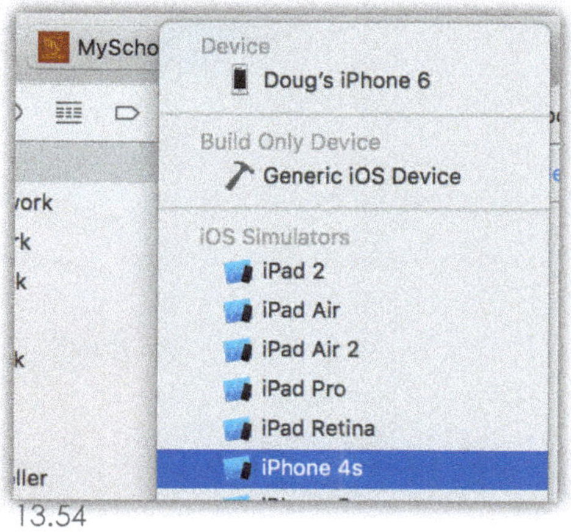

13.54

Go back to *iTunes Connect* and select *Other Sizes* from below the big grey space reserved for the largest iPhone screen sizes. Apple have recently let developers upload screenshots for the largest device and then they automatically use this for all devices. However, as our app isn't optimised for the larger iPhones, we need to set screenshots manually for 3.5-inch screens and 4-inch screens:

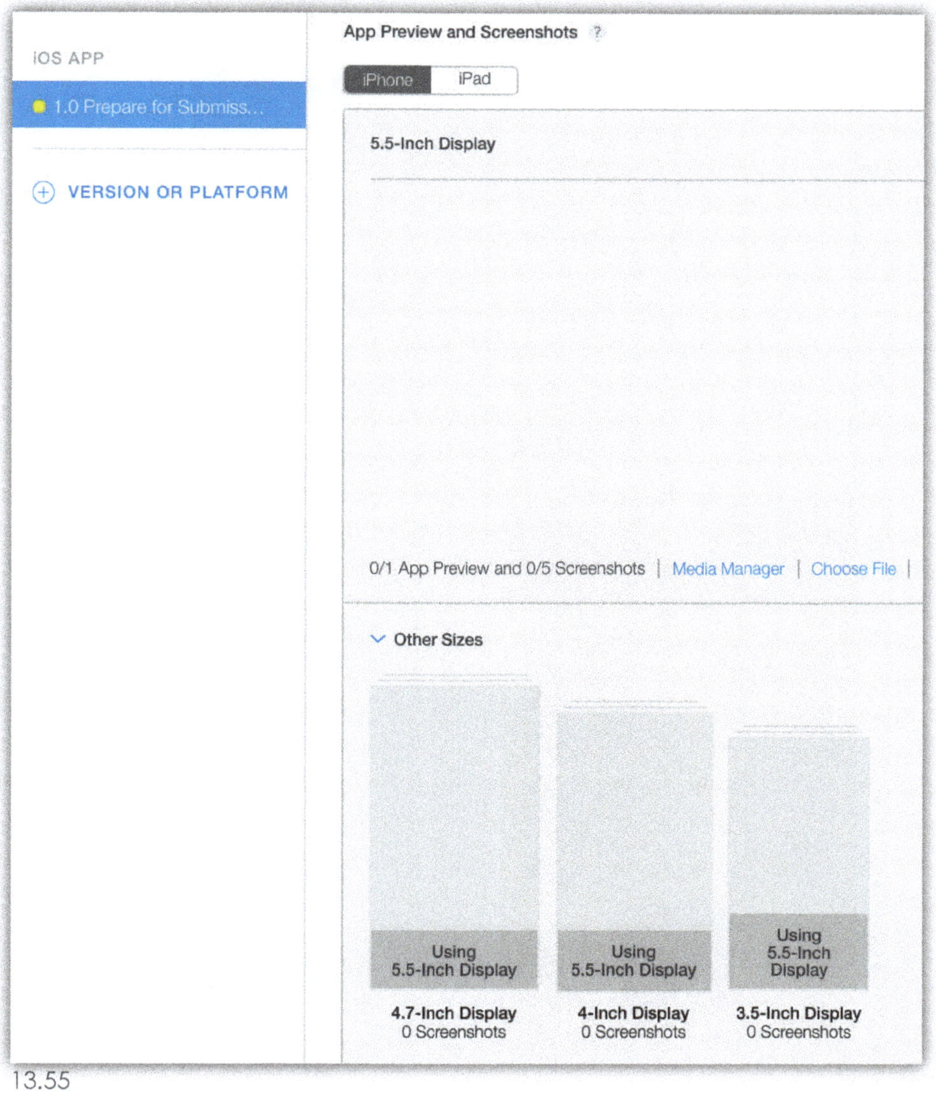

13.55

Select the smallest screen size and a new screen will appear:

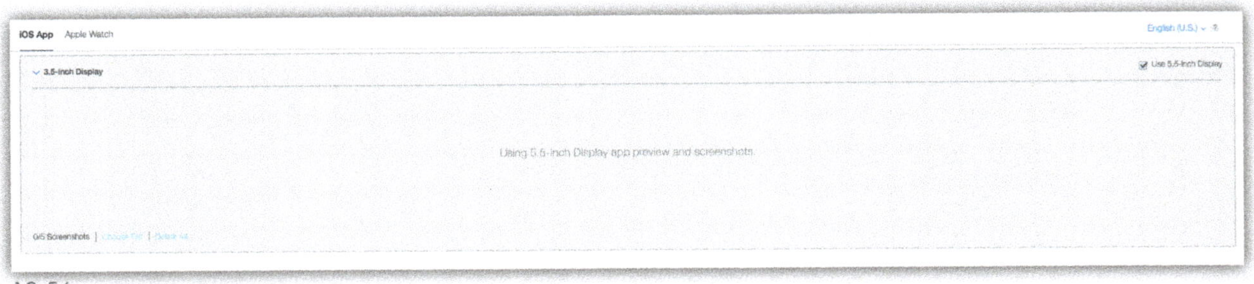

13.56

Can you see that small box on the right (you might need to scroll across)?

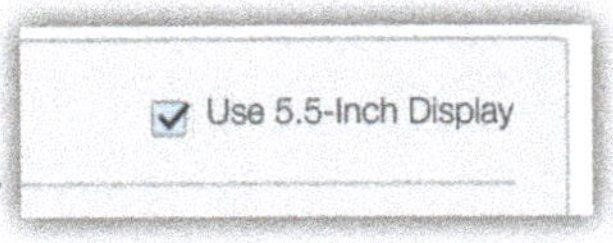

13.57

It is ticked by default to tell it to use the *5.5-inch display* screenshots. But as we aren't uploading any, that's no good to us so you need to untick that box. Once that's done, simply drag your iPhone 4 screenshot from your desktop to the grey box in your web browser:

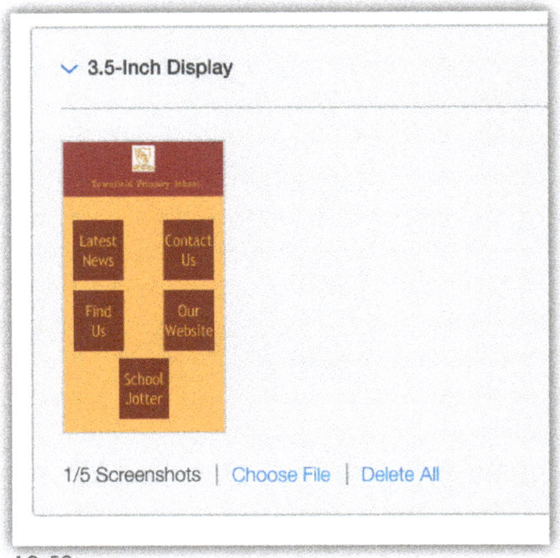

13.58

Then, drag your screenshot from the Desktop into the grey box beneath the menu bar:

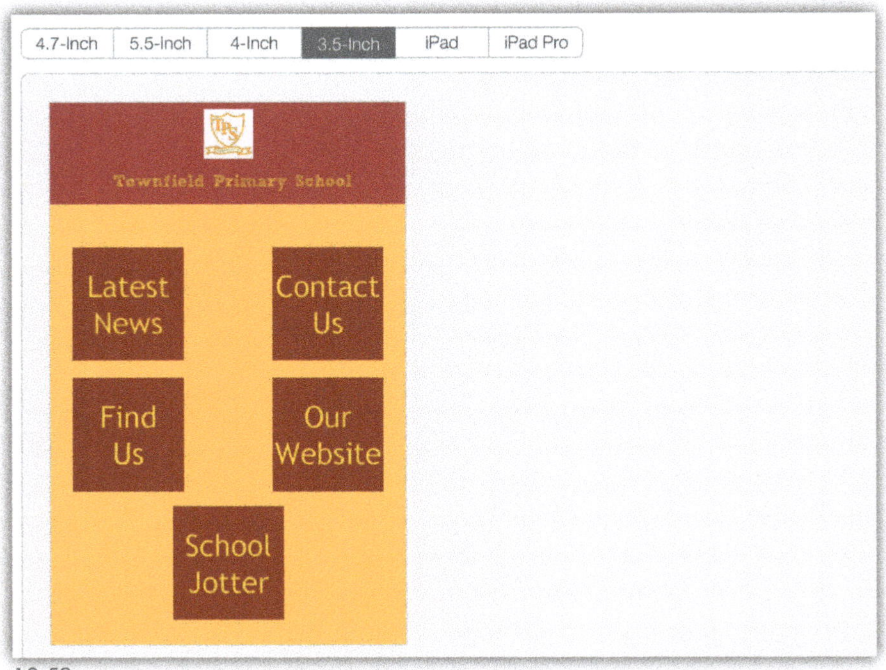

13.59

As if by magic, it will appear.

Now, run your app on the iPhone 5S or iPhone SE simulator, take a screenshot and drag that one into the '4-inch' section - making sure you untick that 'Use 5.5-inch Display' box first:

13.60

The minimum is one screenshot for each device you support but it's a good idea to put a few up to show what your app does.

Make sure you don't add screenshots for devices your app doesn't support as otherwise, when you upload your app later, it won't accept it.

That's the screenshots done. Save where you are up to by pressing the blue *Save* button in the top right.

Move down to the next section by scrolling past the screenshot section.

Here's the next bit:

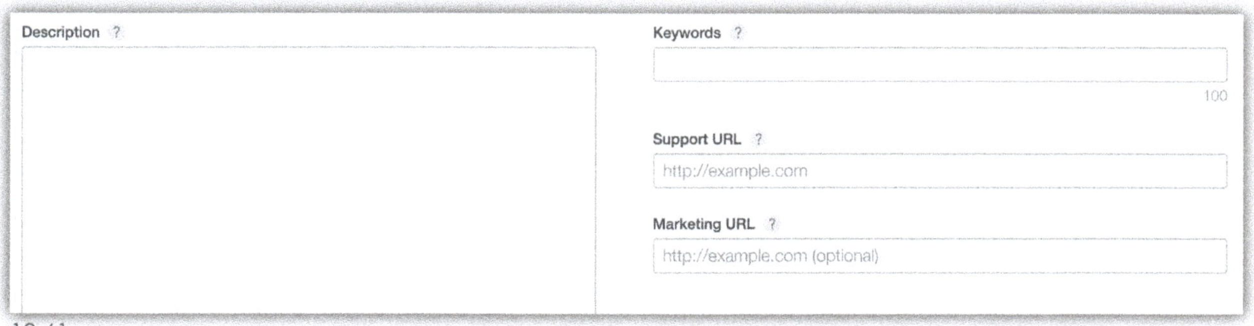

13.61

This is straightforward. In the *Description* box, add a description of what you app does and who it is for. Be careful not to include references to the *Android* operating system or trademarks as Apple may reject your app for that.

In *Keywords* you have 100 characters to input some words that users can type to search for your app. You don't need to use the words in your app name description as they are used automatically.

In *Support URL* put the link to your school's website so people can contact you if there's an issue with your app.

You can leave *Marketing URL* blank.

Once you've filled everything in, save your work.

Scroll down and find the *General App Information*:

13.62

Here, we have to add the full size icon. So press *Choose File* under *App Icon* and locate your 1024 x 1024 icon image. Put your school's name in the *Copyright* box:

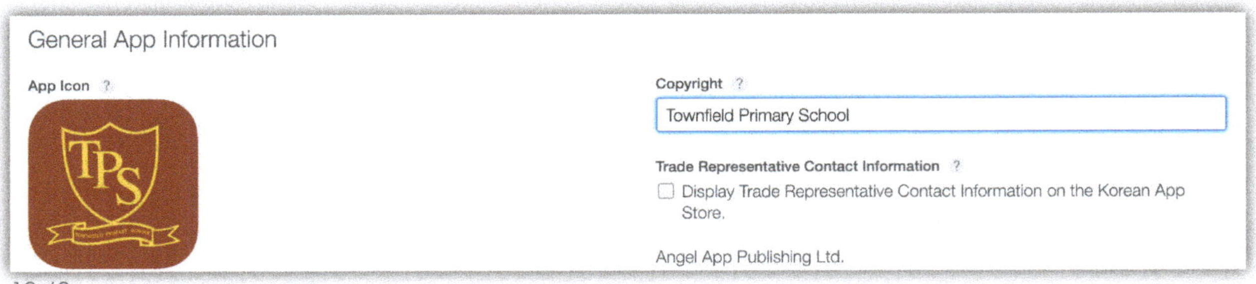

13.63

You'll also see your contact information on the right-hand side. You don't need to do anything with that.

Scroll down a little bit more:

13.64

Next to the word *Rating*, press *Edit*. This will bring up the options for age-suitability. Your app shouldn't have anything dodgy in it so you're safe to tick *None* for all the options:

Apple Content Description	None	Infrequent/Mild	Frequent/Intense
Cartoon or Fantasy Violence	●	○	○
Realistic Violence	●	○	○
Prolonged Graphic or Sadistic Realistic Violence	●	○	○
Profanity or Crude Humor	●	○	○
Mature/Suggestive Themes	●	○	○
Horror/Fear Themes	●	○	○
Medical/Treatment Information	●	○	○
Alcohol, Tobacco, or Drug Use or References	●	○	○
Simulated Gambling	●	○	○
Sexual Content or Nudity	●	○	○
Graphic Sexual Content and Nudity	●	○	○
	No	Yes	
Unrestricted Web Access	●	○	
Gambling and Contests	●	○	

13.65

The only thing to be careful of is to make sure your school website doesn't have an option to search the entire web. Otherwise, you'll have to tick *YES* for *Unrestricted Web Access* and this will make your app suitable for 17+ only.

When you're happy, press *Done*. Then press the blue *Save* button again.

Next, scroll down to the *App Review Information* section:

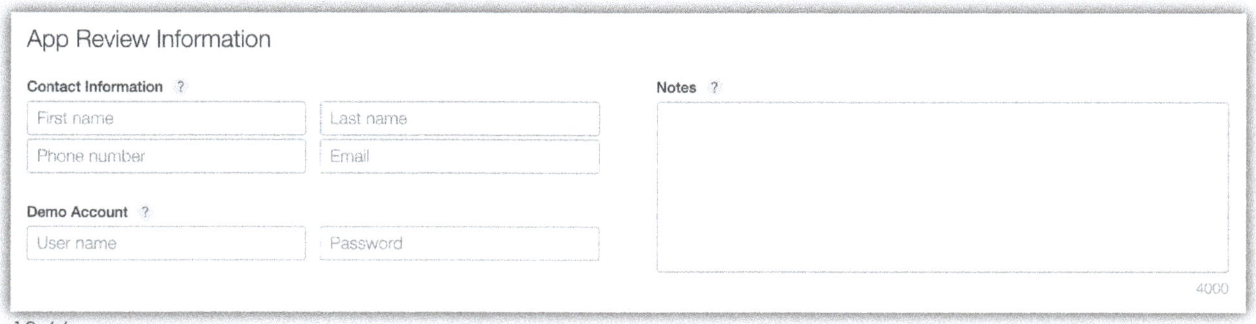

13.66

Here, you need to put your contact information so that Apple can contact you if there's a problem reviewing your app. I've done this hundreds of times and they've never contacted me yet.

In the *Notes* section, explain that your app is a school app and outline some of the things it does. I'm not sure anyone ever reads that box anyway.

You can leave *Demo Account* blank. That's for apps that ask their users to log in.

Press the *Save* button again.

We now need to upload our app to *iTunes Connect*. We do this in *Xcode* so head back there and we'll get this finished.

Uploading your App to iTunes Connect

Sending our app to Apple is pretty easy. Go to the section in *Xcode* where you select which simulator to build your app to and select *Generic iOS Device*:

13.67

Now, in the top *Xcode* menu, go to *Product* and select *Archive*:

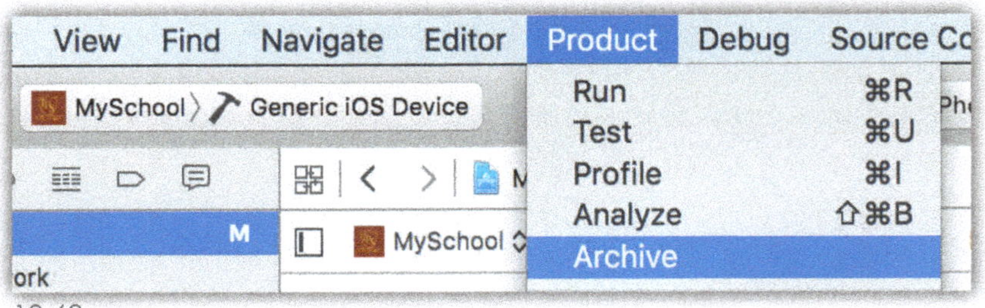

13.68

Your app will build and a new window, called the *Organizer Window*, will appear:

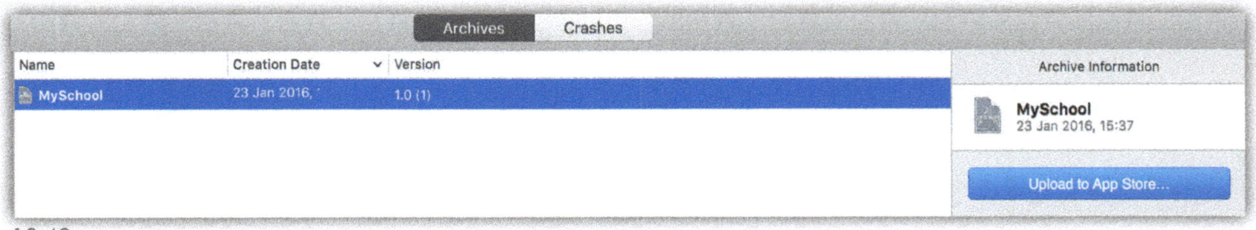

13.69

No prizes for guessing which button to press. That big blue *Upload to App Store...* button.

Go ahead, press it. You'll see this screen. Make sure your Developer account is listed like mine is here:

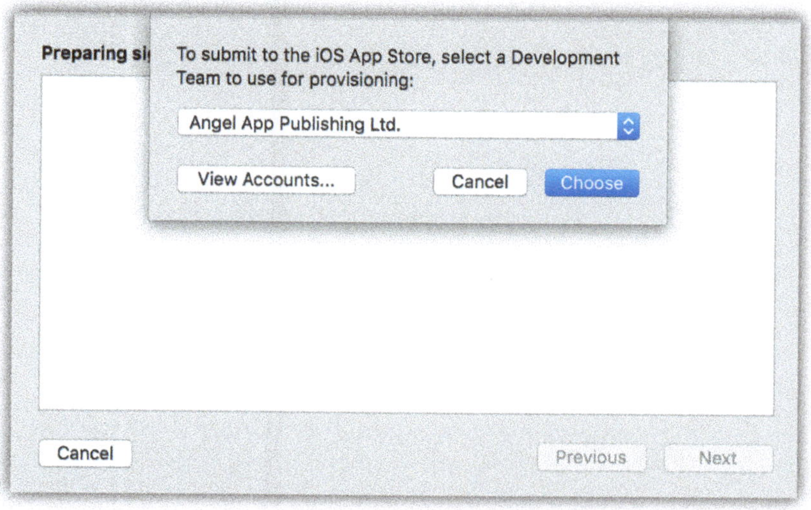

13.70

Press the *Choose* button.

After about 30 seconds, you will see this screen:

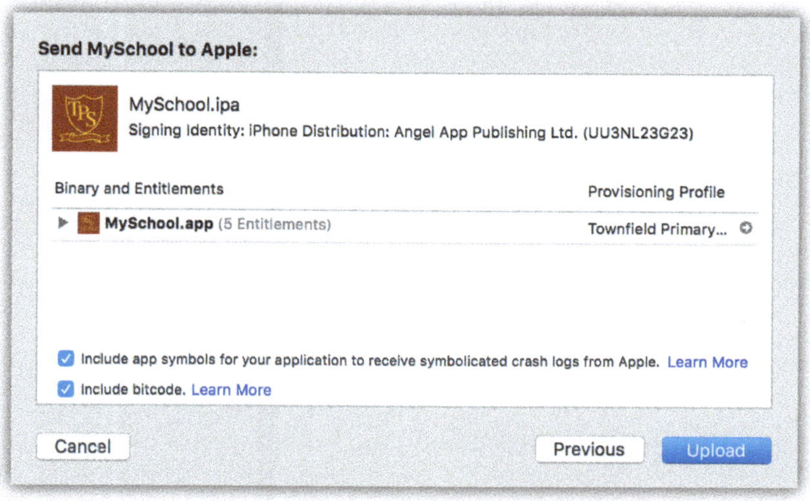

13.71

Press the blue Upload button. The app will then be sent to Apple. The time this takes depends on the size of your images and your internet speed. But it should look like this:

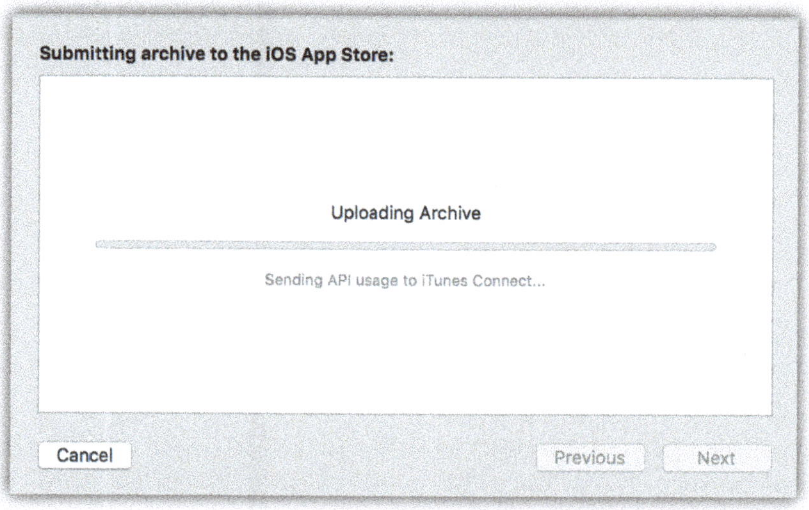

13.72

If everything goes well, this screen should appear:

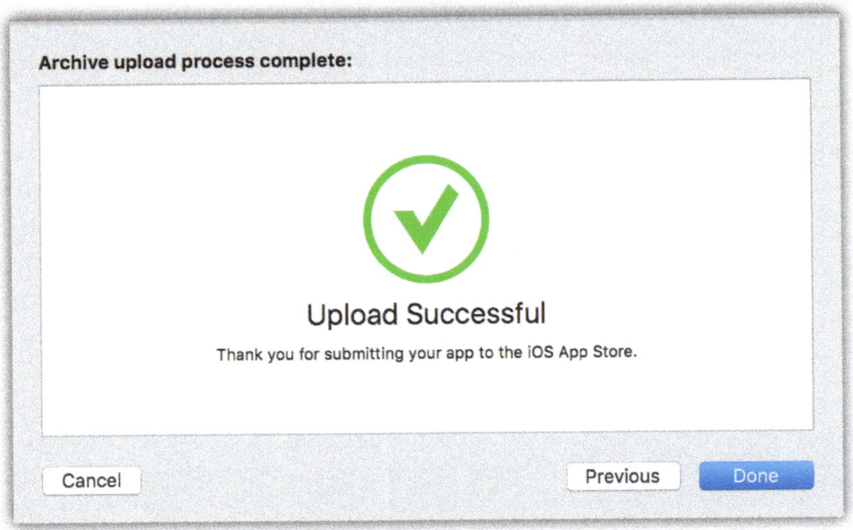

13.73

You can safely press *Done*.

We are now completely finished in *Xcode*. So close it if you want.

When you upload an app to Apple, it can take anything from two minutes to a few hours for them to 'process' it. I have no idea what 'processing' means but until it's processed, we can't finish the submission.

Complete the Submission Process

You may receive an email from Apple telling you your app has been processed. Alternatively, to see if Apple have finished processing our app, go back to *iTunes Connect*, log in and make sure you are working within the *My Apps* section.

Find the *Build* section in the *1.0 Prepare for Submission* section:

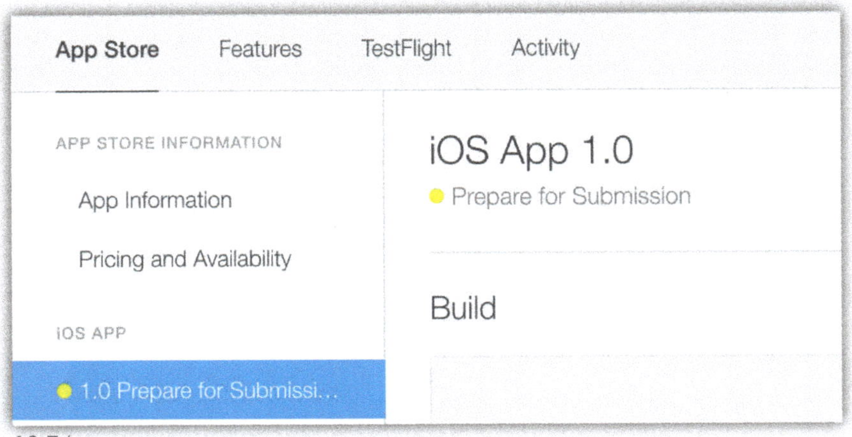

13.74

If you can see a little blue '+' sign next to the word Build, your app is probably ready. If not – as in the screenshot above - you'll have to wait a little bit longer.

Once you've waited, refresh the page. And the '+' should appear:

13.75

Press it to bring up this box:

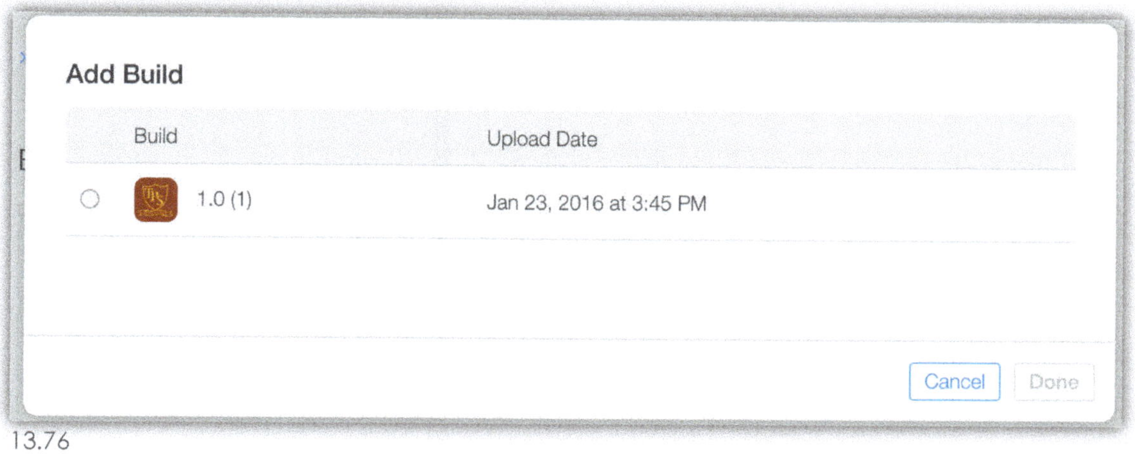

13.76

Select your app and press the *Done* button.

Then press the blue *Save* button in the top right.

You're now ready to press the *Submit for Review* button:

13.77

(If you have missed any sections out, you will be told where there are errors on the page. Correct them and press the button again.)

When everything is okay, you will see this screen:

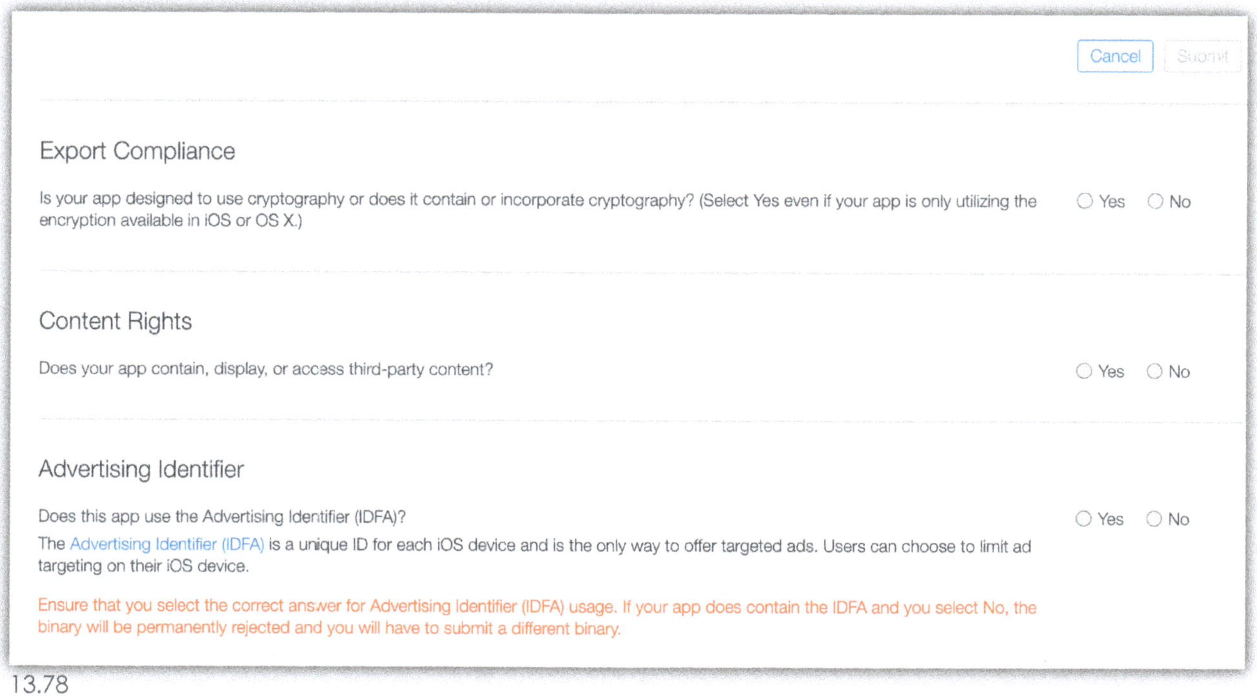

13.78

You can safely tick the *No* box for all three questions and then press the *Submit* button.

You've submitted your app for review. Our journey into iOS app development is nearly over.

There are a few things you still need to know but that's the process… from idea to App Store.

http://www.alanpeat.com/build-an-app/Chapter13

CHAPTER FOURTEEN WRAPPING UP

Presuming you've successfully followed every stage in this book, congratulations, you've done it. From learning how to make a simple 'Hello, World' app to creating a fully functional school app that has been passed to Apple for review.

Apple review all their apps and the process can take anything from a few days to a few weeks but on average, it takes about seven days. You'll get an email when your app goes 'into review' and another one when it is approved.

Should they reject it, you will get an email telling you that there is an issue with your app. The email will contain a link to *iTunes Connect* where you can find out what the issue is and either communicate with the App Review team or resolve the issue and resubmit the app.

It's a lengthy process. But it makes the App Store the most secure of the various app stores available. Dangerous and rubbish apps are much less likely to appear in the Apple store than in the Android store.

Once your app is approved, give it about four hours to appear in the App Store and then you can send the link to everyone you know.

It's important to remember the limitations of what we have done as well as celebrate our success. We haven't delved too deeply into the code syntax – the way you need to write the code to make it make sense.

But if you're intrigued and want to find out more, head over to **https://developer.apple.com/library/mac/documentation/Cocoa/Conceptual/ProgrammingWithObjectiveC/Introduction/Introduction.html** for a full breakdown of the language.

Alternatively, you may decide that you'd like to use Apple's newer language, Swift, to code your apps in. The process we've been through is the same but the code is slightly different. To read more about Swift, go to **https://developer.apple.com/library/ios/documentation/Swift/Conceptual/Swift_Programming_Language/TheBasics.html** where Apple talk you through the language.

Remember, we chose to use Objective-C because it's been around longer and there are more examples online to help you out.

If you're anything like me, you're probably desperate to find out more and try out some ideas for apps. The internet is full of help. One of the best sites for tutorials (in Swift and Objective C) is **http://www.raywenderlich.com/** where you'll find complete projects with more emphasis on the coding elements and the language.

Having learnt so much about using *Xcode* in this book you'll be able to easily follow a range of tutorials.

And if you get stuck on a specific problem, you may wish to consider joining a forum - **http://iphonedevsdk.com/** is a great one for asking questions. Many experts are on there and willing to assist you with your questions.

Like anything, it takes a while to become truly adept at building apps. This book assumed no prior knowledge and in doing so, it gave you some.

You are ready to extend your journey into the world of app development.

But most importantly, you are fully equipped to teach this to your children.

Within this book, you have a breakdown of skills that you can teach at a pace to suit the ability of the students and a clear road-map to producing an app.

Feel free to adapt the School App model. You could, for example, make an app for a specific club. Or you could add multiple news feeds. There are lots of ways to develop your app and improve it.

Every inch of code you need is provided in the screenshots and the instructions we have been through.

However, if something's gone wrong and you can't find the issue, then the full code to my Townfield app is available at **www.alanpeat.com** (CHANGE FOR CORRECT LOCATION).

I hope you've found the process fun. But most importantly, I hope your children have been able to share in your learning journey and worked with you to create their own school app.

Feel free to contact me at **dougstitcher@angelapplications.co.uk**
or tweet me at **@theRenegade78**
or follow our Facebook page at **www.facebook.com/angelapplications**

I will do my best to help you with any issues you may come across.

And that is it. One real iPhone app. Built from scratch.

We've done it. You've done it. Your kids have done it.

GLOSSARY

algorithm - a set of instructions used by a computer to complete a task

array - a collection of different objects held in the computer's memory. For example, a collection of images or text

autolayout - a feature provided by Xcode to allow you to create one user interface file for different sized devices by positioning objects using relative positions

autoshrink - a property of text within an app that allows the text to resize automatically if there is not enough space on the screen

binary - the complete app written as only a series of 0s and 1s. This term is often used to describe the final file of the app that you upload to the App Store

blog - abbreviation of 'Web Log' - a website which is updated regularly with information

bundle identifier - the unique reference name for your app

certificate - a security feature used to digitally sign your app to prevent other apps from pretending to be your app

class - a collection of objects and methods that are related to each other

debug - the process of finding issues within your app

debugger - a tool used to find issues within your app

device orientation - whether your device is presented landscape or portrait

display name - the name of your app that appears beneath the icon on the actual device

dynamic text - text which will change over the course of the app's lifecycle

first responder - the object which is accessing the device's keyboard

frameworks - a set of pre-written code that adds extra features to your app

groups - a way of organising your files in Xcode

HTML - the programming language used to create websites

IBAction - a method that is activated by linking it to an object in your user interface file

IBOutlet - a way of telling Xcode that your object is in your user interface file

icon - the image that is displayed on the home screen of the device to represent your app

IDE - Integrated Developer Environment - software used to create a computer program

Interface Builder - the part of Xcode that allows you to design the user interface

iOS - the name of the operating system used on iPhones and iPads. The operating system is the software that runs in the background - like Windows on a PC

iOS simulator - a simulated version of an iPhone or iPad used to test apps

Launch Screen - the screen that is displayed for a few seconds when an app loads
Method - a set of commands that are called either by a user interaction or by another method

minimum font scale - the smallest size you will allow a font to be displayed should it need to be resized to fit on the screen

modal - presenting a new view on top of the previous view

NSString - a collection of letters e.g. "This is a string"

NSUserDefaults - a way of storing small amounts of data within your app that are not deleted when the app is closed

Object Library - a collection of objects you can use within your app, such as labels, buttons and views

Objective-C - the language originally used to create iOS apps

pixels - the smallest part of an image that can displayed on the screen

properties - attributes you can give to an object. For example, giving a font size to some text

provisioning profile - a small file that links your app to your developer account to enable you to submit it to Apple

QR code - an image that can be scanned by a camera on a phone and then tell the phone to open a specific website or perform an action

resolution - the maximum number of pixels that can be displayed on a screen

RSS Feed - a feed of information provided by a website that can be read by other programs

static text - text that never changes throughout the life-cycle of an app

Status Bar - the information such as the time and service provider that is displayed at the top of an iPhone or iPad

storyboard - a collection of user interface files that link together to map out the flow of the app

Supporting Files - a group provided in the Navigator pane in Xcode used to organise images and sounds in your app

Swift - a new language created by Apple used to create iOS apps

Third-party code - code that has been written by somebody else and used within your app

UIActivityIndicatorView - the spinning circle that appears on iOS devices to show that something is happening

UIButton - a button that can be either text or an image

UIImageView - a view used to hold an image

UILabel - a view used to hold some text

UISegmented Control - a button divided into a number of different buttons

UITableView - a scrolling table used to display information in a number of cells

UITextView - a view that displays multiple lines of editable text

UITextField - a view that displays one line of editable text and is often used for entering text on apps

user interface - the visible part of the app with which the user interacts

Wireframe/Mock-Up - a non-functioning demonstration of the flow of the app

WordPress - a free provider of blog websites - used to create RSS feeds

Xcode - the software provided by Apple to create apps

xib - a single user interface file

XML - the language RSS Feeds are generally written in